Smalltalk and Object Orientation

An Introduction

773-787-7228

Springer
London
Berlin
Heidelberg
New York
Barcelona
Budapest
Hong Kong
Milan
Paris
Santa Clara
Singapore
Tokyo

John Hunt

Smalltalk and Object Orientation

An Introduction

 Springer

John Hunt, BSc, PhD, MBCS, C.Eng

Computer Science Department, The University of Wales,
Penglais, Aberystwyth, Dyfed SY23 3DB, Wales

ISBN 3-540-76115-2 Springer-Verlag Berlin Heidelberg New York

British Library Cataloguing in Publication Data
Hunt, John Edward
  Smalltalk and object-orientation : an introduction
  1.Smalltalk (Computer program language)   2.Object-oriented
  programming (Computer Science)
  I.Title
  005.1'33
  ISBN 3540761152

Library of Congress Cataloging-in-Publication Data
Hunt, John, 1964-
  Smalltalk and object-orientation : an introduction / John Hunt.
      p.   cm.
  Includes bibliographical references and index.
  ISBN 3-540-76115-2
  1. Smalltalk (Computer program language)   2.(Object-oriented
  programming (Computer science) I. Title.
  QA76.73.S59H86 1997
  005.1'17- -dc21   97-995

© Springer-Verlag London Limited 1997
Printed in Great Britain   4-24-98

Typesetting: Camera ready by author
Printed and bound by Creative Print and Design, Wales
34/3830-543210 Printed on acid-free paper

Preface

This book was originally written to support an introductory course in Object Orientation through the medium of Smalltalk (and VisualWorks in particular). However, it can be used as a book to teach the reader Smalltalk, to introduce object orientation as well as present object oriented design and analysis.

It takes as its basic premise that most Computer Scientists / Software Engineers learn best by doing rather than from theoretical notes. The chapters therefore attempt to introduce concepts by getting you the reader to do things, rather than by extensive theoretical discussions. This means that these chapters take a hands-on approach to the subject and assume that the student/reader has a suitable Smalltalk environment available to them.

The chapters are listed below and are divided into six parts. The reader is advised to work through Parts 1 and 3 thoroughly in order to gain a detailed understanding of object orientation. Part 2 then provides an introduction to the Smalltalk environment and language. Other chapters may then be dipped into as required. For example, if the reader wishes to hone their Smalltalk skills then the chapters in Part 4 would be useful. However, if at that point they wish to get on and discover the delights of graphical user interfaces in Smalltalk, then Part 5 could be read next. Part 6 presents some more advances subjects such as metaclasses and concurrency which are not required for straight forward Smalltalk development.

Content Summary

Part 1: Introduction to Object Orientation

Chapter 1: Introduction to Object Orientation
The aim of this chapter is to provide an introduction to the range of concepts and ideas which make up object technology. It presents the background which led to the acceptance of object orientation as a mainstream technology and discusses the pedigree of the Smalltalk language.

Chapter 2: Elements of Object Orientation
This chapter provides a more formal definition of the terminology introduced in Chapter 1. It also considers the advantages and disadvantages of an object oriented approach compared to more traditional procedural approaches.

Chapter 3: Constructing an Object Oriented System
A typical problem for many people when being introduced to a new approach is that they understand the terminology and the concepts but not how to use them. This chapter aims to alleviate this problem by presenting a detailed worked example of the way in which an object oriented system may be designed and constructed. It does so without reference to any particular language so that language issues should not confuse the discussion.

Part 2: The Smalltalk Language

Chapter 4: An Introduction to Smalltalk
The aim of this chapter is to provide some background on the history of Smalltalk and the development environments which are available to support it (such as the VisualWorks system). It also considers some of the tools the reader will encounter.

Chapter 5: A Little Smalltalk
This chapter presents a number of other tools such as the inspectors and debuggers available in VisualWorks. It then uses a worked example to help the user to use some of the development tools available.

Chapter 6: Smalltalk Building Blocks
The chapter introduces the basic elements the Smalltalk language, it discusses the concept of classes in Smalltalk and how they are defined.

Chapter 7: Smalltalk Constructs
This chapter presents further details of the Smalltalk language including the representation and use of numbers, strings and characters.

Chapter 8: An Example Smalltalk Class
In Chapter 7, the reader is presented with a detailed worked example of software development in Smalltalk. This example presents a very simple class definition which uses only those concepts which have been introduced at this stage. The intention is to illustrate how the constructs and language elements can be combined in a real (if simple) program.

Chapter 9: Control and Iteration
This chapter introduces how control and iteration are achieved in Smalltalk. To do this a number of concepts which are unique to Smalltalk are also discussed (such as the block object). To simplify this process for the reader, equivalent C constructs are illustrated beside Smalltalk constructs (where they exist).

Chapter 10: The Collection Classes
This chapter discusses probably the most widely used class hierarchy in Smalltalk; the collection class hierarchy. It presents the hierarchy in general and some of the commonly used collection classes. It also illustrates how these classes can be used to construct other collection style classes such as queues and stacks.

Chapter 11: Further Collection Classes
This chapter concludes the examination of the collection classes available in Smalltalk and presents an application constructed using these classes.

Chapter 12: An Object Oriented Organizer
This chapter presents a detailed example application constructed using the collection classes. The Organizer is intended as an electronic personal Organizer. It therefore possesses an address book, a diary (or appointments section) and a section for notes. The remainder of this chapter describes one way of implementing such an Organizer.

Chapter 13: Streams and Files
This chapter discusses the second most used class hierarchy in Smalltalk; the Stream classes. The Stream classes are used (amongst other things) for accessing files. The Binary Object Streaming Service for storing objects in files is also discussed.

Chapter 14: The Magnitude Class Hierarchy
This chapter considers the magnitude class and those classes which inherit from it. This includes the Number hierarchy. The classes Character, Time and Date are also considered.

Chapter 15: Some More Tools of the Trade
This chapter introduces the use of breakpoints in Smalltalk, the purpose of the change list file and how to file in and file out Smalltalk code.

Part 3: Object Oriented Design

Chapter 16: Object Oriented Analysis and Design
This chapter introduces the concepts of object oriented analysis and design. It reviews a number of the more popular techniques such as OOA, OMT, Objectory and Booch. It also briefly considers the unification of the OMT and Booch notations.

Chapter 17: The Unified Modeling Language
The Unified Modeling Language (or UML for short) is a third generation object-oriented modeling language which adapts and extends the published notations used in the Booch, OMT and Objectory methods. It is intended that the UML will form a single, common, widely usable modeling language for a range of object oriented design methods (including Booch, Objectory and OMT). It is also intended that it should be applicable in a wide range of applications and domains. This chapter (and the next) summarize the UML notation.

Chapter 18: UML: Dynamic Modeling and Deployment
This chapter continues the description of the Unified Modeling Language (UML) started in the last chapter.

Chapter 19: The Object Modeling Technique
This chapter, and the next, discuss the influential design method referred to as the Object Modeling Technique (OMT). It summarizes the main phases of OMT using the UML notation. One extension to OMT is the introduction of use case models from Objectory to improve the requirements analysis process. This is motivated by the inclusion of use case diagrams in the UML.

Chapter 20: More Object Modeling Technique
This chapter continues the description of the Object Modeling Technique (OMT).

Chapter 21: Frameworks and Patterns for Object Oriented Design
The aim of this chapter is to introduce the concept of frameworks and in particular patterns. This is still a relatively new idea within Object Orientation, but one which is growing in popularity at an incredible rate.

Part 4: Testing and Style

Chapter 22: Testing Object Oriented Systems
Object oriented systems may make code easier to reuse and may be supported by object oriented analysis and design methods, but they do not guarantee that the code is correct. This chapter looks at some of the issues behind testing object oriented systems.

Chapter 23: Method and Class Testing
The last chapter discussed the problems facing the tester of an object oriented system (and in particular a Smalltalk system). This chapter considers current best practice in testing object oriented systems.

Chapter 24: Smalltalk Style Guidelines
The aim of this chapter is the promotion of readable, understandable, concise and efficient Smalltalk code. A point to note is that style guidelines for languages such as Pascal do not cover many of the issues which are important in Smalltalk. As in any programming language there are a number of acknowledged bad practices which are not specific to Smalltalk, for example the use of global variables! Such guidelines are familiar to programmers of most languages. This section will therefore try to concentrate on those style issues which are specific to Smalltalk.

Part 5: Graphical Interfaces in Smalltalk

Chapter 25: The Perform and Dependency Mechanisms
In this chapter the use of perform to provide an alternative method for sending messages is considered. This is followed by a practical discussion of the dependency mechanism. This includes what the dependency mechanism is, why you might want to use, how you construct a dependency and the effect that it has.

Chapter 26: The Model-View-Controller Architecture
The Model-View-Controller (or MVC) architecture is the basis upon which user interfaces are constructed in Smalltalk. The architecture separates out the application from the user interface. This chapter introduces the MVC architecture and explains the motivation behind it. A worked example is presented to illustrate the theoretical description.

Chapter 27: Graphic User Interface Construction Tools

The user interface construction facilities in Smalltalk are subject to the widest variation between dialects of any aspect of the language. This chapter concentrates on the facilities provided by the user interface building facilities in VisualWorks.

Chapter 28: A Visual Organizer
This chapter describes a detailed worked example of how a user interface can be constructed for the Organizer application constructed earlier in the book.

Chapter 29: Using a View Within a Window
This chapter explains how to use MVC applications within a VisualWorks window. It is useful to be able to do this as not all user interfaces can be accommodated directly by the user interface builder in VisualWorks.

Part 6: Further Smalltalk

Chapter 30: Memory Management and Garbage Collection
This chapter considers why automatic memory management is desirable. It also discusses how Smalltalk's memory is structured and the garbage collection strategies used. It concludes by considering how to force VisualWorks to place long term objects in the most appropriate region of memory.

Chapter 31: Concurrency in Smalltalk
This chapter presents and explains a short example of how time slicing can be accomplished within Smalltalk.

Chapter 32: The Metaclass Framework
The aim of this chapter is to discuss the concept of classes, what they actually are, what they are really used for and why they are important. To do this it introduces the concept of a metaclass and considers how they are used to provide inheritance and the creation of instances. It also discusses whether it is important for the Smalltalk programmer to be aware of the existence of the metaclass.

Part 7: The Future

Chapter 33:The Future for Object Technology
This chapter brings the many threads in this book together and considers the future of object oriented systems.

Appendix

Appendix A: The Smalltalk Language Syntax

Obtaining Source Code Examples

The source code for the examples in this book is available on the web at URL:
http://www.aber.ac.uk/~jjh/SmalltalkBook/

Typographical Conventions

In this book the standard typeface is Times, however `courier` is used to identify source code. For example, `a := 2 + 3`.

Trademarks

ParcPlace, VisualWorks, Smalltalk-80, Smalltalk/V are registered trademarks, and BOSS is a trademark, of ParcPlace-Digitalk Systems, Inc. Sun and Java are trademarks of Sun Microsystems, Inc. MS-Windows and Windows 95 are registered trademarks of Microsoft Corporation. Apple is a registered trademark of Apple Computer, Inc. UNIX is a registered trademark of AT&T. The X Window System is a trademark of the Massachusetts Institute of Technology. All other brand names are trademarks of their respective holders.

Acknowledgments

The content of this book has been refined by a large number of students in both academia and industry. Many of these people have provided useful feed back and constructive comments. A number of them have actively suggested topic areas which might be covered or which were poorly described; thank you all for your interest. In particular thanks to Peter Holland, Paul Jones, Dave James, John Counsell, Clive King, Andy Whittle and others who I am sure I have forgotten to mention. I would also like to thank Rebecca Moore, of Springer-Verlag, for her patience and thoroughness during the preparation of this book. Finally, thanks to my wife, Denise Cooke, for suffering my disappearances to the study most evenings to work on "the book" and for helping with my many "printing" problems.

Contents

Part 1: Introduction to Object Orientation

Part 2: The Smalltalk Language

Part 3: Object Oriented Design

Part 6: Further Smalltalk

Introduction to Object Orientation

1. Introduction to Object Orientation

1.1 Introduction

This book is intended as an introduction to object orientation for computer science students or those actively involved in the software industry. It assumes familiarity with standard computing concepts such as stacks, memory allocation etc. and with a procedural language such as C. It uses this background to provide a practical introduction to object technology. To do this it uses Smalltalk, one of the earliest pure object oriented languages.

The approach taken in this book is to try to introduce a variety of concepts through practical experience with an object oriented language. It also tries to take the reader beyond the level of the language syntax to the philosophy and practice of object oriented development.

In the remainder of this chapter we will consider the various programming paradigms which have preceded object orientation. We will then examine what the primary concepts in object orientation are and consider how to enable object orientation to be achieved.

1.2 Programming paradigms

Software construction is still more of an art than a science. Despite the best efforts of many software engineers, software systems are still delivered late, over budget and not up to the requirements of the user. This situation has been with us for many years (indeed the first conference to raise awareness of this problem was the NATO Software Engineering Conference of 1968 which coined the term *software crisis*). Since then there have been a variety of programming paradigms which have either been developed explicitly to deal with this issue or which have been applied to it.

A programming paradigm is a particular programming style which embodies a particular philosophy. These philosophies usually represent some sort of insight which sets a new type of *best practice*. For a programming language to support a particular programming paradigm it must not just allow adoption of that paradigm (you can use object oriented programming techniques in assembler - but would you want to?) it must actively support implementations based on that paradigm. This usually means that the language must support constructs which make development using that paradigm straight-forward.

The major programming paradigms which have appeared in computer science include:

Functional Lisp is the classic example of a functional language (although by no means the only one for example, ML is a very widely used functional language). These languages place far more emphasis on applying a function (often recursively) to a set of one or more data items. The function would then return a value - the result of evaluating the function. If the function changed any data items then this was a side effect of the function. There is (was) limited support for more algorithmic solutions which might rely on repetition via iteration. The functional approach turned out to be extremely useful as a way of implementing complex systems for early AI researchers.

Procedural as exemplified by languages such as Pascal and C. These were an attempt to move programming languages to a higher level (than the earlier assembler languages). The emphasis was now on algorithmic solutions and on procedures which operated on data items. They were extremely effective, but software developers still encountered difficulties. This was partly due to the increased complexity of the systems typically being developed. It was also because, although high level procedural languages removed the possibility of certain types of error occurring and increased productivity, developers could still cause problems for themselves. For example, the interfaces between different parts of the system might be incompatible, but this might not become obvious until integration testing or system testing.

Modular Languages such as Modula-2 and Ada employ modularization. In these languages a module hides its data from module users. The users of the module can only access that data via defined interfaces. These interfaces are "published" so that users know what interfaces are available (and their definitions) and can check that they are using the correct versions.

Object oriented This is the most recent "commercial" programming paradigm. This approach can be seen as taking modularization a step further. Not only do you have explicit modules (in this case objects) but these objects can inherit features from one another. We can of course ask "why another programming paradigm?". The answer to this partly lies in the failure of many software development projects to keep to budget, remain within time scales and to give the user what they want. Of course, it should never be assumed that object orientation is the answer to all these problems, it is really just another tool available to software developers.

This book is about this last programming paradigm. It attempts to introduce this paradigm through the medium of an object oriented programming language. It assumes that the majority of readers will have a background in at least one procedural language (in particular with a C-like language). It therefore compares and contrasts the facilities provided with such a language at appropriate times.

It should be seen from the above list, that object orientation, even though it is quite different in many ways from the procedural approach, has developed from it. You should therefore not throw away all that you have learnt using other approaches. Many of the good practices in other languages are still good practices in an object oriented language. However, there will be new practices to learn as well as new syntax. It will be much more than a process of learning a new syntax - you have a new philosophy to learn.

1.3 Revolution versus evolution

In almost every area of scientific endeavor there are periods of evolution followed by periods of revolution and then evolution again. That is, some idea or theory is held to be "accepted" (not necessarily true but at least accepted). During this period the theory is refined by successive experiments / discoveries etc. Then at some point, the theory is challenged by a new theory. This new theory is typically held by a small set of extremely fervent believers. It is often derided by those who are staunch supporters of the existing theory. As time continues, either this new theory is proved wrong and disappears, or more and more are drawn to the new theory until the old theory has very few supports.

There are many examples of this phenomena in science. For example, the Copernican theory of the earth rotating around the sun, Einstein's theory of relativity and Darwin's theory of evolution. Men such as Darwin and those who led him to his discoveries were revolutionaries. They went against the current belief of the times and introduced a new set of theories. These theories were initially derided but have since become generally accepted. Indeed we are now in an evolutionary phase, with regard to the theory of evolution, where Darwin's theories are being refined. For example, Darwin believed that the mechanism of fertilization of an egg was derived from an old Greek theory referred to as Pangenesis. Every organ and tissue was assumed to produce granules, called gemmules. These were combined to make up the sex cells. Of course we now believe this to be wrong and it was Darwin's own cousin, Francis Galton, who helped to disprove the Pangenesis theory. Whether we will enter a new revolutionary phase where the theory of evolution will be over-turned is probably unlikely, however, Einstein's theory of relatively may well be (and is already being) challenged.

Programming is another example of this revolution / evolution cycle. The move from low level to high level programming was one such revolution (and you can still find people who will insist that low level machine code programming is best). Object orientation is another revolution, which in this case is still happening. Over the past ten years object orientation has become much more widely accepted and you will find many organizations, both suppliers and users of software, giving it lip service. However, you will also find many in the computer industry who are far from convinced. A senior colleague of mine recently told me that he believed that object orientation was severely over-hyped (which it may be) and that he really couldn't see the benefits it offered. Hopefully, this book will convince him (and others) that object orientation has a great deal to offer.

It is likely that something will come along to challenge object oriented programming, just as it has challenged procedural programming, as the current software development approach to use. It is also likely that a difficult and painful battle will ensue with software suppliers entering the market and leaving the market. Many existing suppliers will argue that their system always supported approach *X* anyway while others will attempt to graft the concepts of approach *X* onto theirs. When this will happen or what the new approach will be is difficult to predict, but it will happen. Until then, object orientation will be a significant force within the computer industry.

1.4 History /pedigree of object oriented languages

In the horse or dog breeding world, the pedigree of an animal can be determined by considering its ancestry. Whilst you can't determine how good a language is by looking at its predecessors, you can certainly get a feel for the influences which have led to features it possesses. The current set of commercial object oriented languages have all been influenced to a greater or lesser extent by existing languages. Figure 1.1 illustrates some of the relationships between the various languages.

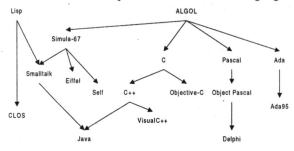

Figure 1.1: Partial Smalltalk Family Tree

Figure 1.1 only partially illustrates the family relationships, as for example, ADA95 should have a link to Smalltalk (or possibly C++). However, this figure attempts to illustrate the most direct influences evident in the various languages. The diagram is also ordered in roughly chronological order. That is, the further down the diagram a language is, the more recent it is. This illustrates for example, that Smalltalk predates C++ and that Java is the most recent object oriented language. Note that Lisp, ALGOL, C, Pascal and Ada are not object oriented and that Simula itself, is at most object based.

The extent to which a language can be considered to be a *pure* object oriented language (i.e. one in which object oriented concepts are consistently adhered) as opposed to a *hybrid* object oriented language (i.e. one in which object oriented concepts lie along-side traditional programming approaches) tends to depend on their background.

A pure object oriented language only supports the concept of an object. Any program is made up solely of interacting objects which exchange information with each other and request operations or data from each other. This approach tends to be followed by those languages which most directly inherit features from Simula (C++ is a notable exception). Simula was designed as a language for discrete event simulation. However, it was itself influenced by many of the features from ALGOL 60 and was effectively the first language to use concepts which we now refer to as

6

object oriented. For example, it introduced the concepts of class, inheritance and polymorphism which we shall discuss below.

The primary language to inherit most directly from Simula is Smalltalk. This means that its ALGOL heritage is there for all to see in the form of structured programming constructs (although the syntax may at first seem a little bizarre). It is a pure object oriented language in that the only concepts supported by the language are object oriented. It also inherits from Lisp (if not any syntax, then certainly the philosophy). This means that not only does it not include strong typing, it also provides dynamic memory management and automatic garbage collection (just as most Lisp systems do). This has both benefits and drawbacks which we will discuss at a later stage. In contrast Eiffel, another pure object oriented language, attempts to introduce "best software engineering practice" rather than the far less formal approach of Lisp. Self is a recent, pure object oriented language, which is still at the research stage.

Many language designers have taken the *hybrid* approach. That is, object oriented constructs have either been grafted onto, or intermixed with, the language. In some cases the idea has been to enable a developer to take advantage of object orientation when it appears appropriate. In other situations it has been to ease the transition from one approach to another. The result has often been a less than satisfactory state of affairs. Not only does it mean that many software developers have moved to their new object oriented language believing that it is just a matter of learning the new syntax, (it isn't), they have proceeded to write procedural programs in which the use of objects is limited to holding data, believing that this will be sufficient (it won't). It is really only safe to move to a hybrid language once you have learnt about object technology using a pure object oriented language.

1.5 Fundamentals of object orientation

The object oriented programmer's view of traditional procedural programming is of procedures wildly attacking data which is defenseless and has no control over what the procedures do to it. This has been called the rape and pillage style of programming. The object oriented programmers view of object oriented programming is of polite and well behaved data objects passing messages to one another, each data object deciding for itself whether to accept the message and how to interpret what it means.

The basic idea is that a system is seen as a set of interacting objects which are organized into classes (of objects). For example, Figure 1.2 illustrates a (simplified) cruise control system from a car. The figure illustrates the objects in the system, the links between the objects and the direction that information flows along these links. The object oriented implementation of this system would mirror this diagram exactly. That is, there would be an object representing each box. Between the boxes would be links allowing one object to request a service from another, or provide information to another. For example, the cruise control electronic control unit (ECU) might request the current speed from the speed sensor. It would then use this information when asking the throttle to adjust its position. Notice we do not talk

7

about functions or procedures which access information from data structures and then call other functions and procedures. There is no concept such as the ECU data structure and the ECU main program. This can be a difficult change of emphasis for some people and we shall try to illustrate it further below.

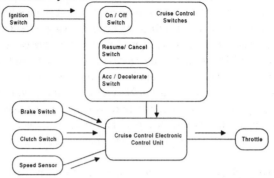

Figure 1.2: A cruise control system as a set of objects

The aim in object oriented programming is to shift the focus of attention from *procedures that do things to data* round to *data which is asked to do things*. The task is not to define the procedures which will manipulate data but to define data objects, their attributes and the way in which they may be examined or changed. Data objects (and procedures) can communicate with data objects only through narrow, well defined channels.

1.6 The four catechism of objèct orientation

The four catechism of object oriented programming are:

Encapsulation or data hiding. Encapsulation is the process of hiding all the details of an object that do not contribute to its essential characteristics. Essentially, it means that what is inside the class is hidden; only the external interfaces are known (by other objects). That is, as the user of an object you should never need to look inside the box!

Inheritance. In many cases objects may have similar (but not identical) properties. One way of managing (classifying) such properties is to have a hierarchy of classes. In this hierarchy of classes a class inherits both from its immediate parent class, above it in the hierarchy, and from classes above the parent. (See the hierarchy in Figure 1.4). This inheritance mechanism permits common characteristics of objects to be defined once, but used in many different places. Any change is thus localized.

Abstraction. An abstraction denotes the essential characteristics of an object that distinguishes it from all other kinds of objects and thus provides crisply defined conceptual boundaries, relative to the perspective of the viewer. That is, it states how a particular object differs from all others.

8

Polymorphism. This is the ability to send the same message to different instances which may appear to perform the same function. However, the way in which the message is handled will depend on the class of which the instance is an example.

An interesting question to ask yourself is how do the following languages relate to the four concepts related above? ADA, C and LISP. An obvious issue to consider is related to inheritance. That is, if we define a concept animal and we then define a concept dog, we don't have to redefine all the things which a dog has in common with other animals. Instead we inherit these features by saying that a dog is a **subclass** of animal. This is a feature unique to object oriented languages. It is also the concept which promotes (and achieves) huge amounts of reuse.

1.7 Encapsulation

1.7.1 The concept

Encapsulation or data hiding has been a major feature of a number of programming languages. For example, Modula-2 and Ada both provide extensive encapsulation features. But what exactly is encapsulation? Essentially, it is the concept of hiding the data behind a software "wall". Those outside the wall cannot get direct access to that data. Instead they must ask intermediaries (usually the owner of the data) to provide them with the data.

The advantage of encapsulation is that the user of the data does not need to know how, where or in what form the owner of the data stores that data. This means that if any changes are necessary in the way in which the data is stored, the user of the data need not be affected. That is, they will still ask the data owner for the data in the same way and it is only the data owner who must change the way in which they proceed in fulfilling that request.

Different programming languages have implemented encapsulation in different ways. For example, in Ada the prevalent concept which enables encapsulation is the package. A package possess both data and procedures. It also specifies a set of interfaces which publish those operations the package wishes to make available to users of the package. These interfaces may for example implement some operations or may provide access to data held within the package.

1.7.2 How OO languages provide *encapsulation*

Object oriented languages provide encapsulation facilities which present the user of an object with a set of external interfaces. These interfaces say what requests the object will respond to (or in the terminology of object orientation, which the object will understand). These interfaces not only avoid the need for the caller to understand how the internal details of the implementation work, they actually prevent the user from obtaining that information. That is, the user of an object cannot directly access the data held by an object as it is not visible to them. In other words, a program that calls this facility can treat the facility as a black box; the program knows what the facility's external interfaces guarantee to do, and that is all it needs to know.

It is worth pointing out a difference between the object oriented approach and the package approach used in Ada. In general a package will be a large unit of code providing a wide range of facilities with a large number of data structures. For example the Text IO package in Ada. In an object oriented language, the encapsulation is provided at the object level. While objects may well be as large and as complex as the typical Ada package, they are often much smaller. In languages such as Smalltalk where everything is an object, this means that the smallest data and code units also *naturally* benefit from encapsulation. Attempting to introduce the same level of encapsulation in Ada can be done, but it is not *natural* to the language.

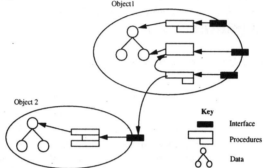

Figure 1.3: Object structure and interaction

Figure 1.3 illustrates the way in which encapsulation works within object oriented languages. It shows that anything outside the object can only gain access to the data the object holds via a specific interface (the black squares). In turn these interfaces trigger procedures which are internal to the object. These procedures may then access the data directly, use a second procedure as an intermediary or call an interface on another object.

1.8 Inheritance

1.8.1 What is inheritance?

A class is an example of a particular type of thing (for example mammals are a class of animal). In the object oriented world a class is a definition of the characteristics of that thing. Thus in the case of mammals, we might define that they have fur, are warm blooded and produce live young. Animals such as dogs and cats are then instances of the class mammal. This is all quite obvious and should not present a concept problem for anyone. However, in most object oriented languages (the language Self being an exception) the concept of the class is tightly linked to the concept of inheritance.

Inheritance allows us to state that one class is similar to another class but with a specified set of differences. Another way of putting it, is that we can define all the things which are common about a class of things, and then define what is special about each sub grouping within a subclass.

For example, if we have a class defining all the common traits of mammals we can define how particular categories of mammals differ. Take for example the Duck-billed platypus. This is a quite extraordinary mammal which differs from other mammals in a number of important ways. However, we do not want to have to define all the things which it has in common with mammals twice. Not only is this extra work, but we then have two places in which we have to maintain this information. We can therefore state that a Duck-billed platypus is a class of mammal that differs in that it does not produce live young (we might also want to mention its beak etc. but for now we will ignore these issues).

1.8.2 An example of inheritance

An example which is rather closer to home for most computer scientists is illustrated in Figure 1.4. For this example we will assume that we have been tasked with the job of designing and implementing an administration system for our local University. This system needs to record both employees of, and students attending, the university. For students we need to record what department they are in, what subjects/classes they are taking (referred to as modules) or what their thesis is about. For employees we need to record the department they work in, what their salary is, what subjects they lecture or research. If they are a professor we need to record that fact. In the case of professors we might also want to record the government bodies they work for.

Figure 1.4 illustrates a class hierarchy diagram for this application. That is, it illustrates each of the classes we have defined and from where they inherit their information. There are a number of points you should note about this diagram:

Inheritance versus instantiation. Stating that one class is a specialized version of a more generic class is different from saying that something is an example of a class of things. In the first case we might say that a lecturer is a category of university employee and that a professor is another category of university employee. Neither of these categories can be used to identify an individual. They are, in effect, templates for examples of those categories. In the second case we say that "John" is an example of a lecturer (just as "Chris", "Myra" and "Denise" may also be examples of lecturers). "John" is therefore an instance of a particular class (or category) of things known as Lecturers. It is important to get the concept of specializing a class with a subclass clear in your mind. It is all too easy to get *instances of a class* and a *subclass of a class* confused.

11

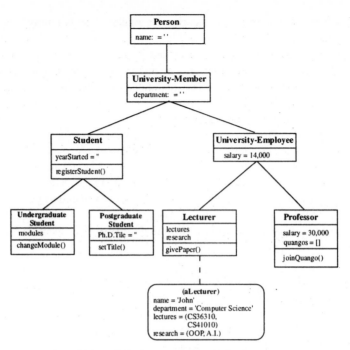

Figure 1.4: An example of inheritance

Inheritance of common information. We have placed common concepts together in a single class. For example, all people have a name, all University-Members have a nominated department (whether they are students or employees). All students have a year in which they started their studies, whether they are undergraduates or postgraduates. In turn all classes below University-Member *inherit* the concept of a department. This means that not only will all Professors and Lectures have a department, but "John" has a department which in this case is "Computer Science".

Abstract classes. It is also worth noting that we have defined a number of classes of which we have no intention of making an example. These include University-Member, University-Employee and Student. These are termed abstract classes (we will come back to this terminology later). They are intended as place holders for common features rather than as templates for a particular category of things. This is quite acceptable and is common practice in most object oriented programs.

Inheritance of defaults. Just because we have stated that all University-Employees earn a default salary of £14,000 a year does not mean that all university employees have to have that default. In the figure, Professors have a default of £30,000 illustrating that one class can over write the defaults defined in one of its parents.

Single versus multiple inheritance. In Figure 1.4 we have only illustrated single inheritance. That is, one class can inherit from only one other class. This is the case in many object oriented programming languages such as Smalltalk. However, other languages such as C++ and Eiffel allow multiple inheritance.

The idea behind multiple inheritance is that you can bring together the characteristics of two classes in order to define a new class. For example, you might have a class Toy and a class Car which could be used to create a class Toy-Car. Multiple inheritance is a controversial subject which is still being debated. Those who think it is useful fail to see why other languages don't include it and vice versa. Java the most recent object oriented language does not include multiple inheritance.

1.9 Abstraction

We have already touched on the subject of abstraction in the previous section. However, abstraction is much more than just the ability to define categories of things which can hold common features of other categories of things (e.g. Student is an abstract class of Undergraduate-Student and Postgraduate-Student). It is in fact a way of specifying what is particular about a class of things. Often this means defining the interface for an object, the data that such an object will hold and part of the functionality of that object.

For example, we might define a class DataBuffer. This class may be used to define an abstract class for things that hold data and return them on request. This class may define how the data is to be held and that operators such as put() and get() will be provided to add data to the DataBuffer and remove it from the DataBuffer respectively. In turn the implementation of these operators may be left to those implementing another class which is a subclass of DataBuffer.

The class DataBuffer might, for example, be used to implement a Stack or a Queue. Stack could implement get() as *return the most recent data item added* while Queue could implement it as *return the oldest data item held*. In either case, a user of either class will know that put() and get() are available and will work in an appropriate manner.

In some languages it can also be related to protection. For example, both C++ and Java have the ability to state whether subclasses are allowed to overwrite data or procedures (and indeed whether they have to overwrite them or not). Smalltalk does not provide the ability to state that a procedure cannot be overwritten, but it does allow the developer to state that a procedure (or method) is a subclass responsibility. That is, a subclass is expected to implement the procedure in order to provide a functioning class.

Abstraction is also associated with the ability to define Abstract Data Types (or ADTs). In object oriented terms these are classes (or groups of classes) which provide some sort of behavior (e.g. DataBuffer above) which acts as the infrastructure for a particular class of data types (e.g. things like stacks and queues). However, it is worth pointing out that ADTs are more commonly associated with procedural languages such as Ada. This is because the concepts in object orientation essentially supersede ADTs. That is, not only do they encompass all the elements of ADTs, they extend them by introducing inheritance.

1.10 Polymorphism

Polymorphism is a strange sounding (Greek derived) word for a relatively simple concept. It is essentially the ability to request that the same operation be performed by a wide range of different types of things. How that request is processed will depend on what it is that received the request. However, you as a programmer, need not worry about how the request is handled, only that it is. For example, you might ask a range of objects to provide a printable string describing themselves. This would mean that if you wished to ask an instance of the Lecturer class (presented above or the system) or a compiler object or a database object to return such a string, you would apparently use the same interface call (such as printString in Smalltalk).

The name *Polymorphism* is unfortunate and often leads to confusion. Of course, it also makes the whole process sound rather grander than it actually is. There are two types of polymorphism used in programming languages: overloading and overriding. The difference in name relates to how the mechanism used to resolve what code to execute is determined. The difference between the two is significant and is important to understand. To understand what polymorphism actually is, it helps to understand how these two different mechanisms work.

1.10.1 Overloading operators

This occurs when procedures have the same name but are applied to different data types. The compiler can therefore determine which operator will be used at compile time and can use the correct version of the operator. Ada uses exactly this type of overloading. For example, you can define a new version of the '+' operator for a new data type. Other programmers would use a '+' for addition and the compiler would use the types associated with the '+' operator to determine which version of '+' to use. In C, although the same function is used to print a value (namely printf), this is not a polymorphic function. Instead, the user must explicitly make sure that they are using the correct options in the format specifier to ensure that a value is printed correctly.

1.10.2 Overriding operators

This occurs when a procedure is defined in one class (for example, Student) and also in one of its subclasses (for example, Undergraduate-Student). This is referred to as overriding. This means that all instances of Student or Undergraduate-Student will respond to requests for this procedure (assuming it has not been made private to the class). For example, let us assume that we had defined the procedure printString in these classes. The pseudo code definition of this in Student might be:

```
printString
        return 'I am a student'
```

Where as in the Undergraduate-Student it might be defined as:

```
printString
    return 'I am an Undergraduate student'
```

The procedure in Undergraduate-Student replaces the version in Student for all instances of Undergraduate-Student. That is, if we made an instance of Undergraduate-Student and asked for the result of printString, we would get the string 'I am an Undergraduate student'. If you are confused, think of it this way:

> "If you have asked an object to perform some operation, then to determine which version of the procedure will be run, look in the class used to create your instance, if the procedure is not defined there, look in the class's parent class. Keep doing this until you find a procedure which implements the operation requested. This is the version which will be used."

In languages such as Smalltalk and Java the choice of which version of the procedure printString to execute is not determined at compile time. Instead it is chosen at run time. This is because the compiler would have to be able to determine what type of object will be operated on and then find which version of the procedure will therefore be run. In Smalltalk's case it cannot determine the type of object in most cases.

The technical term for this process of identifying which procedure to run at run time rather than compile time is called "late binding" and we shall look at this issue in more detail later in the book.

1.11 Summary

In this chapter you have been introduced to the background/history which led to object orientation. You have explored the main concepts which are the underpinnings of object orientation and have encountered some of the (sometimes arcane) terminology used. There is a great deal of new information in this chapter which can at times appear to make obsolete all that you already know.

The object oriented view of the world can be daunting for a programmer who is used to a more procedural view of the world. To have to adjust to this new view of the world is hard (and some never do). Others fail to see the difference between an object oriented programming language and a language such as ADA (ADA here refers to the pre-Ada 95 version of the language). However, object orientation will become second nature to many once they have worked with object oriented systems for a while. The key thing is to try things out as you go along and if possible have someone around who understands a bit about object orientation - they can often illuminate and simplify an otherwise gloomy network of tunnels.

1.12 Further reading

There are of course a great many books available on object orientation some of the best known include [Booch 1994; Budd 1991; Wirfs-Brock *et al* 1990; Cox and Novobilski 1991]. An excellent book aimed at managers and senior programmers who want to learn how to apply object oriented technology successfully to their projects is [Booch 1996]. Another good book in a similar style is [Yourdon 1994].

Other books which may be of interest to those attempting to convince themselves or others that object technology can actually work are [Harmon and Taylor 1993], [Love 1993] and [Meyer and Nerson 1993]. Other places to find useful references are the Journal of Object Oriented Programming, Pub. SIGS Publications, ISSN 0896-8438 and the OOPSLA conferences. These are a set of world wide conferences on Object Oriented Programming: Systems, Languages and Applications (hence OOPSLA). They are held every year, references for some recent ones are listed at the back of this book. There is also a European Conference on Object Oriented Programming called ECOOP. Some of these conference proceedings are also listed at the back of this book.

For further reading on the software crisis and approaches aimed at solving it see [Brooks 1987] and [Cox 1990]. For a discussion of the nature of scientific discovery, refinement and revolution see [Kuhn 1962].

2. Elements of Object Orientation

2.1 Introduction

This chapter is intended to reinforce what you have already learnt in Chapter 1. It concisely defines the terminology introduced in the last chapter and attempts to clarify issues associated with hierarchies. It also discusses some of the perceived strengths and weaknesses of the object oriented approach. Some guidance on the approach to take in learning about objects is also offered.

2.2 Terminology

In Chapter 1 a number of terms were introduced during the discussion of object orientation. Here we recap on those terms and introduce a number of new ones.

Class. A class is a definition for a combination of data and procedures which operate on those procedures. Instances of other classes can only access that data or those procedures via specified interfaces. A class acts as a template when creating new instances. That is, a class does not hold any data, the data is held in the instance. However, the class specifies what data will be held. This will be considered in more detail in Part 2 of this book. The relationship between a class, its superclass and any subclasses is illustrated in Figure 2.1.

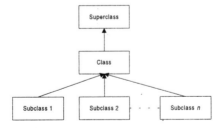

Figure 2.1: The relationship between Class, Superclass and Subclass

Subclass. A subclass is a class which inherits from another class. For example, in the last chapter, Undergraduate-Student was a subclass of Student. Subclasses are of course classes in their own right. The term subclass merely indicates what is inherited by what. Any class can have any number of subclasses.

Superclass. A superclass is the parent of a class. It is the class from which the current class inherits. For example, in the last chapter, Student class was the superclass of Undergraduate-Student. In Smalltalk a class can only have one superclass.

Instance / Object. An instance is an example of a class. All instances of a class possess the same data variables but have their own data in these data variables. Each instance of a class will also respond to the same set of requests.

Instance variable. This is the special name given to the data which is held by an object. The "state" of an object at any particular moment relates to the current values held by its instance variables. (In Smalltalk there are also class variables but a discussion of these will be left until later). Figure 2.2 illustrates a definition for a class in pseudo code. This definition includes some instance variable definitions fuel, mileage and name.

Method. Method is the name given to a procedure defined within an object. The name stems from its use in early versions of Smalltalk where it was a method used to get an object to do something or return something. It has since become more widely used with languages such as CLOS and Java also using the term. Two methods are defined in Figure 2.2, one calculates the miles per gallon while the other one sets the name of the car object.

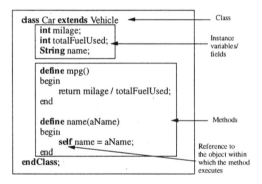

Figure 2.2: A pseudo code definition of a class

Message. This is a request from one object to another object requesting some operation or data. It is traditional to say that one object sends a message to another object requesting it to do something. The idea is that objects are polite well behaved entities which carry out functions by sending messages to each other. In other languages it might be consider akin to a procedure call (again this issue will be discussed later in part 2).

Self. This is a reference to the object within which the method is executing (see Figure 2.2). This means that it is possible to send messages to this object (i.e. ones' self).

Single/Multiple inheritance. Single and multiple inheritance refer to the number of superclasses that a class can inherit from. Smalltalk is a single inheritance system. This means that a class can only inherit from one superclass. C++ is a multiple inheritance system. This means that C++ classes can inherit from one or more classes.

2.3 Types of hierarchies in object orientation

This can be an area of confusion. In most object oriented systems there are two types of hierarchy, one refers to inheritance (whether single or multiple) while the other refers to instantiation. The inheritance hierarchy (or is-a hierarchy) has already been described. It is the way in which an object "inherits" features from a superclass.

The instantiation hierarchy relates to instances rather than classes and is important during the execution of the object. There are in fact two types of instance hierarchy, one indicates a part-of relationship while the other relates to a using relationship. Figure 2.3 illustrates the differences between the two.

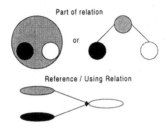

Figure 2.3: Instance relationships

The difference between an *is-a* relation and a *part-of* relationship is often confusing for new programmers (and sometimes for those who are experienced in one language but are new to an object oriented programming language such as Smalltalk). Figure 2.4 should make it clear. This figure illustrates that a student *is-a* type of person where as an engine is *part-of* a car. That is, it does not makes sense to say that a student is *part-of* a person nor that an engine *is-a* type of car!

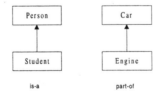

Figure 2.4: is-a does not equal part-of

In Smalltalk, the *is-a* relationship is generally implemented via the subclassing mechanism. It is thus possible to build up large and complex class hierarchies which express these *is-a* relationships. These classes express the concept of inheritance, allowing one class to inherit features from another. The total set of features are then used to create an instance of a class. In contrast, the *part-of* relationships tend to be implemented using instance variables in Smalltalk.

However, *is-a* relationships and classes are not exactly the same thing. For example, if you wished to construct a *semantic network* consisting of explicit *is-a* relationships between instances you might have to construct such a hierarchy manually. The aim of such a structure is to represent some sort of knowledge and the relationships between elements of that knowledge and not for the construction of instances. This is outside the scope of the subclassing mechanism and would therefore be inappropriate.

Another confusion between *is-a* relationships and classes is that John might be an instance of a class Person. It would be perfectly (semantically) correct to say that John *is-a* Person. However, here we are obviously talking about the relationship between an instance and a class rather than a subclass and its parent class.

A further confusion can occur for those encountering Smalltalk who have first encountered a strongly typed language. These people might at first assume that a subclass and a sub type are essentially the same. However, they are not the same, although they are very similar. The problem with classes, types and is-a relationships is that on the surface they appear to capture the same sorts of concepts. For example, see Figure 2.5. In this figure, the four diagrams all capture some aspect of the use of the phrase is a. However, they are all intended to capture a different relationship.

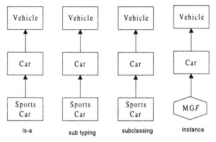

Figure 2.5: Satisfying four relationships

All of the confusion highlighted above is due to the fact that in modern English we tend to over use the term *is-a*. We can distinguish between the four different types of relationship by being more precise about our definitions in terms of a programming language such as Smalltalk. For example, in Table 2.1 we define the meaning of the four different relationships identified above.

Table 2.1: Types of is-a relationships

type	substitutability relationship. That is an example of one type that can be used interchangeably with another (sub)type.
subclassing / inheritance	an implementation mechanism for sharing code and representation
specialization	specifying that one thing is a special case of another
instantiation	one thing is an example of a particular category (class) of things

To illustrate this point consider Figure 2.6. This figure illustrates the differences between the first three categories. The first diagram illustrates the potential relationships between a set of classes defining the behavior of different categories of vehicle. The second diagram presents the sub type relationships between the categories while the third diagram illustrates a straight specialization set of relationships. Note that although the *estate car* is a specialization of a *car with hatch*, its implementation (the subclassing hierarchy) indicates that it does not share any of its implementation with the *car with hatch* class.

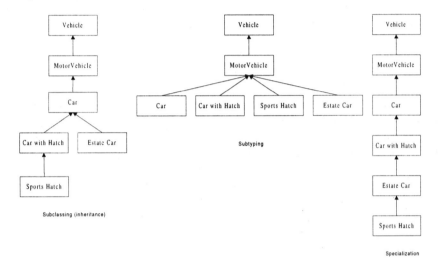

Figure 2.6: Distinguishing between the relationships

It is worth noting that another difference between type and subclassing is that type relationships are specifications, while classes (and subclasses) are implementations of behavior.

2.4 Why bother?

We have already stated that the transition from a procedural view point to an object oriented view point is not always an easy one. This begs the question "why bother?". As you are reading this book you must at least be partly convinced that it is a good idea. Of course this could be because you have noticed the number of job advertisements offering employment for those with object oriented skills. However, that aside, why should you bother learning a new programming paradigm?

Hopefully, some of the reasons why you should bother will become clear during your reading of this book. However, it is worth considering at least some of the issues at this point.

2.4.1 Software industry blues

There is still no silver bullet for the problems in the software industry. Object oriented technology does not take away the problems which exist in constructing complex software systems, it just makes some of the pitfalls harder to fall into and provides ways of simplifying traditionally difficult problems. However, difficulties in software development are almost inevitable, many of them arise due to the inescapable intangibility of software and not necessarily all by accident or poor development methods.

We should not however just throw up our hands and say "well if that's the case, it is not our fault". Many of the problems which have beset our industry relate to some deficiency in how programmers build software today. For example, if a software development is running late then just adding more people to that late project is likely to make matters worse rather than get the project back on time.

Of course object technology is not the first attempt at addressing these issues. However, past attempts have met with mixed success. This is for a number of reasons, only some of which we will consider below. However, as these issues are particularly pertinent to object technology, we will therefore consider each in turn.

2.4.1.1 Modularity of code

Traditional, procedural systems, typically relied on the fact that not only would the data they were using not change (e.g. its type) but the way in which they got that data would not alter. Invariably, it was the function (or functions) using the data, that actually went and got that data. This meant that if the way in which the data was accessed had to change, all the functions which used that data had to be re-written. Those among you who have attended any sort of software engineering course will of course say that what was required was a function to obtain the data. This function could then be used in many different places. However, such application specific functions tend not to get used in "real world" systems. This occurs for several reasons including:

- Small subroutines are too much effort. Although many people talk about reusable code, they often mean relatively large code units. Small functions of one, two or three lines tend only to be defined by a single programmer and are rarely shared amongst a development team, let alone development teams.
- Too many subroutines leads to too little reuse. The larger the number of subroutines available, the less likely that they will get reused. It is very difficult to search through a code library of small subroutines trying to find one which does what you want. It is often much quicker to write it yourself!
- Identifying that a function may be reusable may not be obvious. If you are a programmer working on one part of a system, it may not be obvious that the function you are writing would be of generic use. If these functions are small then they will not have been identified by the designer as being useful reusable components.

2.4.1.2 Ability to package software

Another issue is the way in which programming languages package up software for reuse. Many systems assume that the software should be partitioned into modules, which are then integrated at compile time. Such fixed compile time integration can be good for some types of problem, but in many cases it is too inflexible. For example, while this approach can ensure that the modules being reused are compatible, the developer many not know until run time which modules they wish to use. They would therefore require some form of run time binding.

The UNIX pipes and filters are examples of software systems which can be bound at run time. They act as glue allowing the developer to link two or more programs in sequence together. However, in this case there is absolutely no error protection. It is quite possible to link two incompatible systems together.

What would be really useful would be a combination of these features. That is, the ability to specify either compile time or run time binding. In either case there should be some form of error checking to ensure that you are integrating compatible modules. An important criteria is to avoid the need for extensive recompilation, for example just because one line has been altered. Finally, such a system should by definition enforce encapsulation and make packaging of the software effortless.

2.4.1.3 Flexibility of code

In early procedural languages there was little or no flexibility, for example, C or Pascal. However, more recent procedural languages have introduced some flexibility but need extensive specification to achieve this. The result is internal flexibility at the cost of interface overheads, for example Ada. Object technology allows code flexibility (and data flexibility) with little overhead.

2.4.2 The claimed advantages of object orientation

There are a range of benefits which can be identified for object oriented programming languages. Not all of these are unique to object oriented technology, but that's okay, we are talking about the good things about object orientation here. The main benefits can be summarized as:

Increased code reuse. Languages such as Smalltalk encourage reuse. Every time you specify that one class inherits from another (and you do it all the time in Smalltalk) you are involved in reuse. In time most developers start to actively look to see where they can restructure classes to improve the potential for reuse. As long as this is not taken too far, this is an extremely healthy thing to do.

Data protection for little effort. Due to the encapsulation facilities provided as part of the language you get your data protected from unscrupulous users. Unlike languages such as Ada, you don't have to write reams of specification in order to achieve this protection.

Encapsulation eases integration. As users of an object cannot access the internals of the object they must go via specified interfaces. As these interfaces can be published in advance of the object being implemented, others can develop to those interfaces knowing that they will be available when the object is implemented.

Encapsulation eases maintenance. This point is really a variation on the last point. As users of an object have been forced to access the object via the specified interfaces, as long as the external behavior of these objects appears to remain the same, the internals of the object can be completely changed. For example, an object could store an item of data in a flat file, read it from a sensor or obtain it from a database. However, external uses of the object need never know.

Simplified code - polymorphism. With polymorphism you don't need to worry about exactly what type of object you will get at run time, only that it must respond to the message (request for a method to be executed) you send it. This means that it is a great deal easier to write reusable, compact code, than in many other languages.

More intuitive programming paradigm. It has been argued that object orientation is a more intuitive programming paradigm than approaches such as procedural. This is because we humans tend to perceive the world in terms of objects. We see dials, windows, switches, fuel pumps, automated teller machines (ATMs). These *objects* respond to our use in specific ways when we interact with them. For example, an ATM will require a card, a PIN number etc. in a particular sequence. Of course those of us who have programmed before bring with us a lot of baggage including preconceptions of what a program should be like and how you develop one. Hopefully, this book is about to turn all that on its head for a while, before putting everything back together again.

2.4.3 What are the problems/pitfalls?

Of course no programming language / paradigm is without its own set of problems and pitfalls. Indeed part of the skill in becoming fluent in a new programming language is learning what the problems are and how to avoid them. In this section we will concentrate on the damning statements usually leveled at object orientation. We will deal with common software problems in a later chapter.

2.4.3.1 Lots of confusing terminology

This is actually a fair comment. As you have already seen, object orientation is littered with new terms and definitions for what appears to have already been defined quite acceptably in other languages. It is difficult to argue against this and one may ask the question why this is the case? Certainly, back in the early 70s when Smalltalk was being researched, many of the terms we now take for granted were already quite well established. It would be unreasonable to assume that even if the inventors of the language like their own terminology early users would have tried to get the terminology changed.

One possible answer to this is that in the past (that is, during the early and mid eighties) object oriented languages, such as Smalltalk, tended to be the preserve of academics and research institutions. (Indeed I myself was introduced to it while working on a research project at a British university during 1986/87 having worked with Lisp Flavors for a few years). It is often the case that these people enjoy the mystique that a language with terminology all of its own can create. By now it is so well established in the object oriented culture that you as a new comer will just have to adapt. The important point to remember is that the concepts are actually very simple, although the practice can be harder. To illustrate this, consider the following table, this attempts to illustrate the parallels between object oriented terminology and procedural terminology:

These approximations should not be taken too literally as they are intended only to help you visualize what each of the terms means. Hopefully, by the end of the book you will have gained your own understanding of their meaning.

Table 2.2: Approximate equivalents

Procedural term	OO term
procedure	method
procedure call	message
non-temporary data	instance variables
record + procedures	object

2.4.3.2 Yet another programming paradigm to master

In general people tend to like the things they are used to. This is why many people will buy the same make of car again and again (even when it gives them trouble). It is also why computer scientists will refuse to move to a new word processor / editor / operating system or hardware. Over the years I have had many "discussion" with people over the use of Latex versus Word versus WordPerfect, the merits of Emacs and Vi or of UNIX versus Mac or Windows/DOS. In most cases the issues raised and points made indicate that those involved in the discussions (including myself) are biased, have their own "hobby horse" to promote and don't understand fully what the other approach is about.

Object orientation both benefits and suffers from this phenomena. There are those who hold it up almost like a religion and those who cast it aside because it is so different from what they are used to. Many justify this latter approach by pointing out that procedural programming has been around for quite a while now and many systems are successfully developed using it. This is of course a reasonable statement and one which promotes the status quo. However, the fact that object orientation is a new software paradigm, which is quite different from the procedural paradigm, should not be a reason for rejecting it.

The important points to note about it are that it explicitly encourages encapsulation (information hiding), promotes code reuse and enables polymorphism. Most procedural languages have of course attempted to present these advantages as well, however they have failed to do so in such a coherent and concise manner. Take Ada for example, not only is it a large cumbersome language, it requires an extensive specification to be written to enable two packages to work together. Any error in these specifications and the system will not compile (even if there are no errors or incompatibilities in the code). It is also interesting to note that Ada 95 has introduced the concept of objects and classes into the language. Although for most object technology practitioners, the way in which it has done this, is both counter intuitive and unwieldy.

2.4.3.3 Many OO environments are inefficient

Historically, object oriented development environments have been inefficient, processor intensive and memory hungry. Such environments tended to be designed for use on powerful workstations or mini-computers. Examples of such environments have included Lisp Flavors (which even required specialist hardware e.g. the Symbolics Lisp machine), Self and Smalltalk-80 (the fore runner of VisualWorks). These machines were expensive, sometimes non-standard and aimed at the research community.

With the advent of the PC, attempts were made to rectify this situation. For example, Smalltalk/V was designed specifically to run on the PC and the first version of Smalltalk used by the author was on a 286 PC. The current versions of products such as VisualWorks are now extremely efficient and optimized for use on PC platforms. Although in the case of VisualWorks the use of 16 megabytes of RAM is advisable, any 486 machine or above provides ample performance. The issue of 16 MEG rather than the current 8 MEG is not large, as an additional 8 MEG can be purchased at reasonable rates and many industry pundits predict that 64 MEG (and more) will soon become industry standards. Indeed systems are now emerging which assume that a user will have access to larger memory (such as J++ which requires a minimum of 24 MEG to run the debugger).

Of the course the whole of this section is not really relevant to C++ and object oriented versions of Pascal (such as Delphi) as they are no more memory or processor intensive than any non-object oriented language. However, it is worth noting that these languages do not offer the same level of support for the programmer as for example Smalltalk. In particular they do not provide automatic memory management and garbage collection. However, we will discuss this issue in more detail later in the book.

2.4.3.4 Smalltalk environments are not geared up for project development

Smalltalk environments such as VisualWorks, are derived from the early Smalltalk development systems (see chapter 4). These early development environments were originally designed for a single programmer to develop their own personal programs. This means that the environment provides a great deal of support for developing a single system within a single process, however it provides little or no support for group working. This means that when Smalltalk is used as the basis of a group project (such as is the norm in today's software industry), the project team members must use the facilities provided by the host operating system to share data and code.

In most development environments the above issue is not a problem. However, in VisualWorks the situation is rather different. This is because of the way in which source code and executable code are held by the "environment". It actually takes a conscientious act on the part of the programmer to "extract" their code from the environment and save it onto the host operating system's file system. It is therefore all to easy to get out of "sync" with other members of the team, to forget to obtain the latest version of source code or to have problems when attempting to merge code written by different developers for the same class.

This obviously means that Smalltalk is unsuited to this type of development! Doesn't it? In fact, it is not difficult to provide suitable protocols to ensure that the above situation does not happen. These can in some cases be used to program extensions to the basic environment to make group working easier. It is also possible to purchase support software which does provide extremely good support for group project working. It is therefore incorrect to say that Smalltalk does not support team based software development.

2.5 The move to object technology

At present you are still acclimatizing yourself to object orientation. It is extremely important that from now on you do your utmost to immerse yourself in object orientation, object technology and (in the case of this book) Smalltalk. This is because, when you first encounter a new language/paradigm, it is all to easy to say that it is not good because you can't do what you could do in language/paradigm X. We are all subject to the "better the devil you then the devil you don't" style syndrome. If you embrace object orientation, warts and all, at least for the present, you will gain most.

In addition, it is often a fact of life that most of us tend to fit in learning something new around our existing schedules. This may mean for example, that you are trying to read this book and do the practicals presented while working in C, VisualBasic, Ada etc. either for various assignments or for your employer. From personal experience, and from teaching others about Smalltalk, you will gain most by putting aside a significant amount of time and concentrating on the subject matter involved. This is not only because object orientation is so different, but also because you need to get familiar not only with the concepts but also with Smalltalk and its development environment.

So have a go, take a "leap of faith" and stick with it until the end. If at the end you still can't see the point then fair enough, but until then accept it.

2.6 Summary

In this chapter we have reviewed some of the terminology introduced in the previous chapter. We have also considered the types of hierarchy which occur in object oriented systems and which can at first be confusing. We have then considered the pros and cons of object oriented programming. You should now be ready to start to think in terms of objects. As has already been stated, this will at first seem a strange way to develop a software system, but in time it will become second nature. In the next chapter we examine how an object oriented system might be developed and structured. This will be done without reference to any source code as the intention is to familiarize you, the reader, with objects rather than Smalltalk. This is because it is all to easy to get through a book on Smalltalk, C++, Java etc. and understand the text but still have no idea how to start developing an object oriented system.

2.7 Exercises

Research what other authors have said about single and multiple inheritance. Why should languages such as Smalltalk and Java not include multiple inheritance?

Look for terms such as class, method member, member function, instance variable and constructor in the books listed in the further reading section. When you have found them, read their explanation of these terms and write down you own understanding of their meaning.

2.8 Further reading

Suggested further reading for this chapter include [Coad and Yourdon 1991], [LaLonde and Pugh 1991] and [Meyer 1988]. In additional all the books mentioned in the previous chapter are still relevant.

3. Constructing an Object Oriented System

3.1 Introduction

This chapter takes you through the design of a simple object oriented system. It does not concern itself with implementation issues nor with the details of any particular language. Instead, the aim of this chapter is to illustrate how the concepts described in the last two chapters can be used to construct a software system. In the remainder of the chapter we describe the application to be constructed. We then consider where to start looking for objects and from there, what the objects should do and how they should do it. We conclude by discussing issues such as class inheritance and answer questions such as "where is the structure of the program?".

3.2 The application: windscreen wipe simulation

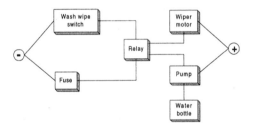

Figure 3.1: The windscreen wash wipe system structure

The aim of this system is to provide a system diagnosis tutor for the equipment illustrated in Figure 3.1. That is, rather than use the wash wipe system from a real car, students on a car mechanics diagnosis course will use this software simulation. The software system will provide a simulation whose behavior will mimic that of the actual system, thus the behavior of the pump will depend on information provided by the relay and the water bottle.

The operation of the wash wipe system is controlled by the wash wipe switch which can be in one of 5 different positions. These are: *off, intermittent, slow, fast* and *wash*. Each of these settings places the system into a different state:

OFF. The system is inactive.

INTERMITTENT. The wiper motor wipes the wiper blades across the windscreen (or windshield if you are American) every few second.

SLOW. The wiper motor continuously wipes the wiper blades across the windscreen.

FAST. The wiper motor continuously wipes the wiper blades quickly across the windscreen.

WASH. The wash setting is a power wash in which the water pump sprays water onto the windscreen. This water is drawn from the water bottle.

For the pump or the wiper motor to work correctly, the relay must function correctly. In turn the relay must be supplied with an electrical circuit. This electrical circuit is negatively fused and thus the fuse must be intact for the circuit to be made. Note cars (automobiles) are negatively switched as this reduces the chances of short circuits which lead to unintentional switching of circuits.

3.3 Where do we start?

This is often a very difficult point for those new to object oriented systems. That is, they have read the basics, understand the simple diagrams they have been presented with, but "where do they start?". It is the old chestnut, "I understand the example but don't know how to apply the concepts myself". This is not unusual and in the case of object orientation is probably normal.

The actual answer to the question "where do I start?" may at first seem somewhat obscure, you should start "with the data". Remember that objects are based around the idea of having things which exchange messages with each other. These things possess the data which is held by the system and the messages which request actions to be performed that relate to this data. Thus an object oriented system is fundamentally concerned with these data items.

Before we go on to consider the object oriented view of the system, let us stop and think for a while. Ask yourself "where would I start if I was going to develop such a system in C or Pascal or even Ada? In most cases the answer will be with some form of "functional" decomposition. That is, you might think about the main functions of the system and then break them down into sub functions and so on. As a natural part of this exercise the data required to support the desired functionality would be identified. Note that the emphasis would be on the system functionality.

Let us take this further and consider the example presented above and the functions we might identify:

Wash	pump water from the water bottle to the windscreen.
Wipe	move the windscreen wipers across the windscreen

We would then identify important system variables as well as sub functions used to support the above.

Now let us go back to the object oriented view of the world. In this view we place a great deal more emphasis on the data items involved and consider the operations associated with that data (which is effectively the reverse of the functional decomposition view). This means that we start off by attempting to identify the primary data items in the system, next we look to see what operations are applied to / performed on these data items. Finally, we group these data items and operations together to form objects. Note that in identifying the operations to perform we may well have had to consider additional data items. These additional data items might be separate objects or attributes of the current object. Identifying which is which is mostly a matter of skill and experience.

Note that the OO approach makes the operations a far less important aspect of the design than the data and their relationships. In the next section we will examine what objects might exist in our simulation system.

3.4 Identifying the objects

As was indicated in the last section we start off by identifying the primary data objects. In this case we might look at the system as a whole and ask ourselves what indicates the state of the system. We might then say that the position of the windscreen wash switch is important or that the status of the pump is significant. This might result in the following table of data items:

Table 3.1: Data items and their associated state information

switch setting	is it off, intermittent, wipe, fast wipe or wash
wiper motor	is it working or not
pump state	is the pump working or not
fuse condition	has the fuse blown or not
water bottle level	the current water level
relay status	whether current is flowing or not

How these are identified in general will be considered in greater detail in Part 6 of this book. At this point, merely note that we have not yet mentioned the functionality of the system nor how it might fit together, only what are the significant items.

As this is such a simple system we could now assume that each of these elements will be an object and illustrate this in a simple object diagram.

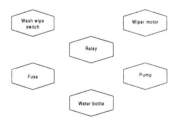

Figure 3.2: Objects in simulation system[1]

Notice that I have named the objects after the element associated with the data item (e.g. the element associated with the fuse condition is naturally the fuse itself) and that the actual data items involved (e.g. the condition of the fuse or the level of the water in the bottle) is an instance variable of the object. This is a very common way of naming objects and their instance variables. We now have the basic objects required for our application.

3.5 Identifying the services/methods

At the moment all we have are a set of objects each of which can hold some data. For example, the water bottle can hold an integer indicating the current water level. However, although object oriented systems are structured around the data, we still need some procedural content to change the state of an object or to make the system achieve some goal. Therefore, we also need to consider what operations a user of each object might require. Note that the emphasis here is on the *user of the object* and what they will *require of the object* rather than what operations will be performed on the data.

Let us start with the switch object. The switch state can take a number of values such as 'off', 'wash' and 'wipe'. As we don't want other objects to have direct access to this variable we must identify the services which the switch should offer. As a user of a switch we want to be able to move it between its various settings. As these settings are essentially an enumerated type, we can have the concept of incrementing or decrementing the switch position. A switch must therefore provide a moveUp and a moveDown interface. Exactly how this is done will depend on the programming language used. For now we will just concentrate on specifying the required facilities.

If we continue examining each object and identifying the required services we could end up with the following list:

switch	moveUp	increment switch value as above
	moveDown	decrement switch value as above
	state?	return a value indicating the current switch state
fuse	working?	indicate if the fuse has blown or not
wiper motor	working?	indicates whether the wipers are working or not
pump	working?	indicates whether the pump is active or not
water bottle	fill	fill the water bottle with water
	extract	remove some water from the water bottle
	empty	empty the water bottle

Note that we have generated the list by examining each of the objects in isolation. The aim was to identify the services which might reasonably be required. We may

---

[1] The hexagonal shape used in this figure for instances is based on the structured cloud used in version 0.8 of the Unified Modeling Language described in Part 6 of this book.

well identify further services when we attempt to "put it all together" but for the moment we will stick to these.

Each of these services should relate to a method within the object. For example, the `moveUp` and `moveDown` services should relate to methods which change the `state` instance variable within the object. Using a generic pseudo code, the `moveUp` method, within the `switch` object, might resemble:

```
define method moveUp()
        if state = 'off' then
                state := 'wash'
        elseif state = 'wash' then
                state := 'wipe'
        endif
end define method
```

This method will change the value of the state variable in switch. The new value of the instance variable will depend on its previous value. `moveDown` could be defined in a similar manner. Note that the reference to the instance variable illustrates that it is global to the object. Also notice that the method `moveUp` requires no parameters. This is common in object oriented systems. That is, few parameters need to be passed between methods (particularly of the same object) as it is the object which holds the data anyway.

3.6 Refining the objects

If we look back to Table 3.1, we can see that *relay, fuse, wiper motor* and *pump* possess an interface 'working?'. This is a first hint that these three objects may have something in common. Each of them presents the same interface to the outside world. If we then consider their attributes, they all possess a common instance variable. At this point it is too early to be able to say whether relay, pump and fuse are all instances of the same class of object (e.g. a Component class) or whether they are all instances of their own classes which may inherit from some common super class (see Figure 3.3). However this is something we will need to bear in mind later.

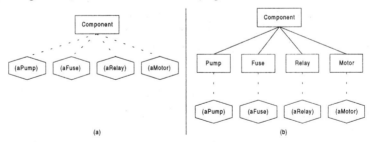

Figure 3.3: Possible classes for components in the simulation

33

3.7 Bringing it all together

So far we have identified the primary objects in our system and the basic set of services they should present. These services were based solely on what data the objects held. We must now consider how to make our system function. To do this we need to consider how it might be used. In the introduction it was suggested that this system would be part of a very simple diagnosis tutor. The idea being that a student would use the system to learn about the effects of various faults on the operation of a real wiper system, without the need for expensive electronics. We therefore wish to allow a user of the system to operate in the following manner:

1. change the state of a component device,
2. ask the motor what is its new state.

Point 1 is already supported by the moveUp and moveDown operations on the switch. Similar operations could be provided for the fuse, the water bottle and the relay. In the case of the fuse and the relay we might provide a changeState interface. This interface might be implemented by a method which used the following pseudo code algorithm:

```
define method changeState()
        if state = 'working' then
                state := 'notWorking'
        else
                state := 'working'
        endif
end define method
```

Point 2 above is more complicated. For the first time we have encountered a situation where we want one object's state (the value of its instance variable) to be dependent on information provided by other objects. If we were to write down procedurally how the value of other objects affected the status of the pump, we might get:

```
if fuse is working then
    if switch is not off then
        if relay is working then
                pump status := 'working'
        endif
    endif
endif
```

This algorithm says that the pump status depends on the relay status, the switch setting and the fuse status. This is the sort of algorithm you might expect to find in a main() program. It links all the sub functions together and processes the data.

Of course in an object oriented language (such as Smalltalk) we don't have a main program. In an object oriented system we have well mannered objects passing messages between one another. How then do we achieve the same effect as the above algorithm? The answer is that we must get the objects to pass messages requesting the appropriate information. One way to do that would be to define a method in the pump object which would get all the required information from the other objects and determine the motors state. However, this would require that the pump had links to all the other objects so that it could send them messages. This is a little contrived and loses the structure of the underlying system. It also loses any modularity in the system. That is, if we want to add new components then we would have to change the pump object, even if the new components only affect the switch. This approach also indicates that the developer is thinking too procedurally and not really in terms of objects.

Now let us consider the object oriented view of this system. The pump object only really needs to know what state the relay is in. It should therefore request this information from the relay. In turn the relay must request information from the switches and the fuse. This is illustrated in Figure 3.4.

This figure illustrates the chain of messages initiated by the pump object. That is, the pump object sends a message working to the relay, then:

1. relay sends a message *state* to the switch
   the switch replies to the switch
2. relay sends a second message *working?* to the fuse
   the fuse replies to the relay
3. the relay replies to the motor

If at this point the pump is working, then the pump object sends on the final message to the water bottle.

4. pump sends a message *extract* to the water bottle.

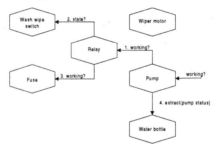

Figure 3.4: Collaborations between the objects for wash operation

In this last case a parameter has been passed with the message, this is because, unlike all the previous messages which were merely requesting state information, this message is requesting a change in state. The parameter indicates the rate at which the pump is drawing water from the water bottle.

Note that the water bottle should not record the value of the pump's status as it does not own this value. That is, if it should ever need the motor's status in the future it should request it from the pump rather than using the (potentially obsolete) value passed to it.

For completeness let us consider the algorithm used in the pump to initiate this process. In Figure 3.4 we assumed that the pump provided the interface working?

which allowed this process to start. Thus the pseudo code of working? for the pump object is:

```
define method working?()
        self status := relay working.
        if self status = 'working' then
                water bottle extract (self status)
        endif
end define method
```

You should note a number of points about this method. Firstly it is a lot simpler than the procedural program presented earlier. Secondly, this algorithm only shows us part of the story. It only shows us what is directly relevant to the pump. This means that it can be much more difficult to deduce the operation of an object oriented system merely by reading the source code. Smalltalk alleviates this problem, to some extent, through the use of sophisticated browsers. Finally, at no point do we change the value of any variables which are not part of the pump, although they may have been changed as a result of the messages being sent.

3.7.1 Where is the structure?

One of the points made at the end of the last section can be very confusing and off putting to someone new to object orientation. This is because they have lost one of the key elements that they use for helping them understand and structure a software system - the main program body. This is because we are dealing with objects and thus it is the objects and the interactions between them which act as the corner stone of the system comprehension. In many ways Figure 3.4 is the object oriented equivalent of a main program. This also highlights an important feature of most object oriented approaches - graphical illustrations. Many aspects of object technology are most easily explained graphically, e.g. object structure, class inheritance and message chains. This has led to many object oriented design methods being heavily graphical.

Let us now consider the structure of our object oriented system. The structure in this case is dictated by the messages which will be sent between objects. That is, an object must possess a reference to another object in order to send it a message. The resulting system structure is illustrated in Figure 3.5.

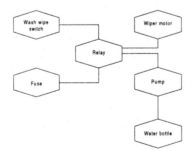

Figure 3.5: Wash wipe system structure

In Smalltalk this structure would be achieved by making instance variables reference the appropriate objects. How this is done will be considered at a later date. The point to note is that this is the structure which exists between the instances in the system and does not relate to the classes which act as the templates for the instances.

Earlier we discussed the relationship between the fuse, the relay and the pump. We will now come back to this issue to consider the classes used to create the instances. We could just assume that each object is an instance of an equivalent class. This is illustrated in Figure 3.6.a. However, as has already been noted, some of the classes bear a very strong resemblance. In particular, fuse, relay and motor all share a number of common features. Table 3.2 compares the features (instance variables and methods) of these three objects.

Table 3.2: Comparison of Components

	fuse	**relay**	**motor**	**pump**
instance variable	state	state	state	state
services	working?	working?	working?	working?

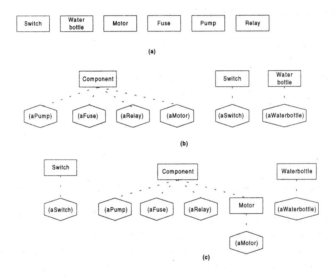

Figure 3.6: Possible class inheritance relationships

From this table it appears that the only way in which they differ is that they have different names. This would suggest that they are all instances of a common class such as Component (see Figure 3.6.b). This class would possess an additional instance variable name to simplify object identification. However, the problem with making them all instances of a common class is that they must all behave in exactly the same way. This is not the case. We want the pump to start the analysis process off when it receives the message working?. Thus the definition of working? that it possesses must be different from fuse and relay. However, in other ways it is very similar to fuse and relay. Therefore, what we want is for fuse and relay to be instances of a class (say Component) and for pump to be an instance of a class which

37

inherits from Component (but which redefines working?). This is illustrated in Figure 3.6.c.

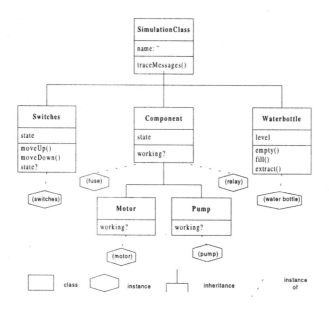

Figure 3.7: The final class hierarchy and instance diagram

3.8 Summary

In this chapter you have seen how one, very simple system, can be broken down into objects. These objects combine to provide the overall functionality of the system. You should have seen how the data to be represented determines the objects used and that the inter object interactions determine the structure of the system. You should also have noted that the identification of the objects, their classes, the methods and instance variables is more of an evolutionary process than that used in non object oriented languages.

3.9 Exercises

Take a system with which you are familiar and try to break it down into objects. Carry out a similar set of steps to those described above. Do not worry about how you would implement the objects you identify or the classes required to generate these objects. Finally, use whatever representation best fits your way of working for describing what the methods do. If you wish, use a pseudo code, or use a programming language such as C or Pascal if you prefer. You could even use a flow chart if that is what you are most comfortable with. It is very important that you try and do this as it is a useful exercise in learning to think in terms of objects.

3.10 Further reading

A good place to start further reading on building object oriented systems is with the first few chapters of [Rumbaugh *et al* 1991]. In addition [Wirfs-Brock *et al* 1990] is an excellent, non-language specific introduction to structuring object oriented systems. It uses a rather simplistic approach which is ideal for learning about object oriented system design, but not really generally applicable. This is not a problem here as what you want to do at the moment is get the background rather than specific techniques. Another good references for further reading is [Yourdon 1994].

The Smalltalk
Language

4. An Introduction to Smalltalk

4.1 Introduction

During the nineties the Smalltalk tools market has grown hugely, for example in 1994 in the US the market was worth about $56 million which was a 60% increase on the previous year [Shan 1995]. This is not just an American phenomena, Smalltalk is now taught in universities in China and Russia and the number of American universities teaching Smalltalk doubled in 1994. The growing interest in Smalltalk is fueled by two factors: alleged failures of C++ based projects and stories of successful Smalltalk developments. For example, EDS (Electronic Data Systems) re-implemented a PL/I based application in Smalltalk in order to compare the development costs of the two languages. The results showed a 3:1 or 4:1 productivity increase in design and programming with little or no performance degradation [Taylor 1992]. This has resulted in Smalltalk becoming the natural successor to COBOL (as opposed to C++) in many organizations. For example, of 137 MIS sites using COBOL in the US, that have approved the migration to object oriented techniques, the majority have opted for Smalltalk and of the remainder, 26% of the C++ developers would recommend Smalltalk [Shan 1995].

In this chapter we encounter Smalltalk, its development environment (and in particular VisualWorks) and some of the tools available in that environment. We also learn a little bit about the history of Smalltalk and consider what Smalltalk comprises (in the way of a programming language, a programming system and a development environment).

4.2 What is Smalltalk

Smalltalk can be viewed from a number of different perspectives. This differs from most other programming languages in that they can be viewed as a programming language and nothing else. However, Smalltalk (at least as embodied by systems such as VisualWorks) is far more than just a programming language. Below we consider some of the ways of classifying Smalltalk:

- *An object oriented programming language.* It certainly provides an OO language, that is the syntax and semantics of the language. The language is supported by a number of compilers which take programs written in Smalltalk and produce an executable. As you will see later, they actual tend to produce a byte code form which is then run on a virtual machine. But

43

more on that later. As for the Smalltalk language itself, it is actually very small and rather compact, unlike languages such as Ada, which are very large.

- *A programming environment.* We refer here to the presence of the 'system' provided objects rather than any particular development environment. Unlike many languages (including C++) Smalltalk has associated with it a large (and fairly standard) set of classes. These classes (which run to over a thousand in some versions of Smalltalk) make Smalltalk very powerful. You will spend most of your time extending the "system" rather than programming from scratch.

  In a number of cases these classes provide facilities which would normally be considered to be part of the language in Ada, C and Pascal. The result is that Smalltalk is anything but a *small* programming system. In many ways Smalltalk takes to the extreme the approach that some other languages take, in that, the basic language is very small and is really little more than a set of building blocks, but these building blocks can be used to provide more complex constructs. However, unlike many other languages Smalltalk does so by providing a common set of facilities.

- *An application development environment (ADE).* Because of Smalltalk's history, it has an extremely well developed ADE which provides far greater integration and openness than many other systems. As the browsers, inspectors and debuggers are all derived from the same source, there is also consistency between (some of) the various implementations. In addition, the source code for these tools is also available with the ADE.

  Other languages now have similar environments (most notably Visual C++) however, most of them are modeled on those found in Smalltalk implementations and few of them illustrate any pretence of consistency between vendors.

Thus it is quite possible to say that Smalltalk is a programming language, a set of extensible classes, a development environment or even a user interface development tool. It is, in fact, all of these.

4.3 Objects in Smalltalk

In Smalltalk everything is an object (or should be treated as an object). For example, the following expression:

$$2 + 3.$$

should be read as the object 2 is sent the message +, with the argument the object 3. In fact in this case for efficiency sake the + message is hard coded into the virtual machine (you will learn about this later). However, if you search for the method + it is there, it is just that its implementation is hidden from you.

This pure object view has some interesting side effects on the language constructs such as conditional statements. They are really messages to the objects *true* or *false* rather than being part of the language syntax. Another example are the iterative control statements (the Smalltalk equivalent of *for* or *while* loops in procedural languages) which are messages to numeric intervals or blocks. You will learn more about these from Chapter 6 onwards.

4.4 History

The original goals for Smalltalk were described by Alan Kay in the early 1970s. The initial sketches that formed the basis for Smalltalk were heavily influenced by the idea of classes as an organizing principle (taken from Simula-67), of turtle graphics (taken from the LOGO project at MIT) and of what is now called "direct manipulation" interfaces (inspired by the sketchpad drawing system, developed by Ivan Sutherland at MIT Lincoln Laboratories in the early 1960s, and by Kay's Ph.D. thesis on the FLEX machine).[1]

Between 1971 and 1975, Kay's group at Xerox PARC designed and implemented the first real Smalltalk language, environment and applications. This system included a number of technical innovations:

- *The language was based entirely on the Simula concepts of class and message.*
- *The language had no fixed syntax.* Each class was responsible not only for its own behavior and state definition, but even for parsing the token stream that followed a mention of an instance.

The innovations in the development environment were equally radical. At that time bit mapped displays were considered expensive and arcane. Nevertheless, Kay persuaded PARC to allow him to use bit mapped displays, which enabled Kay and his team to implement bit-mapped text in multiple sizes and styles, using multi-windowing environments, plus high level support for bit operations and graphics operations.

The Smalltalk-72 system further took the view that there was no reason for a separate operating system, since the object paradigm could manage all hardware resources at least as easily as any other approach.

By 1975-76, it had become clear that the lack of attention to issues of performance and scale were hampering further investigations. Kay's group proceeded with a major redesign of all aspects of the Smalltalk system. In the language area:

- The idea of inheritance and subclass hierarchy was incorporated into Smalltalk.
- The syntax of the language was fixed. This enabled compilation into an efficient, interpretable, compact (byte encoded), instruction set.

---

[1] Note this section is based on information described in a paper by L. Peter Deutsch, called *The Past, Present and Future of Smalltalk*, which was presented at ECOOP'89 [Deutsch 1989].

- Introduction of the Browser by Larry Tesler. The Browser vastly increased the productivity of a Smalltalk programmer.

All previous versions of Smalltalk had been implemented on specialist hardware, until in 1977-78, Bruce Horn and Ted Kaehler ported Smalltalk-76 to a system which incorporated dual Intel 8086 processors with a custom display (called the NoteTaker). Only 10 such systems were produced, however it was a positive demonstration that it would be possible to implement Smalltalk on conventional processors.

4.4.1 Smalltalk-80

In 1979-80, partly due to the NoteTaker project, the attention of the Smalltalk team was drawn to the possibility of marketing Smalltalk beyond Xerox PARC. The team designed and implemented yet another generation of Smalltalk systems, this time with some changes specifically aimed at portability and exploitation of standard hardware. These included:

- The adoption of the ASCII character set rather than the special character set used in Smalltalk-72 and -76.
- Smalltalk-80 removed the ability of primitive methods to directly access any memory location. Instead Smalltalk-80 introduced a dozen primitive methods which provided the required functionality. This significantly helped portability.
- The Smalltalk-80 language introduced the concept of metaclass, to provide a way of talking about behavior (messages) that were specific to an individual class. More about this towards the end of this book.
- The Model-View-Controller (MVC) system was introduced for interactive applications. More about this later in the book.

Finally, by 1981 a significant number of the Smalltalk team felt that it was important to take direct action to propagate Smalltalk beyond Xerox PARC. Adele Goldberg, who had by now replaced Alan Kay as head of the group, and Dave Robson, a long time group member, decided to write a series of books about Smalltalk. These books include descriptions of both the language and its implementation. One of the first external implementors of the system was Digitalk. A company set up by Digital to develop and market Smalltalk systems.

4.4.2 VisualWorks and commercial versions of Smalltalk

VisualWorks is the commercial product developed and supplied by ParcPlace-Digitalk and is probably the most widely used commercial Smalltalk system. This is at least one of the reasons why this book has a VisualWorks emphasis.

The language itself is now well established in the market place and in 1995 had about 17% of the market in client-server systems development in the USA. Smalltalk systems are now available for Macs, PCs and UNIX boxes and in some cases the same system is available on them all (e.g. VisualWorks).

In the case of VisualWorks, it provides not only the basic set of classes but also screen painting facilities, database connectivity, business graphics as well as interfaces to C and other compiled languages. It also provides generic window support for the programmer, which is translated to whatever windowing system is being used. This means that it is possible to develop a system on a Mac but deliver it on a PC or UNIX box. It is interesting to note that the market in Smalltalk systems (and VisualWorks in particular) is growing rapidly while the market for C++ systems appears to have begun to shrink.

Currently there are a number of implementations of Smalltalk available. These include Smalltalk/V and Visual Smalltalk also from ParcPlace-Digitalk, Smalltalk Express, versions of Smalltalk produced by Fuji Xerox, Sony and NEC in Japan and the GNU project's public domain gSmalltalk. IBM is a relatively new player in this field with its IBM Smalltalk (a standard interface based Smalltalk) and VisualAge (a version of Smalltalk with a VisualWorks style interface). Hewlett Packard also market a distributed version of Smalltalk called Distributed Smalltalk.

During 1995 there was a big shake-up in the Smalltalk vendor world when ParcPlace systems (the Xerox spin off) and Digitalk merged to form ParcPlace-Digitalk. At the time these two vendors had the lion's share of the Smalltalk market. Their merger produced the largest single Smalltalk vendor. Quite what the future holds for the products produced by ParcPlace-Digitalk is still unclear. Current reports mention a product called JigSaw which appears to provide the best features of VisualWorks combined with the best features of Visual Smalltalk. It is likely that this will mean that the VisualWorks development tools will remain, while Visual Smalltalk's integration with the PC platform will be exploited. This is one of the reasons that this book uses VisualWorks as the basis of the development environment described - future products from ParcPlace-Digitalk are likely to look very similar.

It should be noted, however, that unlike many other programming languages there is currently no international standard for Smalltalk (although one is in the pipe line - see the ANSI X3J20 draft standard). This means that, although very similar, each of the commercial versions of Smalltalk is slightly different. The major differences are associated with their graphical interfaces and database connectivity (if any). However, there can be subtle differences between the versions such as the scoping of variables within blocks of code. The examples described in this chapter and those that follow (as well as the tools described) are all taken from the VisualWorks system and should be usable with version 1.0 upwards of VisualWorks. They have been tested on versions 1.0, 2.0 and 2.5.

4.5 The Smalltalk environment

One of the major differences between environments such as VisualWorks, and those you may have been used to, is how development proceeds. You are going to be in for a shock if you have been used to having a completely un-integrated environment in which you write the program with your favorite editor (for example, Vi or EMACS), then run that through a compiler (for example, gcc), possibly needing to use a linker before you are able to create an executable, which you can then run to test if it works.

Even if you have been used to a rather more integrated environment, as is often found on personal computers or from commercial software suppliers (e.g. ALSYS Ada), you will be surprised just how integrated Smalltalk is. For example, as soon as you have written some code, you can accept it (which not only checks the syntax and attempts to correct spelling mistakes; it also compiles it) and then run it.

To run a piece of code, you don't even have to leave the window you are in, you can just select a statement which will execute the whole "lump" of code in the same editor window and ask the system to execute it, which, of course, it will. This means that you can "try out pieces of code" without having to write large amounts of code which act as a program harness[2].

As can be seen from this example, the edit / compile / link / execute cycle does not really exist in Smalltalk. You should therefore try to forget it and attempt to work in a much more *exploratory* and *interactive* manner.

4.5.1 The implementation of Smalltalk

Smalltalk is different to other development environments you may have used in another way; when you write Smalltalk code it does not execute on your host machine, even when it is "compiled". Instead it executes in a Virtual Machine, which in turn executes on your host computer[3]. In fact this is part of the secret behind VisualWorks' portability - you can write code on one hardware platform and, without re-compilation, run it on another hardware platform with a completely different windowing system. In effect, your Smalltalk code is always running on the same machine; the Smalltalk Virtual Machine. There is therefore no concept of an "executable" in Smalltalk terms.

Instead of an executable file, what you build up in Smalltalk is called an "Image". This however, holds not only your executable code, but also the compiler, the editors, debugging tools, class definitions, instance definitions etc. available within Smalltalk. The image is literally an image of the state of your development environment when you saved it. Figure 4.1 illustrates the structure of the VisualWorks system.

---

[2] This is not necessarily a new feature for those used to a number of A.I. systems such as POPLOG or LISP, but for those used to Ada or UNIX and gcc, it may be a revelation.

[3] When you compile your Smalltalk it is compiled into a byte code format rather than a machine executable format. These byte codes are then executed by the virtual machine which has been heavily optimized to give very fast run times.

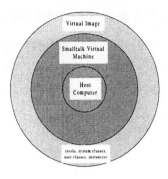

Figure 4.1: VisualWorks system structure

When you deliver systems to clients it is possible to cut down to a minimum what you deliver (e.g. you probably won't need to give a client the compiler classes). To do this a number of tools are available including the *stripper* tool (which strips out those parts of the image you don't need) provided as a utility with VisualWorks.

When you work with a Smalltalk system you should be aware of at least two files (besides your own source files). One is referred to as the *Virtual Machine* (this is also known as the Object Engine) and one is referred to as an *Image* file (see Figure 4.2). The image file is an "image" of the state of your development at a particular point in time as described above. To actually use VisualWorks you need to run the image on the virtual machine. This means that you can have different images on your file system possessing different sets of classes, in different states, all of which can be run by the same virtual machine. It should be noted, however, that it is only possible to run one at a time on a single invocation of the virtual machine.

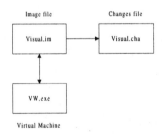

Figure 4.2: Primary files in VisualWorks

Finally, another file that you should be aware of is the changes file. This file lists all the modifications you make to any class, as well as the instructions you issue to the system (e.g. to accept some code). In fact it is the changes file which holds the uncompiled version of your source code. The relationship between the files in VisualWorks is thus that illustrated in Figure 4.2. Note that there are in fact other files used by the system (e.g. such as the VisualWorks sources file - called Visual.sou). However, at present you do not need to worry about them.

4.5.2 The VisualWorks Launcher and Transcript

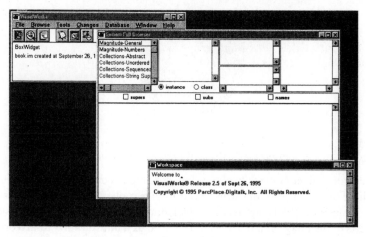

Figure 4.3: The VisualWorks Launcher and Transcript, a System Browser and a Workspace

When VisualWorks is first started up, the user will see the Launcher and the system Transcript as illustrated at the top of Figure 4.3. This illustrates VisualWorks on a Windows-95 system, however, it looks identical on a Macintosh or a UNIX box.

We shall consider the Launcher and Transcript separately as they will be used by the developer in different ways.

4.5.2.1 VisualWorks Launcher

The VisualWorks Launcher is the primary way in which you will access the tools within the VisualWorks environment. You should think of it as the top menu bar across most PC and Macintosh applications, like the start button on Windows-95 or like the pop-up menu used with many X windows desktops. It is your interface to VisualWorks. From the Launcher you can access all the system browsers (for browsers also read editors), the screen painting tools, the database tools, help, file access tools etc. As you use VisualWorks more and more you will come to know where these tools are and how to use them.

For speed of access a number of the most used tools have button icons below the menu bar. These are (from left to right):

- *The file tool* (for browsing directories, editing files on the host file system and filing in (a bit like compiling) files.
- *The System Browser*, which is described below.
- *Open a Workspace* (see below for an explanation of Workspaces).
- *The Screen Painter* which is used to easily and quickly construct graphical interfaces.
- *The Resource Finder* which is used to find window and icon definitions.
- *Database tools* for working with relational database systems
- The on-line *help* system.

50

The most important operations other than those covered above are **Exit VisualWorks ...** and **SAVE AS**. Both of these operations are found under the **File** menu. The **Exit VisualWorks ...** operation allows the user to quit from VisualWorks at any time. This operation brings up a pop-up window with three options, **Exit**, **Save + Exit** and **Cancel**. The **Exit** options quits VisualWorks and the current state of the system is not saved and thus anything that you have done (including coding) since you last saved will be lost. Remember that when you define new classes and methods you are only doing so within the VisualWorks environment, you are not saving anything to file. There is a way to recover anything you have done, if you quit and have forgotten to save your image, which involves the **changes list** which we won't look at yet. The **Save + Exit** option first saves the image and then exits VisualWorks while the **Cancel** option, returns the user to the VisualWorks environment.

The **SAVE AS** operation saves the current state of your VisualWorks environment as an **image**. Look back in this chapter if you are not sure what an image is. This image can be re-started again at a later date.

4.5.2.2 System Transcript

The System Transcript is a text window which has the additional property of supporting display operations from expressions as they are executed. It can be referred to using the name **Transcript**. In effect, it is the output window of the VisualWorks system. It is where the system itself reports important information such as when the image was last saved etc.

It is also very useful as a quick way of outputting information, for example by placing trace statements within code to see exactly what is happening or for displaying the results of computations which do not require sophisticated presentation. For example:

```
Transcript show: 'John'.
```

You can do this anywhere within any part of your code because Transcript is actually a *global variable* and an instance of a class called TextCollector. The Transcript (and other TextCollectors) respond to the message:

```
show aString
```

Other useful messages understood[4] by the Transcript include: cr (starts a new line in the Transcript.), space (puts a single space in the Transcript) and tab (puts a 'tab' in the Transcript).

The Transcript only knows how to print strings. Therefore, to make it easy to print anything in the Transcript, you can use a message called printString. All objects understand this message (as it is implemented in the class Object). When sent to an object, the result is a printable string which represents the object. The

---

4 This is an example of Smalltalk terminology. Rather than say that some procedure has been defined for an object, Smalltalkers say that it understands it.

result will be different depending on the class of the object, but you are guaranteed something you can print. The way to use printString is:

```
Transcript show: someObject printString
```

Type the following into the Workspace (this is the window at the bottom right of Figure 4.3, more information on this window is provided in the next chapter). Once you have typed it in, select it with the left mouse button. Now use the right mouse button to bring up the window menu[5]. This menu has a number of options on it, half way down you will see an option called **do it**. Select this option. The code will then be executed and the results will be printed in the Transcript.

```
Transcript show: 'Hello World'.
Transcript show: (3 + 4) printString.
Transcript cr.
```

You have now written your first piece of Smalltalk. This illustrates an important point, that with Smalltalk you will get the most out of any book or course by trying things out. So try things out; explore, be adventurous; it is the quickest way that you will learn.

4.5.3 The System Browser

The System Browser allows the user to inspect the definition of any object in the system, and to modify it if required. More than one browser can be displayed simultaneously (indeed it is often useful to have a number of browsers open at the same time so that different classes can be considered at the same time).

The **System Browser** is made up of five subviews (or windows) and two complementary items marked **instance** and **class**. By default, the **instance** item is selected; this means that the messages displayed are the ones sent to *instances* of a class rather than to the class itself. Note that each of the subviews has an independent scroll bar. The System Browser is illustrated in the middle of Figure 4.3. In the figure, the object class has been selected (this is indicated in the second window across the top).

From left to right, the top four panes in the System Browser are :

Class categories. These are groups of classes which are categorized for convenience. One of these categories may be selected (as in the figure); the classes in this category are then presented in the next subview.

Class Names. Classes in the selected category are presented. One of these classes may be selected (for example, the class object is selected); various categories of messages are then presented in the next subview.

---

[5] This assumes that you are using a two button mouse, for example on a PC. If your mouse has only one button please refer to the VisualWorks system manuals to find out what the appropriate key sequence is to mimic the second and / or third mouse button. If you have a three button mouse then the middle button is the equivalent of the right button on a two button mouse.

Message categories. These are the categories of messages which can be sent to either instances of the selected class (**instance** selected) or to the class itself (**class** selected). One of these categories may be selected; all message selectors in this category are presented in the right-most subview.

These message categories are also known as **protocols**. In the reminder of the chapters we shall refer to this window (pane) as containing protocols and thus it is the protocol window.

Message Selectors. All of the message selectors (essentially method names) in the protocol are presented. One of these messages may be selected, its *method* (the code executed when this message is received) will be shown in the lower (code view) area. For example, in Figure 4.3 the isNil message is selected.

The code view window. This window is used to browse and define classes, write methods etc.

You will find that off the right mouse button (if you have a three mouse button then it is the middle button) each window will produce a different menu. These are the window specific menus. You will make extensive use of them, so get familiar with what is on each menu. Figure 4.4 illustrates each of the menus for each of the five different windows.

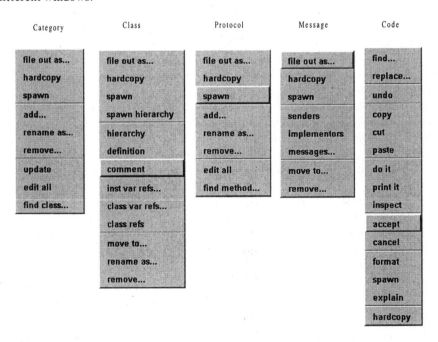

Figure 4.4: The System Browser Menus

There are a number of other browsers and inspectors in the Smalltalk system, for example the **Protocol Browser** and the **Method Browser**. They are condensed versions of the System Browser which possess specific views onto the class hierarchy or onto a particular class. If you have obtained the advanced programmer's tools with VisualWorks you will also be able to use the **Full Browser**. This is an excellent browser which possesses a few more features than the basic system browser.

4.6 Further reading

A good paper giving some of the (historical) background on Smalltalk is [Deutsch 1989]. As an introduction to the language of Smalltalk and the VisualWorks environment you would be hard pushed to find a better book than [Lewis 1995]. If you are only going to buy one other book on Smalltalk, buy this one. Of course there are also the four Smalltalk-80 books produced by the Xerox people [Goldberg and Robson 1983], [Goldberg and Robson 1989], [Goldberg 1984] and [Krasner 1983].

5. A Little Smalltalk

5.1 Introduction

In the last chapter we looked at browsers and the System Transcript, in this chapter we examine Workspaces and inspectors. Workspaces and inspectors are the next most important tools in the Smalltalk system. We then consider the debugger, one of the most useful tools available to the developer. Having looked at all the major development tools you will use (at least for the time being) you are introduced briefly to the Smalltalk language. You will then use the tools available to write some Smalltalk.

5.2 The Workspace

Workspaces are a kind of direct interface to the system compiler. They act a bit like an editor in that you can type Smalltalk code into them, and execute that code immediately. You can define temporary and global variables, create instances of classes, perform arithmetic calculations etc. The only thing you cannot do is define classes and methods (that must be done in one of the browsers). In the following figure, the Workspace is being used to calculate the average of a set of numbers.

To compile code within a Workspace you first select the code using the left mouse button. You then bring up the Workspace operations menu using the right mouse button (if you have a three mouse button you will use the middle button). This menu is also illustrated in Figure 5.1. The fourth grouping on the menu contains **do it**, **print it** and **inspect**. The **do it** and **print it** operations will compile and execute the code. **do it** will merely run the code, while the **print it** operation will also print the result of executing the last expression selected. The result is left highlighted so that you can delete it with the delete key if you no longer require it. Try them out and see for yourself. The **inspect** operation will first compile the code (if required) and then open an inspector (see below) on whatever you currently have selected. It the system was consistent, this option would be called "inspect it".

You can have as many Workspaces as you require open, you are not limited to a single Workspace. Of course on a standard PC or Macintosh screen, you may be limited by space. This highlights another issue, for developing Smalltalk systems, it is often useful to have as much screen "real estate" as you can get. Bigger really is better in this case.

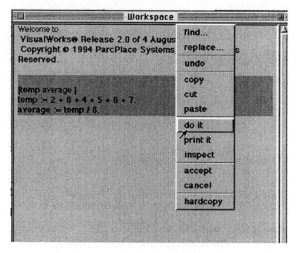

Figure 5.1: Using the Workspace

5.3 Inspectors

Another type of tool available in the Smalltalk environment are *Inspectors*. Inspectors permit the internal state of an individual object to be viewed. In particular they allow the user to view *and change* instance variables directly. In effect inspectors are to instances as browsers are to class definitions. Unlike other programming language development tools, you can use an inspector to change the state of an instance (for example, to set up an object ready for testing a piece of code) as well as examine its contents.

The inspector window is divided into two as shown in Figure 5.2. The left hand side shows the instance variables of the object, while the right hand side shows the contents of those variables. For example, in the figure, the prefs instance variable has been selected (in the left hand side) while the dictionary contained by that instance variable is displayed (in the right hand side). If the contents is a composite object (that is an object which contains other objects e.g. such as the dictionary shown), then you can open another inspector which will present the contents of that object. To do this you select the **inspect** option off the right (middle on the three button mouse) button menu in the left hand side.

The right hand view of the window not only allows you to examine and change the contents of instance variable, it also allows you to evaluate expressions (just as you can in a Workspace) except that the evaluation happens within the context of the instance. This means that instance and class variables can be referenced in the same way as they can within any method definition.

Note that two inspectors are built into the bottom of the debugger window and can be extremely useful when attempting to decide why something unexpected has happened.

The use of inspectors provides a powerful debugging and testing tool. All objects respond to the message `inspect`; the basic inspector method is implemented in the class `Object`'s instance protocol. Most objects respond by opening an inspector window, labeled with the class of the receiver.

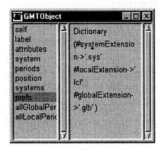

Figure 5.2: An example inspector

5.4 Notifiers

You should also get familiar with the system notifier, such as those you will encounter when you type in an incorrect Smalltalk expression. These notifiers are there to help you. For example, in Figure 5.3, I have mis-typed show, the system recognizes this and informs me of the fact. If I select the **correct it** option, it will try to find what it thinks I was trying to type. In this case it will give a select list containing the show: message, which I can select. This will replace my misspelling and the code will successfully execute.

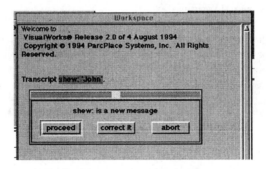

Figure 5.3: A system notifier

Notifiers can be displayed under a number of circumstances. They can be caused:

- **Accidentally**, by sending a message to an object which has no corresponding method. This is the usual response to a program error.
- **Deliberately**, by typing 'CTRL-C' or equivalent to break into the current execution.
- **Deliberately**, by inserting a breakpoint. We will discuss these later.

- **Accidentally**, by the system running out of memory.
- **Accidentally**, by recursion occurring in the system error handling.

5.5 Error processing

Handling run time errors in Smalltalk is slightly different to the way in which run time errors are handled in some other languages. Unlike, for example, C++ on a UNIX box, you do not need to take your core dump and analyze it using another piece of software. Instead, the system indicates the fault and gives you a chance to decide what to do next. One possibility is to interactively fix the problem. This was what was done during the exercise at the end of the last chapter.

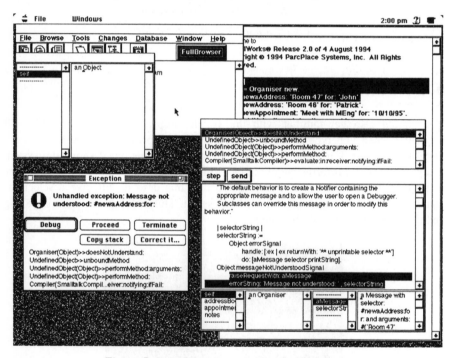

Figure 5.4: An inspector, notifier and debugger

Figure 5.4 illustrates an exception notifier warning that a message (newaAddress:for:) has been sent to an object which does not understand that message. It also illustrates the debugger which would be displayed if the debug option was selected. Finally, it illustrates an inspector examining an instance of class Object.

5.5.1 Exception notifiers

When a message is sent to an object with no corresponding method, then an exception notifier window (as illustrated in the bottom left hand corner of Figure 5.4) is displayed. This notifier is also displayed if a halt message (a breakpoint) is encountered. The exception notifier has a number of options which allow the programmer to determine what should happen next. The options are:

- **Debug** This closes the notifier view and opens a debugger view on the error condition.
- **Proceed** Continue as if the error had not occurred.
- **Terminate** This terminates the current evaluation.
- **Copy Stack** This copies the current state of the execution stack.
- **Correct it** This allows the user to correct the fault.

5.5.2 Types of run time error

When encountering a new language for the first time, it is quite common to get extremely frustrated while you attempt to determine why a piece of code is causing a run time error. This often turns out to be caused by a trivial fault which would have been dealt with immediately if you had been working in a language with which you were familiar. This sort of problem afflicts us all and is the source of a great deal of resistance to change. However, the problems can be eased somewhat if you are aware of the types of root causes for different failures. The following list attempts to ease this sort of problem. It presents the types of run time error (other than incorrect message sends) which can occur:

- Sending a message to an object which does not respond to that message.
- Trying to create an instance of Character or Boolean.
- Trying to create instances with inappropriate instance creation messages.
- Evaluating a block (instance of BlockContext) with the wrong number of arguments.
- Numeric errors, such as divide by zero, or square root of a negative number.
- Lots of collection errors, such as trying to remove an element not in a collection, or trying to use the add: message on a collection class which does not support add: for example Array etc.
- Sending a message to an object where the corresponding method should have been defined in a subclass. This can be identified by finding the following statement in a method:

```
self subclassResponsibility
```

- Control messages to objects which are not Booleans (ifTrue) or Blocks such as [] (whileTrue:).

5.6 Some Smalltalk

Let's look at a little Smalltalk, just to get you going. You have already seen (and possibly written) some Smalltalk when you typed in the Smalltalk version of the

"Hello World" program in the last chapter. Now let's add two numbers together. First we shall do it in a non-object oriented language such as Pascal. For example, we might write:

```
int a, b, c;
a := 1;
b := 2;
c := a + b;
```

This says something like, "create three variables to hold integer values (call them a, b and c). Store the value 1 into the variable a and 2 into variable b. Add the two numbers together and save them into the third variable c".

Now let's look at how we could write the same thing in Smalltalk.

```
| a b c |
a := 1.
b := 2.
c := a + b.
```

As you can see this looks basically the same (apart from the use of a full stop (also known as a period) instead of a semi-colon). We also apparently forget to declare the types of the variables a, b and c (and put some bars around them).

However, although the affect is the same, and the look similar, the meaning is *dramatically* different. In Smalltalk, this actually says:

> "Define three temporary variables a, b and c (we don't care what they will hold). Assign the object 1 to variable a. Assign the object 2 to the variable b. Take the object in a, which has the value 1, and send it the message "+", which includes the argument b, which in turn has the value 2. Object a, receives the message and performs the action requested. This action is to add the value of the argument to itself. Create a new object and return this result as the result of evaluating the message. Then save this object into the variable c."

These concepts of messages, receivers, objects etc. will be explained in a later chapter. Hopefully, by the end of this book you will read the above definition and say "of course".

5.7 Working with Smalltalk

5.7.1 Open a VisualWorks image

First of all start up your current VisualWorks image, for example, on a UNIX system you might enter:

visualworks Visual.im

If this is not local you may need to specify a path name for the object engine or the image. For example, if you are on a UNIX system:

/usr/local/ visual/bin/visualworks   /usr/jjh/visual.im

If you are using a Macintosh or a Windows-95 PC then you just double click on the image file and the VisualWorks virtual machine will be used to open it.

Once you have started VisualWorks, save the image to your own file store and exit. To do this, first select the **save as** option off the file menu on the VisualLauncher. You will be requested to provide a name for your image. Note that if you do not give a path name as well as the image name, the image file will be saved in the current directory.

Once you have created the image file, you can exit from VisualWorks. To do this you select the Exit option (again from the File menu on the VisualLauncher).

5.7.2 Selecting, compiling and executing Smalltalk

If you have not already done so, type the following into the Workspace:

```
Transcript show: 'Hello World'.
Transcript cr.
Transcript show: (3 + 4) printString.
Transcript cr.
```

Select the text and **do it**. That is, select the text with the left mouse button, then bring up the right (or middle on a three button mouse) mouse menu and select the **do it** option. You should then see the phrase "Hello World" and the number 7 appear in the Transcript window.

5.7.3 Using some VisualWorks tools

In many books you are presented with some source code to type in and execute, but are given very little guidance on how to deal with errors etc. Therefore in this section, you get to type in some (intentionally buggy) Smalltalk code and to compile it. This forces you to use tools such as the debugger to identify and correct the errors. After all, at this stage, it is likely that you will write buggy Smalltalk rather than perfect Smalltalk.

Type in the following exactly as it is (there are errors included so that you get some practice using the tools available in Smalltalk).

```
| temp |
temp := Set New.
temp add: 'John'.
temp add: 'Paul'.
temp add: Peter.
temp do: [:item | Transcript show item].
temp inspect.
```

Now select all the code and "do it" as before. You should now get a dialog box such as that illustrated below:

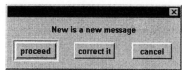

This dialog box indicates that New is not understood by the class Set (note the terminology). This is an example of how Smalltalk (and VisualWorks in particular) attempts to help you if it finds a message it does not understand. In this case it did not understand "New". It identified this as a problem and is now allowing you (the user) to

- **Abort** and correct the error yourself,
- **Proceed** as though nothing had gone wrong (however it would probably fail in another way immediately) or to
- **Correct it,** the error, with the system's help.

The correction option is illustrated below. Click on the "correct it" option. You will then see the following selection box:

Select "OK".

This is an example of how Smalltalk attempts to help you if it finds a message it does not understand. In this case it did not understand "New", but it found that Sets do understand "new". As "new" is very similar to "New", Smalltalk presented it as a possible alternative.

Once you have selected "OK" on the selection dialog, you should then see the following dialog.

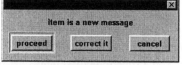

For the moment select "proceed". The problem here is not actually with item, but is a feature of another problem which we will come back to later. Once you have selected "proceed" you will then see:

This dialog was generated because, Peter, does not have single quotes around it (single quotes are used to indicate a string). The system therefore assumes that it is a variable which has yet to be defined.

At this point press "cancel". You should find that `Peter` is highlighted in the Workspace. This illustrates how VisualWorks attempts to point out where the problem is. Now place single quotes around `Peter`, e.g.

```
temp add: 'Peter'.
```

Next re-select the whole lot and "do it" again. You will again see a dialog warning you that item isn't defined. For the moment select proceed.

You will now get an Exception raised. This is because the Transcript object does not understand the message "show". The dialog you see should look like this:

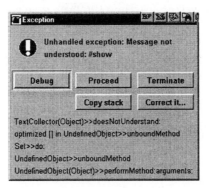

Select the "Debug" option. This will open a debugger on the error code. Now select the second line down in the top window. This should start with `optimized [ ]`. The debugger with this line selected is illustrated below:

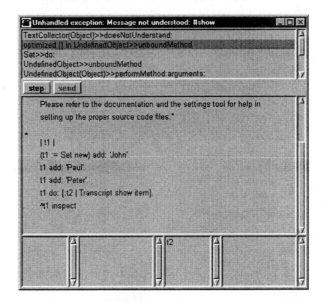

In the top scrollable window of the debugger you see each method which has been executed, in the window below this, you see the source code relating to the method. In this case you see a "decompiled" version of the code you wrote in the Workspace displayed. It is decompiled because you typed the original code into the Workspace rather than into a class. It therefore had no class to refer back to. You will know decompiled code from original source code for two reasons. Firstly, there will be a comment telling you that it has been decompiled and secondly the variables will have names such as t1 and t2 rather than the variable names you chose.

In the debugger you can identify the point at which the error was caused because it will be highlighted. That is, the message "show" will be in bold. You can correct the error by changing "show" to "show:".

You could now fix the problem here (and when you are debugging methods on actual classes you may well do so). However, there is no point doing so this time, as this is the decompiled version of your original. Thus any changes you make here will be lost once this run is completed (in addition the item following show has not been compiled yet and therefore remains as item where as the temporary variable at the beginning of the do: statement has been decompiled to t2 - rather than item). It would therefore be better to go back to the Workspace and fix it there.

You should change the show statement to read:

```
temp do: [:item | Transcript show: item]
```

Now select all the code and "do it" again. This time the contents of the set should be printed in the Transcript.

Notice that the order in which you input the strings may differ from the order in which they are printed. This is due to the way add: works (why not have a look and see for yourself).

Finally, you should see an **inspector** window displayed. Try clicking on some of the left hand items.

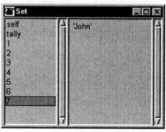

The left hand view of the window shows instance variables (such as tally) and positions (e.g. 1 - 7) and the right shows the contents of the variables (e.g. the string 'John').

Here is a question for you to ponder on and experiment with: *"What happens when the 8th item is added to this set?"*[1].

---

[1] Answer: it grows. Try it for yourself - remember to use the inspector to examine the contents of the set.

5.8 Summary

By now you have used a number of Smalltalk tools, run VisualWorks (or whatever Smalltalk system you are using) and written some Smalltalk code. You have also had the chance to use some of the tools available to help you debug your code. You are now ready for the Smalltalk language itself!

5.9 Further reading

If you are going to do any serious development in Smalltalk then you should consider obtaining at least Vol. 1. of Inside Smalltalk [Lalonde and Pugh 1991] (which concentrates on the language) if not Vol. II. [Lalonde and Pugh 1991b] (which concentrates on the graphical facilities).

However, by far my own favorite book is [Hopkins and Horan 1995]. This is a very good introductory book on Smalltalk using the VisualWorks 2.0 system. Indeed it is based closely on the courses that were run by the University of Manchester by the authors and by the commercial suppliers of VisualWorks. This means that the material in the book has been "debugged" over a number of years. In particular it covers much of the same material as is in Part II of this book but spends much more time on the use of the graphical facilities in Smalltalk. It also goes into a great deal of detail about the tools in VisualWorks and how to use. However it does not cover issues such as 'what is object orientation in much detail', nor does it attempt to guide the novice through the application of object orientation to developing a system.

6. Smalltalk Building Blocks

6.1 Introduction

The aim of this chapter is to present an introduction to the Smalltalk Programming Language. The scope of this chapter is to describe some of the features of the Smalltalk language. As such it is not intended to be a comprehensive guide to the Smalltalk language. For a detailed description of the Smalltalk language's syntax and most commonly used constructs see, Appendix 1.

The remainder of the chapter is structured in the following manner: Section two introduces the basic elements of the Smalltalk language. Section three discusses the concept of classes and instances in Smalltalk and how they are defined. Section four presents methods and method definitions.

6.2 The basics of the language

Smalltalk is a completely object oriented language and as such has no other concept other than object. The actual language is very, very small, however the Smalltalk system (as exemplified by VisualWorks) is very big. All Smalltalk programmers make extensive use of the existing classes even when they are writing relatively trivial code. For example, even when a programmer writes the following version of the traditional "hello World" program they are reusing existing classes (rather than just using the language):

```
| myName |
myName := 'John Hunt'.
(myName findString: 'Hunt' startingAt: 1)
        ifTrue: [Transcript show: 'Hello ' , myName]
        ifFalse: [Transcript show: 'Hello World'].
```

In this example, I have reused the String class to represent the string 'John Hunt' and to find a substring in it using the message selector findString:startingAt:. Some of you may say that there is nothing unusual in this and that in many languages string handling facilities are extensions to the language. However, in this case, the result of the test is an instance of either True or False (subclasses of Boolean) and that this message receives the message ifTrue:ifFalse:. What is printed to the Transcript object depends on which object actually receives the message. Thus, ifTrue:ifFalse: is not part of the language but a method defined in a class. In most languages the if-then-else construct would be an inherent part of the language - in Smalltalk it is not. This is because everything is an object in Smalltalk, thus all language constructs are messages sent to objects. This feature also illustrates the extent to which existing classes are reused - that is, you can't help but reuse existing code in Smalltalk because you do so by the very act of programming.

As well as possessing a completely object oriented programming paradigm, Smalltalk also possesses an inheritance mechanism. It is this feature which separates Smalltalk from object based languages such as Ada - they do not possess inheritance.

The availability of inheritance is very important in Smalltalk. For example, it promotes the reuse of classes as well as enabling the explicit representation of abstract concepts (such as the class Collection) which can then be turned into concrete concepts (such as the class Set). It is also one of the primary reasons why Smalltalk is so successful as a rapid application development tool - you inherit much of what you want and only define the ways in which your application differs from what is already available.

6.2.1 Some terminology

We will now recap some of the terminology introduced in Part 1 of this book, however we will explain this terminology with reference to Smalltalk.

In Smalltalk programs are run or actions are performed by passing *messages* to and from objects. A message is a request for some procedure (referred to in Smalltalk terms as a *method*) to be performed by the object receiving the message (referred to as the *receiver* of the message). The object which sent the message in the first place is referred to as the *sender*. Just as procedure calls can contain parameters, so can messages. In addition, just as in some functional languages, all method executions result in a *response* being returned to the sender.

Smalltalk is not a *strongly typed* language. That is, you do not specify that a variable will take a certain type of data structure. Nor does the compiler attempt to check what types a variable possesses. However, it is not true to say that Smalltalk is not typed. Each object is an instance of a class. These classes give an object a type (as defined by the class). It is possible to send a message to an object to determine the type of its class. Smalltalk is thus a dynamically typed language. This is a feature of Smalltalk which promotes its abilities as a rapid application development tool. It also enables the polymorphic facilities available to be utilized appropriately.

6.2.2 The Smalltalk message passing mechanism

The Smalltalk message passing mechanism is somewhat like a procedure call in a conventional language. That is:

- The point of control is moved to the receiver; the object sending the message is suspended until a response is received.
- However, the receiver of a message is *not* determined when the code is created (at *compile time*) it is identified when the message is sent (at *run time*).

This *dynamic* (or *late*) binding mechanism is the feature which gives Smalltalk its polymorphic capabilities (see Chapter 1 for a discussion of polymorphism).

Another difference between the message passing mechanism of Smalltalk and the procedure call mechanisms of other languages, is that much of what one would consider the basics of the language are implemented using message passing (for example the equivalent of control and iterations structures). This means that not only is message passing fundamental to the language, it is also a critically important feature of the performance of the language.

6.2.3 Smalltalk statements

In the remainder of this chapter you will encounter a number of pieces of Smalltalk. It is therefore useful to introduce you to one of the features of the Smalltalk language; the statement terminator. In Smalltalk this is the full stop (or period). For example:

```
Transcript show: 'Hello World'.
```

Thus the majority of statements will terminate with a '.'. There are a few situations in which it is not necessary to terminate a statement with a full stop. However, in these situations it is often a good idea to do so. In this and following chapters, we shall adopt the convention of always terminating a statement with a full stop (period).

6.3 Classes

A class is the basic building block in Smalltalk. Classes act as *templates* which are used to construct instances. This means that programmers can specify the *structure* of an object (i.e. what instance variables etc. it will possess) and the function of an object (i.e. what methods it will have) separately from the objects themselves. This is important, as it would be extremely time-consuming (as well as inefficient) for the programmer to have to define each object individually. Instead, they define a class and create *instances* of that class.

6.3.1 Class definitions

In Smalltalk the format of a class definition is the following:

```
NameOfSuperclass subclass: #NameOfClass
        instanceVariableNames: 'instVarName1 instVarName2'
        classVariableNames: 'ClassVarName1 ClassVarName2'
        poolDictionaries: ''
        category: 'Class protocol'
```

It is not necessary to remember this format precisely as the Smalltalk browsers will present the above as a template for you to fill out whenever you wish to define a new class. The following is an example of a class definition:

```
Object subclass: #Person
    instanceVariableNames: 'name age'
    classVariableNames: ''
    poolDictionaries: ''
    category: 'Example classes'
```

This definition states that I wish to define a new class, Person, which will be a subclass of the Object class. My new class will possess two *instance variables* called **name** and **age**. It will has no class variables or pool dictionaries (we will discuss these later). Finally, it will be part of the class category 'Example Classes'. This last field is normally filled in for you by the system. It is derived from whatever class category you are in when you attempt to define the new class.

Note that our class name is currently a symbol (see below for an explanation of a symbol) denoted by a #. This is because we have not defined it yet and it is therefore not a class name. An error would be raised if we tried just to use it as class name in the definition. As soon as the definition is complete, we can forget about the #.

However, classes are not just used as templates, they have three further responsibilities which include; actually holding the methods, providing facilities for inheritance and creating instances. We shall consider each of these separately below.

6.3.2 Classes and messages

When a message is actually sent to an object requesting it to perform some service, it is not the object which possesses the method but the class. This is for efficiency reasons. For example, if each object possessed a copy of all the methods defined for that class then there would be a great deal of duplication. Instead, only the class possesses the method definitions. Thus when an object receives a message, it searches its class for a method with the name in the message. If its own class does not possess a method with the appropriate name, it goes to its class's superclass and searches again. This search process continues up the class hierarchy until either an appropriate method is found or the class hierarchy terminates (with the class Object). If this happens an error is raised.

If an appropriate method is found, then that method is then executed *within the context of the object*. This means that although the definition of the method resides in the class, the method executes within the object. Thus different objects can be executing the same method at the same time but without any conflict.

Do not confuse methods with instance variables. Each instance possesses its own copy of the instances variables (as each instance possesses its own state). Figure 6.1 illustrates this idea more clearly.

6.3.3 Instances and instance variables

In Smalltalk *objects* are *instances* of *classes*. All instances of a class share the same responses to messages (methods), but they will contain different data (i.e. they will possess a different "state"). For example, the instances of class Point will all respond in the same way to messages inquiring about the value of the x coordinate, but may provide different values.

The class definition consists of variable declarations and all method definitions. The different state of each instance is maintained in one or more instance variables.

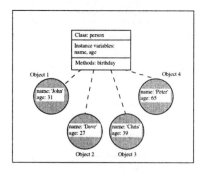

Figure 6.1: Multiple instance variables but a single method

In Figure 6.1 there are four instance of the class Person. Each instance contains copies of the instance variable definitions for name and age. Thus enabling them to have their own values for these instance variables. In contrast, each instance references the single definition for the method birthday which is held by the class.

6.3.4 Classes and inheritance

It is through classes that an object can inherit facilities from other types of objects. That is, a subclass inherits properties from its superclass. For example, in the Person definition above, we stated that Person was a subclass of Object. Therefore, Person inherits all the methods and instance variables etc. which were defined in Object (except those that were overwritten in Person). Thus, subclasses are used to refine the behavior and data structures of a superclass. It should be noted that Smalltalk supports single inheritance while some of the object oriented languages (most notably C++) support multiple inheritance. Multiple inheritance is where a subclass can inherit from more than one superclass. However, difficulties can arise when attempting to determine where different methods will be executed.

6.3.4.1 An example of inheritance

To illustrate how single inheritance works consider Figure 6.2. We will assume that we have three classes called Class1, Class2 and Class3. Class1 is a subclass of Object, Class2 is a subclass of Class1 and Class3 is a subclass of Class2.

When an instance of Class3 is created, it contains all the instance variables defined in classes 1 to 3 and class Object. If any instance variable possesses the same name as an instance variable in a higher class, then only one instance variable of that name will be created. We do not need to consider which one is created as they are both instance variables which can take any value (Smalltalk is not strongly typed remember!).

When we have an instance of Class3 we can send it a message requesting that a particular method is executed. Remember that methods are held by classes and not by instances. This means that the system will first find the class of the instance (in this case Class3) and search that class for the required method. If the method is found, then it is executed and the search stops. However, if the method is not found, then the system will search Class3's immediate superclass; in this case Class2. This process is repeated until the method is found. Eventually, the search through the superclasses may reach the class Object (which is the root class in the Smalltalk system). If the required method is not found here, then the search process terminates and the doesNotUnderstand: method in the class Object is executed instead. This method causes an exception to be raised stating that the message sent to the original instance is not understood.

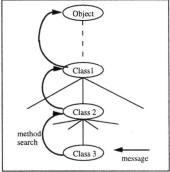

Figure 6.2: Class inheritance in Smalltalk

This search process is repeated every time a message is sent to the instance of Class3. Thus, if the method which matches the original message sends a message to itself (i.e. the instance of Class3), then the search for that method starts again in Class3 (even if the original method was found in Class1).

6.3.4.2 The Yo-Yo problem

The process described above can pose a problem for a programmer trying to follow the execution of the system by tracing methods and method execution. This problem is known as the Yo-Yo problem (see Figure 6.3). It occurs because, every time you encounter a message which is sent to "self" you must start searching from your own class. This may result in the programmer jumping up and down the class hierarchy.

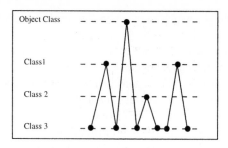

Figure 6.3: The Yo-Yo Problem

The problem occurs because you know that the execution search will start in the current instances class, even if the method which sends the message is defined in a superclass of the current class. In the figure, the programmer starts the search in Class3, but finds the method definition in Class1, however this method sends a message to "self" which means that the programmer must restart the search in Class3. This time, the method definition is found in the class Object etc. Even with the browsing tools provided, this can still be a tedious and confusing process (particularly for those new to Smalltalk).

6.3.5 Instance creation

Classes are also the things which construct the instances. They do so in response to a class message. It is probably confusing, but classes can possess class specific methods as well as class instance variables. These are often referred to as class side methods and variables. They can then respond to a message as an instance would (this is because classes are in fact special instances - we will discuss this in a later chapter. For the moment merely accept that classes can be sent messages).

The message most commonly sent to a class is the message new. This message causes a method to execute which constructs a new instance of the class. This process is referred to as instantiation. You do not need to know the details of this process. An example of sending the message new to a class Person is presented below:

```
Person new.
```

The result of sending this method is illustrated in Figure 6.4 along with the structure of a class. The class Person receives the message new which causes the class method new to execute which generates a new *instance* of the class, with its own copy of the instance variables age and name.

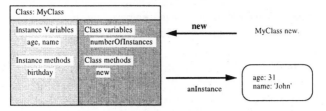

Figure 6.4: Instance creation

The issue of classes having methods, some of which are intended for an instance of the class, and some of which are intended for the class, is not as complicated as it may at first seem. Not least because the tools used with Smalltalk tend to keep the two *sides* of the classes pretty well distinct. In an attempt to make it clearer here are some definitions:

- **Instance variables**: Defined by the class, but a copy is maintained in each instance which has its own value for that instance variable.
- **Class variables**: Defined in the class with a single copy in the class accessible by instances of the class.
- **Class instance variables**: Defined in the class with a single copy in the class and only accessible by the class.
- **Instance methods**: Defined in the class with a single copy maintained in the class but executed within the context of an object.
- **Class methods**: Defined in the class with a single copy maintained in the class and executed within the context of the class.

Some of these concepts will be considered in greater detail later.

6.3.6 Classes in Smalltalk

There are very many classes in any Smalltalk system, e.g. in VisualWorks there over 1,000 classes. However, you will only need to become familiar with a very few of them. The remaining classes provide facilities that you use without even realizing it.

6.4 Method definitions

Methods provide a way of defining the behavior of an object i.e. what the object does. For example, a method may change the state of the object or it may retrieve some information. A method is the equivalent of a procedure in most other languages. A method can only be defined within the scope of an object (and there is no concept such as the main method as there is in C). It has a specific structure:

```
messagePattern arguments
    "comment"
    | temporaries |

    statements
```

where the **messagePattern** represents the name of the method and the **arguments** represent the names of arguments. These arguments are accessible within the method.

The **"comment"** field is a comment describing the operation performed by the method and any other useful information. Note that comments cannot be nested in Smalltalk. This can be awkward if you wish to comment out some code for later. For example, consider the following piece of Smalltalk which I have just commented out:

```
⁽Ꙩ⁾
x := 12 * 4.
ꙨNow calculate y Ꙩ
 y := x * 23.
Ꙩ
```

The Smalltalk compiler would read this as a comment, followed by the code *Now calculate y*, followed by another comment. This is (almost) certainly going to cause an error.

The | **temporaries** | format is used to define variables which are local to the method. They must be declared at the beginning of the method (just after the message pattern) and are initially nil.

The **statements** represents any legal set of Smalltalk statements. These statements are used to implement the behavior of the method.

One of the uses of methods is in providing an interface between an object's internal data and the outside world. Such methods are often termed accessor methods. Such a method retrieves the value of an instance variable and makes it available to other objects. For example, the class Employee has two instance variables age and name. A method implemented in Employee returns the age of an employee. Thus in response to the message age, this method would be executed and the value of the employee's age returned to the object sending the message.

In this situation the employee's age is held explicitly. An equally valid internal representation for an Employee would be to have an instance variable dateOfBirth. The method age, would now need to take the date of birth away from the current date, in order to obtain the employees' age.

Note that this would be a change to the implementation of Employee, but there would be no *visible* change as far as any other object in the system is concerned. This illustrates the encapsulation possible within Smalltalk (and other OOP languages).

6.4.1 The ^ (or return) operator

Once a method has finished executing, an answer is returned to the sender of the message. By default the object returned is the receiver itself (i.e. self). However, other objects can be returned by use of a *return* expression - an expression preceded by an up arrow (^). The return expression must be the last expression executed in a method. This does not mean that it must be the last expression in the method, merely that it is the last executed. For example:

```
      C Version                    Smalltalk

  if (x == y)                 (x = y)
          return x;                 ifTrue: [^x]
  else
          return y;                 ifFalse: [^y] .
```

In this case, either the value of x or y will be returned depending upon whether x and y are equal or not.

6.4.2 An example method

Let us compare a procedure definition in a language such as C with the Smalltalk equivalent. We will assume that we wish to define a procedure to take in a number, add 10 to it and return the result.

```
int myAdd (int x)             myAdd: aNumber
   { int result;                 | result |
     result = x + 10;            result := aNumber + 10.
     return result;              ^result.
   }
```

From this example you will see that although the format is different you should soon be able to get used to it. Let us look at some of the constituent parts of the method definition. The method name (and its message selector) is myAdd: . Note that because this method takes a parameter, the method name must have a trailing colon. It has one parameter called aNumber. Just as in any other language, this parameter variable is limited to the scope of this method. The method also defines a temporary variable (result) which is also limited to the scope of this method.

Variable names are identifiers containing only letters and numbers which must start with a letter. Some examples are:

      anObject   MyCar   totalNumber

A capitalization convention is used consistently throughout Smalltalk and most Smalltalk programmers adhere to this standard which it is therefore advisable to follow:

- *Private variables* (instance/temporary variables) start with a lower-case letter.
- *Shared variables* (class/global/ pool variables) start with an upper-case letter.

Note that *message selectors* should start with a lower-case letter.

Another convention worth noting is that if a variable or a message selector combines two or more words, the convention is to capitalize the first letter of the second word onwards. E.g. displayTotalPay, returnStudentName.

If we consider our new method above, we have still to consider what happens in the assignment statement (:=). We shall look at this in the next chapter along with the range of arithmetic functions available.

7. Smalltalk Constructs

7.1 Introduction

This chapter presents more of the Smalltalk language. Section two considers the representation and use of numbers in Smalltalk while Section three considers strings and characters. Section four discusses variables in Smalltalk and Section five literals and variables. Sections six considers messages, message types and their precedence.

7.2 Numbers and operators

7.2.1 Numeric values in Smalltalk

Numbers in Smalltalk are all objects, that means that they are instances of a class. For example, integer numbers such as 2 are an instance of the class `SmallInteger`. In fact there are a number of classes which together provide for the types of numbers normally used, these include `SmallInteger`, `LargePositiveInteger`, `LargeNegativeInteger`, `Float` and `Double`. These will all be considered in greater detail later in the book. For the moment we will just consider what numbers look like in Smalltalk.

Just as in most programming languages, a numeric value in Smalltalk is a series of numbers which may or may not have a preceding '-' and may contain a decimal point. For example:

```
25      -10     1996    12.45   0.13451345    -3.14
```

It is also possible to specify numbers in bases other than 10. This is done by preceding the number with the base and the letter r (which stands for radix). For example:

```
2r101   16r452
```

Numbers can also be expressed using scientific notation using the 'e' (for exponent) or 'd' (for double-precision) suffix plus the exponent in decimal. For example:

```
10e3 which equals 1000
```

In addition to integers and real numbers, Smalltalk also explicitly supports fractions (e.g. 7/8) and <u>radians</u>. In all other ways numbers in Smalltalk are just like numbers in any other language.

7.2.2 Arithmetic operators

Table 7.1: Numeric operators

+	addition	*	multiplication
-	subtraction	/	division
//	modulus	quo	quotient
rem	remainder	\\	remainder from modulo division
<	less than	<=	less than or equal to
>	greater than	>=	greater than or equal to
max:	maximum	min:	minimum
ceiling	roundup	floor	round down
rounded	round to nearest	truncate	round down

In general, the arithmetic operators available in Smalltalk are essentially the same as in any other language. For example, there is addition, subtraction, multiplication and division operators (+,-,*,/). There are also comparison functions and truncation functions all of which are summarized in Table 7.1.

7.3 Characters and strings

7.3.1 Characters

Just like numbers, characters in Smalltalk are instances of an associated class. In this case the class `Character`. Again we will consider this class and the operations it provides in greater detail later. For the moment we will consider what characters look like. In Smalltalk, a single character is defined by prefixing it with the $ (dollar) sign. For example:

```
$a $Z $@ $1 $$
```

All the above specify a single character, in this case the characters a, b, @, 1 and $.

7.3.2 Strings

`Strings` in Smalltalk are part of the `Collection` class hierarchy. As such they are made up of individual elements in a similar manner to strings in C. However, this is the only similarity between C strings and Smalltalk strings. Smalltalk strings do not need to be terminated by a null character, nor should they be treated as arrays of characters. In Smalltalk, a string should be treated as an object in its own right which responds to an appropriate range of messages (e.g. for manipulating or extracting substrings).

In Smalltalk, a string is defined by one or more characters placed between single quotes. For example:

```
'John Hunt'     'Tuesday'        'dog'
```

Note the use of single quotes rather than the double quotes used in some other languages (e.g. C and Ada). This can be the source of much confusion and frustration when an apparently correct piece of code will not work. Remember that double quotes indicate a comment in Smalltalk. Thus, the following code will compile, but will generate a run time error:

```
a := "John Hunt".
```

This is because there is nothing to assign to the variable a as the comment "John Hunt" does not return a value. Also be wary of assuming that a string containing a single character is equivalent to that single character. It is not. For example:

```
'a' /= $a
```

The string 'a' and the character $a are instances of different classes, the fact that the string contains only one character is just a coincidence. This can be particularly confusing for C programs as 'a' indicates the character *a* in C.

7.3.3 Symbols

Symbols are special strings which are always unique in the system. They do not respond to many of the usual string manipulation messages, but they can be more efficient for some tasks than strings. A symbol is indicated by a preceding hash (#). For example:

```
#john   #Week   #System42
```

They are more efficient for storage and certain logical operations (such as =) and so may be used instead of strings if their values will not be altered and substring operations are not required.

7.4 Assignments

A variable name can refer to different objects at different times; *assignments* can be made to variable names. The ":=" symbol is used in Smalltalk to indicate assignment. It is often read as "become equal to" although some do read it as "colon equals". Some examples are:

```
currentEmployeeIndex := 1.
newIndex := oldIndex.
myName := 'John Hunt'.
```

Assignments return values (like other expressions), so that several assignments can be made together:

```
nextObject := newObject := oldObject.
```

The above example also illustrates a feature of Smalltalk style - the specification of variable names which indicate what they contain. This technique is often used where a more meaningful name (such as currentEmployeeIndex) is not available, i.e. where temp might be used in other languages.

It is worth reiterating the point that variables in Smalltalk are not strongly typed as in languages such as Pascal and ADA. Instead, Smalltalk is dynamically typed. That is, a variable is not un-typed, rather its type is determined by its current contents. Thus, it is possible to determine the type contained in a variable by sending it a message asking for its type. Of course, by type we really mean class. It is also possible that a variable which is currently holding a string, may then be assigned an integer. This is quite legitimate and often happens, for example:

```
myVariable := 'John'.
myVariable := 1.
myVariable := #(1 2 3 4).
```

An important point to note is that assignment is by reference. This means that in the following example nextIndex, newIndex and oldIndex all refer to the *same* object.

```
new := old := (Bag new).
next := new.
```

The effect of these assignments is illustrated in Figure 7.1.

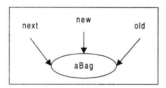

Figure 7.1: The result of a multiple assignment

As all three variables point to an instance of a container class (in this case Bag), if an update was made to the contents of any one of the variables, it would be made for all three!

7.5 Variables

7.5.1 Types of variable

There are a number of different types of variable available in the Smalltalk language. Some of these have already been discussed. The following provides a review of some of the different types:

1. instance variables - discussed above
2. class variables - will be discussed later in the book
3. class instance variables - will also be discussed later in the book
4. temporary variables - see below
5. global variables- see below

7.5.1.1 Temporary variables

These exist only for the duration of some activity (e.g. the execution of a method). They are denoted by being placed between two bars, e.g. | x y z | indicates that the variables x, y and z are temporary variables. Try typing the following into the Workspace window:

```
| x y z|
x := 5.
y := 6.
z := x + y.
Transcript show: z printString.
```

Now select all the text you typed in. Now use the right mouse button (middle if you have a three button mouse) and select the **do it** option on the menu. You should now see the value 11 printed in your Transcript window.

7.5.1.2 Global variables

These are shared by all instances of all classes. These can be useful during testing if you want to keep hold of a particular object. They always start with a capital letter and can be deleted by looking at the Smalltalk system dictionary. This can be accessed from the global variable Smalltalk (you can use the inspect message to examine the contents of the variable Smalltalk). To delete a global variable from the current system, use:

```
Smalltalk removeKey: #<global variable name>.
```

It is interesting to note that class names start with a capital letter and are therefore actually global variables!

7.5.2 Pseudo variables

There are a number of *pseudo variables* in Smalltalk which can be referenced within a method. A pseudo variable is a special variable, whose value is changed by the system but which cannot be changed by the programmer. That is, the value of these variables is determined by the current context within which the code around it is executing. There are two such pseudo variables; they are self and super:

self   This refers to the receiver of a message itself. When a message is received, the search for the corresponding method starts in the class of the receiver. It is the way in which a method in one object can initiate the execution of another method in that same object.

super   Also refers to the message receiver, but the method search starts in the superclass of the class in which super is used. This is often used if the functionality of a method is to be extended rather than overwritten. For example:

```
myMethod: anObject
        new code before super.
        super myMethod.
        new code after super.
```

Don't worry about the syntax or the meaning of this at the moment just make sure you get the idea of things.

7.5.3 true, false and nil variables

These variables represent the two boolean states, true and false and a null value (referred to as nil). This should not be confused with the null pointer in languages such as C. It really means *nothing* or *no value*. The three variables are:

- nil The single instance of class Undefined Object (the non-value).
- true Represents truth. It is the only instance of class True.
- false represents falsehood. Which is the only instance of the class False.

True and False are subclasses of Boolean which implements boolean algebra and control structures.

7.6 Messages and message selectors

7.6.1 Message expressions

Message expressions describe messages to receivers. They are composed of a receiving object (the receiver), the message selector (which indicates which method to execute) and zero or more parameters. Figure 7.2 illustrates the main components of a message expression.

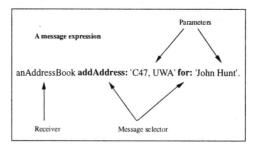

Figure 7.2: The components of a message expression

The value of the expression is determined by the method it invokes. For example, in the following example, the result returned by the method `marries:` is saved into the variable `newStatus`.

```
newStatus := thisPerson marries: thatPerson.
```

7.6.2 Message types

There are three different forms which a message can take. From the programmers point of view they are essentially the same. They are only distinguished by the format they take and by the precedence they have. The following description explains each of the three types of message and states their precedence. The only exception to this is that parenthesized expressions take precedence over all message expressions.

Messages without any arguments are termed *Unary Messages*, for example:

```
#($a $b 23 'john') size.
13 odd.
Time now.
```

Messages with a single argument, where the selector is composed of one or two non-alphanumeric symbols are termed *Binary Messages.* They have a higher precedence than keyword messages, but a lower precedence than unary messages. Examples of binary messages include:

```
a >= b. 24 * 7.          recordCount + 1.
```

The second character in a binary message selector *cannot* be a minus sign.

Messages with one or more arguments, separated by part of the method selector and composed of alphanumeric symbols and a trailing colon, are called *Keyword Messages*. For example:

```
Transcript show: 'Hello John'.
10 max: 20.
aDictionary at: 'UK' put: 'United Kingdom'.
```

82

In the above examples show:, max: and "at:put:" are the keywords (termed selectors). This means that the name of a message selector is spread amongst the arguments. These can be any simple identifier with a trailing colon. The argument can be an expression representing any object. Keyword expressions have the lowest precedence.

7.6.3 Message selectors

A message selector is the term used to describe the method interface provided by one object to other objects. For example, if an object possesses a method with the following definition then it possesses a message selector of "addAddress:for:".

```
addAddress: anAddress for: aName
        addressBook at: aName put: anAddress.
```

Notice that the method selector only consists of the method name and does not include any of the parameters dispersed amongst that name.

7.6.4 Precedence

Smalltalk has slightly different rules regarding precedence than many other languages. For those of you who are unclear about precedence, this refers to the order in which operators are evaluated in an expression. Many languages, such as C, have quite complex rules regarding precedence, which determine the order in which an expression such as:

```
2 + 5 * 3 - 1 / 2.
```

would be evaluated. Smalltalk is rather more intuitive. Essentially it handles parsing in a left to right manner. For example, in the above example, 5 is added to 2, the result (7) is multiplied by 3 (to give 21). 1 is subtracted from this (giving 20) which is divided by 2. The result of this expression is therefore 10. That is, there is no precedence difference between +, -, * or /. If you wish to alter the way in which the arithmetic calculations are performed, then you can use round brackets. For example:

```
2 + (5 * 3) - 1 / 2.
```

This expression will be evaluated to the value 8. This rule also includes unary messages. For example:

```
arraySize := #('a' 'b' 'c' 'd') size even
```

the message size is sent to the array object, and even is sent to the resulting object. The result of this is then assigned to the variable arraySize.

Keyword messages are a special case, in that although they too are parsed in a left to right manner, the system assumes that all the keywords within one expression are part of the same message selector. Thus an expression such as:

will be parsed as calling a message name:age:. If this is not the intention then the programmer must indicate to the system that what is required is that the message name: and then a separate message age: should be sent to aDog. For example, either as separate messages to aDog or using the cascading mechanism. A potential point of confusion here is when the intention is to send the second method to the result obtained from the first. For example:

```
anArray at: 1 max: 10.
```

This will try and send the message at:max: to anArray. Here it is necessary to use round brackets to ensure that it is the object returned as a result of accessing position 1 in the array which receives the max: message. For example:

```
(anArray at: 1) max: 10.
```

7.6.5 Parsing rules

Although the order in which expressions are evaluated is left to right, there are three levels of precedence amongst the categories of message which affect this evaluation. The three categories each have a different precedence as indicated by the following table:

Message category	Precedence	Example
unary	1	size, rem, odd
binary	2	*, /, - , +
keyword	3	max:, min:, at:put:

This means that a unary message will be evaluated before a binary or keyword message. In turn a binary message will be evaluated before a keyword message. If this order is not what is desired then round brackets can be used to alter the evaluation sequences as above. For example:

```
2 * 3 max: 3 * 4 odd.
```

This would generate an error, because, the odd message at the end of the expression has the highest precedence. This means that the result of sending the message odd to the value 4 would be used as the parameter for the message '*' to be sent to the value 3. As this would result is multiplying 3 by false, the system would generate a run time error. To ensure that we obtain the correct result, we might place brackets around parts of the expression, thus:

```
((2 * 3) max: (3 * 4)) odd.
```

This can be a common source of errors. If you have a problem with any of the parsing rules a quick and easy way to make sure the system parses an expression in the way that you want, is to put brackets around parts of the expression to describe your requirements. Then select the **format** menu option in one of the VisualWorks browsers. This option not only formats the code according to Smalltalk standards, it also removes any unnecessary brackets.

7.7 Summary

In this chapter you have learnt about classes in Smalltalk, how they are defined, how instance variables are specified and how methods are constructed. You have also encountered many of the basic Smalltalk language structures.

7.8 Further reading

Two good books to have a look at now, if you have not already done so, are [Lewis 1995] and [Hopkins and Horan 1995].

8. An Example Smalltalk Class

8.1 Introduction

You should now be ready to write some Smalltalk code. So this chapter will take you through a worked example. It is a very simple example, in which you will create a new class, define some instance variables and write a couple of methods.

8.2 The class *Person*

The Person class will provide a very basic set of features. It will record a person's name and their age. It will also allow a person to have a birthday (and thus increment their age).

8.2.1 Creating the class

The first thing you should do is to create a new class category to put your class into. This is done in the class category window of the System Browser. Use the right button menu (middle on a three button mouse) and select the **add** option. This option will prompt for a category name. It is best if you use a meaningful category name. I have used the category name "Example Class".

Once you have provided a category name it will be immediately created. However, note that it will add the category at the bottom of the list of categories or, if you have selected (highlighted) an existing category, immediately above that category. This means that if you have accidentally selected a category in the middle of the list, your new category will be added in the middle of the category list. It is easier to find your own categories if they are not mixed up with other categories. It is therefore advisable to make sure that no categories are selected when you create a new one.

Next define a new class. You can do this by filling out the template in the bottom window (commonly called the code view) of the System Browser to mirror the following:

```
Object subclass: #Person
        instanceVariableNames: ' name age '
        classVariableNames: ''
        poolDictionaries: ''
        category: 'Example Class'
```

That is, define the class Person as a subclass of Object and give it two instance variables name and age. (Note that if you have called your class category something other than "Example Class" the category field will be different).

Notice in Visualworks, that the template fills in the superclass, the class name and the variable fields with default values, e.g.:

```
NameOfSuperclass subclass: #NameOfClass
    instanceVariableNames: 'instVarName1 instVarName2'
    classVariableNames: 'ClassVarName1 ClassVarName2'
    poolDictionaries: ''
```

If you do not delete these fields, they will be included in the compiled class. For example, it is easy to find that you have four instance variables and two class variables. The additional variables having names such as instVarName1 and ClassVarName1.

If you have defined the new class correctly, then at this point your browser should look like that in Figure 8.1. Do not worry if the list of class categories in the right most window is different, the important points are that the class definitions match and that the highlighted text is the same.

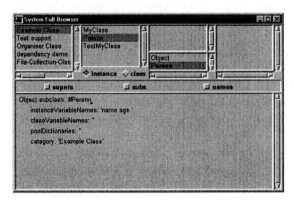

Figure 8.1: Defining a new class

8.2.2 Defining a class comment

The next thing you should do is to define the class comment. It is generally a good idea to do this, but if you wish to omit it, it will not effect how your class operates. If you do wish to add a comment then select the **comment** option off the menu presented from the right mouse button (middle on a three button mouse) in the class window. The comment I have defined is illustrated in Figure 8.2. Once you have typed in the text of your comment you must "accept it". This can be done from the right mouse button (middle button on a three button mouse).

This is a good example of some common uses of the class comment. Note that I have not only specified the intention of the class, what the instance variable of the class are and what they take, but also how the class might be used.

8.3 Defining methods

Now you are ready to start defining methods for the class. The first method you should define is one which will be used to initialize the instance's state (i.e. initialize the instance variables). Traditionally, methods such as initialize, which are not intended for general use, are placed in a method protocol called "initialize-release". If you look at the methods defined in the system classes you will note that similar names are used for protocols possessing similar types of methods, "initialize-release" is an example of such a protocol name. You should therefore place the method `initialize` within the protocol `private`.

8.3.1 The "initialize-release" protocol

To create the initialize method, you will first have to create the message protocol in which to place the method definition. To do this, you use the **add** option off the right button menu (middle if you have a three button mouse) in the message protocol window. This is the third window along in the System Browser. This causes a dialog to be displayed requesting the name of the new protocol. This will either be blank or contain the name of the last protocol you visited. If it is not *initialize-release*, then type in "initialize-release". Again the new protocol will be either placed at the end of the list of protocols or it will be placed above the protocol currently selected (if one is selected).

You will then be presented with a new message protocol in the message protocol window. This protocol will be selected and the following template will be displayed in the code window:

```
message selector and argument names
     "comment stating purpose of message"

     | temporary variable names |
     statements
```

You can now define the initialize method. In this case, the method is very simple as it merely sets the instance variable age to 0 and name to a null string ' '. To do this type in the following method definition into the code view window, replacing the method template displayed there.

```
initialize
     "This method is used to initialize any variables etc."
     self name: ''.
     self age: 0.
```

Once you have typed in the method you can **accept** it. When you do so, the system will inform you that the two methods age: and name: are undefined[1]. From the dialogs you should select the **proceed** option as we will define these methods later. Figure 8.3 illustrates the System Browser at this point.

---

[1] Note that if you have objects in the system which define these messages, then VisualWorks will not tell you that they are undefined, even though they are undefined for Person!

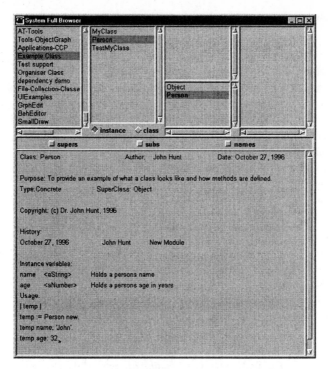

Figure 8.2: Defining a class comment

8.3.2 The "accessing" protocol

Now we will define the "accessing" protocol. Again this is a protocol name which is widely used within the system classes. If you adhere to the standard protocol names you will find it easier to follow the system classes (and other peoples classes). Define the new protocol as before and then define input the following method.

```
age
        "This is an example accessor method"
        ^age
```

This is an example of another feature of Smalltalk style, that is, if you write a method to return an instance variable's value, you do not call it *returnAge*, instead you give it the same name as the instance variable; in this case age. The system is able to determine whether you mean the instance variable or the method from the way you call it. These methods are termed *accessor* methods.

The next method will be called age: this illustrates another Smalltalk style element in this example. This method updates an instance variable. The method is therefore given the same name as the instance variable but with a trailing colon. We do not call it *setAge*: or *updateAge*:. You may not like this convention at the moment, however it is used throughout Smalltalk, it is therefore advisable to use it.

```
age: anInteger
        "This method sets age."
        age := anInteger
```

This method illustrates another feature of Smalltalk programming style, the use of class names as parameter variable names. For example, in this method we are expecting one parameter. Smalltalk is untyped, therefore the contents of this parameter could be anything. However, the programmer of this method has indicated to us that they expect the value passed into the method to be an integer. At least now, if the system encounters a run time error and we enter the debugger, we can see if the contents of anInteger is an integer or not. If it is not, then we may have found the source of the problem.

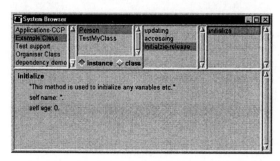

Figure 8.3: The System Browser displaying part of the Person definition

The equivalent methods for accessing and updating the value of the instance variable name are presented below. They are very simple and should not come as a surprise. They are therefore merely listed and are not discussed in detail.

```
name
        "This retrieves the contents of name."
        ^name

name: aString
        "This sets the contents of name."
        name := aString
```

8.3.3 The "updating" protocol

Having defined all the methods for the "accessing" protocol, we will now define a new protocol called "updating". This protocol should be created in exactly the same way as the last two protocols. This protocol is intended for methods which cause a change in the state of the object due to some calculation or operation. This protocol will be used to define the birthday method (see Figure 8.4).

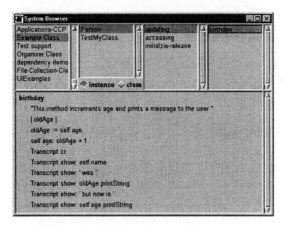

Figure 8.4: Defining the birthday message

This last method uses the other methods in order to change the current value of the instance variable age and to print a meaningful message to the user.

8.4 Creating an instance

As was suggested in the class comment, create an instance of the class and send it some messages. You can do that by typing the code in Figure 8.5 into the Workspace and selecting it. Then use the **do it** option off the right mouse button menu (middle mouse button if you have a three button mouse).

The result of running this code should be that the following is printed into the Transcript:

```
0
Bob was 0 but now is 1
```

Once you have done this and are happy with what is happening, why not try and change the method definitions or add a new instance variable called `address` and define the appropriate methods for that variable.

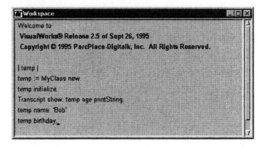

Figure 8.5: Creating an instance of Person

9. Control and Iteration

9.1 Introduction

This chapter introduces how control and iteration are achieved in Smalltalk. To do this a number of concepts which are unique to Smalltalk are also discussed (such as the block object). To simplify this process for the reader, equivalent C constructs are illustrated beside Smalltalk constructs (where they exist).

The remainder of this chapter is structured in the following manner. Section two introduces the concept of cascading, Section three discusses blocks and Section four describes the control structures available in Smalltalk.

9.2 Cascading

Cascading is a syntactic form that allows multiple messages to be sent to the same object. The aim of this is to reduce the need for tediously repeating the same object over and over again, because a whole set of messages must be sent to that one object. The intention is to produce more concise code which is easier to read, and to avoid the need for additional temporary variables.

Cascading is achieved by using the semicolon delimiter. This is slightly confusing for those coming from a C or Ada background as the semicolon is used there as a expression terminator. Instead, in Smalltalk, it should be read as send the next message to the same object as the last message. For example, the expressions:

```
Transcript cr.
Transcript tab.
Transcript show: 'Hello World'.
Transcript cr.
```

can be written in a shorter form as:

```
Transcript cr;
          tab;
          show: 'Hello World';
          cr.
```

The programmer should be wary of using the cascade mechanism. Although it was intended to simplify code, it can often have the opposite effect. For example, in a very long cascaded expression, which appears all on the same line, it can become difficult to determine exactly what is happening. It is therefore often the case that a set of message expressions are easier to understand when they are not written using cascading.

9.3 Blocks

9.3.1 Block definition and evaluation

Earlier in this book you were told to treat Blocks as the same as Begin/End constructs in Pascal and ADA or { }'s in C. This was, however, not exactly the truth. They are in fact objects in their own right (and are instances of BlockClosure) which represent code that can be executed (or evaluated) now or at a later date. *Block expressions* therefore describe deferred activities.

Blocks are represented by square brackets '[ ]' and obviously have a very different meaning to round brackets '( )'. This can be yet another point of confusion for those new to Smalltalk. The round brackets will return the result of evaluating what they contain, at the point at which the expression is encountered. The square brackets will return a block object. This block object will contain zero or more statements. These statements will only be executed when the block is *evaluated*. This is achieved by sending the message value to the block. For example:

```
[counter := counter + 1] value.
```

However, if we don't want to execute the statements in this block until later, we don't have to. In fact as the block is actually an object, we can assign the block to a variable. Then when we are ready we can evaluate the block held by the variable. For example:

```
myBlock := [counter := counter + 1].
....
myBlock value.
```

Thus when a block expression is encountered, the statements enclosed are *not* executed immediately. In other words, the contents of the square brackets are stored until a value message is sent to it. Thus in the above example, counter will only be incremented when the message value is sent to myBlock.

It is important to note that the block will execute within *the context in which it was defined* and not necessarily in the current context. This means that the value used for counter will be the value it had wherever the block was created.

As was explained in Chapter 6 all expressions return a value. In the case of a block, when it is evaluated, the result returned is the result of evaluating the last expression in the block. Thus the value 18 is assigned to the variable result in the following example:

```
result := [2 * 4. 3 * 6].
```

9.3.2 Block parameters

Blocks can also take parameters. This is done by preceding the statements in the block by a vertical bar and the input parameter. This parameter has a preceding colon. For example:

```
[:counter | counter * 2.]
```

This block takes one input parameter and possesses a single statement which multiples the input value by 2. This can then be evaluated with a single parameter. This is achieved by sending the block the keyword message value: ; the argument is the value to bind to the block parameter counter. For example:

```
[:counter | counter * 2] value:10.
```

This would produce the value 20. It is possible to pass in more than one parameter to a block. For example, if we want to specify that a block takes two parameters, then we could use the following definition:

```
[:x :y | x * y ]
```

This block would be evaluated using the value:value: message.

```
[:x :y | x + y] value: 10 value: 20.
```

The same number of arguments must appear in the block and the message. In fact there are also value:value:value: and value:value:value:value: messages for blocks which take three and four arguments. There is also a valueWithArguments: message for blocks taking more than four arguments.

9.3.3 Block temporary variables

Blocks can also possess their own temporary variables. These variables are defined between two vertical bars and after any input parameters. For example:

```
[:x |
  |temp1 temp 2|
  temp1 := x.
  temp2 := temp1 * 3.]
```

A block can actually have up to 256 temporary variables in VisualWorks. However this figure does vary from implementation to implementation.

9.3.4 Typical block usage

Finally, blocks are often used for control structures:

```
aNumber even
        ifTrue: [aString := 'even']
        ifFalse: [aString := 'odd'].
```

94

Effectively this means send the message value to one of the blocks, depending on the result of testing aNumber to see if it is even or odd. We shall look at the use of blocks in condition and iteration statements later in this chapter.

9.4 Control structures

9.4.1 Flow of control

As has previously been mentioned, the if-then constructs in Smalltalk are actually methods defined on the class Boolean. However, ignoring that issue for a moment, the actual use of the structures is very straight forward. The basic formats of the if-then expression are:

```
aBoolean                          aBoolean
      ifTrue: aBlock                    ifTrue: aBlock.
      ifFalse: anotherBlock.

aBoolean                          aBoolean
      ifFalse: aBlock                   ifFalse: aBlock.
      ifTrue: anotherBlock.
```

The boolean object is often generated dynamically via some form of logical test (e.g. a < b). That is, the first operation is to create the boolean object, which is then sent the message ifTrue:ifFalse:. This is why the boolean test is often bracketed with round brackets. Then if the value of the boolean is true, the code in the ifTrue block is executed, if it is false the code in the ifFalse block is executed. Consider the following example:

<table>
<tr><td>C version</td><td>Smalltalk Version</td></tr>
</table>

```
if (count < 100)                  (count < 100)
      count++;                          ifTrue:  [count := count + 1]
else  {                                 ifFalse: [Transcript show:
      printf("Overflow\n");                       'Overflow'.
      count = 0;                                   Transcript cr.
}                                                  count := 0.]
```

In both cases the code increments the value of a counter if its maximum count has not been reached; if the maximum count has been reached, the code resets the counter and prints an error message. Nested if-then statements can be constructed as in any other language. For example, in Smalltalk:

```
(count < 100)
      ifTrue: [(index < 10)
                    ifTrue: [....]
                    ifFalse: [.....]]
      ifFalse: [.....]
```

However, it is easy to get confused and therefore one must be careful. A facility not provided explicitly by Smalltalk is the if-then-elseif-else type of structure. For example, in C it is possible to write:

```
if (n < 10)
        printf ("less than 10");
else if (n < 100)
        printf ("greater than 10 but less than 100");
else
        printf ("greater than 100");
```

In Smalltalk it is necessary to nest ifTrue:ifFalse constructs as above. However, it is easier to see if you have a dangling else problem as the built-in formatter available in the various browsers can be used to see if the code formats in the expected manner.

There is also no such thing as a case statement in Smalltalk. Instead, the functionality required is usually achieved using a dictionary.

```
map := Dictionary new.
map at: $^ put: [Transcript show: 'It is a caret'].
map at: $> put: [Transcript show: 'It is greater than'].
map at: $< put: [Transcript show: 'It is less than']
            :
result := (map at: char) value.
```

This is the Smalltalk equivalent of the following in C:

```
switch (char) {
case '^':
        printf("It is a caret");
        break;
case '>':
        printf("It is a greater than");
        break;
        :
```

This is actually an example of how Smalltalk is truly object oriented. That is, even what would considered standard control structures in other languages, have to be implemented by using objects and message passing. A point to note is that the control structures which do exist in Smalltalk may at first seem to be similar to the control structures in other languages. However, this is both persuasive and misleading. They are of course messages to objects (e.g. true, false or a block object). Internally they perform something which is similar in nature to what we have done above for the switch statement. If you find this confusing, don't worry, but if you can see what is meant by this then you have gone a long way down the round to understanding Smalltalk.

9.4.2 Repetition

Iteration in Smalltalk is accomplished with the timesRepeat:, whileTrue:, whileFalse: and enumerating messages (such as do:). The enumerating messages will be considered in more detail when we discuss the collection classes. For the moment we shall limit ourselves to a simple form of the do: message and the `timesRepeat` message. In the next subsection we will consider the while-based messages.

Like their counter-parts in other languages, the `timesRepeat:` and `do:` messages repeat a sequences of instructions a fixed number of times. In C, this construct is provided by the for loop. For example:

```
for (n = 1; n <= 10; n = n + 1)
        printf("%3d", n);
```

This assigns *n* the initial value 1, it then repeats while the middle test is true during which the last expression increments the value of *n* after each execution of the printf statement. In Smalltalk this can be achieved using the `do:` message. This message is actually sent to an interval (which is discussed elsewhere):

```
(1 to: 10) do: [:n | Transcript show: n printString]
```

The brackets round the 1 to: 10 are required, because we create an interval object with the range 1 to 10 which is sent the message `do:` with a block as its parameter. However, it has exactly the same effect as the C version presented above.

It should be noted that what is happening here is that the block object passed as the parameter to the `do:` message actually takes a parameter itself. In fact it is passed the values 1 through 10 in turn. Each value is then bound to the block variable *n*. This is achieved by sending the message `value:` with a different element of the interval to the block within the `do:` message.

In situations where you merely require a piece of code to execute a given number of times, without the requirement to reference any loop variable, it is possible to use a very simple control structure. This structure is the `timesRepeat:` message. This message is sent to an integer and causes the associated block to be executed *n* times, where *n* is the integer the message is sent to. For example:

```
10 timesRepeat: [Transcript show: 'Hello'; cr.].
```

this will cause Hello to be printed ten times in the Transcript window.

Blocks with arguments are also used to implement functions to be applied to all elements of a data structure. For example (using an array):

```
sum : = 0.
#(3 5 8 4 6) do:
        [:item | total := total + ( item * item )]
```

The variable `item` takes the value of each element in the array. The result of these expressions is the sum of the squares of the values in the array. This is a very useful construct.

9.4.3 While loops

The while loop exists in almost all programming languages. In most cases it has a basic form such as:

Because in Smalltalk a while loop is achieved by sending a message to an expression the format is slightly different. In Smalltalk the basic format is:

```
[condition] whileMessage:
        [statements]
```

where *condition* is the control expression in the form of a Block Context. *Statements* are the controlled set of Smalltalk code also in a block context. The control of this statement is determined by the *whileMessage* that can actually take a number of forms which will be discussed below.

The basic while messages are the `whileTrue:` and `whileFalse:` messages. For the `whileTrue:` message, if the value of the control expression in the receiving block is true, then the controlled statements are executed. After this the control expression is evaluated again and so on. This is actually achieved in Smalltalk by sending the receiver block the message `value`; if the response is *true*, then the argument block is sent the message `value`. This repeats until the receiver block answers *false*.

For example:

C Version

```
n = 1;
while (n <= 10)
{
        printf("%3d", n);
        n++;
}
```

Smalltalk Version

```
n := 1.
[n <= 10]
        whileTrue:
        [Transcript show: n.
         n := n + 1].
```

This should be read as: The block object is sent the message whileTrue: with one parameter which is also a block object. If the first block object evaluates to true when sent the message value, (i.e. if the value of *n* is less than or equal to 10) then the message value is sent to the second block object. If this message is sent, then the current value of *n* is printed in the Transcript and is then incremented by one. This is repeated until the first block returns false (i.e. n = 11). Note, as in any other language *n* must be assigned an initial value before the condition expression. This is because the while message begins by evaluating the control expression, if no initial value is provided for n it will default to nil. Comparing nil with a numeric value will result in an exception being raised.

As you can see the equivalent C code is not that different, but the semantic meaning is completely different.

The `whileFalse:` message has exactly the same format as the `whileTrue:` message. The only difference is in the condition used to decide whether to evaluate the second block or not.

```
n := 1.
[n > 10] whileFalse:
        [Transcript show: n.
         n := n + 1].
```

In some cases we want to do all the work in the receiver block. These versions of the while message can be viewed as being similar to the do statement in C. To support such a feature there are two versions of the while loop which do not require the second block to be provided. These are the `whileTrue` and `whileFalse` messages (note the absence of the ':'). For example:

```
        C Version                          Smalltalk Version

do {                               [n := Transcript getNumber.
    scanf("%d", &n);                Transcript show: n; cr.
    printf("%d\n", n);              n < 1000] whileTrue.
} while (N < 1000);
```

Both of these segments of code are expected to read in a number, print it back out and then check to see if it is less than 1000. If it is the sequence of steps is repeated, otherwise the loop is terminated. For example, this could be used to ensure that some input is in the desired range.

9.5 Summary

You now know virtually everything about Smalltalk except the classes which make up the very large library of reusable components available to the developer. You have learnt the basics of the language in chapter 6 and in this chapter you have learnt about cascading, blocks and their use in iteration constructs. You have also learnt about conditional statements and their use of blocks. You are now ready to explore the class structure in Smalltalk.

9.6 Further Reading

As ever, the Hopkins and Horan book [Hopkins and Horan 1995] is a good reference source for the Smalltalk language. Other useful books are [Lalonde and Pugh 1991] and [Goldberg and Robson 1989].

10. The Collection Classes

10.1 Introduction

This chapter discusses probably the most used class hierarchy in Smalltalk; the collection class hierarchy. The collection classes are the basis upon which data structures are constructed in Smalltalk. Section two introduces the collection class hierarchy and the common functionality provided by all collection classes. Section three presents a decision tree to help identify the most appropriate collection class to use. Sections four, five and six present the Bag class, the Set class and the OrderedCollection class (respectively). Section seven then presents how the OrderedCollection class can be used to construct Stack and Queue classes.

10.2 The Collection class hierarchy

A *collection* is a group of objects (these objects are called the *elements* of the collection). Collections are the Smalltalk mechanism for building data structures of various sorts; it is therefore important to become familiar with the collection hierarchy and its functionality.

Class Collection is the abstract superclass of all collections in the system. Figure 10.1 summarizes the collection classes in VisualWorks. Some of the classes illustrated are abstract classes on which others build. In fact the collection class hierarchy is a classic example of the use of abstract classes and how they can be used to group together functionality as well as indicate what is expected of subclasses. Now might be a good time stop and examine the collection class itself. Abstract classes in this hierarchy include:

- Collection. This is the abstract root class for the whole hierarchy.
- SequenceableCollection. This is the abstract class for collections which have a defined sequence. That is, the subclasses of this class support the notion of having an *order* associated with the elements.
- ArrayedCollection. This is the abstract class for those classes which have an array like behaviour. That is, subclasses of this class support the notion of an externally defined ordering.

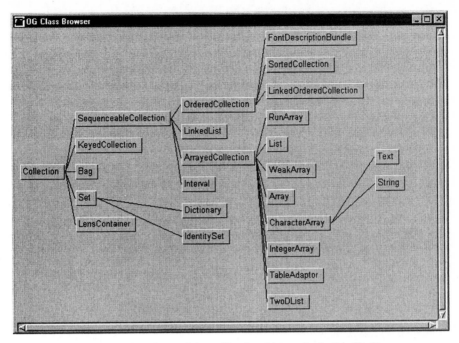

Figure 10.1: Part of the collection hierarchy in Smalltalk

The concrete classes in the collection class can either be ordered or unordered and may or may not possess duplicates. Concrete classes which are unordered include:

- `Bag`. A `Bag` contains all the objects put in it, in no particular order. Duplicate objects are permitted.
- `Set`. Sets contains all the elements put into it, in any order. Duplicates are not kept; adding equal objects many times results in only one such object in the Set.
- `Dictionary`. Class `Dictionary` is a subclass of `Set` and represents a set of *associations* between pairs of objects.

Concrete classes which are ordered include:

- `OrderedCollection`. A collection where the ordering is given by the order in which elements were added.
- `Array`. A collection which provides array like behaviour.
- `String`. An indexed collection of `Characters`.
- `SortedCollection`. A collection of objects, which are sorted according to an ordering defined in the instance of SortedCollection.
- `Symbol`. A subclass of `String`. All symbols are unique, while there can be two different Strings containing the same characters.
- `Text`. A class which understands a notion of a collection of *fonts* associated with a string.

101

A relatively new class which incorporates some of the more useful features of the `Array`, `OrderedCollection` with `SortedCollection` classes is the `List` class.

The basic operations that are performed by the collection data structures include adding and removing elements, determining the size of the collection, querying the presence or absence of elements and iterating over the elements.

10.3 Choosing a Collection class

It can sometimes be confusing for those new to Smalltalk to decide which collection class to use. Some make the mistake of always using an array (because it is similar to the constructs that they are used to). However, this is failing to understand the way one should work with collections (data structures) in Smalltalk. To this end the following decision tree may be of use.

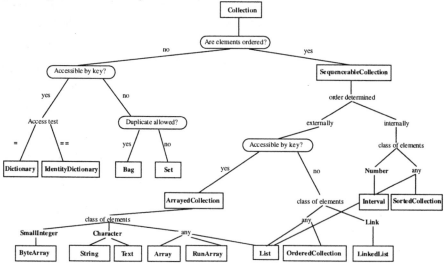

Figure 10.2: Selecting which Collection class to use

The most commonly used collection classes are, `Array`, `SortedCollection`, `OrderedCollection`, `List`, `Dictionary` and `Set`.

10.4 The Collection class

The collection class is the abstract superclass which acts as the root of all collection classes. It provides facilities for creating instances of a collection class, adding an element to a collection, accessing elements in a collection, removing an element from a collection and indicating the size of the collection. It also provides facilities which allow an operation to be applied to all elements of the collection (in a similar fashion to the mapcar function in Lisp). It also provides a number of conversion routines which allow one collection to be converted into another.

With one or two exceptions (e.g. `ByteArray`) any object can be stored into any collection. The only message that these operations must be able to respond to is = (although objects to be placed in a Sorted collection must also respond to <=). This means that a collection can be a very flexible way of holding other objects. Typically, collections are used as data structures in Smalltalk systems. They can also be used as temporary holding places for groups of calculations, results, operations etc.

The `Collection` class assumes that a new subclass will provide at least the following:

- `add`: This adds an object to the collection
- `remove:ifAbsent`: This removes an object from the collection. If it is not present in the collection, the block provided as the parameter to ifAbsent: is evaluated.
- `do`: This applies the associated block to each element in the collection
- `copyEmpty`: (if the subclass possesses named instance variables). This creates a copy of the receiving collection which contains no elements.

The `Collection` class defines the common protocols to which all types of collection are expected to respond. For example, objects may be added to collections using:

- `aCollection add: anObject` Subclasses redefine this message such that it will add a single instance of anObject to the collection. In some classes this is dependent on the current contents of the collection (e.g. class Set).
- `aCollection addAll: oldCollection` Add each element in oldCollection to aCollection. This method uses add: and therefore does not need to be redefined in a subclass.
- `size`. The current size of the collection (i.e. the number of objects it contains) may be obtained using the `size` message: aCollection size.

Objects may be removed using one of the following:

- `aCollection remove: oldObject`. Remove the first element which equals `oldObject`
- `aCollection remove: oldObject ifAbsent: aBlock`. Subclasses redefine this method. The intention is that the method will remove the first instance of `oldObject`. They will run `aBlock` if that object is not present in the collection.
- `removeAll: aCollection`. This method removes all of the element contained in `aCollection` from the receiving collection.

The `Collection` class also defines a range of test methods which can be used to identify the current state of a collection or determine if an object is a member of a collection. The test operations supported include:

- `aCollection includes: anObject`. This tests whether an element is currently a member of a collection. This method uses the = test.
- `aCollection isEmpty`. This message returns true or false depending on whether the collection contains any objects or not.
- `aCollection occurrencesOf: anObject`. This message returns the number of times `anObject` is present in the collection. Again this uses the #= test.

Additional protocols are implemented by subclasses to support operations suitable only for that class. For example, `OrderedCollection` supports `first`, `atFirst:`, `after:` and `add:before:` while arrays understand `at:` and `at:put:`.

10.5 Bag

Abstractly a `Bag` can be considered to be any collection of objects, which can be of any class; these objects are the elements of the `Bag`. It is a general place holder for collections of objects. There is no order assumed. It is the most general form of collection available in Smalltalk. (In many implementations each entry in the bag is actually an association which indicates the object and the number of times it has been placed in the bag. This is intended as a performance enhancement and is normally transparent to the user.)

If you are confused by this description of a bag, think of it as a shopping bag. At a supermarket, you pick objects up from the shelves and place them in your shopping bag. For example, you pick up a pint of milk, a box of corn flakes, a packet of biscuits, three bags of potato crisps, and a few bananas (see Figure 10.3).

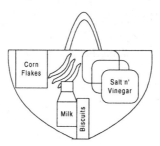

Figure 10.3: A shopping bag

Each of the objects in the bag is a different type of thing, with different characteristics etc. There is no particular order to them, they will have moved about in the bag while you were shopping and while you brought them home. When you reach into the bag at home to remove the objects, the order in which they come out will not be predictable. If you think of a bag collection in these terms then you will not be far off the mark.

As with any other class we create an instance of Bag by sending the message new to the class Bag. For example:

```
| temp |
temp := Bag new.
```

The bag object responds to the add: message to add objects as well as the add:withOccurrences: messages which can be used to add an object *n* times. For example:

```
temp add: 'John'.
temp add: 'Hello' withOccurrences: 2.
```

At this point the bag object will contain three objects, the string 'John' and two copies of the string 'Hello'. We can examine the contents of the bag using the inspect message, for example:

```
temp inspect.
```

You will notice that the bag object does not record the objects in the order in which they were added. Instead, the order is not specified (it is actually determined for efficiency). You will also notice that there are instance variables numbered 1 - 7. This is because collections are a special type of object whose instance variables are defined dynamically as and when required. They are termed "variable" classes.

It is also possible to remove objects from a set using either the remove: ifAbsent: message or the removeAllOccurrencesOf: ifAbsent: message. The first is used to remove a single reference to an object, while the second is used to remove all references to an object. In both cases a block must be supplied which is executed if the object is not a member of the bag. For example:

```
temp remove: 'Paul' ifAbsent: [].
temp remove: 'Paul' ifAbsent: [Transcript show: 'No Record of Paul'].
```

In the first example, if the string 'Paul' is not in the bag then the empty block will be executed, which will result in nothing happening. In the second example, a message will be printed to the Transcript.

10.6 Set

The class Set is basically the same as the class Bag, with the exception that it does not allow duplicates. That is, it is only possible to hold a single reference to an object in a set. For example, try the following out in a Workspace:

```
| temp |
temp := Set new.
temp add: 'John'.
temp add: 'Paul'.
temp add: 'Peter'.
temp add: 'John'.
temp inspect.
```

You will find that only one occurrence of the string 'John' was added to the set. The second addition was ignored.

There is also a version of the collection class Set called IdentitySet. This type of set performs an identity test to determine if an object is a duplicate or not. That is, it uses the == test rather than the = test. This means that rather than an object having the same value as an object already in a set, it must actually **be** that object. If it is only equivalent then the object will be added to the set. In this way it may appear that duplicates have been added to the set. However, they are not the same object and are therefore allowed.

The IdentitySet can be useful if you know that duplicate elements to be added to the set will be the same object. In such cases the Identity set can be used as it is more efficient than the standard set.

10.7 OrderedCollection

The OrderedCollection class can hold any type of object. It does so in a specified order. That order is determined by the order in which objects are added to the OrderedCollection instance. An instance of OrderedCollection is created by using either new or new:. The second version of new allows an integer to be provided which indicates the maximum size of the collection required. This can be useful in situations where this number is known and time is optimal. That is, it is not necessary to waste time incrementally growing the collection.

OrderedCollection can be used in situations where the order in which the objects were added to the instance must be preserved. For example, try out the following example of using an OrderedCollection:

```
| x |
x := OrderedCollection new.
x add: 'one'.
x add: 'two'.
x add: 'three'.
x inspect.
```

You will find that the strings 'one', 'two' and 'three' remain in the order in which they were added (unlike instances of Bag and Set).

There is a wide range of order related messages which allow objects to be added and accessed with reference to the order in the OrderedCollection instance. For example, it is possible to access an object "before" or "after" another object by using the before: or after: messages, e.g.:

```
x after: 'two'.
```

It is also possible to add an object either before or after another object. For example:

```
x add: 'five' after: 'one'.
x add: 'six' before: 'three'.
```

To remove an object from the collection use remove:ifAbsent:, this removes the first instance of the object specified in the collection. If the object is not present, then the absent block will be executed. For example:

```
a remove: 'John' ifAbsent: [Dialog warn: 'John not present'].
```

The OrderedCollection class can be used to construct a Stack or Queue class. An example of how to do this is presented in the next section. Notice how little code has to be written and how much is inherited.

10.8 Stack and queue classes in Smalltalk

In this section we will work through an example illustrating how we can define new collection classes (data structures). We shall put both classes we will define into a class category called "Additional-Collections".

10.8.1 The Stack class

The first class we will define is the Stack class. The class definition of the Stack is illustrated below[1]. Note that we are making Stack a subclass of OrderedCollection. This is because the elements of a stack are ordered, and may be duplicated within the stack. Also note that we are not defining any new instance variables. The functionality of the Stack will come solely from extending the interface, the structure of the class will be completely inherited from the OrderedCollection class.

```
OrderedCollection variableSubclass: #Stack
        instanceVariableNames: ''
        classVariableNames: ''
        poolDictionaries: ''
        category: 'Additional-Collections'
```

As before I am also providing a class comment (see Figure 10.4). Again it is up to you to decide whether you wish to provide one as well (although I strongly recommend doing so - it is a good habit to get into).

---

[1] As OrderedCollections are variable in size the variableSubclass: class creation message is used. Don't worry too much about this as the tools provided with environments such as VisualWorks ensure that the appropriate message is always used.

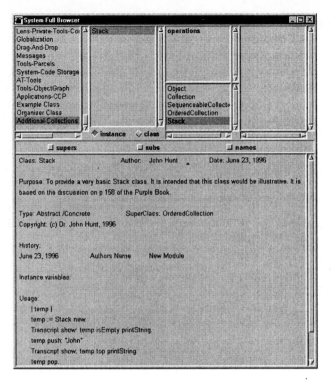

Figure 10.4: The Stack class comment

Next we will define a message protocol called "operations". It is within this protocol that we will define all the methods which will provide the functionality of the Stack. These methods will be push:, pop and top.

The push: method is used to push something onto the top of the stack. It takes one argument, (an object) and adds it to the top of the stack. To do this it uses the addLast: method inherited from OrderedCollection.

```
push: newObject
        self addLast: newObject
```

Next we will define the pop method. This method removes the top element from the stack and returns it as the result of evaluating pop. Again it uses methods inherited from OrderedCollection to do this.

```
pop
        self isEmpty
                ifTrue: [^nil]
                ifFalse: [^self removeLast].
```

Finally, we will define the method top. This method is like pop, except that it does not remove the top most element from the stack. To do this we use the message last inherited from OrderedCollection.

```
top
        self isEmpty
                ifTrue: [^nil]
                ifFalse: [^self last].
```

This class is an excellent example of why Smalltalk is so powerful. We have defined a class which provides the functionality of a `Stack` (no matter what the contents of that stack will be) in just a few lines of code. Consider the amount of work required to achieve the same result in a language such as Pascal or C (without purchasing additional libraries).

10.8.2 The Queue class

This class definition is very similar to the Stack example, it is therefore presented here with little additional comment.

```
OrderedCollection variableSubclass: #Queue
        instanceVariableNames: ''
        classVariableNames: ''
        poolDictionaries: ''
        category: 'Additional-Collections'
```

Again a class comment should be defined. This is left an an excersie for the reader. The methods should again be placed in a protocol called "operations". Each of the methods are listed below.

```
add: newObject
        self addLast: newObject.

delete
        self isEmpty
                ifTrue: [^nil]
                ifFalse: [self removeFirst].

next
        self isEmpty
                ifTrue: [^nil]
                ifFalse: [^self first].
```

The state of the class definition at this point is illustrated in Figure 10.5.

10.9 Summary

In this chapter you have encountered for the first time, one of the most important class hierarchies in Smalltalk. The various collection classes will form the basis of the data structures you build and will be the corner stone of most of your implementations. So far you have looked at `Bags`, `Sets` and `OrderedCollections`. For those of you coming from a Lisp style language these concepts won't have seemed too strange. However, for those of you coming from languages such as C, Pascal or Ada you may well have found the idea of a bag and a set quite bizarre. Stick with them, try them out, implement some simple programs using them and you will soon find that they are easy to use and extremely useful. You will very quickly come to wonder why every language doesn't have the same facilities!

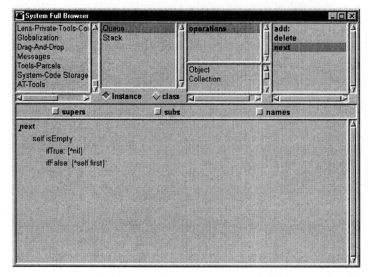

Figure 10.5: The System Browser after the "next" method has been defined

10.10 Further reading

Almost any good book on Smalltalk includes a detailed discussion of the collection classes. However, particularly good references can be found in [Lalonde and Pugh 1991]. Useful references for the Queue and Stack classes can be found in [Goldberg and Robson 1989].

11. Further Collection Classes

11.1 Introduction

This chapter continues the discussion of the collection class hierarchy. It concentrates on the ordered collections and builds on the previous chapter. Sections two, three and four present the SortedCollection class, the List class and the Interval Class. The Array class, Dictionary class and String class are presented in Sections five to seven. Section eight describes how to iterate over collections while Section nine explains how to convert between collections. Figure 11.1 illustrates the relationships between some of the ordered collection classes.

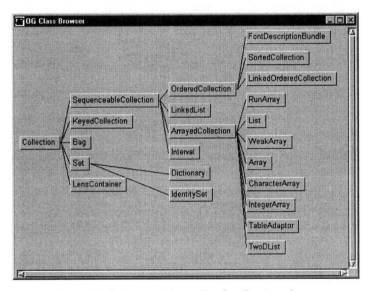

Figure 11.1: Some of the ordered collection classes

11.2 SortedCollection

A SortedCollection is a collection class in which the order of the elements is determined by a specified sorting criteria (for example $x_i < x_{i+1}$). This is specified by the sort block associated with every sortedCollection object. That is, the ordering is defined by a special block of code (for example, [:x :y | x>= y]). This

111

block can be replaced by the user of the class so that any type of ordering can be applied to the objects within the collection. Why not browse the class using the class browser. Try and find out what type of sorting algorithm is being used.

Try out the following in a Workspace:

```
| x |
x := SortedCollection new.
x add: 5.
x add: 6.
x add: 7.
x add: 1.
x inspect.
```

This is a very powerful class which greatly simplifies the production of ordered lists of information. You can change the block controlling the sort by sending the message sortBlock: to the sortedCollection instance with a new block definition.

11.3 List

The List class is a recent addition to the collection classes in VisualWorks (which is not yet available in other implementations of Smalltalk such as Visual Smalltalk). The List class combines some of the more useful features of the Array, OrderedCollection, SortedCollection classes and the Model class. The order of its elements is initially determined by the order in which the elements are added (as in OrderedCollection). These elements can then be accessed via an index (as in Array). However, the elements can also be sorted using either the default ascending order, or a custom sort block can be provided (as in SortedCollection). In addition a List keeps a record of dependents to which it should send updates (as in class Model). However, as we have not yet looked at the Model class, we will ignore this part of the class's operation.

The set of features provided by this class make it one of the most widely used types of collection, in some cases supplanting the older OrderedCollection and SortedCollection classes. It responds to a combination of the Ordered and Sorted Collection class protocols. Therefore it understands after:, before:, sort, sortWith:, add:, add:after: and add:before:. It also responds to addLast:, addFirst:, remove:ifAbsent:, removeFirst, removeLast etc.

To create a new instance of class List use either new or new: depending on whether you wish to specify an initial size or not.

For example, try this out in a Workspace.

```
| temp |
temp := List new: 10.
temp add: 'John'.
temp addFirst:'Paul'.
temp add: 'Peter' before: 'John'.
temp inspect.
```

11.4 Intervals

Instances of class `Interval` represent *finite arithmetic progressions*. Such progressions are given by a starting number, a (finite) limit, and a method of computing the next number. Once created, new elements cannot be added or removed from the `Interval`.

Intervals can be created using the class messages:

```
from: start to: stop
from: start to: stop by: step
```

`start`, `stop` and `step` can be any kind of `Number`. Intervals are common enough that a shorthand form has been provided. This shorthand form is achieved by sending `to:` or `to:by:` to a kind of `Number`. For example the following are equivalent:

```
Interval from: 10 to: 100 by: 2
10 to: 100 by: 2
```

These are equivalent to a `for i = 10 to 100 step 2` type loop. However, they actually create an interval containing all the objects to be processed before any further processing occurs. This allows them to be used with a do loop.

Intervals respond to the message `do: aBlock` by evaluating `aBlock` for each of its values in sequence. Thus, an `Interval` can be used to construct the equivalent of a FOR loop. For example:

```
(10 to: 100 by: 2) do: [:each | Transcript show: each printString].
```

This is therefore roughly equivalent to the C *for* loop:

```
for (i = 0; i <= 100; i := i + 2)
    printf ("%d", i);
```

This construction is so common that the `to:do:` and `to:do:by:` are also implemented in `Number` so that the brackets can be omitted if desired. For example:

```
10 to 100 do: [:each | Transcript show: each printString].
```

11.5 Array

Essentially the `Array` class is just the same as an array in any language. In an array of *n* locations there will be 1 to *n* indexes in which objects can be stored. For those of you familiar with C, be warned attempting to access the value of location 0 will result in an error. However, one major difference between arrays in languages such as C and those in Smalltalk is that you do not specify the type that each element in the array will take. For example, in C you might specify that an array will be of type

113

int. That is all elements in the array will be integers. Instead, an array in Smalltalk can hold any type of object.

Note that it is also not necessary to specify the size of your new array, you can just create a new array (e.g. Array new.). However, this will typically only allocate you 7 array locations. If you want more, the system will dynamically allocate you with more. However, this is slow and time consuming. If you know you want a hundred locations then say so when you create the array (i.e. Array new: 100). Now let's look at an example:

C Version   Smalltalk Version

```
int x[10]
x[0] := "one";
x[1] := "two";
x[2] := "four";
x[3] := "five";
printf ("%s", x[4]);
```

```
| x |
x := Array new: 10.
x at: 1 put: 'one'.
x at: 2 put: 'two'.
x at: 4 put: 'four'.
x at: 5 put: 'five'.
Transcript show: (x at: 4)
                        printString.
x inspect.
```

Notice that the `at:put:` message is used to put values at specific locations, and the `at:` message is used to retrieve elements. Also notice that it was not necessary to specify the type of the array. As it happens all the elements are strings, but there is no reason why the element at location 3 can't be any type of object at all.

The typical way to access an element in an array is to access it via its index. This means that if you wish to access all the elements in the array x in turn you might use a do loop. For example:

C Version   Smalltalk Version

```
for (i = 1; i <= 5; i++)
        printf ("%s", x[i]);
```

```
1 to 5 do: [:i |
        Transcript show: (x at: i)].
```

These pieces of code are fairly similar and perform the same function. However, this is not the most appropriate way to process the elements of the array in Smalltalk. Smalltalk provides a number of other constructs (referred to as iteration messages) which are not only more efficient but usually implement the required functionality rather more elegantly. These will be considered in more detail later.

11.6 Multi dimensional arrays

Multi dimensional arrays can be created in Smalltalk, and there are two ways of doing this. One provides a two dimensional array (with list like features) which is fixed in size, while the second provides any dimension size but requires additional programmer support. For example, in C to create a two dimensional array of 3 by 4 integer elements we could write:

114

```
int table [3] [4];
```

In Smalltalk we can either use a TwoDList or create the two dimensional structure manually. For example, if we used the TwoDList class:

```
| aTwoDList |
aTwoDList := TwoDList columns: 3 rows: 4.
```

We could then place the string 'John' into position 1, 1 using the atPoint:put: message. We can then retrieve this string using the atPoint: message. Note these messages take a point object as the position. A point object can be created using the @ form. For example:

```
aTwoDList atPoint: (1 @ 1) put: 'John'.
Transcript show: (aTwoDList atPoint: (1 @ 1)).
```

As this class possesses list like behaviour it can be used in a similar manner to an instance of list. For this reason it is often used with the user interface facilities provided in VisualWorks. For example, with the table widget. However, we cannot change the size of a TwoDList once it is created. Nor do we have the ability to use higher dimensions. It is sometimes therefore necessary to manually construct multidimensional arrays. For example:

```
temp := Array new: 3.
temp at: 1 put (Array new: 4).
temp at: 2 put (Array new: 4).
temp at: 3 put (Array new: 4).
```

We could then access elements of the object in the following manner:

```
((temp at: 1) at: 1)
```

If you find yourself having to do this often then it probably means that you are thinking too procedurally and need to reconsider your design.

11.7 Dictionaries

A Dictionary is a set of Associations, each representing a key-value pair. It is a subclass of Set. The elements in a Dictionary are unordered, but each has a definite name or *key*. Thus a Dictionary can be regarded as an unordered collection of object *values* with external keys. Part of the protocol for dictionaries is listed below:

- at: aKey returns the value associated with aKey.
- at: aKey put: aValue puts aValue into a dictionary with the external key aKey.
- associationAt: aKey answers with the *association* given by the key (i.e. the value and the key).

- keyAtValue: aValue answers with the name (key) associated with aValue.
- keys answers with a Set of keys from the receiver.
- values answers with a Bag of the values in the receiver. Note that values are not necessarily unique (hence they are returned as a Bag rather than as a Set).

Here is a simple Dictionary example you might like to type in and try out.

```
| x |
x := Dictionary new.
x at: 'John' put: 'jjh'.
x at: 'Myra' put: 'msw'.
x at: 'Chris' put: 'cjr'.
x at: 'Denise' put: 'dec'.
Transcript show: (x at: 'Chris') printString.
Transcript show: (x keyAtValue: 'jjh') printString.
x inspect.
```

This has some similarities to a hash table found in some other languages (e.g. Common LISP) or in libraries available for other languages (e.g. C). The great advantage of Smalltalk is that everyone has the same type of Dictionary. In Pascal or C almost everyone would have to re-invent their own or purchase a library to get the same functionality. This, of course, leads to problems of consistency between implementations.

Another form of the Dictionary collection also exists. This form is termed the IdentityDictionary. Like the IdentitySet it uses the == test rather than the = test. This means that for an object to be returned, the object used as the key must be the *same* object as was used to create the key and not just an equivalent object. Like the IdentitySet it is more efficient that the standard Dictionary class and may be used in certain circumstances.

11.8 Strings

Strings are represented in Smalltalk as collections of characters. Unlike in languages such as C, there is no need to provide special string processing functions such as strcpy(). Instead, we can treat strings as collections (and iterate over their contents) or as "strings" in their own right. This is because we are inheriting the collection class (and the subclasses between the collection class and the class String) methods and are using the methods defined in the class String.

Useful String operations include the concatenation of strings, searching for substrings and pattern matching between strings. For example, sameAs: aString answers whether the receiver and aString match precisely (ignoring case differences).

To concatenate two strings together use a comma. For example:

```
myName := 'John' , ' E ' , 'Hunt'.
```

Notice that you do not have to specify the length of the string. Remember they are just objects and a variable can hold any object.

Substring operations are essential in any language and Smalltalk provides a variety of features for searching for substrings and pattern matching between strings. For example, the `findString: startingAt:` message. This message searches the receiving string for the string passed as a parameter to the method. For example:

```
'John Hunt was here' findString: 'Hunt' startingAt: 1.
```

There are two pattern matching methods defined for strings, `sameCharacters:` and `match:`. The first method counts the number of beginning characters which are the same. The second method is more powerful and can include two types of wild card (# which can represent any single character and * which can represent zero or more characters). For example:

```
'Dr. * Hunt' match: 'Dr. John Hunt'.
```

This expression *evaluates to true*. There is a variant of the match: method which can either ignore or consider case; `match:ignoreCase:` (which takes either true or false as the second argument).

Instances of class `String` also respond to boolean operators such as '<'. This is because strings have an ordering (defined by the alphabet). For example:

```
'john' < 'Denise'
```

There are similar methods for '<=', '>' and '>='. Strings can also be converted into lower or upper case using `asLowerCase` and `asUpperCase`. Finally, as strings are types of collection they can respond to the iteration message described above. These can be used for performing some operation on each character in a string in turn.

11.9 Iterating over collections

A number of messages are available which allow the same operation to be applied to each element in a collection and in some cases the results of this operation can be automatically collected. These messages are referred to as the iteration messages, they include do:, `select: reject:`, collect: and detect:. For all the messages (except do:), the result is a new collection 'just like the receiver'. The elements of this object depend on the criteria specified in the block associated with the message. Note the result can be an empty collection.

11.9.1 The do: message

The do: aBlock message evaluates aBlock for each of the elements in the receiver (a Collection). aBlock should have one argument. (Note that you have not yet encountered blocks. For the time being treat them as begin/ends as in other languages such as Pascal or ADA. We will look at them in more detail later.)

The following example illustrates the use of do:

```
count := 0.
letters do: [:each | each == $a ifTrue: [count := count + 1]].
```

This expression counts the number of 'a's in the collection *letters*. The do statement iterates over the elements in the letters collection. Each element is bound to the temporary variable "each" in turn. It then compares each with the character "a". If the result of this comparison is the object true (remember all expression return an object of some form) then the ifTrue: message will execute the code in its associated block.

Compare it with C style code for the same task:

```
count = 0; i = 0;
max_num = length(letters);
for (i = 1, i <= max_num, I++) {
    if (letters[i] == 'a') {
        count++;
    }}
```

Notice that in the Smalltalk version we did not need to calculate the length of the collection letters. Also notice that we only specified the variable "each" which was local to the do block within the loop.

11.9.2 The select: message

The select: aBlock message evaluates aBlock for each element in the receiving collection. It returns a result which is a collection object containing the objects selected when the result of evaluating aBlock was *true*. For example:

```
(letters select: [:each | each == $a] ) size
```

This creates a new collection containing only 'a's then counts the number of elements. That is, it only stores the elements of the collection letters which return true for the test presented in the block. The equivalent Pascal style code might be:

```
count := 0; i := 0; index := 0;
max_num := length(letters);
for i = 1 to max_num do
    if (letters(i) ='a') then
        newList(index) := letters(i);
        index := index + 1;
    endif;
endfor;
```

As you can see the Smalltalk construct is rather more elegant.

11.9.3 The reject: message

The reject: aBlock message evaluates aBlock for each element in the receiving collection. The result of this message is then a collection containing the objects selected when aBlock evaluated to *false*. For example:

```
(letters reject: [:each | each == $a] ) size
```

This will return a collection containing all the elements in letters which weren't the lower case 'a' character. That is, this message returns all the elements in letters which fail the comparison test.

11.9.4 The collect: message

With the collect: aBlock message aBlock is again evaluated for each element in the receiving collection. The resulting returned collection object is the same size as the receiving collection. The returned collection contains the result of evaluating the block for each of the elements in the receiving collection. For example:

```
(letters collect: [:each | each == $a] ) size
```

This will return a collection of the same size as letters, with either true or false in each element depending on the outcome of the comparison.

11.9.5 The detect: message

In some cases we want to retrieve the first element in a collection which passes some test. The detect: aBlock message does this for us. It evaluates aBlock for each element in the receiving collection and answers with the first element where aBlock evaluates to true. For example:

```
letters detect: [:each | (each asUppercase == $A) |
                         (each asUppercase == $B)]
```

This can be extremely useful if you have a collection of records and you need the first one which matches some test.

11.10 Inserting into a collection

The insert message is a very useful and very efficient operation. For example, if you have a collection of numbers which you wish to total you would either need to iterate over the collection using a do loop or convert the collection to an array and use an interval to mimic a Pascal style *for* loop.

In Smalltalk, however, this type of operation (i.e. where you want to initialize some values and then perform the same thing on all elements in a collection) is so common that an extremely efficient construct is provided. This construct is called the inject: mechanism. For example, assume you have a bag of integers and real numbers which you want to sum. You can use inject: to do this, for example:

```
| aBag result |
aBag := Bag new.
aBag add: 12; add: 24; add: 23.56; add: 7.
result := aBag inject: 0 into: [:sum :item | sum + item ].
```

This injects the initial value zero into sum and item. It then binds item to each of the elements of the bag in turn. Each time it does so, it adds item to the current value in sum and saves the result into sum. This is therefore equivalent to writing:

```
| sum aBag |
aBag := Bag new. sum := 0.
aBag add: 12; add: 24; add: 23.56; add: 7.
aBag do: [:item | sum := sum + item].
result := sum.
```

An interesting exercise is to create a very large bag and an array (e.g. over 100,000 numbers) and time the performance of the inject: message versus the do: message on the two objects. The result of doing this for bags and arrays of 100, 1000, 10000, 100000 and 1,000,000 is interesting. The performance of the array is noticeably faster, however the differences between the inject: and do: messages (for the same class) are negligible.

The Smalltalk facility which allows the developer to time their code is millisecondsToRun:. This is used to calculate the processor time taken to execute the code in the block passed to it. For example:

```
| anArray time1 aNumber |
anArray := Array new: 10000000.
1 to: 10000000 do: [:i | anArray at: i put: i].
time1 := Time millisecondsToRun:
            [anArray inject: 0 into: [:sum :item | sum + item ]].
Transcript cr; show: 'Inject '; show: time1 printString.
```

11.11 Conversion

An instance of one collection can be converted into a different sort of collection with certain conditions. For example, it is possible to convert a Bag instance into a Set instance, but any duplicate objects in the Bag instance will be removed. For example:

```
| a b |
a := Bag new.
a add: 'John'.
a add: 'Paul'.
a add: 'John'.
b := a asSet.
```

120

It is quite common to want to take a set or a bag and to sort it in some manner. The easiest way of doing this is to convert it to a sorted collection. For example:

```
| aBag aSortedCollection |
aBag := Bag new.
aBag add: 'John'; add: 'Paul'; add: 'Denise'; add: 'Fiona'.
aSortedCollection := aBag asSortedCollection.
aSortedCollection do: [:item | Transcript cr; show: item].
```

This results in the list of names being printed alphabetically in the Transcript (see Figure 11.2).

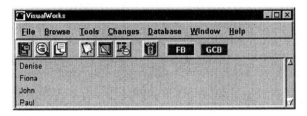

Figure 11.2: Printing a sorted list in the Transcript

You should note that these conversion messages do not affect the receiving object in anyway. That is, it does not actually convert the collection, rather it creates a new collection of the correct class and fills it with the objects in the receiving collection.

The other commonly used conversion messages include:

- asBag. This will return a bag collection
- asSet. This returns a set collection. Note if duplicates existed in the receiving collection, they will have been ignored.
- asOrderedCollection . This returns an OrderedCollection with elements from the receiver. The ordering is arbitrary.
- asSortedCollection. This creates a SortedCollection, sorted so that each element is less than or equal to (<=) its successors. An error will be generated if the elements within the collection do not respond to this message.
- asSortedCollection: aSortBlock This uses aBlock to sort the elements in the SortedCollection The aBlock must take two parameters. For example

```
#( 5 1 3 7 9 2) asSortedCollection: [:x :y | x>= y]
```

will produce a sorted collection of the numbers.

12. An Object Oriented Organizer

12.1 Introduction

This chapter presents a detailed example application constructed using the collection classes. The Organizer is intended as an electronic personal Organizer. It therefore possesses an address book, a diary (or appointments section) and a section for notes. The remainder of this chapter describes one way of implementing such an Organizer. At the end of this chapter is a programming exercise for you the reader.

12.2 The Organizer

This example involves more than one class and has a more complex architecture than anything you have seen so far. The architecture is illustrated in Figure 12.1. This example illustrates another important concept in object orientation, that of an object within an object. These are often referred to as *part-of* hierarchies, i.e. one object is *part-of* another. This should not be confused with the class hierarchy which is a *kind-of* hierarchy.

Figure 12.1: The structure of anOrganizer Object

As illustrated in Figure 12.1 an instance of the Organizer class contains three other objects. These objects are held in the instance variables addressBook, appointments and notes. The instances within addressBook and appointments are dictionary objects, while the notes instance variable holds a bag object.

12.3 The class definition

We shall put all Organizer class in a class category called *Organizer Class*. As illustrated in the above figure the class definition possesses three instance variables, addressBook, appointments and notes. Figure 12.2 illustrates the class definition.

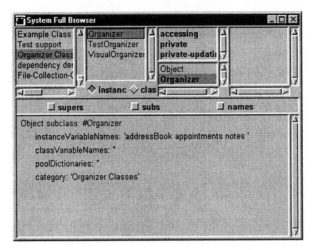

Figure 12.2: The Organizer class definition

The class comment has been defined as follows. Remember providing a class comment is a good habit to get into.

```
Class: Organizer    Author: John Hunt   Date: 27 September 1995

Purpose: This is a class definition which provides some of the
facilities of a personal Organizer.

History:
27 September 1995    John Hunt                New Class

Instance variables:
addressBook    <aDictionary>        Holds names and addresses.
Appointments   <aDictionary>        Holds dates and things to do.
notes          <aBag>               Scratch pad for notes

Usage:
To try the class out select the following and 'do it'.
|temp |
temp := Organizer new.
temp newAddress: 'Room 47' for: 'John'.
temp newAddress: 'Room 46' for: 'Patrick'.
temp newAppointment: 'Meet with MEng' for: '10/10/95'.
temp addNote: 'I must do all my work'.
temp addNote: 'Today is a brand new day'.
temp addressFor: 'John'.
temp appointmentFor: '10/10/95'.
temp printNotes.
temp inspect.
```

12.4 The *initialize-release* protocol

The first protocol we will define will be the "initialize-release" protocol. As usual we will define the initialize method. This method will be used to initialize each of the

123

instance variables with appropriate objects. This is necessary for the other methods to function correctly. The addressBook is initialized to hold a Dictionary object as is the appointments instance variable, while the notes instance variable holds a Bag. Note however, that we do not access the instance variables directly, even though we can as we are within the same class. This is because, by using the updater methods we can ensure that any modification relating to how the Organizer class represents an addressBook, appointments or notes will be localized to the methods which access and update the instance variables. Otherwise, if we changed the internal representation we would have to modify every method which accessed them. This could make maintenance very difficult.

Figure 12.3 illustrates the System Browser with the initialize method for the Organizer class. Your definition should look like this.

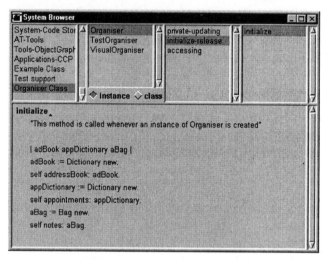

Figure 12.3: Defining the initialize method in the Organizer class

12.5 A class side method

We shall now do something we have not yet done. We shall define a class method. To do this, first select the class radio button below the class list window. You will now be on the *class side* of the Organizer class. You should see that the code view window has changed and now indicates the class instance definition. You will also see that your *initialize-release* protocol and initialize message have disappeared. This is because you are now on the *class side* and they are part of the *instance side* definitions.

We are now going to define a class message protocol. Just as before, to do this you must first define the protocol name. You do this using the right button menu in the protocol window. Call the new protocol "instance creation". Now define a method in the code view window called new. Follow the example illustrated below exactly.

new
```
^super new initialize
```

Note you must make sure that you include the return symbol "^", otherwise you will get the class `Organizer` returned in response to the message `new`, rather than the new instance you wanted. The main purpose of this method is to make sure that the *instance* method `initialize` is sent to the new instance of an Organizer, before anything else happens. This is a common use for redefining `new`, i.e. doing something before anything else can get its hands on it. The System Full Browser (available with the advanced toolkit) is illustrated in Figure 12.4. This figure presents the state of the system after the class side method has been defined.

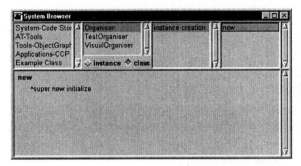

*Figure 12.4: Defining the class side **new** method*

12.6 The *private-updating* protocol

Next we return to the instance side of the class (by selecting the instance radio button in the System Browser) and define each of the methods in the *private-accessing* protocol. Remember you *MUST* move back to the instance side of the class by selecting the *instance* radio button below the class list. Notice that the name of this protocol is comprised of two names "private" and "updating". This is because, it is not intended for use by users of this class. Rather it is used by the initialize method to set up an instance of this class. The methods there are "private" to the object and are used for "updating" the state of the object.

The `addressBook:` method is an updater method for the `addressBook` instance variable. It is used to accept a new dictionary object to use for the `addressBook`. It is intended only for use with the instance creation method of the `Organizer` class.

addressBook: aDictionary
```
addressBook := aDictionary
```

The `appointments:` method is an updater method for the `appointments` instance variable. It is used to accept a new dictionary object to use for the appointments. It is intended only for use with the instance creation method of the `Organizer` class.

```
appointments: aDictionary
        appointments := aDictionary.
```

Finally, the `notes:` method gives the `notes` instance variable a `Bag` to hold its contents.

```
notes: aBag
        notes := aBag.
```

Figure 12.5 illustrates the state of the System Full Browser at the end of these steps.

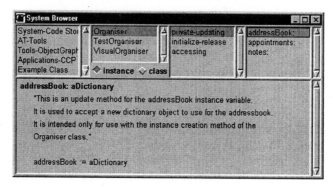

Figure 12.5: The private-updating protocol

12.7 The *accessing* protocol

Now we will define the methods for the *accessing* protocol. First define the protocol then each of the following methods in turn. We will first define the instance variable accessors and then the Organizer specific methods. As before, the accessor methods have the same name as the instance variables. We will also define methods which are used to set the contents of instance variables.

The `addNote:` method adds a new note to the `notes` instance variable.

```
addNote: aNote
        notes add: aNote.
```

The `newAddress:for:` method is used to add a new address to the address book. It is illustrated in Figure 12.6.

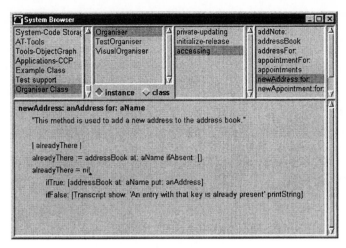

Figure 12.6: The newAddress:for: method

The method for adding a new appointment is essentially the same as the
`newAddress:for:` method.

```
newAppointment: anAppointment for: aDate
        "This method is used to add a new appointment to the
        appointments dictionary."

        | alreadyThere |
        alreadyThere := appointments at: aDate ifAbsent: [].
        alreadyThere = nil
                ifTrue: [appointments at: aDate put: anAppointment]
                ifFalse: [Transcript show:
                                'An entry with key is already present']
```

The remaining accessor methods in this protocol are relatively straight forward,
they are therefore listed below with no additional commentary.

```
addressBook
        "This is an accessor method for the addressBook instance variable"
        ^addressBook

appointments
        "This is an accessor method for the appointments instance variable"
        ^appointments

notes
        "This is an accessor method for the notes instance variable"
        ^notes
```

Now we will define the methods used to access information within the instance
variables. These are Organizer specific operations. The `addressFor:` method is
used to retrieve an address from the address book.

```
addressFor: aName
        | anEntry |
        anEntry := addressBook at: aName ifAbsent: [nil].
        ^anEntry
```

The `appointmentsFor:` method is used to retrieve an appointment from the `appointments` instance variable.

```
appointmentFor: aDate
    | anEntry |
    anEntry := appointments at: aDate ifAbsent: [nil].
    ^anEntry
```

Finally, the `printNotes` method is used to display all the notes which have been made in the Organizer.

```
printNotes
    Transcript cr.
    notes
        do:
            [:item |
            Transcript show: item printString.
            Transcript cr.]
```

Once you have defined all the methods, you are ready to use your Organizer. Figure 12.7 illustrates how the Organizer might be used. For example, I have used the Workspace to create a new Organizer and put some entries in it. Try your Organizer out in a similar way. Try extending it by adding additional functionality. For example, provide a way of deleting an address or replacing it with a new one.

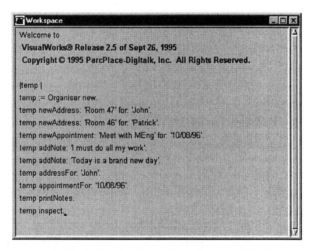

Figure 12.7: Using the Organizer class in a Workspace

12.8 The Financial Manager project

At certain points throughout the remainder of this book you will be asked to develop a small project. This project will provide the basic functionality of the Financial Manager application.

The aim of the Financial Manager application is to keep a record of deposits and withdrawals from a current account. Associated with this, it should keep an up to date balance, as well as allow statements to be printed.

You should be able to:

1. Add deposits to the account for a specified amount.
2. Make payments (withdrawals) from the account for specified accounts.
3. Get the current balance.
4. Get a statement of all payments and deposits made, in the order in which they happened. This statement should be printed to the Transcript.

To do this you should use a collection class to hold the statement in conjunction with a new class subclassed off the class Object, which will hold the current balance and handle deposits and withdrawals.

Assuming the class you define is called FinancialManager, then you should be able to run the following Smalltalk:

```
| aFinancialManager |
aFinancialManager := FinancialManager new.
aFinancialManager deposit: 25.00.
aFinancialManager withdraw: 12.00.
aFinancialManager deposit: 10.00.
aFinancialManager deposit: 5.00.
aFinancialManager withdraw: 8.00.
Transcript show: 'The current balance is
                        FinancialManager balance printString.
Transcript cr.
aFinancialManager statement.
```

The result of evaluating this code should be:

```
The current balance is 20
Statement:
deposit 25.00
withdraw 12.00
deposit 10.00
deposit 5.00
withdraw 8.00
```

13. Streams and Files

13.1 Introduction

This chapter discusses the second most used class hierarchy in Smalltalk; the Stream classes. The Stream classes are used (amongst other things) for accessing files. The remainder of the chapter is structured in the following manner: Section two describes the Streams classes. Section three describes how the stream classes can be used for file access. Section four describes an example of using files and streams.

13.2 Streams

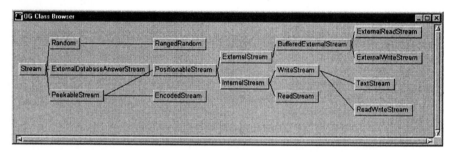

Figure 13.1: The structure of the Stream class hierarchy

Streams are the second most used set of classes. Streams are objects which serve as sources or sinks of data. At first this concept can seem a bit strange. The easiest way to think of streams are as streams of data (as opposed to water) either flowing from a pool of data or into a pool of data.

There are a number of different types of stream in the Smalltalk system, and each can have a surprisingly wide range of uses. Figure 13.1 illustrates the structure of the stream class hierarchy. The Stream class is the root class of this hierarchy. Below this are stream classes for reading, writing, for accessing external files etc.

A stream may be input only (ReadStream), output only (WriteStream) or input and output (ReadWriteStream). They can be internal streams (i.e. that act as a source or sink for data internal to the image) or external streams (i.e. the source or sink for the data is external to the current image. A file is a typical example of an external source or sink). Peekable streams also have an internal record of their current position and can look ahead in the stream for information.

Streams have various access methods defined which allow the next item to be obtained or provided. Some of the more useful methods include:

- `next` Answer the next object in the receiver stream and advance the position indicator by one.
- `peek` Answer the next object in the receiver stream, but do not advance the position indicator.
- `nextPut: anObject` Write `anObject` at the current position.
- `nextPutAll: aCollection` Write all elements of the collection to the receiver stream.
- `atEnd` Answer true if the stream is at the end else answer false.

Others include `next: anInteger`, `peekFor: anObject` and `skipTo: anObject`. What operations can be performed on Streams depends on the class of stream being used. Figure 13.1 illustrates the structure of the stream hierarchy.

Typically streams are connected to files (using one of the ExternalStream's subclasses) or to a collection of data (using one of the InternalStream's subclasses). If a stream is connected to an external device (including a file) then it essentially acts as an interface to that external device. It thus allows messages to be sent to and received from an external device object enabling it to accomplish various activities including input and output. If a stream is connected to a collection (such as a string) it can act as a means for processing the contents of a collection. In both cases the stream views the source (or sink) of the data as being able to provide (or receive) a data item on request.

13.3 ASCII files

13.3.1 Working with ASCII files

There are a wide range of file handling facilities available within Smalltalk. Most are provided by one of the subclasses of the class Filename and Stream. The Filename class is an abstract superclass in which the basic framework for files is defined. Most of the work of this class is actually performed by one of its (platform specific) subclasses. It is this which is one of the facilities which allows you to ensure that your code can run on any platform, even if you are accessing the host platform's file system! In the remainder of this section we shall look at some of the most common operations.

13.3.2 Creating, reading and writing a file

To create a file you must first have a filename to work with. A filename is created by sending the message asFilename to a string. This converts the string into an appropriate form for the host operating system. You now have a filename, however you need to link this file name with an actual file. To do this you use an instance of one of the streams classes (see earlier in chapter). This can be done by sending the message *writeStream*, *readStream* or *readWriteStream* to a filename (it is rarely a good idea to use the readWriteStream option. It is invariably better to use either the readStream or writeStream messages). In effect this links the resulting instance directly to the actual file. In the case of creating a new file, it also creates the file for you when the first character is written to it. You now have something to which you can send ASCII text.

You may wish to check to see if a file exists before attempting to open it (e.g. to be sure there is something to read from or to make sure you don't overwrite an existing file). You can do this with the *exists* message. This message returns true if the file is already present and false if it does not exist.

To close the file once it has been opened there is a close message. This message closes the associated file as well as the data stream to that file.

Try typing the following into the Workspace and evaluating it.

```
| filename stream |
filename := 'temp.txt' asFilename.
(fileName exists)
   ifTrue:
     [Dialog warn: 'file ' , fileName asString, ' already exists'.]
   ifFalse: [
             stream := fileName writeStream.
             stream nextPutAll: 'Hello World'.
             stream close.].
Transcript show: fileName fileSize printString.
```

This example creates a file called "temp.txt" in the current working directory, assuming that one does not already exist. It then puts the string "Hello World" in that file and closes the file. It then prints the size of the file in the system Transcript. For example, using VisualWorks 2.5 on a Windows-95 PC, this results in the value 11 being printed in the Transcript. If the code is evaluated a second time, it results in a dialog box (illustrated in Figure 13.2) being displayed which warns that the temp.txt file already exists.

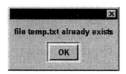

Figure 13.2: A file exists dialog

Notice that in this example we used the message nextPutAll: to save the single string 'Hello World'. Remember that strings are actually collections and what this says is save the whole contents of this collection to the file.

An important point to note about files is that it may sometimes be necessary to access a file which is in a different directory to the working directory. This can be a cause of problems when porting between platforms unless care is taken. If you hard code the name of a directory structure into your system then you will need to modify the system code before it will work on a different platform. There is a way around this using the `construct:` message. This constructs a path name which is appropriate for the platform on which you are working. For example:

```
(('dcs' asFilename construct: 'jjh')
                    construct: 'visual' )
                    construct: 'examples'.
```

Try typing the above into a Workspace and inspecting the result. The actual pathname you obtain will depend on your host operating system. For example, on a Windows-95 PC you should see the style of pathname illustrated in Figure 13.3.

Figure 13.3: Inspecting a filename on a PC

Other messages which may be of use include:

- `directory` Return the directory containing the receiving file.
- `isDirectory` Check to see if a filename is actually a directory.

It is also possible to obtain information on the date and time a file was modified, accessed or had its status changed. To do this first use the message `dates` (this is another aspect which can differ from one Smalltalk implementation to another). This is sent to a filename, which returns a dictionary of associations. Then the key `#modified` will access the most recent modification, the key `#accessed` will return the last access date and the key `#statusChanged` will provide the date of the most recent change in the files status (or privileges). For example Figure 13.4 illustrates checking when a file was last accessed, modified and its status changed.

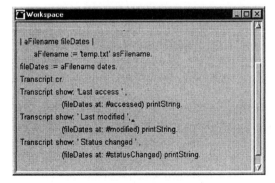

Figure 13.4: Accessing a files details

133

The result of evaluating the code in Figure 13.4 on the `temp.txt` file created earlier might look like:

```
Last access #(June 24, 1996 11:00:00 pm) Last modified #(June 25, 1996
1:56:54 pm) Status changed nil
```

You can also copy, move and delete files, get the contents of directories and files as well as setting file permissions and printing files all from within Smalltalk. The messages used for these functions are all fairly intuitive and readily available in the Smalltalk documentation.

13.3.3 Handling file IO errors

You should always wrap your file access code up in a block and use the `valueNowOrOnUnwindDo:` message to evaluate it. This is a special version of value, which will execute the block passed to it as a parameter if an exception is raised, while the block it was sent to is executing. For example, if you try and read to a file which does not exist, then an exception will be raised and your system will be left in an unstable state with streams still open. However, if you use the `valueNowOrOnUnwindDo:` message, then you can define what should happen if such an event occurs. For example, you could specify that the stream should be closed. This is a very good way of ensuring that your file accesses are handled tidily.

For example, consider the `load:` method defined below. This method accesses a file, reading each line at a time. Once all the lines in the file have been accessed it terminates.

```
load: filename
    |newFile newLineChar stream readingBlock item student |
    newFile := filename value asFilename.
    newFile exists
      ifTrue:
        [newLineChar := Character cr.
         stream := newFile readStream.
         contents := OrderedCollection new: 250.
         readingBlock :=
                [[stream atEnd]
                       whileFalse:
                             [item := stream upTo: newLineChar.
                              contents add: item.]].
          Cursor read showWhile:
                 [readingBlock valueNowOrOnUnwindDo:
                                    [stream close]]].
       ifFalse: [Dialog warn: 'File does not exist!!']
```

There are three things to note about this method from a Smalltalk point of view.

- The first is that we read in one line of the file at a time by telling the (read) stream that we wanted to read up to a carriage return. To do this we send the `upTo:` message to the stream with the `newLineChar` as the parameter. You can use this to read in text up to any character in the input stream.
- If the file exists, a block is created which contains the code which will read in the data in the file. This block is assigned to a variable `readingBlock`. This block

is evaluated by sending it the `valueNowOrOnUnwindDo:` message. Notice that if anything happens to raise an error during these operations (e.g. the file system becomes full), the block passed as a parameter to the `valueNowOrOnUnwindDo:` message will be executed. In this case, it will close the stream (i.e. it will close the file). Thus, if anything goes wrong during the processing of the file, the file will be closed and the system left in a stable state. Indeed when the last statement has been executed in the write block, the block passed as a parameter will be executed. Thus the stream will also be closed. This is a very good way of handling the process of closing the link to files.

- The other point is that the whole of the read expression (i.e. `readingBlock valueNowOrOnUnwindDo: [stream close]`) is passed in a block to the `showWhile:` message. This message is part of the cursor protocol and is used to specify the type of cursor to be displayed while a particular operation is being performed. In this case, the *read cursor* will be displayed while the text file is being read in. This provides some visual feedback to the user.

13.4 The Binary Object Streaming Service

The Binary Object Streaming Service (or BOSS for short) is a very useful and effective way of storing information in the form of objects (instances). If you were to save information to an ordinary text file, then all you could save would be the ASCII version of the data held by the object. You would then need to reconstruct the data into objects when you read the text file. This would mean that you would have to invent some way of indicating that certain data was associated with certain objects and that certain objects were related (if you were dealing with a composite object). All of this would be very time consuming and error prone. It would also be very unlikely that the ASCII data written out by someone else would be in the right format for your system.

The BOSS is provided by VisualWorks as a way around this. It allows objects to be directly stored to a file in a compact and encoded form. You do not need to convert the objects into anything special nor do you need to worry about reconstructing the objects when you load them back in. In addition everyone else who uses the BOSS will be able to read and write to your BOSS files. The action of writing objects to a BOSS file is referred to by Smalltalkers as BOSSing out (or in) the objects.

13.4.1 Saving to BOSS

It is possible to "BOSS out" a single object, a series of objects or a whole collection of objects. It is also possible to BOSS out a composite object. If an object references another object, then both the original object and the objects which it contains are saved to the BOSS file. The BOSS file is an incremental file so it is possible to add objects to a BOSS file at different times (i.e. in different executions of the same image). It is also possible to read the BOSS file one object at a time (assuming the objects were written incrementally). This means that you do not have to read the whole file to access the third object etc.

The procedure for creating a BOSS file is relatively straight forward and is outlined below:

1. Create a data stream to write the objects to. This is usually a write stream onto a specified filename.
2. Create the BinaryObjectStorage system (BOSS) object. This is done using the instance creation method onNew: with the data stream as the parameter.
3. Using the nextPut: message save each object to the BOSS object. Each object you wish to save is passed as the parameter of the nextPut: message.
4. Once you have finished BOSSing out the object you can close it by sending it the message close.

If you want to save a whole collection of objects to the BOSS file you can do so by using the nextPutAll: message (instead of the nextPut: message). Each object will be stored separately, which allows each object to be retrieved separately at a later date.

If you wish to append an object to an existing BOSS file then you create a read-append data stream (rather than a write data stream), then create the BOSS file using the onOld: message (rather than the onNew: message). Finally, you need to move the file pointer to the end of the BOSS file. You can do that by sending the setToEnd message to the BOSS object.

A simple example of creating and saving to a BOSS file is presented below. The bosFileName is set to a string representing an appropriate file on the host computer system.

```
valuesFileStream := bosFileName asFilename writeStream.
bosFileStream := BinaryObjectStorage onNew: valuesFileStream.
bosFileStream nextPutAll: aList.
valuesFileStream close.
```

This example saves all the elements in the variable aList to the bosFile indicated by the bosFileName. It then closes the file.

A point to note is that it can be a good idea to wrap the writing of objects to the BOSS file with a valueNowOrOnUnwindDo: message. This message is used to ensure that the BOSS file you are writing to is closed safely even if an abnormal interruption occurs. That is, the file will be closed and freed up in an appropriate manner. The message is sent to a block in which you define the write expression. It takes a second block as its argument, which executes if there is a problem or when the first block terminates. For example, we could have written the *write* part of the above as:

```
[bosFileStream nextPutAll: aList] valueNowOrOnUnwindDo:
                                      [valuesFileStream close].
```

136

13.4.2 Reading from BOSS

You can either load the whole contents of a BOSS file, read individual objects from a BOSS file (or if you know the position of the object you are interested in) access a single object from any position in the file. This last technique is much faster than reading *n - 1* objects to get to the *nth* object, but it does assume that you know that the object you are interested in is the *nth* object.

The procedure to follow is presented below.

1. First create a data stream to be used to read the BOSS file. This is typically achieved by send a `readStream` message to a file name which represents the name of the BOSS file.
2. Now create a BOSS object by sending an `onOld:` creation message with the newly created data stream as the parameter. You can optimize this process if you know that you are not going to write to the BOSS file. To do this you can use the `onOldNoScan:` message (rather than the `onOld:` message).
3. Obtain the objects in the BOSS file using the appropriate access message (e.g. `contents` or `next`).
4. Once you have finished reading from the boss file you should close it.

The `next` message listed in item 3 above will return a single object which can then be saved into an appropriate collection / data structure etc. The `contents` message will return an array of objects which can then be manipulated in the same way as any other array of objects. For example:

```
| valuesFileStream bosFileStream|
valuesFileStream := bosFileName asFilename readStream.
bosFileStream := BinaryObjectStorage onNew: valuesFileStream.
aBag := Bag new.
[[bosFileStream atEnd]whileFalse: [aBag add: bosFileStream next]]
                        valueNowOrOnUnwindDo: [valuesFileStream close].
```

This example illustrates two things, first it illustrates the equivalent of a while not end of file (EOF) style construct for BOSS files. This construct is the `atEnd` message. This message is used to test whether the end of the BOSS file has been reached. It is therefore possible to use it in a while loop which says "read while not end of file". The other thing this illustrates is the practical use of a `whileFalse:` loop. Many other languages would force a construct such as not (fileName EOF) onto the programmer. The `whileFalse:` construct is far more elegant.

Finally, the `position:` message is used to position the BOSS file pointer so that a single object can be read from a specific point in the BOSS file. However, a record must have been maintained of what the position is (note the third object stored is unlikely to have been stored at position 3). This message could be used to create a file based version of a collection class. We shall look at this in more detail in the next section and so will leave a detailed discussion of this message until then.

13.4.3 Warnings about BOSS files

You should only use BOSS files to store data objects and never for interface objects. This is because the objects you BOSS out will lose their reference to onscreen objects. You should also avoid BOSSing out any objects associated with the execution machinery of VisualWorks. Finally, you should take care never to BOSS out a circular references as this can confuse the BOSS system.

13.5 Using files with the Financial Manager

This application builds on that carried out in the last chapter. The aim of that FinancialManager application was to keep a record of deposits and withdrawals from a current account. Associated with this, it kept an up to date balance as well as allowing statements to be printed.

A problem with that version of the application was that there was no way of permanently storing the account information. As soon as the FinancialManager object was destroyed (or reference to it lost) then all the information associated with it was also lost.

The aim of this exercise is to extend the existing application by adding the following features:

1. The ability to save the current statement to a file.
2. The ability to load an existing statement from a file.

This means that you should provide two new interfaces to your application, one to load a file and one to save a file. These files will contain a formatted version of the information held in the statement. The format of the text file might be: <type of action> <amount> newline. For example:

```
deposit 24.00
withdraw 13.00
```

Note you should try to use a BOSS file as this will make accessing the contents of the file much easier. Other points to note include:

- Check to see that the file exists before loading it.
- Define a save: method which will save the current statement to the specified file.
- Define a load: method which will load a statement into the statement collection.

If you are successful then you should be able to evaluate the following in a Workspace and get the same result from both FinancialManager objects.

```
| aFinancialManager anotherFinancialManager|
aFinancialManager := FinancialManager new.
```

```
aFinancialManager deposit: 25.00.
aFinancialManager withdraw: 12.00.
aFinancialManager withdraw: 8.00.
Transcript show: 'The current balance is ' ,
                      aFinancialManager balance printString.
Transcript cr.
aFinanacialManager statement.
aFinanacialManager save: 'account1'.

anotherFinancialManager := FinancialManager new.
anotherFinancialManager load: 'account1'.
Transcript show: 'The current balance is ' ,
                      anotherFinancialManager balance printString.
Transcript cr.
anotherFinancialManager statement.
```

13.6 Summary

In this chapter you have encountered streams and their use in file input and output. Many simple Smalltalk applications never need to worry about file access, however, if you are ever going to do something where information needs to be stored or shared between images, then you are going to need to interact with the host file system. You have now seen the basic facilities available, the Binary Object Streaming Service (BOSS) approach to storing and accessing information in files is particularly useful. You should now spend some time exploring the stream and file facilities available in your Smalltalk system.

14. The Magnitude Class Hierarchy

14.1 Introduction

This chapter considers the magnitude class and those classes which inherit from it. This includes the Number hierarchy. We also consider the classes Character, Time, and Date.

14.2 The class Magnitude

The Magnitude class is the abstract super class of all classes which possess some concept of a size and the comparison of objects of different size (see Figure 14.1). This means that all types of numbers inherit (eventually) from Magnitude, although they are in fact all subclasses of another class Number, which acts as the abstract superclass for all numbers. This abstract class inherits all of its size related behavior from the Magnitude class. Other classes which have some concept of size and thus can be compared via logical operators such as <, = and > include Time, Date and Character. The subclasses of Magnitude will be considered later in this chapter, in this section we will concentrate on the Magnitude class.

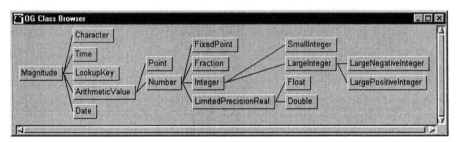

Figure 14.1: The top of the Magnitude class hierarchy

The Magnitude class provides protocol for comparing objects which possess size and which can use their size to rank themselves. The relationship of this size to their peers is class dependent and is not defined by the Magnitude class. The comparing protocol in Magnitude defines the methods < and = :

- <. The intention is that this method will determine if the receiver is less than the argument object. This method is a subclass responsibility. It is used by numerous other methods and is defined here to indicate which methods should be redefined by subclasses.

- =. This method is another subclass responsibility. It is intended to determine equality between the receiver and the argument object.

Other comparison methods defined include; <=, > and >= all of which are defined in terms of < and =. The protocol also defines max: and min: messages used to return either the maximum or minimum of two numbers respectively. For example:

```
10 max: 15.
10 min: 15.
```

The first expression returns the result 15 and the second 10. Magnitude also provides a test method which checks to see if a value is between two other values. For example:

```
10 between: 1 and: 9.
```

14.3 The class Date

Class Date, a subclass of Magnitude, represents a particular day, in a particular month of a particular year. A date object can be created in a number of ways. For example, it is possible to request the date today and thus create a date object:

```
todaysDate := Date today.
```

It is also possible to create a date object for an explicit date, using the newDay:month:year:. For example:

```
birthDate := Date newDay: 23 month: #Sep year: 1964.
```

Note that only the first three letters of the month name are significant and that if the century is not provided in the year parameter (e.g. if 64 had been passed in rather than 1964), then the current century is used as a default.

The Date class also allows date objects to be compared, added, subtracted etc. by virtue of its inherited abilities from Magnitude. For example:

```
(todaysDate < birthDate) ifTrue: [Transcript show: 'Weird!'].
Transcript show: (todaysDate subtractDate: birthDate) printString.
```

This will calculate the difference between today's date and the 23rd of September 1964. The result will be printed in terms of the difference in days. To convert this into (an approximate) number of years, you can divide by 365. This ignores leap years. For example:

```
Transcript show: ((todaysDate subtractDate: birthDate) // 365).
```

Question: Why have I used // rather than / ? Answer, because / will return a fraction if the number of days cannot be divided exactly by 365, where as // will ignore any remainder.

There are also a range of other messages which are supported by the class Date. These messages allow you to determine if the date object is in a leap year, which day of the year it is, which month the date object is in, which year it is part of etc. Some examples using todaysDate are presented below:

```
todaysDate day.
todaysDate leap.
todaysDate monthName.
todaysDate weekday.
todaysDate year.
```

Class Date also supports a range of messages itself. These messages provide additional behavior related to dates. For example, the Date class will respond to messages requesting the number of days in a particular month for a particular year:

```
Date daysInMonth: #Feb forYear: 1997.
```

Another class method can be used to determine if a given year is a leap year or not. This is done using the leapYear: message to the Date class:

```
Date leapYear: 1999.
```

14.4 The class Time

The class Time, provides a similar set of features for objects which represent a specific instant of time (to a particular second) as the class Date does for a specific calendar date. A new instance of the class Time can be created using the instance creation message now or by reading from a string. The string can contain hours, minutes and seconds separated by colons ('11:59:20'). It can also contain an AM or PM designation. For example:

```
currentTime := Time now.
previousTime := Time readFromString: '1:10:20 am'.
```

Just as with the class Date, these times can be compared, added and subtracted. For example:

```
(currentTime = previousTime) ifTrue:
                [Transcript show: 'Time has stood still!'].
differentTime := currentTime subtractTime: previousTime.
```

However, the usefulness of the subtractTime: message is somewhat limited. For example, having evaluated this expression I obtained the result *2:57:18 PM*, when what I really wanted to know was the difference in hours. In the case of time, I can obtain this by converting the time into seconds and dividing by 3600 (the number of seconds in an hour). For example:

```
| currentTime previousTime differentTime |
currentTime := Time now.
previousTime := Time readFromString: '1:00:20 am'.
differentTime := currentTime asSeconds - previousTime asSeconds.
differentTime // 3600.
```

There are two class side messages which may be of general use. The first is
millisecondClockValue. This message returns a value indicating the number
of milliseconds since the system clock was reset. It can be useful as a means for
generating an unique name for a temporary file etc. The uniqueness of such a
filename cannot be guaranteed as there is a vague chance that a file with the same
name may have been left around from an execution of the system prior to the
resetting of the system clock (although the chances of a temporary file being created
with a name derived from the same millisecond clock reading are remote). For
example:

`Time millisecondClockValue.`

The second class side message is the millisecondsToRun: message. This
takes a block as a parameter and generates a report on the time required to evaluate
that block. This message is most often used when determining the performance of
various constructs. For example, in the last chapter it was used to compare the do:
loop with the inject: construct on two collection classes Bag and Array. For
example:

```
Time millisecondsToRun:
            [1 to: 10000 do: [:i | Transcript show: ' ' , i ] ].
```

On a Pentium 120 PC with 16 megabytes of memory this resulted in a value of
79056 seconds being returned.

14.5 The class Character

Characters such as letters (e.g. A, b or Z) are objects in their own right in Smalltalk.
When they are written alone they are preceded by a dollar sign. For example:

`$A, $b, $Z`

These objects can be combined together to form strings (which are actually
collections of characters).

As the Character class inherits from Magnitude, you can compare
characters to determine if one is greater, less than or equal to another. For example:

`Transcript show: ($A < $a) printString.`

In addition, Character adds another comparison method called sameAs:. This method ignores case. Thus it is possible to evaluate the following and have true printed in the Transcript:

```
Transcript show: ($A sameAs: $a) printString.
```

The Character class also understands the differences between alphabetic characters, numeric characters, vowels, uppercase and lowercase letters etc. These are provided by methods in the testing protocol, which include:

```
aCharacter isAlphabetic.
aCharacter isDigit.
aCharacter isLetter.
aCharacter isLowercase.
aCharacter isVowel.
```

It also provides some useful conversion methods, including:

```
aCharacter asUppercase.
aCharacter asLowercase.
aCharacter asInteger.
```

The first two messages would convert the contents of aCharacter either to an uppercase character or a lowercase character while the third message would return the ASCII code a letter or number.

Just like the classes Date and Time, the Character class provides some useful class side protocol. The methods provided on the class side provide access to non-alphanumeric characters. These can be extremely useful when processing text (as was illustrated in the example presented earlier in the book). The facilities available allow you to obtain the character for carriage return, backspace, space, new page and tab (amongst others). For example:

```
newlineChar := Character cr.
spaceChar := Character space.
tabChar := Character tab.
```

14.6 Further reading

The Object Reference manual supplied with your Smalltalk system will provide a detailed description of all the classes described in this chapter. For a detailed description of the Number hierarchy see [Hopkins and Horan 1995].

15. Some More Tools of the Trade

15.1 Introduction

In this chapter you are introduced to the use of *breakpoints* and user initiated *exceptions*. Breakpoints in particular are extremely useful and you will find that you will make extensive use of them, not just for debugging but also to help you understand how objects are behaving. The use of the *file in* and *file out* facilities for saving classes onto your host file system are also discussed. These are important as without this ability you would loose any source code you developed when you started a new image. Finally the use of the *changes* file and *projects* are discussed.

15.2 Errors and breakpoints

As in most languages, it is possible to generate user specified errors (sometimes known as mishaps or exceptions in other languages). This is achieved by sending the message `error` to an object. Errors are usually intended to force the user of the system (which may be another developer) to stop executing and investigate the problem. A similar operation is provided by the `halt` message. The only real difference is that the halt message is intended as a debugging aid, while the error message is intended for use in undesired situations.

15.2.1 Programmer generated errors

Programmer generated errors are really exceptions, which are not handled by the system. These exceptions are generated by the message `error`. For example:

```
self error
```

This message would result in an exception dialog being displayed. These dialogs allow the user a number of options, however, you should notice that the "proceed" option is grayed out. This is because proceeding is not an option if an error has been encountered.

If you wish, you can use a version of the error message which will take a string as a parameter. This string is displayed to the user and can act to provide further information about the error. For example:

```
self error: 'This is not allowed!'.
```

Note that an error message is a message just like any other. You can therefore use it anywhere that you would use a message expression, this means for example that you can conditionalize the call to error:

```
(x < 0)
        ifTrue: [self error: 'Divide by zero coming'].
z := y / x.
```

Have a look at the add: method defined within the Array class of objects for an example of an error handling method. You can do this by selecting the "find class" option off the right mouse button (middle on a three button mouse) in a browser.

15.2.2 Breakpoints

Breakpoints are often useful in determining what is really happening inside the system. In Smalltalk, breakpoints simply provide a controlled mechanism for entering the debugger at a known point in the execution.

Breakpoints may be placed in a method by using the halt breakpoint method. This can be used with or without arguments. For example:

```
self halt. or self halt: 'An example breakpoint'.
```

This form of the halt message is useful if more than one breakpoint exists within the system as it allows the breakpoint to be identified. For example, the result of executing the above halt message expression is illustrated in Figure 15.1. Notice that, the dialog is actually entitled "Exception". This is because both error messages and halts raise a signal which is caught by the exception handler. Notice, that unlike the result of encountering an error message, the user can proceed after evaluating a halt message.

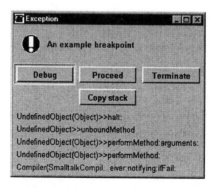

Figure 15.1: An example breakpoint dialog

When a halt expression is encountered, the message halt is sent to the receiver. The corresponding method is implemented in Object so all objects respond to it. This opens the halt notifier from which point you can proceed as if the halt had never been encountered, terminate or select the debug option if you wish to analyze the

146

state of the object when the breakpoint was encountered. If the **debug** option is selected then a debugger window is opened on the method currently executing.

Note that just like an error message, a halt message can be used anywhere that you would use any other message expression. You can therefore conditionalize the call to halt:

```
(x < y)
        ifFalse: [self halt].
```

15.3 File in/file outs

15.3.1 File out

It is possible to file out any group of definitions using the System Browser (or one of its derivatives). That is, you can save to a file whole class categories, individual classes, whole method protocols or just individual methods. By doing so you create a file on the host system's file system, which contains a plain ASCII definition of the appropriate class, method etc. To save information to file, select the **file out** option in the appropriate browser window.

This ASCII file can be viewed in the same way as any other ASCII file using one of the host system's editors / viewers (e.g. EMACS, vi or more on a UNIX system). However, if you do this, you will notice that some additional characters have been added (these are "!" and used as delimiters) as well as extra statements indicating that something is a class comment or a method protocol name etc. Normally, you would not need to edit this file and indeed, unless you are sure of what you are doing, you should not do so.

The purpose of creating "file outs" can be to provide a permanent storage for your class definitions etc. or to share those definitions with others. If you have created a definition which is particularly important and which you do not want to lose at any cost, it is often a good idea to file it. At least then, if you have a catastrophic failure and have to create a whole new image on a new platform, you can still reconstruct your important work.

Another reason for creating file outs, is that they take up a lot less space than the system image. Therefore, if you have a number of sets of definitions which you wish to retain, but not enough space to maintain a large number of images, then you can create file outs which will allow you to construct the images you require, when you require them.

You can file out a whole class category, a class, a message protocol or a single method. This is done by selecting "**file out**" from the right mouse button menu (middle mouse button on a three button mouse) in the appropriate window from the System Browser (or one of the other available browsers, e.g. the excellent Full Browser).

15.3.2 File in

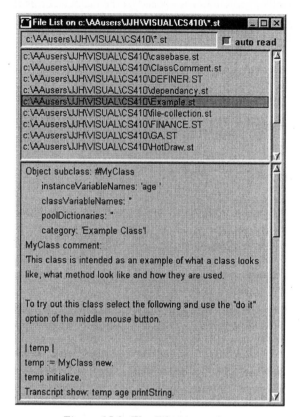

Figure 15.2: The File List tool

If at a later stage you wish to "file in" a "file out" file, you can do so using the file tool. This tool is accessible from the VisualWorks Launcher by clicking on the filing cabinet icon. This presents the user with a (very) basic file editor.

To view files, type into the top pane of the file editor the appropriate path (if required) for your host system, followed by either a specific name or a wild card.

The list of files will be displayed in the middle pane of the file tool. If you select any of these files, their contents will be displayed in the bottom window. If the files are very large the system will ask you whether you really want to see their contents or whether just information on the file (such as its size) will do. You would use the right (or middle) mouse button to file in one of the files. If you do file it in, then a trace of what is being loaded (and compiled) will be printed in the system Transcript window. Once the load is completed, if it is successful you will be able to view it using the System Browser. Note that if you have loaded in a whole class category, you will not be able to view it until you select update in the category pane of any open browsers, or you open a new browser. Figure 15.2 illustrates the file list tool being used to examine the contents of a file called Example.st. This file contains the source of a simple example class.

If a file is selected and displayed in the bottom window, then you can edit that file and save the changes you have made. You can also select part (or all) of the file and then use the "do it" or "print it" options to execute that selected code. This can be a very useful feature.

Note that you can also file in source code under programmatic control. To do this you need to send the message fileIn to a file. For example:

```
'example.st' asFilename fileIn.
```

If the file does not exist you will raise an exception "File not found". Otherwise the result of filing in the file will be printed in the System Transcript window.

15.4 Change list

15.4.1 The changes file

To understand the use of the changes list tool, you must first understand the significance of the changes file. This is a system provided file which has a .cha extension (and is named after the image, for example, if the image is named Visual.im then the changes file will be named Visual.cha). The changes file is always located in the same directory (folder) as the image file (and should never be manually moved).

This file lists all the changes which have been made to VisualWorks for the current image. That is, all the changes to existing classes and methods as well as all new classes and methods which have been defined. It also records all the actions that have created objects and sent messages in the image. Thus as you develop a system within an image, your changes file grows - each time you make a change it is recorded.

In fact, if you manually move your changes file and then attempt to view the code you have written you will find that VisualWorks says that it can't find the changes file and will have to disassemble your code. This is an indication that VisualWorks uses the changes file to store the actual source of the compiled byte encoded class and method definitions.

The main use of the changes file, however, is as a recovery aid. It allows a sequence of changes to be replayed. This may be done following a system crash, or following the accidental deletion of a class or method. The result is that, even if you did not save your work before a system crash, you can get back to where you were by replaying the changes file. This is done using the Change List tool.

15.4.2 Viewing and replaying the changes file

The Change List tool (illustrated in Figure 15.3) is used to view the contents of the changes file. It is made up of:

- a scrollable list selection (referred to as the changes view),
- a set of selection boxes which allow the user to restrict the display of past changes (for example in Figure 15.3 the list has been restricted to references to the same class, in this case the MyClass class.
- a code display area where the result of the change (if any) is displayed. In Figure 15.3 the result of editing the age method is presented.

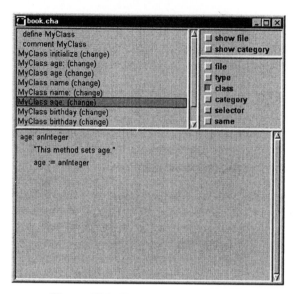

Figure 15.3: The Change List tool

The changes presented in the *changes view* often need to be filtered before being re-run. For example, if the list of changes includes the creation of windows or test objects, you probably don't need to redo those commands. If the system crashed in response to a message sent, you probably don't want to resend that message etc.

Once you have got a list of changes which reflect the set of operations you want to perform you can replay them using one of the replay options from the right mouse button (middle on a three button mouse) menu.

15.5 Working with projects

15.5.1 Projects - what are they?

A project is a way of organizing your development environment. It allows the developer to manage a number of different tasks at the same time within the *same image*. The way to think about this is that if what you see on the screen can be viewed as the VisualWorks desktop, then projects allow you to have multiple desktops for different parts of your work.

Why is this feature useful? Well consider that you are trying to draw a diagram on a flip chart. Then you might see a blank page with a number of pens clipped to the side of it. This would be fine for some diagrams, however, if you need to draw a number of associated diagrams, then you would either need to get a larger flip chart, or you would have to use more pages. Projects allow you to use multiple pages, each page having its own VisualLauncher. When you switch between projects, the layout of the screen will be restored to the state of the screen when you last left that project. If the project has just been created, then you will see only the visual Launcher.

15.5.2 Creating a new project

By default, when you start the VisualWorks image you are in the root project. To create a new project you select the **Open Project** option off the changes menu on the VisualLauncher. In response to this, the system displays the window illustrated in Figure 15.4. This allows you to provide some notes about the project in a scrollable text window (for example, what the project is about, things to do etc.). This is a good idea as it acts as a project documentation tool. It is also a good idea to change the window label to something which indicates the purpose of the project. This can be done using the right mouse button (on a three button mouse). This displays a menu with a **relabel as ..** option.

Figure 15.4: Creating a project

To enter the project select the **enter** button on the window. To exit a project select the **Exit project** option from the VisualLauncher from within the project. Exiting the project in this way will bring you back up a level and your desktop will be restored to the state it was in when you entered the project. You can delete a project by closing the project window. For example, if I wished to destroy the project in Figure 15.4, then I would close that window using the Windows-95 close icon.

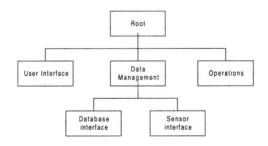

Figure 15.5: Project hierarchy

151

Projects can be nested hierarchically to any depth (although it is rarely useful to go beyond 2 or 3 levels). This means that the project structure illustrated in Figure 15.5 can easily be constructed. In this structure, at the top level the developer sees the *User Interface* project, the *Data Management* project and the *Operations* project. When the user enters the *Data Management* project, then they see the *Database Interface* project and the *Sensor Interface* project.

This means that, when they are working on the user interface project, they do not see the windows they have been using in any of the other projects. They can thus leave one of the other projects in a particular state and come back to it later.

15.5.3 Changes and projects

In addition to the changes file created for the whole image, a project has its own *changes set*. This changes set is a summary of the changes which have been made to that project. This means that, unlike the changes file, it does not include all changes to the system. Instead it lists those classes which have been modified within the current project.

The changes set of a project can be accessed using the **Inspect ChangeSet** option from the changes menu on the VisualLauncher. If you wish to save the changes made to a project, you can do it using the **file out as ..** option from the right mouse button menu (middle on a three button mouse) available from the left hand window of this inspector. This can be a useful way of exchanging changes with other developers.

15.5.4 Warnings about projects

There are two points you should note about projects. The first it that they are only a visual aid to project organization. That is, all the source code changes you make are global to the current image. Many developers when they first encounter projects assume that changes in one project will be limited to that project. They aren't and this can be rather counter intuitive. Care should therefore be taken when modifying classes in one project which may be used in another project. Secondly, as all changes are actually made to the whole image, it is a mistake to assume that when a project is deleted, its affects will also be deleted.

15.6 Summary

In this chapter you have encountered a number of tools which you are likely to make a great deal of use of. At this point you should try some of them out and get familiar with what they do. None of the tools is that complicated and once you understand what they do and why, they can prove to be extremely useful and make your life a lot easier.

Object Oriented Design

16. Object Oriented Analysis and Design

16.1 Introduction

This chapter provides an introduction to Object Oriented Analysis and Design. It will survey the most significant methods to emerge since the late 1980's. This means that we will concentrate primarily on OOA [Coad and Yourdon 1991], Booch [Booch 1991, 1994], OMT [Rumbaugh *et al* 1991], Objectory [Jacobson 1992] and Fusion [Coleman *et al* 1994]. We will also introduce the Unified Modeling Language (or UML) [Booch *et al* 1996; Booch and Rumbaugh 1995].

The aim in this chapter is not to be comprehensive either with regard to the range of methods available, nor with the fine details of each approach. Rather it is to provide an overview of the design process, strengths and weaknesses of some of the important and reasonably representative methods.

In the remainder of this chapter we briefly introduce the Unified Modeling Language, Object Oriented Design (OOD) and then summarize a number of OOD methods.

16.2 The Unified Modeling Language

The Unified Modeling Language (or UML as it is known) is an attempt by Grady Booch, Ivar Jacobson and James Rumbaugh to build on the experiences of the Booch, OMT and Objectory methods [Booch *et al* 1996; Booch and Rumbaugh 1995]. Their aim is to produce a single, common, and widely usable modeling language for these methods and, working with other methodologists, for other methods as well. This means that the UML focuses on a standard language and not a standard process. This reflects what actually happens in reality: a particular notation is adopted as the means of communication on a specific project and between projects. However, between projects (and sometimes within projects) different design methods are adopted as appropriate. For example, a design method intended for the domain of real-time avionics systems may or may not be suitable for designing a small payroll system. The result is that the UML is an attempt to develop a common metamodel (which unifies semantics) from which a common notation can be built. We will discuss the UML in greater detail in a later chapter.

16.3 Object oriented design methods

The object oriented design methods (OOD methods) we shall be considering are all architecture-driven, incremental and iterative. That is, they do not adopt the more traditional waterfall software development model adopting instead an approach which is more akin to the spiral model of Boehm [Boehm 1988]. This reflects developers' experiences when creating object oriented systems - the object oriented development process is more incremental than that for procedural systems with far less distinct barriers between analysis, design and implementation. Indeed some organizations take this process to the extreme and have adopted an *Evolutionary Development* approach. That is a system which is developed around the concept of evolutionary delivery. This means that system functions are delivered to users in very small steps with project plans being revised in light of experience and user feedback. This has proved to be very successful for those organizations who have fully embraced this philosophy and has led to much earlier business benefits and successful end-products from large development projects.

16.4 Object Oriented Analysis

We shall first consider the Object Oriented Analysis Approach (known as OOA) of Coad and Yourdon [Coad and Yourdon 1991]. This is because the identification of objects and classes is a crucial task in OO analysis and design, however, many techniques ignore this issue. For example, both the Booch method and OMT do not deal with this issue at all. They indicate that it is a highly creative process which can be based on the identification of nouns and verbs in an informal verbal description of the problem domain! A different approach is to use a method such as OOA as the first part of the design process and then to use some other OOD method for the later parts of the process.

OOA is aimed at helping designers identify the requirements of their software in detail - rather than how the software should be structured or implemented. It therefore aims to describe the existing system, how it operates and how the software system should interact with it. One of the claims of OOA is that it helps the designer to package the requirements of the system in an appropriate manner (for object oriented systems?) and helps to reduce the risk of the software failing to meet the customer's requirements. In effect, OOA helps to build the Object (systems) Model which we will look at in more detail when we look at OMT.

There are five activities within OOA. These act as the framework used to direct the analyst during the analysis process. They are:

1. Finding classes and objects. This activity aims to identify the objects (and the classes of objects) in the domain.
2. Identifying structures (amongst those classes and objects). Here structures relate to relationships such as *is a* as well as *part of*.
3. Identifying subjects. In essence subjects indicate related objects.
4. Defining attributes. These are the data elements of the objects.

5. Defining services. These are the active parts of objects and indicate what the object does.

These are not five steps (as steps implies a sequential ordering to the activities). Instead, as information becomes available, the analyst performs the appropriate activity. The intention is that the analyst can work in whatever way the domain expert finds easiest for them to express their knowledge. Thus the analyst may drop down deeper into one activity than the others as the domain expert provides greater information on that area. Equally, the analyst may jump around between activities identifying classes one minute and services the next.

16.5 The Booch method

The Booch method (also known as just Booch and Object Oriented Development or confusingly OOD) is one of the earliest recognizable object oriented design methods. It was first described in a paper published in 1986 [Booch 1986] but has become widely adopted since the publication of the book describing the method [Booch 1991] and the more recent second edition [Booch 1994].

The Booch method provides a step by step guide to the design of an object oriented system. Although Booch's books do discuss the analysis phase, they do so in too little detail, compared to the design phase.

16.5.1 The steps in the Booch method

The major steps in the Booch method are the identification of objects and their classes, identification of the semantics of classes and objects, identification of the relationships between classes and objects and the implementation of the classes and objects. Each of these steps is briefly outlined below:

Identification of classes and objects. This involves analyzing the problem domain and the system requirements to identify the set of classes required. This is not trivial and relies on a suitable requirements analysis.

Identification of the semantics of classes and objects. This step involves identifying the services offered by an object as well as those required of an object. A service is essentially a function performed by an object (it is therefore during this step that the overall system functionality is devolved amongst the objects). This is another non-trivial step and may result in modifications to the classes and objects identified in the last step.

Identification of the relationships between classes and objects. This step involves identifying links between objects as well as inheritance between classes. As this step may identify new services required of objects, there is usually an iteration between this step and the last step.

Implementation of classes and objects. This step attempts to consider how the classes and objects will be implemented, how attributes will be defined and services provided. This will involve consideration of algorithms etc. This process may lead to modifications in the deliverables of all of the above steps and may force the designer to return to some or all of the above steps.

During these steps class diagrams, object diagrams, module diagrams, process diagrams, state transition diagrams and timing diagrams are produced. The class diagrams illustrate the classes in the system and their relationships. The object diagrams illustrate the actual objects in the system and their relationships. Module diagrams, in turn, package the classes and objects into modules (these modules illustrate the influence Ada had on the development of the Booch method [Booch 1987].) Process diagrams perform a similar function for processes and processors. The state transition diagrams, together with the timing diagrams, describe the dynamic behavior of the system (while the class, object and other diagrams describe the static structure of the system).

It is notable that Booch recommends an incremental and iterative development of a system through the refinement of different yet consistent logical and physical views of that system.

16.5.2 Strengths and weaknesses

The biggest problem for a designer approaching the Booch method for the first time is that the plethora of different notations are supported by a very poorly defined and loose process (although the revision to the method described in [Booch 1994] addresses this to some extent). It lacks the step by step guidance required. In particular it possesses very few mechanisms for determining the system's requirements. Thus its main strengths are its (mainly graphical) notations which cover most aspects of the design of an object oriented system, whilst its greatest weakness is the lack of sufficient guidance in the generation of these diagrams.

16.6 The Object Modeling Technique

The Object Modeling Technique [Rumbaugh *et al* 1991] is an OOD method which aims to construct a series of models which refine the system design, such that the final model is suitable for implementation. The actual design process is divided into 3 phases:

- the *Analysis Phase* which attempts to model the problem domain;
- the *Design Phase* which structures the results of the analysis phase in an appropriate manner;
- the *Implementation Phase* which takes into account target language constructs.

Each of these will be briefly described below.

16.6.1 The Analysis phase

Three types of model are produced by the Analysis phase; these are the object model, the dynamic model and the functional model.

The *Object Model* describes the objects in the domain, their class and the relationships between the objects. For example, the object model might represent the fact that a department object possesses a single manager (object) but many employees (objects). The object model therefore represents the static structure of the domain. The actual notation used is based on an extension of the basic Entity-Relationship (E-R) notation.

The *Dynamic Model* expresses what happens in the domain, when it occurs and what the effect is. That is, the dynamic model expresses the behavior of the system (although it does not represent how the behavior is achieved). The formalism used to express the dynamic model is based on a variation of finite state machines called statecharts. These were developed by Harel [Harel *et al* 1987, Harel 1988] for representing dynamic behavior in real-time avionic control systems. Essentially statecharts indicate the states of the system, the transitions between states, their sequence and the events which cause the state change.

The *Functional Model* describes how system functions are performed. To do this it uses data flow diagrams (DFD). These illustrate the sources and sinks of data as well as the data being exchanged. They contain no sequencing information or control structures.

The relationship between these three models is important as each model adds to the designer's understanding of the domain. Essentially the relationships are:

- The object model defines the objects which hold the state variables referenced in the dynamic model and are the sources and sinks referenced in the functional model.
- The dynamic model indicates when the behavior in the functional model occurs and what triggered it.
- The functional model explains why an event transition leads from one state to another in the dynamic model.

The construction of these models is not sequential, with changes to any one of the models having a knock on effect in the other models. Typically, the designer will start with the object model, then consider the dynamic and finally the functional, but the process is iterative.

The actual analysis process is described in considerable detail and is supported by step by step guidance. This ensures that the developer knows what to do at any time to advance the three models.

16.6.2 The Design phase

The Design phase of OMT builds upon the models produced during the analysis phase by breaking them down into subsystems and by identifying appropriate algorithms for methods. These two steps are performed during the system design and object design steps.

- The system design breaks the system down into subsystems and determines the overall architecture to be used.
- The object design decides on the algorithms to be used for the methods. The methods themselves are identified by analyzing the three analysis models for each class etc.

Each of these steps possess some guidelines for their respective tasks, however, far less support is provided for the designer than in the analysis phase. For example, systematic guidance for the identification of subsystems is missing. Instead the issues involved are discussed such as resource management, batch versus interactive modes etc. This means that identifying where to start, how to proceed and what to do next can be difficult.

16.6.3 The Implementation phase

The implementation phase represents the process of codifying the system and object designs into the target language. This phase does provide some very useful guidance on how to implement features used in the model-based design process used, but is again lacking in the step by step guidance which would be so useful for those new to object orientation.

16.6.4 Strengths and weaknesses

OMTs' greatest strength is the level of step by step support which it provides during the analysis phase. However it is much weaker in its guidance during the design and implementation phases providing general guidance (and some heuristics).

16.7 The Objectory method

The Objectory method [Jacobson 1991] possesses three phases each of which produce a set of models. The three phases are: the *Requirements phase*, the *Analysis phase* and the *Construction phase*. The driving force behind the whole of the Objectory method is the concept of a *use case*. A use case is a particular interaction, between the system and a user of that system, for a particular purpose (or function). The users of the system may be human or machine and are termed *actors*. A complete set of use cases therefore describes a system's functionality based around what actors should be able to do (with the system).

16.7.1 The Requirements phase

The Requirements phase uses a natural language description of what the system should do to build three models: the *Use case models*, the *Domain Object model* and the *User Interface descriptions*.

The *use-case model* describes all the interactions between actors and the system. Each use case specifies the actions which are performed and their sequence. Any alternatives are also documented. This can be done in natural language or using state transitions diagrams.

The *domain model* describes the objects, classes and associations between objects in the domain. It uses a modified E-R model.

The *user interface descriptions* contain mock ups of the various interfaces between actors and the system. User interfaces are represented as pictures of windows while other interfaces are described by protocols.

16.7.2 The Analysis phase

The Analysis phase produces the analysis model and a set of subsystems. The analysis model is essentially a refinement of the domain object model produced in the last phase. It also contains behavioral information as well as control objects which are linked to use cases. As well as control objects, the analysis model also possesses entity objects (which are objects which exist beyond a single use case) and interface objects which handle system-actor interaction. The subsystem description aims to partition the system around objects which are involved in similar activities and which are closely coupled. This organization is used to structure the remainder of the design process.

16.7.3 The Construction phase

The Construction phase refines the models produced in the analysis phase. For example inter object communication is refined as well as consideration of facilities provided by the target language. Four models are produced by this phase:

- Block models which represent the functional modules of the system.
- Block interfaces which specify the public operations performed by blocks.
- Block specifications are optional descriptions of a block behavior in the form of finite state machines.

The final stage is then to implement the blocks in the target language.

16.7.4 Strengths and weaknesses

The most significant aspect of Objectory is its use of use-cases. These act as the cement which joins the various building blocks of the whole method. As such Objectory is unique in the methods considered here as it provides a unifying framework for the design process. However, it still lacks the step by step support which would simplify the whole design process.

16.8 The Fusion method

The majority of OOD methods currently available, including those described in this chapter, possess some form of systematic approach to the design process. However, in almost all cases this process is rather weak, providing insufficient direction or support to the developer. In addition methods such as OMT rely on a "bottom up" approach. This means that the developer must focus on the identification of appropriate classes and their interfaces without necessarily having the information to enable them to do this in an appropriate manner for the overall system. For example, little reference is made to the system's overall functionality when determining class functionality etc. Indeed, some methods provide little more than some vague guidelines and anecdotal heuristics.

In contrast, fusion explicitly attempts to provide a systematic approach to object-oriented software development. In many ways the fusion method is a mixture of a range of other approaches (indeed the authors of the method acknowledge that there is little that is new in the approach other than the fact that they have put it all together in a single method, for example see Figure 16.1).

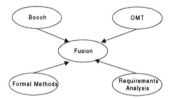

Figure 16.1: Some of the influences on Fusion

As with other OOD methods, fusion is based around the construction of appropriate models that capture different elements of the system as well as different knowledge. These models are built up during three distinct phases. The analysis phase, the design phase and the implementation phase:

- The analysis phase produces analysis models which provide a description of the high level constraints from which the design models are developed.
- The design phase produces a set of models that describe how the system behaves in terms of a collection of interacting objects.
- The implementation phase describes how to map the design models onto implementation language constructs.

Within each phase a set of detailed steps attempts to guide the developer through the fusion process. These steps include checks to ensure the consistency and completeness of the emerging design. In addition the output of one step acts as the input for the next.

Fusion's greatest weakness is its complexity - it really requires the use of a sophisticated CASE tool. Without such a tool it is almost impossible to produce a consistent and complete design.

16.9 Summary

In this chapter we have reviewed a number of OO analysis and design methods as well as the Unified Modeling Language. We have briefly considered what each offers as well as their strengths and weaknesses. It should be noted that a problem encountered with all these systems is that during the design process it is often difficult to identify commonalities between classes at the implementation level. This means that during any implementation phase, experienced OO technicians should be looking for situations in which they can move implementation level components up in any class hierarchy. This can greatly increase the amount of reuse within a software system. This may then lead to the introduction of new abstract classes whose role is to contain the common code. The problem with this is that the implemented class hierarchy no longer reflects the design class hierarchy. It is therefore necessary to have a free flow of information from the implementation phase to the design phase and vice versa in an object oriented project.

17. The Unified Modeling Language

17.1 Introduction

The Unified Modeling Language (or UML for short) is part of a development being carried out to merge the concepts in the Booch, Objectory and OMT methods [Booch and Rumbaugh 1995, Booch *et al* 1996]. This effort has been termed the unification or the Unified Method. The method is still under development (and has taken a much lower profile recently) however the notation underlying this method is nearing completion. This notation has now become the focus of Booch, Rumbaugh and Jacobsons' current work and is receiving a great deal of interest. For example, Microsoft Corporation, Hewlett Packard, Oracle, Texas Instruments have all endorsed the UML.

The UML is a third generation object-oriented modeling language [Rational 1996] which adapts and extends the published notations used in the works of Booch, Rumbaugh and Jacobson [Booch 1994, Rumbaugh et al 1991, Jacobson *et al* 1992] as well as being influenced by many others (such as Fusion [Coleman *et al* 1994], Harel's statecharts [Harel *et al* 1987; Harel 1988] and CORBA [Ben-Natan 1995], see Figure 17.1). It is intended that the UML will form a single, common, widely usable modeling language for a range of object oriented design methods (including Booch, Objectory and OMT). It is also intended that it should be applicable in a wide range of applications and domains. Therefore it should be equally applicable to client-server applications as it is to real-time control applications.

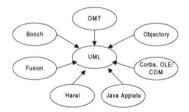

Figure 17.1: The influences on the UML notation

Part of the justifications for this is that different organizations, applications and domains require (and use) different design methods. In many cases organizations have developed their own methods or have modified other methods through experience. In some cases different parts of the same organizations may use different methods. The result is that the notation used acts as a language in which ideas represented in part (or all) of the design are expressed and communicated. For example, the production of shrink wrapped, off the shelf software, is different from the creation of one off bespoke software. However both activities may be carried out by a software company. Such an organization may well wish to exchange ideas, designs or parts of designs amongst its various departments or operational units. This kind of exchange relies on the availability of a common language - UML provides such a language.

At present the UML is in draft form [Booch *et al* 1996], however it is being presented to the OMG (Object Management Group) in the hope that it will be accepted as a standard (this is an on going process and is part of the OMG's call for information on object-oriented methods). For the latest information on the UML (as well as any other developments on the unification front) see the Rational Software Corporation's web site (http://www.rational.com).

This chapter provides a brief introduction to the UML but omits many of the details. For further information on the UML please see version 1.0 of the UML documentation set. There is also a series of books on the UML including a Reference Manual, a User Guide as well as a process book (which at the time of writing were still in the pipe line) that should be referenced for more information.

In the remainder of this chapter we consider how the UML can represent the class, objects, relationships and attributes in an object oriented system. The next chapter considers *sequence* and *collaboration* diagrams, *State diagrams* and *deployment* diagrams.

17.2 The UML Infrastructure

The UML is built upon a common metamodel which defines the semantics of the language. On top of this is a common notation which interprets these semantics in an easily (human) comprehensible manner. Each of these is discussed below.

17.2.1 The Metamodel

A metamodel describes the constituents of a model and its relationships. That is, it is a model (in its own right) which documents how another model can be defined. Such models are important because they provide a single, common and unambiguous statement of the syntax and semantics of a model. It thus allows CASE tool builders to do more than provide diagramming tools. In fact the metamodel serves several purposes including:

- Defining the syntax and describing the semantics of the UML's concepts.
- Providing a (reasonably) formal basis for the UML.
- Providing a description of the elements of the UML.
- Providing the basis for the interchange of models between vendors' tools.

In the normal course of events a user of the UML (or indeed of a tool which supports the UML) need never know anything about the metamodel. It should be, and is, hidden from sight. However, for the developers of the UML and for tool vendors in general it is a valuable, indeed essential, feature.

At present the UML metamodel is defined in terms of the UML and textual annotations (although this may appear infinitely recursive, it is possible). Work on the metamodel is still progressing with the authors of the UML attempting to make it more formal and simpler.

17.2.2 The UML models

The UML defines a number of models and the notations to be used with these models. They are:

Use case diagrams. These diagrams are based on the use case diagrams of Objectory and organize the use cases that encompass a system's behavior.

Class diagrams. These are derived form the Booch and OMT methods and express the static structure of the system. For example the *part of* and *is a* relationships between classes and objects. Note that the class diagrams also encompass the object diagrams. Therefore, in this book, we will refer to them as the *object model* following the name used in OMT.

State machine diagrams. These, like those in OMT, are based on statecharts. They capture the dynamic behavior of the system.

Sequence diagrams. Sequence diagrams (formerly known as message-trace diagrams in version 0.8 of the Unified method draft) deal with the time ordered sequence of transactions between objects.

Collaboration diagrams. Collaboration diagrams (previously known as Object-message diagrams) indicate the order of messages between specified objects. They are complementary to sequence diagrams as they both illustrate the same information. The difference is that the sequence diagrams hi-light the actual sequence, while the collaboration diagrams hi-light the structure required to support the message sequences.

Component diagrams. In version 0.8 of the Unified Method draft these diagrams were called module diagrams. These diagrams represent the development view of the system or how the system should be developed into software modules. They can also be used to represent concepts such as dynamic libraries.

Deployment diagrams. Deployment diagrams (previously known as platform diagrams). As this model attempts to capture the topology of the system once it is deployed, it reflects the physical topology upon which the software system is to execute.

17.3 Use case diagrams

Use case diagrams explain how a system (or subsystem) will be used. The elements which interact with the system can be humans, other computers or dumb devices which process or produce data. The diagrams thus present a collection of use cases which illustrate what the system is expected to do, in terms of its external services or interfaces. Such diagrams are very important for illustrating overall system functionality (to both technical and non-technical personnel). In addition they can act as the context within which the rest of the system is defined.

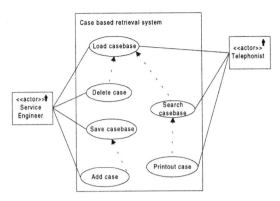

Figure 17.2: Case-based retrieval system Use Case example

The large rectangle in Figure 17.2, indicates the system's boundaries. The rectangles on either side of the system indicate external actors which interact with the system. In this case the Service Engineer and the Telephonist (this assumes a system being used as a telephone help desk adviser).

The actual notation used for actors is based on what are called stereotypes (stereotypes are discussed in more detail later in this chapter). Actors are in fact classes with stereotypes. The <<actor>> indicates the actor stereotype and the stick figure is the actor stereotype icon. Although we have used the class icon (a box) as well as the stereotype icon (the stick man) we could have used only one of them if we had so wished.

The ovals inside the system box in Figure 17.2 indicate the actual use cases themselves. For example, both the actors will wish to be able to "load a casebase". Each individual use case can have a name, have a description explaining what it does as well as a list of its responsibilities, attributes and operations. They may also describe their behavior in the form of a state chart. The most appropriate form of description for a use case will differ from one domain to another and thus the format should be chosen as appropriate. This illustrates the flexibility of the UML as it does not prescribe the actual format of a use case.

It is also possible to use sequence diagrams and collaboration diagrams with use case diagrams to illustrate the sequence of interactions between the system and the actors. Use cases should also be annotated with a statement of purpose to place the use case itself in some overall context.

Finally, the relationship between use case diagrams and class diagrams is that use cases are peers of classes. Depending on the size of the system, they can be grouped with the object model in a package or remain totally independent.

17.4 The object model

This is really the key element of a UML model. The constituent diagrams illustrate the static structure of a system via the important classes and objects in the system and how they relate to each other. The UML documentation currently talks about class diagrams (and within this about object diagrams) stating that "class diagrams show generic descriptions of possible systems and object diagrams show particular instantiations of systems and their behavior". They go on to state that class diagrams contain classes, while object diagrams contain objects, but that it is possible to mix the two. However, they discuss both under the title *class diagrams*. Therefore, to avoid confusion, we adopt the term Object Model to cover both sets of diagrams (following the approach adopted in both the Booch and OMT methods).

17.4.1 Classes and objects

A class is drawn as a solid-outline rectangle with three components. The class name (in bold type) is in the top part, a list of attributes (with optional types and initial values) in the middle part and a list of operations (with argument types and return values) in the bottom part. Figure 17.3 illustrates two classes, one for a class Car and one for a class File. The Car class possesses three attributes called name, age and fuel. Their types are string, integer and string respectively. The class also possesses four operations start(), lock() and brake(), plus accelerate which takes a single parameter "to" which is an integer and represents the new speed.

Figure 17.3: Class with attributes and operations

An attribute has a name and a type specified in the format *name: type = initialValue*. The name and type are strings that are ultimately language dependent. The initial value is a string representing an expression in the target language. Operations have a name and may take one or more parameters and return a value. The format of an operation is *name (parameter : type = defaultValue, ...): resultType*. The operation's constituent parts are strings that are language dependent.

The attribute and operation compartments can be *hidden* from view to reduce the detail shown in a diagram. Omitting a compartment says nothing about that part of the class definition. However, leaving a compartment blank implies that there are no definitions for that part of the class. Additional language dependent and user-defined information can also be included in each compartment in a textual format. The intention of such additions is to clarify any element of the design in a similar manner to a comment in source code.

The class *stereotype* can be shown as a normal-font text string in between << >> centered above the class name (see Figure 17.4). A stereotype tells the reader what "kind" of class it is. Examples of stereotypes are *exceptions, controllers, interfaces* etc. However, UML makes no assumptions about the range of stereotypes which exist and the designer is therefore free to develop their own. Other (language specific) class properties can also be indicated in the class name compartment. For example in Figure 17.4 the Window class is an abstract class, thus the label abstract is printed below (and to the left) of the class name.

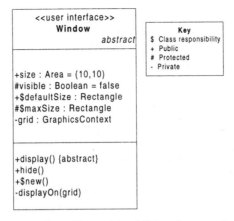

Figure 17.4: Class with additional annotations

Attributes and operations can also have their intended scope indicated in the class definition. This can be useful even for languages such as Smalltalk which do not support concepts such as Public, Private and Protected attributes and operations. The absence of any symbol at all in front of an attribute or operation indicates that the element is a public instance attribute or operation for that class. The significance of this depends on the language. The range of symbols currently supported is indicated in Figure 17.4 and combinations of symbols can be used to indicate (for example) that a method is a class side public method (such as +$new() - a class side operation intended for instance creation).

```
repMobile1 : Car
   name = XK8
   age = 1
   fuel = petrol
```

Figure 17.5: An object (structured cloud)

An object is drawn as a hexagon with straight sides and a slight peak at the top and bottom (as illustrated in Figure 17.5). For those familiar with the Booch clouds this can be thought of as a structured cloud otherwise just accept that this is the object symbol[1]. The object symbol can be divided into two sections. The top section indicates the name of the object and its class in the format *objectName : className.*

---

[1] Note that as of September 1996, the 0.91 addendum to the UML states that objects are now drawn as rectangles with the object name and its class name (separated by a colon) underlined. This is a major notational change which the authors of the UML wish to make so that they do not have to invent different symbols every time they have a type (or class) - instance relationship. However this means that the distinction between objects and classes in diagrams is minimal and can easily lead to confusion. In an attempt to make objects clearly distinguishable in this, and subsequent chapters, we shall continue to use the structured cloud symbol for objects.

For example, in Figure 17.5 the object is repMobile1 and the class is Car (see Figure 17.3 for the definition of the class Car). The object name is optional although the class name is compulsory. The lower compartment contains a list of attributes and their values in the format *name type = value* (although the type is usually omitted). For example in Figure 17.5 the three attributes defined in Figure 17.3 for a Car have the values XK8, 1 and petrol. The bottom compartment can be suppressed for clarity. It is also possible to indicate how many objects of a particular class are anticipated. This is done by indicating the maximum value, range etc. in the top compartment. The lack of any number indicates that a single object is intended.

17.4.2 Associations

Relationships between classes and objects are represented by associations drawn as a solid line between classes or objects (for example see Figure 17.6). An association between classes may have a name with an optional small "direction arrow head" (which is drawn as an arrow head on the association) showing which way it is to be read. For example in Figure 17.6 the relationship is called *hasEngine* and is read from the class *Car* to the class *Engine*. In addition each end of an association is a *role*. Roles may have a name illustrating how its class is viewed by the other class. In Figure 17.6 the engine sees the car as being a name and the car sees the engine as being of a specified type (e.g. Petrol, Diesel, Electric etc.).

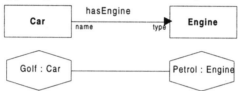

Figure 17.6: Association between classes / link between objects

Each role (i.e. each end of the association) indicates the multiplicity of its class (i.e. how many instances of the class can be associated with one instance of the other class). This is indicated by a text expression on the role. The expression can either be a * (indicating zero or more), a number (e.g. 1), a range (e.g. 0..3) or nothing (indicating exactly 1). These expressions are illustrated in Figure 17.7. It is also possible to specify that the multiple objects should be ordered using the text {Ordered}. It is also possible to annotate the association with additional text (such as {Sorted}) but this is primarily for the readers benefit and has no semantic meaning in UML.

In some situations it is sensible for associations to have attributes of their own. In these situations associations need to be treated as a class. Such a situation is illustrated in Figure 17.8. These associations have a dashed line from the association line to the association class. This class is just like any other class and can have a name, attributes and operations.

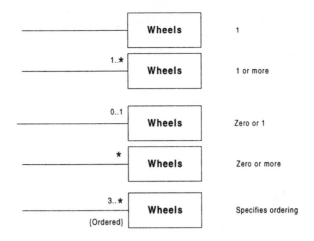

Figure 17.7: Types of association annotations

In Figure 17.8 the associations possess an access permissions attribute which indicates the type of access allowed for each user for each file.

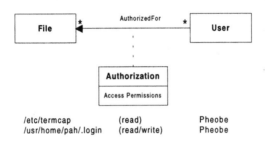

Figure 17.8: Associations with attributes

Aggregation represents *part-whole* relationships. That is, it indicates that one or more objects are dependent on another object for their existence. For example, in Figure 17.9 the Micro Computer is formed from the Monitor, the System box, the Mouse and the Keyboard. All of these objects together are needed for the fully functioning Computer. Aggregation is actually represented as an empty diamond on the role attached to the whole object.

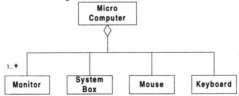

Figure 17.9: Aggregation tree notation

A qualified association is an association which requires both the object and the qualifier to uniquely identify the object involved in the association. It is represented as a box between the association and the class. For example, in Figure 17.10, it is necessary to use the catalog and the part number to identify a unique part. Note that the qualifier is part of the association, not the class.

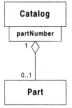

Figure 17.10: Qualified associations

Ternary (or indeed higher order) associations are drawn as diamonds with one line path to each of the participating classes (for example see Figure 17.11). This is actually the traditional entity-relationship model symbol for an association (the diamond is omitted from the binary form to save space). Ternary associations are very rare and higher order associations are almost none existent. However, the facility to model them is available.

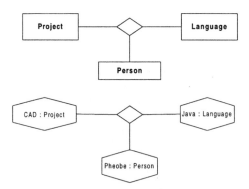

Figure 17.11: Ternary Associations

It is sometimes useful to differentiate between by-value references and by-reference ones. This is done using the aggregation symbol. If the aggregation symbol is hollow, it indicates a by-reference implementation (i.e. a pointer or other reference); if the aggregation symbol is filled, it indicates a by-value implementation, i.e. a class that is embedded within another class (see Figure 17.12).

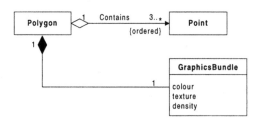

Figure 17.12: Implementation adornment

172

Inheritance of one class by a subclass is indicated by a solid line drawn from the subclass to the superclass with a large (unfilled) triangular arrowhead on the superclass end (see Figure 17.13). For compactness a tree structure can be used to show multiple subclasses inheriting from a single superclass.

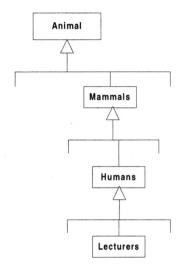

Figure 17.13: Inheritance : specialization - generalization

Multiple inheritance can also be modeled as languages such as CLOS (the Common Lisp Object System) and C++ support it. This is done by drawing multiple inheritance lines from a single subclass to two or more super classes as in Figure 17.14. In this figure the class *Motor powered water vehicle* inherits from both *Motor powered* and *Water vehicle*.

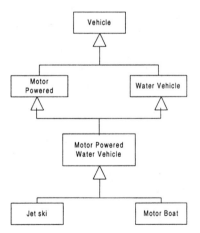

Figure 17.14: Multiple Inheritance

Derived values can be represented by a slash ('/') in front of the name of the derived attribute. Such an attribute requires an additional textual constraint defining how it is generated (as in Figure 17.15). This is indicated by a textual annotation below the class between curly ({ }) brackets.

{age = currentDate - birthdate}

Figure 17.15: Derived values

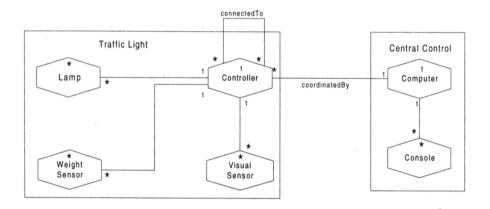

Figure 17.16: Example composites

A class may define a pattern of objects and links that are part of it and that exist whenever the class is instantiated. Such a class is called a composite. It is a class that contains an object diagram. It may be thought of as an extended form of aggregation where the relationships among the parts are valid only within the composite. A composite is a kid of *pattern* or *macro* that represents a conceptual clustering for a given purpose. Composition is shown by drawing a class box around its embedded components (as illustrated in Figure 17.16) which are prototypical objects and links. That is, a composite defines a context in which references to classes and associations, defined elsewhere, can be used.

17.5 Packages

Packages are used to group associated modeling elements such as classes in the object model (or subsystems in component diagrams). They are drawn as tabbed folders as illustrated in Figure 17.17.

Figure 17.17 actually illustrates four packages called *clients, Business model, Persistent store, Bank* and *Network*. In this particular diagram the contents of *Clients, Persistent Store, Bank* and *Network* have been suppressed (by convention these packages have their names placed in their body) with only *Business Model* being shown in detail (with its name in the top tab). This package possesses two classes

174

Customer and Account as well as a nested package *Bank*. The dashed lines between the packages illustrate dependencies between packages. For example, the package *Clients* directly depends on the packages *Business Model* and *Network* (this actually means that at least one element in the package *Clients* relies on at least one element in the other two packages).

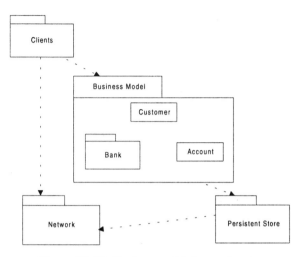

Figure 17.17: Packages with Dependencies

Classes may belong to exactly one package but references may be made to classes in other packages. Such references have the package name followed by the class name (separated by two colons), for example: *Business Model :: Customer*.

Packages allow models to be structured hierarchically, they therefore act to organize the model and control its overall complexity. Indeed packages may be used to enable top down design of a system (rather than the bottom up design typical of many OOD methods) by allowing designers to specify high level system functionality in terms of packages which are "filled out" when and as appropriate.

18. UML: Dynamic Modeling And Deployment

18.1 Introduction

The basic class and association notations of the object model in the Unified Modeling Language (or UML for short) were presented in the last chapter. This chapter presents the *sequence*, *collaboration* diagrams and *state diagrams* as part of the dynamic modeling facilities in the UML. We then consider *deployment* diagrams.

18.2 Dynamic modeling facilities

18.2.1 Sequence diagrams

A *scenario* shows a particular series of interactions among objects in a single execution of a system. That is, it is a history of how the system behaved from one start state to a single termination state. This differs from an *envisionment* which is a description of all system behaviors from all start states to all end states. Envisionments thus contain all possible histories (although they may also contain paths which the system is never intended to take).

Scenarios can be presented in two different ways: *Sequence Diagrams* and *Collaboration Diagrams*. Both these diagrams present the same information although they stress different aspects of this information. For example, sequence diagrams stress the timing aspects of the interactions amongst the objects, where as the collaboration diagrams stress the structure between these objects (which helps in understanding the requirements of the underlying software structure).

Figure 18.1 illustrates the basic structure of a sequence diagram. The objects involved in the exchange of messages are represented as vertical lines (which are labeled with the object's name). For example, Caller, Phone Line and Callee are all objects involved in the scenario of dialing 999 (the Emergency services' number in the UK). Time proceeds vertically down the diagram, as indicated by the dashed line arrow. The horizontal arrows indicate an event or message sent from one object to another. The arrow indicates the direction in which the event or message is sent. That is, the receiver is indicated by the head of the arrow. Normally return values are not shown on these diagrams. However, if they are significant, they can be illustrated by return events annotated with the type of value returned etc.

Time proceeds vertically and can be made more explicit by additional timing marks. These timing marks indicate how long the gap between messages should be or how long a message or event should take to get from the sender to the receiver.

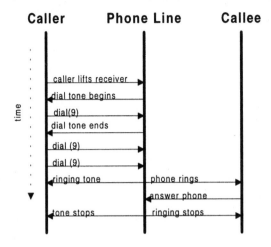

Figure 18.1: A sequence diagram

A variation of the basic sequence diagram (called a focus-of-control diagram) illustrates which object has the thread of control at any one time. This is shown by a fatter line during the period when the object has control (as illustrated in Figure 18.2). Note how the bar representing the object C only starts when it is created and terminates when it is destroyed.

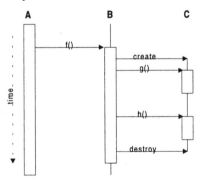

Figure 18.2: Sequence diagram with focus-of-control regions

18.2.2 Collaboration diagrams

As stated above, collaboration diagrams illustrate the sequence of messages between objects based around the object structure (rather than the temporal aspects of sequence diagrams). A collaboration diagram is formed from the objects involved in the collaboration, the links (permanent or temporary) between the objects and the messages (numbered in sequence) that are exchanged between the objects. An example collaboration diagram is presented in Figure 18.3.

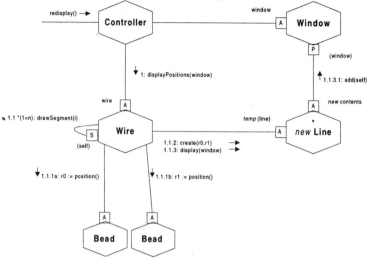

Figure 18.3: An example collaboration diagram

Objects which are created during the collaboration are indicated by the label *new* before the object name. For example the Line object in Figure 18.3. Links between objects are annotated to indicate their type (e.g. permanent or temporary existing for this particular collaboration). These adornments are placed in boxes on the ends of the links and can have the following values:

A - association (or permanent) link
F - Object field (the target object is part of the source object)
G - global variable
L - local variable
P - Procedure parameter
S - self reference

Role names can also be added to distinguish links (e.g. self, wire and window in Figure 18.3). Role names in brackets indicate a temporary link, i.e. one that is not an association.

The messages which are sent along links are indicated by labels next to the links. One or more messages can be sent along a link in either or both directions. The format of the messages is defined by the following (some of which are optional):

1. *A comma-separated list of sequence numbers in brackets:* [seqno, seqno]. The sequence numbers indicate messages from other threads of control that must occur before the current message can occur. This element is only needed with concurrency.
2. *A sequence number containing a list of sequence elements separated by full stops (periods).* These represent the nested procedural calling sequence of the

178

message in the overall transaction. Each element section has the following parts:

- A letter (or name) indicating a concurrent thread. All letters at the same level of nesting represent threads that execute concurrently e.g. 1.2a and 1.2b are concurrent. Omitting the letter entirely is equivalent to another dummy letter and usually indicates the main sequence.
- An integer number. The numbers show the sequential position of the current message within its thread. For example, message 2.1.4 is part of the procedure invoked by message 2.1 and follows message 2.1.3 within that procedure.
- An iteration indicator. This is a star (*), optionally followed by an iteration expression in parentheses. Iteration indicates that several messages of the same form are sent either sequentially (to a single target) or concurrently (to the elements of a set). If there is an iteration expression, it shows the values that the iterator or iterators assume, such as "(i=1..n)"; otherwise the details of the iteration must be specified in text or simply deferred to the code.
- A conditional indicator. This is a question mark (?), optionally followed by a Boolean expression in parentheses. The iteration and conditional indicators are mutually exclusive.

3. *A return value name followed by an assignment sign* (":="). If present this indicates that the procedure returns a value designated by the given name. The use of the same name elsewhere in the diagram designates the exact same value. If no return value is specified, then the procedure operates by side effects.
4. *The name of the message.* This is an event name or operation name. It is unnecessary to specify the class of an operation since this is implicit in the target object.
5. *The argument list of the message.* The arguments are expressions defined in terms of input values of the nesting procedure, local return values of other procedures and attribute values of the object sending the message.

Argument values and return values for messages may optionally be shown graphically using small data flow tokens near a message. Each token is a small circle, with an arrow showing the direction of the data flow, labeled with the name of the argument or result.

18.2.3 State machine diagrams

Scenarios are used to help understand how the objects within the system collaborate, where as state diagrams illustrates how these objects behave internally. That is, state diagrams relate events to state transitions and states. The transitions change the state of the system and are triggered by events. The notation used to document state diagrams is based on that developed by Harel [Harel *et al* 1987, Harel 1988] and termed *Statecharts*.

Statecharts are a variant of the finite-state machine formalism which reduces the apparent complexity of a graphical representation of a finite-state machine. This is accomplished through the addition of a simple graphical representation of certain common patterns of finite state machine usage. As a result, what might be a complex subgraph in a "basic" finite state machine is replaced by a single graphical construct.

Each state diagram (statecharts are referred to as state diagrams in UML) has a start point at which the state is entered and may have an exit or termination point at which the state is terminated. The state may also contain concurrency as well as synchronization of concurrent activities.

Figure 18.4 illustrates a typical state diagram. This state diagram describes a (very) simplified remote control locking system. The chart indicates that the system first checks the identification code of the hand held transmitter. If it is the same as that held in the memory it will allow the car to be locked or unlocked. For the *car locking* situation, the windows are also closed and the car is alarmed.

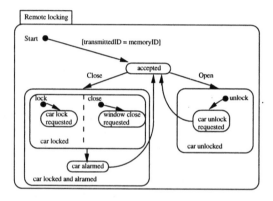

Figure 18.4: An example State diagram

A state diagram consists of a start point, events, a set of transitions, a set of variables, a set of states and a set of exist points. These are described briefly below:

18.2.3.1 A start point

A start point is the point at which the state diagram is initialized. In the figure, there are actually four start points indicated ('Start', 'lock', 'close' and 'unlock'). The 'Start' start point is the initial entry point for the whole diagram, while the other three indicated start points are for sub State diagrams.

Any preconditions required by the State diagram can be specified on the transition from the start point (for example, in the figure the transmittedID must be the same as the memoryID memorized by the system). It is the initial transition from which all other transitions emanate. This transition is automatically taken when the State diagram is executed. Note that the initial 'Start' point is not equivalent to a state.

18.2.3.2 Events

Events are one way asynchronous transmissions of information from one object to another. They can possess parameters with names and types. The general format of an event is: *eventName (parameter:type, ...)*. Of course many events do not have any associated parameters.

18.2.3.3 A set of transitions

These are the statements which move the system from one state to another. In the state diagrams each transition is formed of four (optional) parts:

1. an event (e.g. lock).
2. a condition (e.g. transmittedID = memoryID]
3. the initiated event (e.g. ^EngineManagementUnit.locked)
4. an operation (e.g. /setDoorToLock)

The event is what triggers the transition, however the transition will only occur if the condition is met. If the event occurs and the conditions are met, then the associated operation is performed. An operation is a segment of code (equivalent to a statement or program or method within a programming language) which causes the system state to be altered. Some transitions can also trigger an event which should be sent to a specified object. For example, the above example sends an event *locked* to the *EngineManagementUnit*. The process of sending a global event is a special case of sending an event to a specified object.

The syntax of an event is therefore:

event(arguments) [condition] ^target.sendEvent(arguments) /operation(arguments)

18.2.3.4 A set of state variables

These are variables referred to in a State diagram (for example memoryID is a state variable). They have the format *name: type = value.*

18.2.3.5 A set of states

A state represents a period of time during which an object is waiting for an event to occur. It is an abstraction of the attribute values and links of an object. A state is drawn as a rounded box containing the (optional) name of the state. A state may often be composed of other states (the combination of which represents the higher level state). A state has duration, that is it occupies an interval of time.

A state box can contain two additional sections, one section containing a list of state variables and the other section containing a list of triggered operations (as illustrated by Figure 18.5).

Figure 18.5: State box with state variables and triggered operations

Operations can be of the following types:

- *entry* (executed when the state is entered). These are the same as specifying an operation on a transition. They are useful if all transitions into a state perform the same operation (rather than need to specify the same operation on each transition). Such operations are considered to be instantaneous.
- *exit* (executed when the state is exited). These are less common than entry actions and indicate an operation performed before any transition from the state occurs.
- *do* (executed while the state is active). These are operations which start on entry to the state and terminate when the state is exited.
- *event*. A specified event can also trigger off an operation while within a particular state. For example, the event *help* could trigger the help operation which in the state *active*.

Each operation is separated from its type by a forward slash ("/"). The ordering of operations is:

operation on incoming transitions -> entry operations -> do operations -> exit operations -> operations on outgoing transitions.

State diagrams allow a state to be a single state variable, or a set of substates. This allows for complex hierarchical models to be developed gradually as a series of nested behavior patterns. This means that a state can actually be a State diagram in its own right. For example, *car alarmed* is a single state, however the *car locked* state, is actually another State diagram. Notice that the transition from *car alarmed* to *accepted* jumps from an inner state to an outer state.

The dotted line down the middle of *car locked* state indicates that the two halves of that state run concurrently. That is, the car is locked as the windows are closed.

A special type of state, called a history state, is used to represent a state which must be remembered and used the next time the (outer) state is entered. The symbol for a history state is an H in a circle.

18.2.3.6 A set of exit points

Exit points are used to specify the result of the State diagram. They also terminate the execution of the State diagram.

18.3 Deployment diagrams

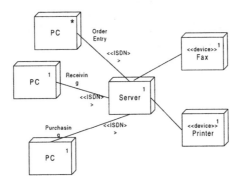

Figure 18.6: Nodes in a Deployment Diagram

The elements in Figure 18.6 are called nodes and represent processors (such as PC's and servers) and devices (such as Printers and Faxes). A node is thus a resource in the real world upon which we can distribute and execute elements of the (logical) design model. A node is drawn as a three-dimensional rectangular solid with no shadows. The <<device>> stereotype designation of the Fax and Printer indicates that these nodes are not processors. That is, they do not have any processing ability (at least not from the point of view of the model being constructed). It is also possible to show how many nodes are likely to be involved in the system. Thus the Order Entry PC is of order * (*0 or more*), while there will be exactly one server, printer, fax etc. Finally, we have also indicated the roles of the associations between nodes and their stereotype. For example the *Receiving* association on one PC which will employ a type of ISDN connection (which has yet to be specified).

18.4 Summary

This chapter (and the last) have presented an overview of the Unified Modeling Language (or UML). The UML is an attempt to develop a third generation object oriented modeling language for use with a variety of object oriented design methods. It can be used for documenting the design of client-server, real-time, distributed as well as batch style applications. It captures the best elements of the notations used by a number of existing design methods including Booch, OMT and Objectory while attempting to remain extensible, simple, clear and (relatively) concise. Many CASE tool vendors are already committed to supporting the UML and it is being presented to the OMG by a consortium of organizations as the basis of a standard notation for object-oriented systems development.

19. The Object Modeling Technique

19.1 Introduction

This chapter provides an overview of the Object Modeling Technique (OMT). It should not be treated as a definitive, nor complete, description of the method. For that the reader should see [Rumbaugh *et al*, 1990] and [Derr 1995]. Instead, this chapter provides an introduction to the basic phases and a summary of the steps which form each phase. As such it should provide an insight into an object oriented design (OOD) method.

The chapter first introduces the OMT methodology. The analysis phase is then described in some detail. The use of use case analysis is included. This is not actually part of OMT (in fact it is part of the Objectory method of [Jacobson *et al* 1992]) but is a useful adjunct to the method. The dynamic and functional models of the analysis phase are described in the next chapter. The design phase (which is then introduced) and the implementation phase are described in detail in the next chapter.

19.2 The OMT methodology

The OMT methodology consists of several phases. These phases progress a design from (relatively) early requirements analysis through detailed design to the implementation. The phases are thus: the analysis phase, the design phase and the implementation phase.

The *analysis phase* is concerned with understanding and modeling the application and the domain within which it operates. The OMT book suggests that the initial input to the analysis phase is a problem statement which describes the problem to be solved and provides a conceptual overview of the proposed system. This problem statement may be a textual description (as suggested by the authors) or it might be a more formal description as provided by a technique such as OOA or one of the structured analysis methods in the software engineering field.

The *design phase* is made up of two sub-phases, the system design phase and the object design phase. The system design sub-phase is concerned with the overall architecture of the system. This architecture is based on the information provided during the analysis phase (in particular the object model).

The object design sub-phase attempts to produce a practical design by refining, optimizing and reviewing the models produced during the analysis phase. This therefore involves moving the focus away from conceptual objects and towards computer implementation objects. It also involves identifying appropriate algorithms, ensuring efficient communication between objects and accounting for the flow of control and concurrency issues.

The final phase, the *implementation phase*, considers how the design should be implemented. It considers, amongst other issues, mapping a design onto an object oriented language, a data base system as well as non object oriented languages.

19.3 Analysis phase

The analysis phase is concerned with producing a precise, concise, understandable, and correct model of the real-world. This is done by constructing a series of models. In particular OMT defines an *object model*, a *dynamic model* and a *functional model*. OMT does not attempt to construct use case diagrams to help understand how the system is used and what the main functions of that system are. However, it is probably a very good idea to start the analysis phase by carrying out a use case analysis. We will therefore consider use case analysis before continuing with the OMT method.

OMT is a prescriptive method, it provides guidance on how the various models it generates should be constructed. In the remainder of this section we will consider the guidelines given.

19.3.1 Use case analysis

The intention of the use case analysis is to identify how the system is to be used and what the system is expected to do in response to this use. This involves identifying the external users of the system (human or machine) and the required system functionality. The users of the system and the roles they play are referred to as *actors* while the functions requested and their sequence are called *use cases*. The combination of the actors and the use cases are referred to as the *use case* model. Each of these will be considered in more detail below.

19.3.1.1 Actors

An actor can be anything which interacts with the system. This means they can be human users, other computer systems, dumb terminals, sensors, devices to be controlled etc. However, they not only represent the user, but also the role that the user plays at that point in time. For example, in a small company the accountant might act as the data entry clerk at one time, the internal auditor at another and as the payroll administrator at yet another time. Each of these roles would be represented by a different actor, even though they would all be performed by the same person. To stress the difference between actors and users [Jacobson *et al* 1992] says that they think of an actor as "a class, that is, a description of a behavior" while a user is described as playing "several roles" which are "many actors".

Identification of the actors in the system is not trivial and as [Jacobson *et al* 1992] point out "all actors are seldom found at once". Jacobson goes on to state that a "good starting point is often to check why the system is to be designed?". Having done this it should be possible to identify the main users of the system and what they will need to do with that system. From these users and their needs, actors can be identified. Identification of such actors is usually relatively straight forward, but it is often much more difficult to identify non-human actors. In general, as the rest of the use case model develops, these actors "come out in the wash".

The notation used (in this book at least) for actors is based on that presented by the UML in the last chapter.

For a simple bank account system the actors may be the *customer*, the *bank clerk* and the *bank manager*.

19.3.1.2 Use cases

When an actor interacts with the system it is for a specified purpose. The achievement of this purpose involves following one or more steps. If there are multiple steps there may be a specific sequence to these steps in order to achieve the desired purpose. For example, if you are attempting to obtain money from a "hole in the wall machine" (cash dispenser/ATM) then you must first input your card, type in your PIN, select the type of transaction your require, specify the amount of case required, take the card and then take the money. If you attempt to change this sequence you will fail to obtain your money (e.g. you type in your PIN before inputting your card!). The combination of the purpose, and the specified sequence of steps, forms a use case.

A use case can be represented in a number of ways, the two most common are as natural language and as state transition diagrams. Whichever approach is adopted, the same information should be captured. The most appropriate form may depend on the availability of support tools for the state machine notation.

The collection of all uses cases for a system defines the functionality of that system. The identification of uses cases is based on the identification of actors. Each actor will need to do one or more things to the system, each of these uses will be a use case. That is, each actor must have at least one use case (and may be involved in many use cases). Whether each use case is unique (or merely a duplication of another use case) may only be determined once all the uses cases are identified and defined. To help in identifying the uses cases, the following questions can be asked [Jacobson *et al* 1992]:

- What are the main tasks of each actor?
- Will the actor have to read/write/change any of the system information?
- Will the actor have to inform the system about outside changes?
- Does the actor wish to be informed about unexpected changes?

Early in the analysis process it is often enough just to identify the possible uses cases and not to worry about their details. Once a reasonable set of uses are identified, it may be possible to analyze the systems requirements in greater detail in order to flesh out the uses cases. Use case identification tends to be iterative and should not be treated as a single step process for all but the simplest of systems.

Having identified the uses cases, we can identify the steps performed within each use case. In many cases this can help to identify omissions and over generalizations in any problem statement or domain understanding, that we may have.

For the simple bank account system mentioned above, a typical use case might be:

```
Check account is started by Customer when they want to find out their
current balance. This is accomplished by:
    1. typing in their account number followed by the PIN
    2. requesting the current balance of their account (this may be on
       screen or on a print out)
    3. receiving the balance
    4. acknowledging receipt of the balance
    5. logging off the system
```

Notice that the first element of the use case is a statement of its purpose. This is then followed by the sequence of steps performed by the use case. The steps described above are referred to as the *basic course* of the use cases. That is, the normal way in which the use case will *execute*. In general uses cases only possess a single basic course. However, they may possess one or more *alternative courses*. These alternatives deal with exceptional situations or errors. For example, what if the customer does not have a current account, what happens if they do not accept receipt of their balance?

19.3.1.3 Use case models

The identification of the actors and the uses cases together help to specify the limits of the system. That is, anything that is an actor is outside the system, whereas anything that is a use case is within the system boundaries. This means that it is possible to draw a line around the uses cases indicating the boundary of the system. This is very useful in helping to identify the bounds of the software project as a whole in terms which both a developer and a user can understand. This can help to clarify misunderstandings between users and developers over what is the system's responsibility and what is not. A partial use case model for the simple account system is presented in Figure 19.1.

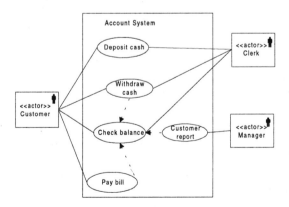

Figure 19.1: Use case model

187

Having defined the actors in the system and the uses they make of the system, the next step is often to specify the interfaces between the actors and the system. For human users of the system, these interfaces may well be graphical user interfaces (GUI's) and may be drawn using a drawing tool or mocked up using some form of interface simulation software. These interfaces can be very useful in confirming the users' needs, their anticipated use, as well as helping to keep them involved in the development. As the use cases specify the sequences of operations to be performed, the GUI's can be made to mimic the desired system behavior. This is a good way of confirming that the use case is correct. For non-human interfaces any proposed communications protocols can be defined and checked (for example, that the interacting system is capable of sending and receiving the appropriate information).

19.3.1.5 Relating the use case model to OMT

The use case model dictates the formation of the models in OMT's analysis phase as indicated in Figure 19.2. For example,

- it helps identify the primary objects in the object model,
- it helps specify the top level behavior of the system in the dynamic model,
- it helps determine the inputs and outputs provided by, and expected by, the actors for the functional model.

In addition use cases may also have an influence on how the system will be organized into subsystems as they indicate associated behaviors. In the implementation phase the use cases may be used to identify suitable scenarios and expected results for integration or system testing.

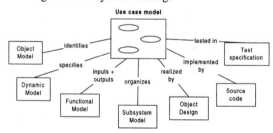

Figure 19.2: How the use case model can be used in OMT

19.3.2 Object modeling

The first step in requirements analysis phase, of the OMT method, is the construction of the object model. The object model is essentially comprised of the class and object diagrams described in the last chapter. As with BOOCH and the UML it is the object model which is the core of the OMT representation. As we have already encountered object models before we will not attempt to explain what they are other than to state that the object model "shows the static data structure of the real-world system and organizes it into workable pieces".

The information for the object model comes from:

- the problem statement (written in natural language according to OMT),
- requirements analysis process such as OOA,
- the domain experts,
- general knowledge of the real world,
- the use case model (if you have constructed one).

An interesting point to note is that OMT claims that object models promote communication between computer professionals and application-domain experts (what do *you* think?).

OMT suggests the following steps as being an appropriate way in which to construct an object model.

1. Identify objects and classes.
2. Prepare a data dictionary.
3. Identify associations (including aggregations) between objects.
4. Identify attributes of objects and links.
5. Organize and simplify object classes using inheritance.
6. Verify that access paths exist for likely queries.
7. Iterate and refine the model.
8. Group classes into modules.

However, you should not take the sequence of these steps too strictly: remember analysis and design are rarely completed in a truly linear manner. It is likely that some steps will be performed to greater depths as the whole process proceeds. In addition, some steps may (will) lead to revisions in other steps and once an initial design is produced it will doubtless require revisions. Therefore you should consider that they are a sequence of processes which should be performed. The order of which may be influenced by the domain, the expertise available, the application etc. However it is probably a good idea always to start with the process of identifying objects and classes.

We will consider each of the above steps in more detail below.

19.3.2.1 Identify objects and classes

The first step in constructing the object model is to identify the objects in the domain and their classes. Such objects may include:

- physical entities such as petrol pumps, engines and locks
- logical entities such as employee records, purchases and speed
- soft entities such as token, expression or data stream
- conceptual entities such as needs, requirements or constraints.

As long as they make sense for the application and the domain then they are a candidate object or class. The only things you should avoid are objects which might relate to the proposed computer implementation.

OMT suggests that you start identifying these candidate objects by looking in the textual problem description. It indicates that classes are often found by identifying nouns in the description and making them into classes. However, if you have a more formal problem specification it might be easier to identify a set of potential classes. If you have used the use case analysis method you may also be able to identify the top most objects directly from the use case diagrams.

Do not worry about getting it right at this point or about identifying classes which should not be there. Inappropriate classes will be filtered out later on - for the moment, attempt to find anything which could be a class.

Once you have a comprehensive list of candidate classes you can discard any unnecessary and incorrect ones. This is done by using the following criteria:

Are any of the classes redundant? That is, two or more classes express the same information. For example, customer and user might just be different names for the same thing.

Are any of the classes irrelevant? That is, are they outside the scope of the system to be built even though they are part of the domain. For example, although porters work in a hospital they are probably not relevant to a hospital bed allocation system.

Are any of the classes vague? That is, do they represent ill defined concepts? For example, history provision is vague - what is it a history of?

Are any of the classes really attributes of other classes? For example, name, address, salary, job title tend to be attributes of an object employee rather than objects in their own right.

This can be a tricky one as it is often possible to represent something as both a class or an attribute. One way of handling this is to leave the decision until later. If the class possesses only one type of information and has no operations then it should probably have been an attribute.

Are any of the classes really operations? If a class appears to describe an operation that is applied to objects and not manipulated in its own right then it is not a class. For example, a telephone call is a sequence of actions performed by a caller. In the implementation you may wish to make this an object, however at this point in the design we are trying to produce a model of the application domain (i.e. not an implementation model).

Does the name of the class represent its intrinsic nature and not its role in the application? For example, the class Person might represent an object in a restaurant booking system, but the class Customer is a better representation of its role in the system.

Is a class really an implementation construct? For example, things such as process, algorithm, interrupt, exception are implementation concepts and tend not to be related to the application domain.

19.3.2.2 Prepare a data dictionary

A data dictionary provides a definition for each of the terms / words being used in the evolving analysis models. Each entry precisely describes each object class, its scope, any assumptions or restrictions on its use and its attributes and operations (once they are known).

19.3.2.3 Identify associations between objects

The next step is to identify any (and all) associations between two or more classes. This is done by looking for references between two classes. OMT suggests that a good place to look for these relationships is to examine the problem description for verbs or verb phrases between known objects. In particular it identifies the following types of relationships:

- physical location (next to, part of, contained in)
- directed actions (drives)
- communication (talks to)
- ownership (has, part of)
- satisfaction of some condition (works for, married to, manages)

Again OMT exhorts you to identify all possible relationships and not to worry at this point about getting it right.

If you have used a method such as OOA you might already have some knowledge about the relationships between the classes in the domain, if not then considering which classes are likely to need to work with which other classes (i.e. the accounts clerk may need to work with the salaries clerk) is also a good place to start. This process will be simplified if you have performed a use case analysis.

Once you have a set of candidate associations, OMT provides a detailed set of criteria to help in refining them. The criteria are:

Is the association one which is between eliminated classes? If one of the classes involved in the association has been eliminated then the association should be eliminated.

Are any of the associations irrelevant or implementation associations? Eliminate any associations that are outside the scope of the application domain (including implementation related associations).

Are any associations transient? An association should be a structural property of the applications domain. For example, *interacts with user* is a temporary association in a hotel booking system.

Are any of the associations ternary? Although the OMT notation and indeed the UML notation allow ternary associations, they are not encouraged. Instead you are encouraged to decompose these associations into binary ones (they are easier to implement, maintain and understand!).

Are any of the associations derivable? OMT suggests that you should remove any associations which can be derived from other associations. However you should be wary of removing such associations as they may be critical to understanding the domain relationships. That is, if an association can be replaced by two existing associations, only do so if the semantic meaning of the two associations can be combined to provide the same semantic meaning as the one to be removed. A good example of this is that a *GrandparentsOf* relationship can be replaced by two *ParentOf* relationships.

Having removed inappropriate associations, you can now consider the semantics of the associations you have left. To do this you should use these criteria:

Are any of the associations misnamed? That is, do they actually reflect what they represent? Are they named after their use or the relationship they indicate?

Add role names where appropriate. As described in the last chapter, role names describe the role that a class plays in the associations from the point of view of the other class.

Are there any qualified associations? That is, are there any associations which require a qualifier to identify a unique object.

Specify multiplicity on the associations. That is, indicate how may objects are involved in the association. By default all associations are 1 to 1 associations. Where no multiplicity is specified check that these really are 1 to 1 links.

Are there any missing associations? Check that all reasonable associations are present. This may need to be done in consultation with the domain expert.

19.3.2.4 Identify attributes of objects

OMT suggests that attributes correspond to nouns followed by possessive phrases, such as "the color of the car" or "the position of the cursor" in the problem statement. Although the authors do admit that attributes are less likely to be fully described in the problem statement and that you must draw on your knowledge of the application domain and the real world to find them. If you have already used a method such as OOA you may already have identified the key attributes. Luckily attributes can (usually) be easily added to objects as and when they are identified - it is rare that the addition of a new attribute will cause the structure of the system to become unstable.

An important point to note is that you should only be trying to identify application domain attributes. This means that attributes which will be needed during the implementation of the system should not be included at this stage. However, link attributes (which might appear to be implementation attributes) should be identified at this stage as they have an impact on the systems structure. A link attribute is a property of the link between two objects, rather than being a property of an individual object. For example, the many to many association between Stockholder and Company has a link attribute of "number of shares".

Having identified the set of candidate attributes for each object you should then challenge these attributes using the following criteria:

Should the attribute be an object? For example, earlier we said that a telephone call should not be an object, however if you are constructing a telephone call billing system, then it is probable that it *should* be an object. You therefore need to think carefully about the domain when deciding whether something is an attribute or an object. Don't worry about getting it wrong (there may be no correct answer) you can come back to it later and refine the model.

Is an attribute really a name? Names are often actually selectors used to identify a unique object from a set of objects. In such situations a name should really be a qualifier.

Is an attribute an identifier? Here identifier relates to a computer based identifier and is an implementation issue and not part of the application domain. For example, objectId is an identifier which is probably not in the applications domain.

Is an attribute really a link attribute? Link attributes are often mistaken for object attributes. Link attributes are most easily identified when it becomes difficult to identify which of two (or more) classes the attribute should belong to. In such situations it is an attribute of the link between the two classes.

Does the attribute represent an internal state of the object which is not visible outside the object? If it does remove the attribute. It is an internal implementation issue and not part of the domain problem.

Does the attribute represent fine detail? If the attribute represents some aspect of the object which is relatively low level then omit it. It will not help with the overall understanding of the domain and will increase the complexity of the object model.

Are any of the attributes unlike the others in their class? Such discordant attributes may either be misplaced (this may indicate that one class should actually be two or more) or that the attribute is not part of the current application (although it may be part of the overall domain).

19.3.2.5 Organize and simplify object classes using inheritance

The next step is to refine your classes using inheritance. This can be done in both directions, that is, either by grouping common aspects of existing classes into a superclass from which the existing classes inherit or by specializing an existing class into a number of more specialized subclasses which serve specific purposes. Again if you have used an analysis method such as OOA, some of this may already have been performed. Note that you are not doing this with a view to implementing the class hierarchy being generated, rather you are trying to understand the commonalities in the domain.

Identifying potential superclasses is easier than identifying specialized subclasses. To find potential superclasses, you should examine the existing classes looking for common attributes, operations or associations. Any common patterns you find may indicate the potential for a superclass. If such a situation is found, then the superclass should be defined with an appropriate name (i.e. one that encompasses the generic roles of the class which will inherit from it). Then move the attributes, associations and operations which are common up into this superclass. Do not try to force unrelated classes to become subclasses of a superclass just because they happen to have similar attributes (or associations or operations). Attempt to make sure that when you do group a set of classes together under a superclass, that grouping makes sense in the application domain. For example, grouping the classes car, truck and bus under a superclass vehicle makes sense. However, adding the class student just because they all share the attribute *registrationNumber* does not make sense!

Identifying specializations can be more difficult, however if you find a class playing a number of specific roles then specialization may be appropriate. Note that you should be wary of specialization as you do not want to over specialize the classes in your object model. This is because you may actually be talking about separate instances of the same class, rather than subclasses.

19.3.2.6 Testing access paths

This step involves checking that paths in the model make sense, are sufficient and are necessary. OMT suggest that you trace access paths through the object model to see if they yield sensible results. The sorts of issues you might wish to consider are:

- Where a unique value is expected, is there a path yielding a unique result?
- For multiplicity "many" is there a way to pick out a unique value when needed?
- Are there any useful (domain specific/application specific) questions which can't be answered?

19.3.2.7 Iterate and refine the model

There are two things you will come to learn about object design, firstly it is still more of an art than a science and secondly (unless the problem is trivial) the first version of the object model will probably not be correct (or complete). Object oriented design is far more iterative in nature than some other design methods and it therefore acknowledges that you will need to iterate over the whole of the above process a number of times to get a reasonable object model. Indeed some changes will be initiated by the development of the dynamic model and the functional model which you have not even considered yet (for example we have not attempted to identify any operations for the object model at this point).

At this point some of the questions you can ask yourself about the object model are:

- Are there any missing objects (does one class play two roles)?
- Are there any unnecessary classes (such a class might possess no attributes)?
- Are there any missing associations (such as a missing access path for some operation)?
- Are there any unnecessary associations (such as those that are not used by anything)?
- Are all attributes in the correct class?
- Are all associations in the correct place?

Cross referencing the object model with the use case model may help answer some of the above questions.

19.3.2.8 Group classes into modules/packages

The final step associated directly with the object model is to group classes into packages. Packages should be identified by looking for classes which work together. Do not base the packages purely on system functionality as this is likely to change and will result in inappropriate packaging. OMT suggests that you ensure that a package can be fitted onto a single drawing surface (be that paper or the screen) as this aids comprehensibility. In addition, packages can be hierarchical and can be a very useful way of partitioning the design of the system amongst a number of designers.

20. More Object Modeling Technique

20.1 Introduction

This chapter continues from where the last chapter finished. It describes the dynamic and functional models of the analysis phase as well as the design and implementation phases.

20.2 Dynamic models

The dynamic models of the analysis phase capture the behavior of the system being analyzed. That is they describe what states the system can be in and what causes a state change to occur.

20.2.1 Dynamic modeling

The dynamic model describes the behavior of the application and the objects which comprise that application. The sequence, collaboration and state diagrams described in the last chapter are the main components of the dynamic model. OMT uses the term event trace to mean a sequence diagram and event flow to mean a collaboration diagram (in UML terms).

The aim of the dynamic model analysis is to identify the important events which occur and their effects on the state of the objects. Thus the first step in this phase is the identification of events and the objects associated with those events. Next the sequence in which those events occur must be identified which allows a state diagram to be drawn.

OMT recommends the following steps are performed in the construction of a dynamic model:

1. Prepare scenarios of typical interaction sequences.
2. Identify events between objects.
3. Prepare an event trace (sequence diagram and collaboration diagram) for each scenario.
4. Build a state diagram.
5. Match events between objects to verify consistency.

20.2.1.1 Prepare scenarios

Scenarios illustrate the major interactions between the system and external actors on that system (whether human or otherwise). These scenarios are essentially the use cases in the use case model, if this has been performed. If not it is necessary to consider the different ways in which the system will be used and to determine the likely interactions. The scenarios can be written down as sequences of steps which describe one path through the systems. You should first prepare scenarios for the normal system interaction and then for exceptional system interaction.

20.2.1.2 Identify events between objects

The scenarios essentially document external events between the system and the actor(s). These events should trigger internal events between the objects in the system. You should trace these events through the system, noting the objects involved and the types of events occurring. Having obtained sets of events you should group together events which have the same effect (even if they have different parameters). For example, an event to close a file has the same effect whichever file is being closed!

20.2.1.3 Prepare sequence and collaboration diagrams

Once you have identified events within the system document them first as sequence diagrams and then as collaboration diagrams. This approach is easier, as sequence diagrams tend to deal with the sequential ordering of the events from one object to another whereas a collaboration diagram may involve a number of objects.

20.2.1.4 Build a state diagram

A state diagram should be constructed for each object class with nontrivial dynamic behavior. Every sequence diagram (and thus collaboration diagram) corresponds to a path through state diagram. Each branch in control flow is represented by a state with more than one exit transition. The procedure for producing state diagrams as described by the OMT method, is summarized below by the following algorithm:

1. Pick a class.
2. Pick one sequence diagram involving that class.
3. Follow the events for the class, the gaps in between the events are states. Give each state a name (if it is meaningful to do so).
4. Draw out a set of states and events linking states based on the sequence diagrams.
5. Now find loops within the diagram. That is, repeated sequences of states.
6. Chose another sequence diagram for the class and produce the states and events for that diagram. Next merge these states and events into the first diagram. That is, find the states and events which are the same and find where they diverge. Now add the new events and states.

7. Repeat step 6 for all sequence diagrams involving this class.
8. Repeat from step 1 for all classes.

After considering all normal events, add boundary cases and special cases. Also consider events which occur at awkward times including error events.

You should now consider any conditions on the transitions between states and any events which are triggered off by these transitions. Note that we still have not really considered the operations which the system will perform.

20.2.1.5 Match events between objects

Having produced the state diagrams you should now check for completeness and consistency across the whole system. Every event should have a sender and a receiver, all states should have a predecessor and a successor (even if they are start points or exit points) and every use case should have at least one state diagram which explains its effect on the system's behavior. You should also make sure that events which are the same but on different state charts have the same name.

20.2.2 Functional modeling

The functional model in OMT describes how values are computed. UML does not possess any notation for representing functional models and this reflects the lack of emphasis placed on functional model style analysis by object oriented design methods. OMT uses Data Flow Diagrams (or DFD's) to represent functional models. In essence the functional model explains how the operations (yet to be added) in the object model and the actions / activities of the dynamic model are achieved. It can also be used to represent constraints amongst the values of the model.

A DFD possesses inputs and outputs, data stores, processes and data flows (arrows). Figure 20.1 illustrates an example DFD diagram.

Data stores are passive objects which store data for later use. That is they merely respond to requests to store and access data. The *Icon Definitions* label between two parallel bars indicates a data store.

Processes are drawn as an ellipse. They possess a fixed number of inputs and outputs which are labeled with their type or name. Processes may be nested and of arbitrary complexity and eventually reference atomic operations.

Data flows are indicated by an arrow labeled with the type of data. They may split or converge. The tail of the arrow indicates the source and the head of the arrow the sink for the data.

Actors (drawn as rectangles) act as the eventual sources and sinks of the whole data flow. For example, the screen buffer is the eventual sink for the data flow in Figure 20.1.

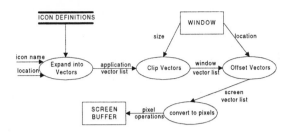

Figure 20.1: A Data Flow Diagram

OMT advises that it is best to construct the functional model after the object and dynamic models. The steps in this phase defined by OMT are:

1. Identify input and output values.
2. Build data flow diagrams showing functional dependencies.
3. Describe functions.
4. Identify constraints.
5. Specify optimization criteria.

20.2.2.1 Identify input and output values

Input and output values are parameters of events between the system and the outside world. You should reference the use case diagram to see whether the actors should provide information to the system or expect a response from the system.

20.2.2.2 Build data flow diagrams

The data flow diagrams are constructed by producing a diagram which groups inputs, processes those values and generates outputs. Each nontrivial process should then be broken down (at a lower level) into smaller steps. This process is repeated until only atomic operations remain. The result is a hierarchical model containing data flow diagrams which implement (higher level) processes.

Objects can also store data for use at a future date. These objects can be identified in a DFD because they receive values that do not result in immediate outputs but instead are used at some future time.

20.2.2.3 Describe functions

Once the DFD for a particular function has been defined you should write a description of that function. This description can be in the form of natural language, pseudo code, mathematical equations, decision tables or any other suitable form. The intention is that the function description places the DFD (which indicates how data is processed) into context.

20.2.2.4 *Identify constraints*

Constraints are functional dependencies between objects. They may be preconditions or postconditions on a function or a relationship which must hold (for example birthDate < currentDate). They may exist between two instances or between different instances at different times. Either way, they need to be documented.

20.2.2.5 *Specify optimization criteria*

Specify any data values which should be maximized (for example, process as many orders in an hour as possible), minimized (for example, ensure that system response is < 2 milliseconds) or otherwise optimized.

20.2.3 Adding operations

It is only at this point that the operations in the analysis models are considered. Note how this differs from the procedural approach in which the operations to be performed would be considered right *up front*. The operations are summarized by the object model (but relate to functions, actions and events in the functional and dynamic models). The criteria used for identifying operations are:

- operations implied by events,
- operations implied by state actions and activities,
- operations from functions,
- application / domain operations,
- simplifying operations.

20.2.3.1 *Operations implied by events*

All the events in the object model correspond to operations (although a single operation may handle multiple events and vice versa). OMT suggests that during analysis "events are best represented as labels on state transitions and should not be explicitly listed in the object model". However, if you find it clearer to list the operations corresponding to the events in the object model; then do so.

20.2.3.2 *Operations implied by state actions and activities*

The actions and activities in the state diagrams correspond to operations. These can be listed in the corresponding classes in the object model.

20.2.3.3 *Operations from functions*

Each function corresponds to one or more operations. The functions should be organized into operations on objects. This is not as straight forward as it might at first seem since we have not yet associated the functions with objects.

20.2.3.4 Domain operations

There may be additional domain operations which are not immediately obvious from the problem description. These should be identified from additional domain knowledge and noted. For example, although a cash point system (ATM system) does not allow you to open and close accounts, such operations are appropriate within the domain and may be important for understanding the domain or for aspects of the application which have yet to come to light.

20.2.3.5 Simplifying operations

Examine the object model for operations which are essentially the same. Replace these operations with a generic one. Note that earlier steps may well have generated the same operation but with different names. Therefore check each object's operations to see if they are intended to do the same thing even if they have very different names. Adjust the other models as appropriate.

20.3 Design phase

The aim of the analysis phase is to identify *what* needs to be done and not *how* it is done. The design phase takes the models produced by the analysis and considers how the requirements can be achieved. It is broken down into two sub-phases. The first, called the system design, breaks the overall system down into components called subsystems, while the second, called the object design, moves the models produced towards the implementation.

20.3.1 System design phase

The subsystem architecture provides the context within which the more detailed design decisions, made during the object design, are performed. The subsystem decomposition defines an architecture which can be used as the basis by which the detailed design can be partitioned among a number of designers, thus allowing different designers to work independently on different subsystems. The steps used to generate this architecture are:

1. Organizing the system into subsystems.
2. Identifying concurrency inherent in the problem.
3. Allocating subsystems to processors and tasks.
4. Choosing an approach for management of data stores.
5. Handling access to global resources.
6. Choosing the implementation of control in software.
7. Handling boundary conditions.
8. Setting trade offs between competing priorities.

Of course not all these steps will be important for all applications. For example, a batch oriented, purely serial process, probably cannot have much concurrency imposed on it.

20.3.1.1 Breaking the system into subsystems/packages

Most systems will be comprised of a number of subsystems, for example, a payroll system might possess a file subsystem, a calculation subsystem and a printing subsystem. A subsystem is not an object nor a function, but a package of classes, associations, operations, events and constraints that are interrelated and that have a reasonably well-defined and (hopefully) small interface with other subsystems. The package notation in the UML can be used to represent subsystems.

A subsystem (or package) is usually characterized by the common (or associated) set of services that it provides. For example, the file package would provide a set of services to do with creating, deleting, opening, reading and writing files. The use case model may be useful in identifying such common services.

Each package therefore provides a well defined interface to the remainder of the system which allows other packages to use its facilities. Such a specified interface also allows the internals of the package to be defined independently of the rest of the system (i.e. it encapsulates the package). In addition, there should be little or no interactions between objects within the package and objects in another package (except via the specified interfaces).

Packages can be hierarchical and may be involved in *client-server* or *peer to peer* relationships with other packages. Client-server relationships are easiest to implement and maintain as one package responds to requests from another package and returns results. In peer to peer relationships both packages must be capable of responding to requests from the other. This can result in unforeseen circularities.

20.3.1.2 Identifying concurrency

Concurrency can be very important for improving the efficiency of a system. However, to take full advantage of concurrency the system must be designed around the concurrency inherent in the application. This can be done by examining the dynamic model for objects which receive events at the same time or perform any state transitions (and associated actions) without interacting. Such transitions are therefore concurrent and can be placed in separate execution threads without effecting the operation of the system.

20.3.1.3 Allocating subsystems to processors and tasks

Each concurrent package should be allocated to an independent process or processor. The system designer must therefore:

- estimate performance needs and the resources needed to satisfy them,
- choose hardware or software implementations for packages,

- allocate packages to processors to satisfy performance needs and minimize inter processor communication,
- determine the connectivity of the physical units that implements the packages.

A deployment diagram can be used to illustrate the results of this step.

20.3.1.4 Management of data stores

The designer must identify appropriate data stores for both internal and external data. This involves identifying the complexity of the data, the size of the data, the type of access to the data (single or multiple users), access times and portability. Having identified these issues decisions can be made about whether data can be held in internal memory, on secondary storage devices, whether it should be held in flat files, relational or object database system.

20.3.1.5 Handling access to global resources

The system designer must identify what global resources are required and how access to them can be controlled. Global resources include processors, disk drives, disk space, workstations as well as files, classes and databases.

20.3.1.6 Choosing the implementation of control in software

The choice of the internal control mechanism used by the system will be mediated by the facilities provided by the implementation language. For example, Ada supports concurrent tasks whereas VisualBasic does not. Smalltalk and Java support light weight processes and therefore can be said to mimic concurrent systems. The choices available are:

- *procedure oriented systems.* Such a system represents a procedure calling mechanism in which the flow of control is passed from one procedure / method to another when the first calls the second.
- *event driven systems.* This is the approach taken by the dynamic model of the analysis phase. Essentially operations are triggered off by events which are received by objects. Many window based interfaces operate in this manner.
- *concurrent systems.* In which the system exists in several processes which execute at the same time. Some synchronization between the processes may take place at certain times, but for the majority of the time they are completely separate.

20.3.1.7 Handling boundary conditions

There are three primary boundary situations which the designer should consider. These are: initialization, termination and failure. Initialization involves setting the system into an appropriate, clean, steady state. Termination involves ensuring the that the system shuts down in an appropriate manner. Failure involves dealing with unplanned termination of the system cleanly.

20.3.1.8 Setting trade offs between competing resources

In any design there are various trade offs to be made. For example, the trade off between speed of access and data storage is a common one in database systems. The larger the number of indexes used, the faster data retrieval can be made (however the indexes must now be stored along with the data). Such design trade offs must be made with regard to the system as a whole (including non-software issues) as sub-optimal decision will be made if they are left for designers concentrating on a single package.

20.3.2 Object design phase

The object design essentially takes the models produced by the analysis phase and *fleshes* them out ready for the implementation. Thus the objects identified during the analysis act as the skeletons for the design. However, the designer must now consider how the analysis objects (partitioned into packages) should be implemented. They must express the operations identified earlier in terms of algorithms which can be implemented and associations as appropriate references from one object to another (taking into account the type of facilities provided by the target language). New classes may need to be introduced to deal with aspects which are important for the design (and ultimately the implementation) but are not significant for the analysis.

The following steps are performed by the designer during the object design:

1. Combine the three models to obtain operations on the classes.
2. Design algorithms to implement operations.
3. Optimize access paths to data.
4. Implement control for external interactions.
5. Adjust class structure to increase inheritance.
6. Design associations.
7. Determine object representation.
8. Package classes and associations into modules.

As stated before, these steps are iterative.

20.3.2.1 Combining the three models

If the implied operations from the dynamic and functional models have not been added to the object model, then they should be added now.

20.3.2.2 Designing algorithms

Each of the DFDs in the functional model needs to be expressed as an algorithm to indicate how they perform the function. The DFD says what it does, but the algorithm says how it does it. The algorithm designer must:

- Choose algorithms that minimize the cost of implementing operations.
- Select data structures appropriate to the algorithms.
- Define new internal classes and operations as necessary.
- Assign responsibility for operations to appropriate classes.

Note that any algorithms defined in pseudo code during the analysis phase were intended to explain the required functionality. It is therefore necessary at this stage to consider what algorithms are required in the implementation. For example, although a bubble sort algorithm may have been used in the analysis phase, an insertion sort may well be a more efficient algorithm to chose for the design.

20.3.2.3 Design optimization

The analysis model was only intended to describe the application and its requirements and did not attempt to take into account efficient information access or processing. These issues need to be considered by the designer at this point. In particular they should consider:

- adding redundant associations to minimize access cost and maximize convenience,
- rearranging the computation for greater efficiency,
- saving derived attributes to avoid recomputation of complicated expressions.

20.3.2.4 Implementation of control

During the system design, an approach for handling the internal control of the system must have been identified. That approach is fleshed out here. This includes determining how the selected approach can be implemented and identifying any constraints this choice imposes on the design.

20.3.2.5 Adjust class structure

As the design progresses the class hierarchy is likely to change, evolve and become refined. It is quite common to produce a design and then to rearrange it in light of commonalities which were hidden at an earlier stage. The designer should:

- rearrange and adjust classes and operations to increase inheritance,
- abstract common behavior out of groups of classes,
- use delegation to share behavior when inheritance is semantically invalid.

20.3.2.6 *Design associations*

Associations are an important aspect of the analysis object model. However, they are conceptual relationships and not implementation oriented relationships. The designer needs to consider how the associations can be implemented in a given language. The choices made for representing associations may be made globally for the whole system, locally to a package or on an association by association basis. The criteria used for determining how associations should be represented in the design are based on how are they traversed. If they are traversed only in one direction then a pointer representation may be sufficient. However, if they are bi-directional then an intermediate object may best represent the association.

20.3.2.7 *Determine object representation*

In most situations it is relatively straight forward to identify how to represent an object. However in some cases consideration needs to be given to decide whether to use a system primitive or an object. For example, in Java there are basic types int and char and there are also classes `Integer` and `Character`.

20.3.2.8 *Package classes*

The system will have been decomposed into *logical* packages in the system design. However, different languages provide different facilities for *physically* packaging a system. VisualWorks provides class categories which can be used in a similar manner to packages but they do not provide any information hiding etc.

20.4 Implementation phase

OMT states that implementation is "an extension of the design process" and that "writing code should be straightforward, almost mechanical, because all the difficult decisions should already have been made". (However implementation still tends to possess unexpected design problems which must be solved. These decisions should be subject to, and determined by, the processes described above). Because of this, OMT places a limited amount of emphasis on the implementation phase, concentrating instead on stylistic points. You should treat the implementation of an object oriented system in just the same way as you would treat the implementation of any software system. This means that it should be subject to, and controlled by, the same processes as any other implementation. In addition it should be subjected to similar testing (as discussed earlier in this book). This is where the use cases may come back into use in helping identifying suitable test scenarios.

20.5 Summary

As can be seen from this chapter, OMT concentrates the majority of its guidance on the analysis phase, the design and implementation phases are far less well supported. It is however one of the most widely used object oriented design methods and is likely to have a very large influence on any method developed by Booch, Rumbaugh and Jacobson to support the UML.

21. Frameworks and Patterns for Object Oriented Design

21.1 Introduction

Designing complex software systems is hard. It is a great deal easier to reuse an existing software system, merely modifying it where necessary, than to build it from scratch. These two facts have led to a great deal of interest in what has become termed software frameworks in the object oriented community. A software framework is "the reusable design of a system or a part of a system expressed as a set of abstract classes [and concrete classes] and the way instances of (subclasses of) those classes collaborate" [Beck and Johnson 1994]. However such frameworks are notoriously difficult to document. For example the Model View Controller (MVC) framework in Smalltalk is very powerful, but it has proved difficult to explain in a clear and simple manner how the MVC should be used [Krasner and Pope 1988].

In the object oriented community a number of researchers have explored the work of an architect who designed a language for encoding knowledge of the design and construction of buildings [Alexander et al 1977, Alexander 1979]. The knowledge is described in terms of patterns which capture both a recurring architectural arrangement and a rule for how and when to apply this knowledge. That is, they incorporate knowledge about the design as well as the basic design relations.

The result is that there is now a growing community exploring how software frameworks can be documented using (software) design patterns (for example, [Johnson 1992] and [Birrer and Eggenschmiler 1993]). Johnson's paper describes the form that these design patterns take and the problems encountered in applying them.

The remainder of the chapter is structured in the following manner: Section two considers what a framework is and the role of patterns in documenting frameworks. Section three introduces the HotDraw framework and Section four presents a very simple pattern documenting how you can use HotDraw to construct a simple editor.

21.2 Patterns and frameworks

21.2.1 What is a framework?

A framework is a reusable design of a program or a part of a program expressed as a set of classes. That is, a framework is a set of prefabricated software building blocks that programmers can use, extend, or customize for specific computing solutions. With frameworks, software developers don't have to start from scratch each time they write an application. Frameworks are built from a collection of objects, so both the design and code of a framework may be reused. However frameworks are not necessarily easy to design or implement. Questions such as "how much will it cost" to produce a framework and "how much will we benefit" from the network are difficult to answer [Moser and Nierstrasz 1996]. In addition reusing frameworks instead of libraries can cause subtle architectural changes in an application calling for innovative management [Sparks, Benner and Faris, 1996].

Frameworks can provide solutions to different types of problem domain. These include application frameworks, domain frameworks and support frameworks:

- **Application frameworks** encapsulate expertise applicable to a wide variety of programs. These frameworks encompass a horizontal slice of functionality that can be applied across client domains. An application framework might provide the basic facilities of a payroll system, or a geographic information system. These facilities could then be used to construct a concrete payroll (or GIS) system with the features required by a specific organization.
- **Domain frameworks** encapsulate expertise in a particular problem domain. These frameworks encompass a vertical slice of functionality for a particular client domain. Examples of domain frameworks include: a control systems framework for developing control applications for manufacturing systems or drawing frameworks such as HotDraw, Unidraw for C++/X windows and DRAW_Master for C++/OS 2 and Windows environments.
- **Support frameworks** provide system-level services, such as file access, distributed computing support, or device drivers. Application developers typically use support frameworks directly or use modifications produced by system providers. However, even support frameworks can be customized - for example when developing a new file system or device driver.

Since frameworks are reusable designs, not just code, they are more abstract than most software which makes documenting them more difficult. Documentation for a framework has three purposes and patterns can help to fulfill each of them. Documentation must provide:

1. the purpose of the framework,
2. how to use the framework,
3. the detailed design of the framework.

21.2.2 Designing object-oriented frameworks

The process of designing and implementing frameworks is not trivial and is, in many ways, harder than designing and implementing a one off application. This is because the framework needs to be complete, robust, generic, easy to use, extensible and flexible if it is to be effective:

- *Complete.* A framework must provide all the infrastructure required to construct applications. This includes documentation, concrete examples as well as the underlying skeleton of the framework. If any of these are missing (in particular the underlying skeleton) then this will act as an impediment to the adoption of the framework.

- *Robust.* A framework that is not robust will soon be ignored as users will not want to have to debug the framework as well as their own code.
- *Generic.* A framework that is not generic (relative to its application area) will be difficult to apply except in very specific ways. This can reduce the incentive for organizations to adopt a framework.
- *Easy to use.* A framework which is difficult to use will not be adopted as few developers have the time to gain the necessary understanding to take advantage of such a framework.
- *Extensible.* Users of the framework should find it easy to add and modify default functionality. That is, the framework should provide hooks so that users can apply the framework in different ways.
- *Flexible.* One of the claimed benefits of frameworks is that they can be applied and used in ways which were not envisaged by their creators. They therefore need to be flexible.

The first step in developing a framework is to analyze the application problem domain such that you know the requirements of any frameworks, the types of frameworks that would be useful and how they might be used. For example, look for the types of subsystems which are built repeatedly. A pseudo natural language parser might be a common subsystem within a range of diagnostic tools.

The next step involves identifying what is common about these systems and what is different. This allows the identification of the primary abstractions for the framework. These are the components which are constant across applications (even though they may have different names in these different applications). Note that it is often easiest to work bottom up in identifying these abstractions (in some cases the designs of the system might be the best starting points and in others the source code).

The third step involves taking these abstractions and constructing a skeleton for the framework. This skeleton should provide the basic infrastructure (comprised of the abstract concepts) for the framework. This is a bit like attempting to produce a set of abstract classes and their interactions for some application, without filling out all (or most) of the concrete classes.

As the framework takes shape you should be continually attempting to refine it by adding more default behavior, more hooks into it as well as additional ways for users to interact with it. You will also need to produce concrete instantiations of the framework to test its functionality and to customizability. These example instantiations should be included with the framework as part of the delivered product (whether it is delivered internally or externally to your organization).

The whole development process is extremely iterative but is by necessity subject to the strictest of software engineering practice. In addition suitable documentation of the framework is essential (and this is where design patterns come into their own) from design, implementation and user perspectives.

Finally, some useful general comments about framework development include:

- Develop frameworks by examining existing applications.
- Develop small focused frameworks (breaking down larger frameworks when the opportunity to do so is identified).
- Build frameworks using an iterative process prototyping how the frameworks will be used all the time.
- Always look out for additional functionality for the framework. For such functionality, determine whether it should be a default behavior of the framework or whether a hook should be provided to allow a user to implement it.
- Good documentation is essential and should include sample instantiations of the framework, descriptions of the framework architecture, descriptions of the framework and its intent, guidelines on using the framework and cookbook examples for particular operations.

21.2.3 What is a design pattern?

Design patterns capture expertise in building object oriented software [Gamma *et al* 1993; Johnson 1992; Beck and Johnson 1994]. A design pattern describes a solution to a recurring design problem. It also contains information on the applicability of a pattern, the trade offs which must be made and any consequences of the solution. Books are now appearing which present such design patterns for a range of applications. For example, [Gamma *et al*, 1995] is a widely cited book which presents a catalog of 23 design patterns. Design patterns are extremely useful for both novice and experienced object oriented designers. This is because they encapsulate extensive design knowledge and proven design solutions with guidance on how to use them. Reusing common patterns opens up an additional level of design reuse, where the implementations vary, but the micro-architectures represented by the patterns still apply.

There are potentially very many design patterns available to a designer. A number of these patterns may superficially appear to suit their requirements, even if the design patterns are available on-line (via some hyper text style browser) it is still necessary for the designer to search through them manually, attempting to identify the design which best matches their requirements.

In addition, once they have found the design which they feel best matches their needs, they must then consider how to apply it to their application. This is because a design pattern describes a solution to a particular design problem. This solution may include multiple trade offs which are contradictory and which the designer must choose between, although some aspects of the system structure can be varied independently (although some attempts have been made to automate this process for example [Budinsky *et al* 1996]).

Patterns seem to be exceptionally well suited for documenting frameworks. They certainly provide guidance on how to use a framework, the purpose of the framework, they can also include concrete examples and can be used to document the design of the framework.

21.2.4 Pattern templates

The pattern template used in [Gamma *et al*, 1995] provides a standard structure for the information which comprises a design pattern. This makes it easier to comprehend a design pattern as well as providing a concrete structure for those defining new patterns. Gamma's book [Gamma *et al*, 1995] provides a detailed description of the template; only a summary of it is presented in Table 21.1.

Patterns are best suited for teaching how to use a framework, but with care they can meet all three purposes identified earlier. By describing the design of a framework in terms of patterns, you describe both the design and the rationale behind the design. As patterns also show how to use the framework for a particular problem, the user gains a better understanding of the framework as a whole. It is essentially a tutorial on using a framework, but one which is more than a cookbook.

The problem with cookbooks is that they describe a single way in which the framework will be used. A good framework will be used in ways that its designers never conceived. Thus a cookbook is insufficient on its own to describe every use of the framework. Of course a developer's first use of a framework usually fits the stereotypes in the cookbook. However, once they go beyond the examples in the cookbook, they need to understand the details of the framework. The problem is that cookbooks tend not to describe the framework itself. But in order to understand a framework, you need to have knowledge of both its design and its use. Patterns provide opportunities for describing both the design and the use of the framework as well as including examples, all within a coherent whole. In some ways patterns act like a hyper-graph with links between parts of patterns. To illustrate the ideas behind frameworks and patterns the next section will present the framework HotDraw and a tutorial HotDraw pattern example explaining how to construct a simple drawing tool.

Table 21.1: The design pattern template

Heading	Usage
Name	The name of the pattern
Intent	This is a short statement indicating the purpose of the pattern. It includes information on its rationale, intent, problem it addresses etc.
Also known as	Any other names by which the pattern is known.
Motivation	Illustrates how the pattern can be used to solve a particular problem.
Applicability	This describes the situation in which the pattern is applicable. It may also say when the pattern is not applicable.
Structure	This is a (graphical) description of the classes in the pattern.
Participants	The classes and objects involved in the design and their responsibilities.
Collaborations	This describes how the classes and objects work together.
Consequences	How does the pattern achieve its objective? What are the trade offs and results of using the pattern? What aspect of the system structure does it let you vary independently.
Implementation	What issues are there in implementing the design pattern.
Sample Code	Code illustrating how a pattern might be implemented.
Known uses	How the pattern has been used in the past. Each pattern has at least two such examples.
Related patterns	Closely related design patterns are listed here.

21.3 An introduction to HotDraw

What is HotDraw? HotDraw is a drawing framework developed by Ralph Johnson at
the University of Illinois at Urbana-Chapaign [Johnson 1992]. It is a reusable design
for a drawing tool expressed as a set of classes. However, it is more than just a set of
classes; it possesses the whole structure of a drawing tool, which only needs to be
parameterized to create a new drawing tool. It can therefore be viewed as a basic
drawing tool and a set of examples which can be used to help you develop your own
drawing editor!

Essentially HotDraw is a skeleton DrawingEditor waiting for you to fill out the
specific details. That is, all the elements of a drawing editor are provided including a
basic working editor., which you, as a developer, customize as required. What this
means to you is that you get a working system much, much sooner and with a great
deal less effort.

21.3.1 The HotDraw framework

HotDraw was first presented at the OOPSLA'92 conference in a paper entitled
"Documenting Frameworks using Patterns" by Ralph Johnson [Johnson 1992] . This
paper is somewhat abstract, however the appendices included with the paper are very
useful as guides for changing the default drawing editor. The concept behind
frameworks is that a set of abstract classes are only so useful, it is much more useful
to capture the design in the classes along with concrete examples. The combination
of design information, concrete examples and an explicit skeleton to work with is
easier to understand. Indeed it is usually the case that concrete examples to follow
and modify are a much better way to learn about a set of classes, than to attempt to
understand the class and work from there (particularly when you are learning
Smalltalk). For example, if a method takes a block as an argument, what is that block
supposed to look like? An example or two are often invaluable.

Every HotDraw application is comprised of a number of elements, these are the
Drawing Editor, the Drawing View, the Drawing Controller, the Drawing, figures in
the drawing, handles, constraints between drawings and creation tools. Each of these
is explained briefly below:

DrawingEditor DrawingEditor is a subclass of Model that represents a
graphical drawing editor. It is the model of the MVC triad that includes a
DrawingView and a DrawingController. It shares the
DrawingView and the DrawingController with a Drawing.

DrawingView A DrawingView is the view component of a MVC triad. The
Drawing and the DrawingController are the other components. A
DrawingEditor also uses the DrawingView in a MVC triad.

DrawingController A DrawingController is the controller component of a
pair of MVC triads. A Drawing and A DrawingView is one pair and a
DrawingEditor and DrawingView are the other pair. A
DrawingController's primary task is to delegate mouse and keyboard activity
to the current tool of the Drawing.

Drawing A drawing is a directed graph of figures (or complex figures). As indicated above it is a model in a MVC triad with the `DrawingView` and `DrawingController`.

Figures A `Figure` is a kind of drawing element or widget which describes how it should be drawn within a `DrawingEditor`. A `CompositeFigure` is a figure which can contain other figures as components, which all have an influence on what the composite figure looks like. `CompositeFigure` also defines a bounding box which is independent of its sub-components. Only components which are wholly within the bounding box are actually displayed. Unlike VisualComponents in VisualWorks, figures keep track of which objects which depend on them.

Handles All figures can potentially have handles. Handles are a way to modify a figure's attributes, for example by resizing the figure, or by linking a figure to another figure and thereby creating a dependency. The Figure class defines a method handles which returns a basic set of handles for resizing a figure. It is therefore common for subclasses of figure to redefine the handles method, either to overwrite this, or to add to it (in which case the method would "call super" handles at some point).

Constraints HotDraw provides `Constraint` objects which are used to express dependencies between objects. A `MultiheadedConstraint`, which is a subclass of constraint, makes the state of one object be the function of the states of many other objects. The one object is the "sink" and the many objects are the "sources". For example, if the value of one cell in a spreadsheet is the sum of five other cells, then the five cells are the sources and the cell with the sum is the sink.

CreationTools These are used to create a new instance of a figure. They are parameterized by the class of the figure to display, the icon to display in the tool palette and the cursor to use while that tool is selected.

21.3.2 Obtaining HotDraw

HotDraw is available by anonymous FTP from the Smalltalk repository at st.cs.uiuc. There are versions available for most of the recent releases of ParcPlace Smalltalk (e.g. VisualWorks version 1.0, 2.0 and 2.5). You should follow the installation instructions and then immediately save the image onto your local file store and exit VisualWorks.

21.3.3 Examples with HotDraw

The examples provided with HotDraw include a Pert Chart tool, a HyperCard clone, HotPaint and Network Editor which allows you to play with nodes in a network which are either attracted or repulsed by each other and a diagramming inspector. If you have access to HotDraw (e.g. via ftp) then explore them! Explore the patterns at the end of this chapter which describes the patterns based on one of these example applications.

Finally, it is interesting to note a comment made in Ralph Johnson's paper "The implementation [of HotDraw for ObjectWorks Rel 4.0] was simpler than previous ones because the design of the user interface framework for release 4.0 was influenced by HotDraw".

21.3.4 Facilities provided by HotDraw

So what does HotDraw provide in this framework. (I will use the term framework to describe the basic HotDraw editor). You get the following facilities:

- A `ToolPaletteView`. This is the tool bar down the left hand side of the display.
- A `DrawingView`. This is the area a user would actually draw in.
- A `DrawingEditor`. This is the model for the DrawingView and Drawing Controller.
- A `Drawing`. This is also a model used by the DrawingView and Drawing Controller.
- A `DrawingController`. which allows you to interact with the application.

All these are already connected together in the appropriate manner, unlike many class-only packages, in which you as the developer must determine how to bring these elements together.

21.4 Where do you start?

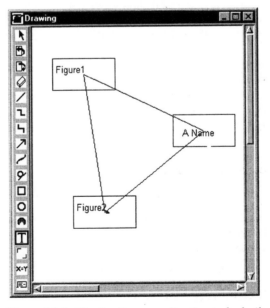

Figure 21.1: The BoxDraw application to be built

215

The remainder of this document is in effect a sample pattern which illustrates how you create a simple extension to the drawing editor. The problem to be addressed by this pattern is:

> *The basic facilities provided by HotDraw make it very easy to construct a simple graphic editor for drawing diagrams. One useful feature of such diagrams is the ability to link figures together and to get those links to move when the figures are moved. Thus there needs to be a way to link two figures together.*

21.4.1 The DrawingEditor

You will almost always start by subclassing the DrawingEditor. This is the basic element of any HotDraw tool. In this case we shall subclass DrawingEditor to create BoxDrawEditor, which will be the basis of our application BoxDraw. The definition of the BoxDrawEditor is presented below:

```
DrawingEditor subclass: #BoxDrawEditor
    instanceVariableNames: ''
    classVariableNames: ''
    poolDictionaries: ''
    category: 'BoxDraw'
```

Note that I have put this class in a category called BoxDraw. Also note that I have not had to define any new instance or class variables - it is not necessary as I inherit all I need from DrawingEditor. In fact I am not even going to define any instance methods for this class. So why have a BoxDrawEditor class at all? Because I want a different set of tools in the toolPalette.

21.4.2 Define the set of tools to use

The next step is therefore to define the set of tools available to a user of BoxDraw. This is done by defining a method called defaultTools on the class side. This method is used to create the ToolPaletteView. This method returns an OrderedCollection of creationTools. Every type of figure will provide a creation tool for example:

```
LineFigure creationTool.
```

We are going to use the default set of tools, with the addition of just one figure, called BoxDrawFigure. We can therefore use the defaultTools method defined in the superclass of BoxDrawEditor and just add a creation tool for BoxDrawFigure to the end of this OrderedCollection. The code for this method is listed below:

```
defaultTools
    "Answer an OrderedCollection of the tools I can use"
    ^(super defaultTools) add: (BoxDrawFigure creationTool); yourself.
```

This method should be defined in a class method category called "defaults".

21.4.3 An example class method

Finally, for the `BoxDrawEditor` class we shall define a class method protocol called "examples". In this protocol we shall define a single method called `example1`. This method will send the message open to the `BoxDrawEditor` which will create a new instance of the `BoxDrawEditor` and will cause the graphic editor we are constructing to be displayed.

```
example1
    BoxDrawEditor open.
```

21.5 BoxDrawFigure

21.5.1 Defining the figure

We now have a drawing editor for BoxDraw with everything we need defined - except what a `BoxDrawFigure` is. This is the next step.

We could make a `BoxDrawFigure` a subclass of a simple figure such as `Rectangle`, `Ellipse` or `PolylineFigure`. However, we want to have a text field in the middle of `BoxDrawFigure` which will represent the name of the figure. This means that `BoxDrawFigure` will have at least one subfigure, we therefore want to make BoxDrawFigure a subclass of `CompositeFigure`.

A `CompositeFigure` is a figure which possesses subfigures, who determine part or all of the look of the figure. `CompositeFigures` are also often used if it is necessary to give a user access to the subfigures (for example to change the text in the text field of the `BoxDrawFigure`). The definition for `BoxDrawFigure` is given below:

```
CompositeFigure subclass: #BoxDrawFigure
    instanceVariableNames: ''
    classVariableNames: ''
    poolDictionaries: ''
    category: 'BoxDraw'
```

21.5.2 Adding an instance creation method

Now we have a class called `BoxDrawFigure`, we need some way of instantiating this class. HotDraw expects a figure's instance creation method to be called `createAt:` (rather than new or open with which you may be more familiar). We will therefore define a method `createAt:` in the protocol "instance creation":

```
createAt: aPoint
    ^self new initializeAt: aPoint
```

This method first creates a new instance of the `BoxDrawFigure` and then sends it an `initializeAt:` message with `aPoint` as the current cursor position. The initializeAt: method will actually draw the figure and its component elements. We will look at this method below.

21.5.3 Defining a creation tool

While we are still on the class side, we shall define the creationTool method which specifies what icon to use in the ToolPalette for a BoxDrawFigure. Rather than define a new creationTool class, we will provide a creationTool method which will return the default creationTool, parameterized for BoxDrawFigure. This method will be defined in the class protocol "tool creation". The creationTool method is:

```
creationTool
    ^Tool
      icon: (Image
              extent: 16 @ 16
              depth: 1
              palette: MappedPalette blackWhite
              bits: #[255 255 255 255 255 255 128 1
                      191 253 160 125 191 253 160 197
                      191 253 160 125 191 253 28 1
                      255 255 255 255 255 255 255 255]
              pad: 8)
      cursor: Cursor crossHair
      class: self
      creationMessage: #createAt:
```

This method is based on that defined in PERTEvent in one of the HotDraw example applications. It returns an instance of CreationTool which uses a particular icon on class BoxDrawFigure and uses a crossHair (rather than origin) style cursor. Note that the creationMessage is specified here. We could have used a different creation message to that used elsewhere in HotDraw. However, to remain consistent with existing HotDraw applications we used createAt:.

21.5.4 The *initializeAt:* method

We now need to define what the elements of this drawing will be. That is, "what the figure will look like". This is done within initializeAt: defined in "initialize" protocol on the instance side of the class. The code for this method is:

```
initializeAt: aPoint
    |  title myFigures aRectangle |
    "Get the bounding rectangle"
    aRectangle := aPoint extent: 90 @ 45.
    origin := aRectangle origin.
    "Position the text field relative to the origin"
    title := FixedTextFigure string: 'A Name' at: origin + (5 @ 5).
    title maxLength: 65.
    "Add the text field to the subelements of this figure"
    myFigures := (OrderedCollection new) add: title; yourself.
    self setFigures: myFigures visibleArea: aRectangle.
    "Draw the bounding box of this figure"
    self showVisibleAreaIndicator.
```

This method first creates a rectangle whose right hand corner is indicates by aPoint and whose extent is 90 by 45. Having done that, it then sets the origin of the figure relative to the rectangle. Next it creates a text field at a particular point and then uses the bounding box of the figure to draw the shape of the figure (in this case a rectangle).

21.5.5 Running the editor

You have now done enough to open a BoxDrawEditor. Do this by evaluating:

```
BoxDrawEditor open.
```

in a Workspace window.

The BoxDrawFigure is the last icon in the ToolPalette. However, all you can do is place a BoxDrawFigure in a drawing and change the label. Note to change the label, select the Text tool (the big 'T') and hold down the shift button while selecting the label with the left mouse button.

21.5.6 Adding handles

To be able to link a BoxDrawFigure to another figure we need to add another handle. Handles provide a way of telling a figure that some operation should be performed. The most common handles are for shrinking or growing a figure. For example, handles on the four corners of a figure. We want to add another handle which will allow us to link one BoxDrawFigure to another BoxDrawFigure.

By default we have inherited the handles defined in the figure. These handles are on the four corners of our figure and allow the user to resize the figure. The method handles in the protocol "accessing" on the class Figure provides for this. We want to add an additional handle which allows links to be created. We shall select the center point. However we do not want to lose the ability to resize our figures, we shall therefore define a new handles method in the "accessing" protocol of the BoxDrawFigure which uses super to obtain the original handles and then add our handle to this collection of handles:

```
handles
    "Add a handle at my center that draws connections to other figures"
    ^(super handles) add: (CommandHandle
                            connectionFor: self
                            at: #center:
                            class: LineFigure); yourself
```

We now have a fully functional BoxDraw application. Open the BoxDrawEditor again and place some BoxDrawFigures on the drawing area. Now select the "arrow" icon on the icon menu. This is the top icon. Next select one of the BoxDrawFigures. You should see a small square (a handle) in the center of the figure. Click on this and drag the resulting line to another BoxDrawFigure. This should connect the two figures together. Now move the figures around. You should find that the link between the two figures moves with you.

21.5.7 Changing a figure menu

To complete this application we shall change the menu available when clicking on a BoxDrawFigure using the middle mouse button. At present the user has the option to show visible area, hide visible area and reset visible area as well as the standard cut, copy and paste options. We only want the user to have access to the standard cut, copy and paste options. To do this we redefine the menu method inherited from CompositeFigure. This method is defined within the accessing protocol:

```
menu
    "Define a pop up Menu for use with BoxDrawFigure"
    ^Menu labels: 'cut\copy\paste' withCRs
        values: #(#cut #copy #paste )
```

21.5.8 The (pattern) solution statement

The ability to specify handles which perform specific functions allows operations to be performed through operation of the mouse. The use of a CommandHandle with a LineFigure can be used to link two figures together.

21.6 Summary

In this chapter we explored the concepts of frameworks and patterns as a method of documenting frameworks. We have briefly considered what we mean by frameworks and how frameworks can be developed. We then discussed what a pattern is and how they may be used to document a framework. Following on from this an extended tutorial describing how the framework HotDraw can be used to develop a simple drawing tool called BoxDraw. This tutorial example was presented in the manner of a very (simplified) pattern.

Testing and Style

22. Testing Object Oriented Systems

22.1 Introduction

Testing object oriented systems is a very important issue as more and more organizations are starting to develop Smalltalk (as well as C++ and Java) based applications. Many such organizations have been forced to come up with their own solutions for assuring the quality of their product. However, little attention has been focused onto this subject at Smalltalk-centered conferences or in Smalltalk literature (see the workshop at OOPSLA-95 for a notable exception). There is a particular scarcity of literature on "how-to" test Smalltalk systems as well as tools to support such testing. For organizations just starting to use Smalltalk for major projects this is a very worrying situation.

Object oriented techniques do not (and cannot) guarantee correct programs. They may well help to produce a better system architecture and an object oriented language may promote a suitable coding style, but these features do not stop a programmer making mistakes. Although this should be self evident, for a long time there was a feeling that object oriented systems required less testing than systems constructed with traditional procedural languages, was prevalent (for example see the book describing the OMT method by Rumbaugh *et al*).

Where the testing of object oriented systems has been considered it is often the user interface of the system which has actually been tested in a principled or systematic manner. These tests usually concentrate on overall system functionality, usability issues (such as the ability of the user to use the system or the speed of response) and stress or exception testing. Stress or exception testing relate to attempting to break the operation of the system by inputting unacceptable data or crashing part of the system (e.g. an associated relational database system) to ensure that the system can recover from such catastrophic failures.

However, this chapter aims to show you that if anything, object oriented systems require more testing, not less testing than traditional programming languages. In the remainder of this chapter we shall consider what effects inheritance, encapsulation, polymorphism and dynamic typing have on testing as well as approaches to method and class (unit) testing, object integration and system testing.

22.2 Why is testing object oriented systems hard?

22.2.1 An example

To illustrate the point consider the following Smalltalk. Let us assume that we have defined a method `returnSymbol` which returns a symbol based on the current state of an object. Let us also assume that we have defined another method `passesTheTest` which returns true or false based on the state of its object. We could then write the following method:

```
myMethod: aCollection and: anObject
| aVariable |
aVariable := anObject returnSymbol.
aCollection do: [:item | (item passesTheTest) ifTrue:
                                    [item perform: aVariable]].
```

In this case it is very difficult to determine statically what is going to happen in this method. This is because until the method is executed, we do not know the content (let alone the type (class) of the objects) in `aCollection`. We cannot determine therefore which objects must respond to the `passesTheTest` message. Nor can we determine which objects will return true from this message and thus which objects will cause the ifTrue block to be evaluated. In this example, the situation is made worse, because the symbol held in aVariable (which is the name of the message to send to the item) is determined by `anObject` which is an object passed into this method. We therefore do not know:

1. What the contents of `aCollection` will be
2. Which classes must respond to the message `passesTheTest`
3. Which instances are likely to result in the ifTrue block being evaluated (this is context dependent).
4. What the message to be sent within the ifTrue block will be (this is content dependent).
5. Which objects must respond to the message we don't yet know.

It could be argued that this is true, but irrelevant. However, the point is that a number of the above issues would be resolved by the compiler at compile time in other languages such as Ada or Pascal. These static compile time checks can identify what type of object will be held in the aCollection, if the type of object receiving the message will understand that message etc. Where as in Smalltalk, it is left up to the developer to ensure that no problems are likely to occur.

As you can see from this very simple (although slightly contrived) example traditional static test generation techniques, although of use in object oriented languages such as Smalltalk, do not provide the whole answer. In the example above, the problems are due to the dynamic typing of Smalltalk and the late binding and polymorphism of object oriented languages.

22.2.2 What makes it hard?

Part of the problem for object orientation is that space of possibilities is so much greater. For example, not only are we concerned about objects sending messages requesting that other objects run specified methods correctly, we are also concerned with which class of object will receive the message and which class of object sent the message as this will therefore have an effect on which method will be used. These issues are related to the polymorphic nature of object oriented languages and the use of abstraction and inheritance as a basic system construction tool.

In addition encapsulation leads to a fundamental problem of observability; as the only way to observe the state of an object is through its operations. This is fine for black box testing, but makes white box testing extremely difficult. This problem is compounded as traditional control flow analysis techniques are not directly applicable as there is no definite sequential order in which methods will be invoked. That is, another object may request that a method is executed at a point which cannot be statically determined (see example in introduction). Indeed, as the state of the object may affect what the method does, it may not even be possible to determine how the method will behave. Of course this does introduce the issue of "what is correct behavior", however we will leave the issue of "correctness" until a later section.

In traditional programming languages the basic unit of test is usually taken to be procedure or function. However, it should be seen from this brief discussion that, the object oriented equivalent i.e. the method, cannot be taken as the basic unit of test. It is affected by the state of the object, possibly by the state of the class (if the class has class variables), may interact in unforeseen ways with other methods and may rely on methods defined elsewhere in the class's superclass hierarchy.

Inheritance also affects testing and introduces the following question "after a change, to what extent should the code currently in the system be re-tested?". In a traditional programming language it is usually quite straight forward to identify what parts of the system code are affected by some change. In an object oriented system it is far less obvious.

The implication of the above is that in object oriented programs, such as those implemented in Smalltalk, the basic unit of test must be considered to be the class. That is not to say that care is not given to exercising individual methods within a class, merely that the individual methods should not be treated in isolation.

22.2.3 Why a lack of emphasis?

Part of the reason for the lack of Smalltalk testing literature or tools is probably due to the background of Smalltalk. In the past it was often used as a single (or at most a few) developer's language. It was often considered to be a personal development environment or a good prototyping tool. However few people considered it suitable for constructing industrial strength systems in. The reasons for this have already been considered in the introductory chapters of this book.

As the types of systems being constructed were experimental, the tools available made code debugging easy and could be done even when the implemented system was executing. This led many people to design the overall system, roughly specify the components, implement them and test the resulting system (not the components) using the user interface. If the system failed (at any time including once development was complete) then a quick fix could sort out the problem. This approach can work well for a single developer-user, non critical, application where the majority of the system is the user interface. However, for serious development this approach is inappropriate.

Smalltalk applications require testing just as any other software requires testing. Indeed the type of testing normally applied to traditional programming languages is also required by object oriented systems. However, object orientation imposes unique requirements on the testing process. Why these requirements exist and how they can be handled is the subject of the remainder of this chapter.

22.3 Inheritance

Inheritance is a fundamental feature of object oriented programming languages. However, it is both a blessing and a curse. For example, many programmers believe that they can inherit many of the features they require in their new classes from existing classes (and often they can). However, they also tend to feel that it is not necessary to test those features they have inherited because they have been tested very many times before (both by the system developers and by the many thousands of users). However, this is misleading because in defining a new subclass they have changed the context within which the methods will execute at least in the subclass. The problem is that each new subclass may not require any re-testing and may very well function acceptably, but you are relying on a continuing hypothesis. Of course this hypothesis may have held many times before, but there is no guarantee that it will hold this time. Interestingly, the same problem also occurs with Ada generics. In this case each instantiation of the generic package may work as intended but equally this time it may fail.

22.3.1 The effects of inheritance

There are a number of ways in which inheritance can affect the testing required in a subclass. The following list summarizes these and lists the type of testing required:

Adding functionality. For example, by adding new methods. In these situations, the tests should concentrate first on the new functionality, to ensure that the class works correctly (relative to its specification). If the new functionality calls on existing methods, then tests should be performed to ensure that these methods continue to function correctly. If any existing instance variables are modified by the new methods, or the methods they call, then the effects of these changes should be determined. This may result in re-testing the whole class.
Over-riding methods. In these situations, the newly defined methods must of course be tested. This should test the new definition to ensure that it handles the same

range of values as the original and produces the same results. If this is not what was desired, then over-riding was not the correct approach.

Next all the methods which invoke the overridden operation must be re-tested. This can be done by using the tools provided with the Smalltalk system to identify all the senders of the messages associated with the changed methods. This will provide the initial test list. If the behavior of inherited methods is changed in any way then this should be treated as adding functionality and tested as above.

Super Class references. If the subclass changes anything used by the super class, for example by referencing a pool variable, then the super class must also be subjected to incremental testing. Again, the process needs to identify the elements of the class which have been affected and to test those elements. In the case of a pool variable, it may also involve testing other classes which reference the pool variable.

22.3.2 Incremental testing

Incremental testing is one obvious answer, i.e. we don't want to re-test the whole class if we don't need to, only those elements which have been affected by the additions in the subclass need to be tested. Of course this is the key issue here: what determines whether or not we "need to" re-test a subclass. One answer is that it is the properties of the class which are affected by the subclass, including which instance variables may be altered and which methods may be directly or indirectly affected, which determine what should be re-tested. For example, a directly affected method may be one which is called by a (re)defined method in the subclass or which directly references an instance variable which is modified by (re)defined methods. Indirectly affected methods are much harder to identify. They are methods which may be affected due to a chain of interactions. For example, suppose that a method "a" references an altered instance variable and modifies another instance variable. This results in a second method operating in a different way generating a different result which is used by a third method. The third method is indirectly affected by the original change in the instance variable. In the worst case, every element of a class may be affected in such a way. In such cases, either the whole class must be re-tested or the developers must use their own intuition and experience to decide how much testing is required.

A subtlety which can often be missed is that although an inherited method has not been changed, a method which it calls may have been redefined in the subclass. Thus the inherited method is directly affected by the subclass and must be re-tested.

However, we want to be sure that any inherited functionality has not been adversely affected in an unanticipated way (note that this implies that we have some sort of specification against which we can compare the functionality of the class). We must therefore also consider some form of regression testing. This can be achieved by defining an appropriate set of regression tests on the class side of the root superclass. These tests can then be performed whenever the root class or one of its subclasses is changed in anyway. Ideally these tests should include their own evaluation so that a report can be generated (to the Transcript or to a file) stating the result of the tests. If appropriate, additional tests can be defined (in subclasses of the root superclass) to test the added functionality. If new tests are defined each time the functionality is extended or modified, then the tests on the class side also act as a repository of testing knowledge which can be exploited by future users of the classes without the need to understand their full functionality.

22.4 Abstract superclasses

Abstract superclasses bring together common features, which are to be used in many subclasses. However, from a testing point of view they are a difficult problem. The definition of an abstract superclass is a class which is never intended to be instantiated and which does not provide, in its own right, enough functionality to be useful. Given these two features, it is extremely important to test abstract superclasses thoroughly. However as they do not provide enough information to create an instance of the class, it is impossible to test the class directly. The tester should provide a subclass which acts as a test harness for the facilities defined in the abstract class (such a class can be easily removed from the Smalltalk image).

The test subclass might provide a wide range of facilities. For example, a method may be defined which sets the state of the instance such that a particular method can be called and then sends a message causing the method (inherited from the parent class) to be executed.

Note that testing the abstract superclass does not mean that exhaustive testing of the methods in the subclasses, which inherit from it, is not required. As each subclass has changed the context within which the method will be run, the same approach to testing as discussed in Section 3 must be performed.

22.5 Encapsulation

Encapsulation is a great bonus from the point of view of the user of an object - they do not need to know anything about the object's implementation, only what its published protocols are. This also means that the developer of the class knows that any potential users will have to come through the front door etc. However, for the tester of the class it is both a benefit and a drawback. It is a benefit because the encapsulated object is clearly designated for unit testing. That is, it is clear what the boundaries of the class are, i.e. anything that is not in the class is in another class and thus does not come into the picture (from the point of view of unit testing). It is therefore possible to test the unit in isolation.

22.5.1 Black box testing

Encapsulation therefore promotes black box testing. Black box testing can be carried out in the normal way with the addition that the state of the object (and possibly the class) must be taken into account. Black box testing (also called specification based testing) is aimed at testing a program against its specification only. That is, the class should be tested regardless of the way in which it has been coded. It is usually accomplished, even in object oriented systems, by identifying a set of messages to send to the object and the parameters to use with these messages. The results of sending these messages are then compared to the original specification (assuming one exists). The product of this comparison is then used to determine if the class has passed the test or not. In general, if some results are not as expected further testing would be used to determine the actual behavior of the class. A decision would then be taken to determine what action was required (i.e. modification of the source code or if appropriate, modification of the specification).

22.5.2 White box testing

Although encapsulation promotes black box testing, it can make white box testing much harder. White box testing (also known as program-based testing) is complementary to black box testing. It consists of examining the internal structure of a piece of code to select test data which will exercise that code thoroughly either because that piece of code is critical or to gain confidence in the code to eliminate it from suspicion (for example if you are attempting to track down the source of some undesired behavior).

A problem with encapsulation is that while it is entirely possible to view the source code and identify the tests to perform, it is not possible to access the instance variables of the object directly, nor is it usually possible to monitor the execution of the methods externally to the object.

Of course in most Smalltalk environments you could use the debugger and the inspector to examine the source code during execution (and indeed this is the intention of these tools). However, using such tools presents problems for both traceability and accountability. Thus it is not possible to trace the tests which have been performed during a project nor is it possible to record these tests and their results for later quality audits. Of course, you can require the developer to note what they are doing, but this is nowhere near as good as having the system do it for you automatically. This approach also fails to support repeatability of tests. That is, once you have completed your testing, it is not possible to re-run the tests and check the results following some change to the class.

22.5.3 Overcoming encapsulation during testing

In Smalltalk it is possible to work around the problems imposed by encapsulation in a number of ways:

22.5.3.1 Use of the halt message

Smalltalk provides a halt message which can be sent to an object. This will cause the object to stop executing at that point and allow the user to enter the debugger. The debugger will then allow the user to view the method that is executing as well as the state of any instance and temporary variables

This may at first seem intrusive, as the developer is modifying the source code of the method by adding the halt message. As has already been stated this is not desirable. However, in this case, it is possible to control the method's execution through the debugger. This means that the developer can ensure that the intended operation of the method remains unchanged before attempting to identify the behavior of the method under test situations. Thus this approach may not be as intrusive as would at first appear.

It is unfortunate that the debugger is so named, as it is not only useful for debugging systems, it is also a particularly useful tool for white box testing. This is because, once you have entered the debugger (e.g. by introducing a self halt message into the source code of a method) it is possible to control the execution of the method in a number of ways. For example, a tester can change the state of an object or the input parameter values using the inspectors at the bottom of the debugger. They can control the execution of the method either by stepping through the method a line at a time, descending into methods called by this method or proceeding to run the whole method as though the debugger had never been entered. By default the tester controls the execution of the method from the point immediately after the halt message. However, it is also possible to re-run the whole method.

22.5.3.2 Subclassing the test class

A more object oriented approach is to define a test subclass for the class being tested (this approach has already been mentioned above). The tester can then define an appropriate set of test harness methods which exercise the class in the desired manner. As the test harness methods have the same ability to access the state of the object as the methods under test, it is possible to determine the object's state before and after a method is executed. The results of these tests can then be written to the Transcript and / or to a file. If the results are written to a file, the tests can be re-run at a later date and the new results compared with the previous results. This is cleaner than writing print statements within the source code of the methods to be tested, however it does not allow the internal operation of the methods to be monitored as closely.

To monitor the actual execution of the desired methods, it is possible to place a self halt. message just prior to any super message. This invokes the debugger and allows the developer to step down into the super method's code. For example:

```
age
    self halt.
    super age.
```

Of course, in practice a combination of all of the above may be necessary to accomplish both black box and white box testing effectively.

22.6 Polymorphism

Polymorphism is the ability of objects to send the same message to instances of different classes which do not have a common superclass. It is made possible by the dynamic binding of messages to objects. That is, it is only at run time that it is possible to determine to which object the messages will be sent. From the point of view of testing, there are a number of problems associated with polymorphism. Each of these is discussed separately below.

22.6.1 Undecidability

Polymorphism allows the programmer to specify which message will be sent to an object, but not which object will receive that message. This will only be determined at run time. It is therefore not possible to provide any form of static check to see that the message will be "understood" by the object (other than checking that at least one class somewhere in the system will respond to that message). In addition, even when it is known that the object receiving the message will understand the message (e.g. all objects in Smalltalk understand printString), it is not possible to identify which version or implementation of the method will be executed. That is, the tester will know that the object will understand the message printString, however, which version of printString will be used will depend on the class of the receiver. It might be that defined in class Object, that defined in class Collection etc.

It is therefore impossible for the tester to know what would be an appropriate range of tests for a polymorhpic message expression. They therefore have to make assumptions about the range of objects which are likely to be sent the message. In some cases this range may be very large indeed. In such situations it is necessary to produce one or more class hierarchies for different implementations of the method. These trees can then be used to identify those classes in which new definitions of the method are provided. The assumptions being used in the tests should, of course, be made explicit in the test report, so that they can be challenged if it is felt that they were inappropriate.

22.6.2 Extensibility of hierarchies

Another problem associated with polymorphism is presented when an operation, which possesses one or more parameters which are polymorphic, is being tested. That is, the operation can be called with a range of different types of object as a parameter. For example, a parameter may be assumed to be a collection, however it could be a set, a bag, an array, a list, a sorted collection or an ordered collection. Each of these have specific features which may or may not affect the operation of the method. They may also contain elements which are of any type, which in turn may or may not affect the method's behavior.

As testing a method consists of checking its effects when executed for various combinations of actual parameters, a test suite must ensure that all possible input types are covered. This of course implies that some form of specification exists which specifies the acceptable range of input types. However, it is impossible to plan a set of tests in which you check all possible parameter values for a method. This is because the range of different types of objects which could be presented to a method is huge in Smalltalk. Remember that the hierarchy of classes is very large (e.g. every class under `Object`) and is freely extensible. For example, I can define my own stack and queue collection classes. However, even if the method I am testing includes a test to see if it has been presented with an instance of a collection class, it could easily encounter a type of collection class for which it was never designed. Remember you (or anyone else) can extend the set of collection classes whenever you wish. If the method is part of a class which is to be provided as part of a set of "highly" reusable classes, either within a single project or for external use, this is a significant issue.

22.6.3 Heterogeneous containers

As has been briefly mentioned above, there are many classes which are designed to hold elements which may be any instance in the system. In Smalltalk, this means that they can hold instances of classes, classes, metaclasses etc. If the tester is considering a method which will be applied to, or will consume, the members of such a heterogeneous container (e.g. a collection), it is almost impossible to ensure that a complete range of tests has been performed. For example, it may be assumed that all the members of such a container are conventional instances of user defined classes, however there is nothing to stop the member of one of these containers being a class or the system dictionary etc.

In such situations care must be taken to ensure that reasonable usage of the method has been tested. In other words, with reference to the classes specification, assumptions must again be made, this time about the use of the method. Again, these assumptions should be documented so that they can be challenged if necessary at a later date.

22.7 Additional Smalltalk specific features

22.7.1 Block evaluations

Blocks introduce another complexity to the testing process which is particular to Smalltalk. Not only are they more difficult to test physically (it is more difficult to get hold of them in isolation), they also execute in the context within which they were created (rather than the context in which they are evaluated). This second issue is important because in many situations a block is defined in one place, and then passed as a parameter to another place, where it is evaluated. If the receiving method is being tested, it is impossible to conceive of all the contexts in which the block could be created and therefore impossible to produce a comprehensive test suite. Again, care must be taken to test the receiving method against its specification and not the assumptions which this led to.

In addition when they are examined in the debugger, they are treated in a different way to general Smalltalk code, which makes it more difficult to follow the thread of execution. Instead of immediately stepping through the code in the block, it is necessary to step down into the value method and then into the block. It is all to easy to step over the block and fail to see the result.

22.7.2 The Perform: message

The perform message takes a symbol as its parameter. It then uses this symbol as the name of a method to execute on the receiving object. As the symbol can be stored in a variable, it is impossible to determine all the possible symbol values which will be passed to the perform message. It is therefore advisable not to use perform unless it is absolutely necessary. However, if the developer has used a perform expression, then a reasonable set of tests should be identified. Once again, the assumptions used to generate this set should be made explicit.

22.8 Summary

In this chapter we have considered some of the special problems which face a developer when testing an object oriented system (with special consideration for Smalltalk implementations). As has been discussed inheritance, abstraction, polymorphism and encapsulation all play a major part in determining the best practice in testing Smalltalk systems. A number of recurring themes have been:

- The importance of specifying what a class or object is intended to do.
- The use of scenarios to aid in the adequate testing of methods and classes.
- The adequacy of testing and the importance of deciding what is sufficient.
- Examples and assumptions need explanation (including their context).

A final comment is that this chapter should not put you off constructing large complex systems in Smalltalk. Rather it should make you aware of the difficulties you will face in testing such a system.

22.9 Further reading

Little has been written about the special problems of testing object oriented systems, however the papers by [Barbey and Strohmeier 1994] and [Barbey, Amman and Strohmeier 1994] are an exception and provide an excellent introduction to the subject of testing object oriented systems. [Perry and Kaiser 1990] a discussion of the effects of inheritance on object oriented testing. The next chapter also provides further reading on the subject of object oriented testing.

23. Method and Class Testing

23.1 Introduction

In the last chapter we discussed the problems facing the tester of an object oriented system (and in particular a Smalltalk system). We also briefly considered some approaches which overcome these problems. In this chapter we will consider the current best practice in testing object oriented systems.

23.1.1 Class and instance sides

As was stated in the last chapter, the basic unit of test in Smalltalk is the class. However, there are two sides to a class, one is referred to as the *class side* and the other the *instance side*. The class side can be tested directly by sending messages to the class. However, the instance side can only be tested by creating instances of the class. That is, although you define the instances' methods in the class, you must test them using an instance. An important point to remember is that, it may be necessary to use both the class and instances of the class together, to adequately test both the class side and the instance side. For example, let us assume we have a class such as that illustrated in Figure 23.1.

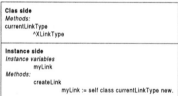

Figure 23.1: Instance and Class method interaction

In this situation, it is possible to test the class side method currentLinkType directly by sending a message to the class and in isolation. However, it is not possible to test the instance method createLink without considering the range of values which may be returned by currentLinkType. In this case, it is the class XLinkType which is returned, however, it could easily be one of a range of values. In addition, the class to which the currentLinkType message is sent, depends on the class of the object in which the createLink method is executing. As the createLink method may be inherited by other classes, we cannot guarantee which class will receive the currentLinkType message.

23.1.2 Testing methods in a class

Each method in a class should first be tested in isolation. However, once all the individual methods in the class have been tested, threads through the methods in the class should be identified. This can be done by postulating scenarios of normal and exceptional usage (which may have been produced when the class was being designed). By tracing the result of these scenarios through the class it is possible to identify threads of execution amongst the methods in the class. An example of a thread of execution is illustrated in Figure 23.2. This thread was obtained by considering a scenario in which a person object has a birthday. This leads to the person object being sent the message birthday. The associated method birthday is presented below:

birthday
```
        Transcript show: 'A happy birthday to ' , self name.
        self incrementAge.
        Transcript show: 'I am now ' , self age.
```

From the scenario that a person might have a birthday and therefore receive the message birthday, and from examining the source code of birthday (and incrementAge) we can obtain the thread in Figure 23.2.

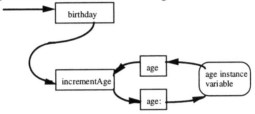

Figure 23.2: A thread of execution through an object

23.1.3 Object state

Another point to bear in mind when testing a class, is that both instances and classes have state. For example, a class may have a class instance variable which is used to keep a record of the number of instances which have been created of that class. This information may be used purely for book keeping or may be used to limit the number of instances created. In the latter case, a test needs to be performed which sets the counter to its limit and then a new instance should be requested. This could be done, either by creating the required number of instances, or by manually setting the counter to the appropriate value (e.g. by using the debugger or inspector).

It is also important to remember that although a method has been tested in the context of a state instance, it is possible that some unintended sequence of message sends could result in the method being executed with the object in an unintended state. It is therefore not possible to test individual methods in isolation thoroughly, nor is it sensible to ignore the state of the object when performing these tests. It is of course quite possible to ignore the state, however the tester does so at their peril.

23.1.4 Private methods

Some methods are defined such that the user of the class is never expected to see them. This may be because they do some housekeeping which is local to the object (for example the initialization method) or because they provide facilities which are relevant to the internals of the object and not to the external interface to the object In Smalltalk, this method hiding is not enforced, it is usually left implicit (unlike C++ or Java in which the equivalent of private methods really are private and are not available as external messages). For example, in VisualWorks Smalltalk this can be done by placing the appropriate set of methods in a protocol entitled private or private-*. The convention is that a user of this class is not expected to use or to need to know about these methods. This is useful from a testing point of view as the tester can test the individual execution of these methods in a black box fashion. They can also use the approaches described above to perform white box testing. However, it also means that a user of the class, if they so wish, can call these methods. As this is not what is intended it is arguably reasonable to ignore this scenario. However, it may be wise in some situations at least to know what the effects will be and whether the object's methods will respond in a meaningful or at least well defined manner. For example, it may be useful to know what will happen if another object sends the message initialize to the current object at some point after the object has started to be used.

23.1.5 Pool variables

An additional problem with testing classes (as opposed to unit testing in other languages) is the presence of pool variables. These are rather like limited scope global variables. They are common to a set of classes and may affect the operation of these classes. As any one of the classes associated with the pool can change their value it is possible for one class (or its instances) to have a profound effect on the operation of a completely different class or its instances elsewhere in the system. This is something which requires careful thought.

23.1.6 Tracing a classes operation

In order to trace a classes operation it would be possible to create a subclass which mirrored the parent classes methods exactly. The subclasses methods could print the value of any parameters into the method before calling the method and then any results returned by the method. If necessary tests could be performed to ensure that the parameters or the returned value were within anticipated ranges. The advantage of testing the class method calls in this way would be to encapsulate all the test information into a test subclass which could be removed from the Smalltalk image for the delivered system.

23.1.7 Sources of test information

The concept of use cases discussed earlier in this book is an important source of test cases. Opportunities for the merging of the use case specifications into test specifications abound.

A style issue, rather than a testing issue, is that it is good style to provide a set of test examples, often on the class side, which exercise some behavior of the objects of the class. These can be used to illustrate how to use the objects of the class. They can also act as a form of regression testing either when the class is modified or when a subclass is defined. If these test methods are placed in appropriate protocols, then the whole protocol can be filed out in one go, thus creating a test file.

23.2 Object integration testing

The above section deliberately only deals with the issue of testing a class in isolation. This involves individual method testing followed by testing combinations of methods. Object integration testing involves testing instances of the same or different classes when they are collaborating in some operation. This is different from traditional procedural integration testing as the structure of traditional programming languages is fairly rigid and is unlikely to vary while the system is executing. It is also different from statically bound procedural programs, because when a language such as Pascal is used, the compiler is able to test to see whether the called procedure or function definition matches the calling definition. For example, if a procedure expects an integer as a parameter the compiler checks that an integer is being presented to it.

In Smalltalk, neither the structure of the objects is fixed nor are the actual types of parameters etc. likely to be known. It is therefore necessary to perform object integration testing in a methodological and principled manner. If the specification of two classes indicates that they are intended to collaborate to achieve some behavior, then those two classes should be tested together. Again the specification should be used to generate scenarios which exercise normal and abnormal interactions. These scenarios can then be used to define tests to perform. Having tested the two classes other cooperations may be identified involving these and other classes. Each of these collaborations also needs to be tested.

Integration testing (like multiple method testing in a single class) relies on the identification of scenarios which will be used to define appropriate test suites. However, consideration should also be given to identifying anticipated message paths. The differences between these two tests are akin to black box and white box testing for a single method. The scenario based testing relies on testing the specification of the behavior of the collaborating objects, while the white box testing is intended to test particular message paths through the classes. Again, the two approaches to testing are intended to be used together.

23.3 System testing

System testing of Smalltalk systems should be carried out in essentially the same way as system testing of any computer system. This is because a system implemented in Smalltalk should be subject to the same types of requirements as a system written in any other language. There are some special situations which you might wish to test for, such as ensuring that the system does not run out of memory before a garbage collection is forced or that the system will still work once the image has been "stripped" of those classes not required by the production system (e.g. the compiler classes etc.). However, in general the system should be subject to the same range of tests as any other.

23.4 Self testing

An approach, suggested by Charles Weir of Object Designers Ltd., would be to provide facilities which enable code self-testing within Smalltalk. A simple technique is to make the code do its own self-testing using assertions. This is a code statement that is always true; it tests that the code is behaving as expected. If the statement is false the assertion stops processing to allow debugging.

An implementation of assertions in Smalltalk is

```
assert
        self value ifFalse: [self halt].
```

This method should be added to the `BlockContext` class and allows the developer to verify assertions wherever required, for example:

```
[range first == 1] assert.
```

Of course in the released version of the system, these tests are redundant and waste processing time. So they could be replaced by a null version of the method:

```
assert
        self.
```

The overhead of the extra method dispatch is relatively small; of course if it is still significant, we could write a utility to find the senders of the method and to comment out the assertion statements.

Assertions are particularly useful for testing preconditions, postconditions and class invariants. The Syntropy design method makes extensive use of such assertions [Cook and Daniels 1994]. It would therefore be possible to use the assertions identified during the design as the basis of the assertions to place in the Smalltalk code.

This approach could be taken further with the introduction of universal quantifiers (there exists and for all). This would allow expression such as if there exists a value x. The introduction of such quantifiers is not without its problems but should be possible. In addition assertions could also be used to ensure that the relationships between pre and post values during some operation is appropriate. Again this would not necessarily be straight forward, but it should be possible.

23.5 Summary

Throughout the chapter, guidance has been given to ways to overcome the problems inherent in testing object oriented systems. In the next chapter we shall consider a simple set of extensions to the basic VisualWorks environment which greatly simplify the whole testing process.

23.6 Further reading

As there is so little written about testing object oriented systems, this section provides an extended set of references on the subject.

In 1994 a special issue of the Communications of the ACM was published which focused on testing object oriented systems [Binder 1994]. In this special issue a number of papers cover topics related to object oriented testing. For example, [Binder 1994b] discusses design for testability in object oriented systems which is a particularly important issue given the effects of inheritance, polymorphism and particularly encapsulation on testing.

Other papers relevant to object oriented testing include [Beck 1994], [Hoffman and Strooper 1995], [Hunt 1995], [Jorgensen and Erickson 1994], [Siepmann and Newton 1994].

The workshops on testing held at the OOPSLA conferences are also a useful source of references. For example the workshop held as the OOPSLA '95 Conference. For more information contact Barbara Yates, OOPSLA Workshop, 2002 Parkside Court, West Linn, Oregon, 97068-2767, USA (Email: barbara.bytesmiths@acm.org).

A good discussion of incremental testing for C++ can be found in [Harrold, McGregor and Fitzpatrick 1992]. While [Feigenbaum 1995] discusses some of the features which could be introduced into Smalltalk which would improve its potential as a development language.

The Syntropy object oriented development method makes explicit use of assertions. This method is documented in [Cook and Daniels 1994].

There are also many references which discuss various aspects of testing which are as appropriate for object oriented systems as they are for procedural systems. For example, [Beizer 1990], [Freedman 1991], [Myers 1979], [Pyle 1991] and [ISO 1993].

24. Smalltalk Style Guidelines

24.1 Introduction

Good programming style in any language helps promote the readability, understandability and clarity of your code. In many languages there are established standards to which many people adhere (sometimes without realizing it). For example, the way in which a C or Pascal program is indented is such a standard. However, style guidelines which have evolved for these procedural languages do not cover many of the issues which are important in Smalltalk. These are issues relating to classes, instances and methods. As non-object oriented languages do not have these concepts, they do not have standards for dealing with them.

Of course you should not forget all the pearls of wisdom and programming practices that you have learnt using other languages. Just as in any other language there are a number of acknowledged bad practices (which are not specific to Smalltalk), for example, the use of global variables! In this chapter (as in the whole of the book) we will assume therefore that you do not need to have the basic concepts explained, instead we will try to concentrate on those style issues which are specific to Smalltalk.

The remainder of the chapter is structured in the following manner: Section two considers style issues associated with variables including temporary variables, instance variables as well as class, class instance and pool variables. Section three provides some guidance on the use of classes within Smalltalk. Section four considers methods, their naming, use and code placement within methods. Section five discusses how to name message protocols for both instance and class methods.

24.2 Variables

24.2.1 Naming variables

In Smalltalk variable names such as t1, i, j, or temp should rarely be used. Instead variable names should either be descriptive (known as semantic variables) or should indicate the type of object which the variable will hold (known as typed variables). Which approach should be chosen depends on both personal style and the situation in which the variables are being used. Instance and class variables, for example, tend to have semantic-oriented names, while parameters to methods often have typed names.

The semantic approach has the advantage that less needs to be assumed about what the variable will be used for. Since subclasses can inherit instance and class variables, the point at which they are defined and the point at which they are used may be very remote. Thus any contextual meaning and commentary, provided with their definition, will have been lost. Examples, of semantic variable names include:

```
score
currentWorkingMemory
TotalPopulationSize
```

The typed approach is often adopted for parameter names as it is easier to see what type of object is required as an argument to a method. For example:

```
add: anObject ifAbsent: aBlock
at: anIndex put: anObject
```

Although some methods mix the use of the two, for example: `at: key put: anObject`.

Temporary variables, which are local to a method, often have a mixture of semantic and typed names. Larger methods often have semantic local variable names due to the additional complexity they represent.

Table 24.1: Variable naming conventions

Variable type	Convention	Variable type	Convention
Global variable	Capitalized	Temporary variables	Lower case
Class variable	Capitalized	Class instance variables	Lower case
Class names	Capitalized	Instance variables	Lower case
Pool variables	Capitalized	Method parameters	Lower case

In addition, if the variable name is made up of more than one word, the words should not be separated by '-' or '_', but by the capitalization of the first letter of all but the first word. For example:

```
theDateToday
employeeRecord
objectInList
```

Whether the first word in the variable is capitalized or not depends on the type of variable being used. Table 24.1 summarizes the conventions.

24.2.2 The role of variables

Instance variables, class variables and class instance variables all play particular roles within a Smalltalk system:

Instance variables should only be used for holding local data or for holding references to other objects. In the latter case, these other objects should be involved in some form of collaboration with the object (otherwise why does the object have a reference to them).

Class variables should only be used as 'constant' values which are referenced by all instances of a class. They should never be used as a form of limited global variable. Such a use is frequently an indication that a solution has not been designed with the proper amount of care and attention. A very nice use of class variable can be found in the database classes of VisualWorks.

Class instance variables are often ignored by most Smalltalk programmers because they are not sure what to do with them. This is partly due to the lack of their use in much of the VisualWorks image and partly due to the rarity of occasions when their use is justified. A class instance variable, is a local variable for the class. They are only accessible by the class itself and each class will hold its own copy of the data.

Class instance variables should only be used when either:

- classes need to hold some local data which instances should not have access to (otherwise use a class variable)
- each class in a particular class hierarchy needs to hold its own copy of some data which should not be shared with other classes.

If you wish to see an example of their use look up `UILookPolicy` in the VisualWorks image.

24.2.3 The role of pool variables

Pool variables are global variables whose scope is limited to those classes which have (explicitly) joined the pool. They should not be used as a cheap way of sharing information amongst a disparate set of classes (for example as a means of providing a global variable without the stigma of a truly global variable). In general their use is really only justifiable within an application framework (a set of cooperating objects of different classes). Such frameworks often require some common shared values. For example, the text style to use in an application, the name of a preference file or the settings obtained from such a file. Pool variables can then be used to record this information once, but allow it to be used by all the objects within the framework.

24.2.4 Adding variables to system classes

Always add class and instance variables to the end of any existing variables in a system class. This is because the interpreter on some Smalltalk implementations accesses the variables of certain classes by *position* rather than by name!

24.2.5 Accessing instance and class variables

In general it is always better to access instance and class variables via intermediate methods, referred to as *accessor* methods, rather than access or set them directly. This is called *variable-free programming*. This promotes the modularity of your methods and insulates the methods against changes in the way the object (or class) holds instance (or class) information. This is a very important concept, as direct access to instance variables can limit the power of subclassing.

It is also possible to protect the instance (or class) variables from undesired changes. For example, you can put preconditions on an access method, or return a copy of the contents of the variable so that it cannot be directly affected.

24.3 Classes

24.3.1 Naming classes

The naming of a class is extremely important. The class is the core element in any object oriented program. Class names are always capitalized. For example:

- Collection
- GraphicalClassBrowser
- EmployeePensionPaymentsHistory

The second and third class names above provide extremely good examples of how a class name can describe the class. This is because the name of the class is used by most developers to indicate its purpose or intent. This is partly due to the fact that it is the class name which will be used when searching for appropriate classes (for example by using the **find class...** menu option).

The class name should therefore be descriptive, for example, classes with names such as MyClass or ProjectClass1 are of little use. However, class names should not be so specific that they make it appear that the class is unlikely to be of use except in one specific situation (unless of course this is the case). For example, in an application to record details about university lecturers, a class with a name such as ComputerScienceDepartmentLecturer is probably not appropriate unless it really does relate only to lecturers in the computer science department. If this is the case, you need to ask yourself in what way are computer science lecturers special over other lecturers.

24.3.2 The role of subclasses

A subclass should only be used to modify the behaviour of its parent class. This modification should be a refinement of the class; this can be accomplished in three ways (or in combination):

- Changes to the external protocol, that is the set of messages that the instances of the class respond to.
- Changes in the implementation of the methods, that is changes in the way the messages are handled.

• Additional behaviour, which references inherited behaviour.

If a subclass does not provide one or more of the above, then it is incorrectly placed. For example, if a subclass implements a set of new methods, but no reference is made to the parent classes' instance variables or methods, then this class is not really a subclass of the parent (it doesn't extend it).

The one exception to this rule are subclasses of Object. This is because Object is the root class of all classes in Smalltalk and as you must create a new class by subclassing it from an existing class, it is typical to subclass off Object when there is no existing appropriate class.

24.3.3 Capabilities of a subclass/class

A subclass or class should accomplish one specific purpose, that is it should capture only one idea. If more than one idea is encapsulated in a class you may be reducing the chances for reuse as well as contravening the laws of encapsulation in object oriented systems. For example, you may have merged two concepts together so that one can directly access the data of another. This is rarely desirable.

This guideline leads to small classes (in terms of methods, instance variables and code). Breaking a class down costs little but may produce major gains in reusability and flexibility. If you find that when you try and separate one class into two or more classes, some of the code needs to be duplicated for each class, then the use of abstract classes can also be very helpful. By placing the common code into a common abstract superclass, you may be able to avoid unnecessary duplication of that code.

The following two guidelines are intended as an aid in identifying when a class should be split:

1. Look in the class comment (if there is no class comment than this is a bad sign in itself). Consider the following points:

   • Is the comment short and clear. If not is this a reflection on the class? If it is, then consider how the comment can be broken down into a series of short clear comments. Now base the new classes around these comments.
   • If the comment is short and clear, do the class and instance variables make sense within the context of the comment? If they do not, then the class needs to re-evaluated. It may be that the comment is inappropriate, or the class and instance variables inappropriate.
   • If the comment is short and clear, do the class and instance methods make sense within the context of the comment? Again if they do not then appropriate action should be taken.
2. Look at the instance variable references (i.e. look at where the instance variable access methods are used). How are the instance variables being used? Is their use in line with the class comment? Again, if the answer to this is *no*, then appropriate action should be taken.

24.3.4 Changes to system classes

In general attempts should be made to avoid making changes to system classes if at all possible. Such changes can produce surprising side effects as well a reduce the portability of your code and others. In addition you may find it difficult to support the changes you have made to the system classes in future releases of the system.

However, there are certain circumstances in which it is necessary and useful to *extend* system classes. However, it is an extremely bad idea to modify an existing method of a system class. This is because if you are not absolutely sure about what you are doing you can affect the behaviour of very many objects. If you really feel you have to modify an existing class's method(s), then it is much better to subclass off the existing system class and modify the method(s) behaviour(s) there. Then if you do something which has unanticipated effects, those effects are localized.

If you are merely adding new methods to an existing system class, then it is a very good idea to place your additions in a separate category. This means that not only is it easier to find these additions, but that you can *file out* the category to a different file so that when updates to the system are delivered, you can easily patch in your extensions.

24.3.5 Creating new collection classes

When working with collections, there is always the question of whether to subclass a new collection class to hold your data (as we did for the Queue and Stack classes) or whether to define a non collection class which will hold a collection within one of its instance variables and then provide methods which will access that instance variable. For example, let us assume that we wish to define a new class called account, which will hold information on deposits and withdrawals. We believe that we should use a dictionary to hold the actual data, but should Account be a subclass of Dictionary or a subclass of something else (for example Object)? The two options are illustrated below:

```
Object
     Account has in an instance variable holding an instance of class Dictionary
```

or would it be better to have:

```
Object
     Dictionary
          Account
```

Of course this point also depends on what you are going to do with the Account class. If it is providing a new collection class (in some way) even if it is only for your application, then the above should be born in mind. However, if what you are actually doing, is providing a functionally complex class which just happens to contain a dictionary, then the above would be the wrong way to do it. In this case it is almost certainly better to make the new class a subclass of Object.

There are two further points to bear in mind about this. The first is that if you define any instance variables in `Account`, then when you examine any instance of `Account` you will find that you get the `Dictionary` inspector which does not display the instance variables. This can be quite infuriating. Of course you can subclass the inspector and extend it so that it does display the instance variables. A second point is that if an instance of `Account` needs to grow, then the contents of the instance variables defined in `Account` will apparently *disappear*, unless you extend the `copyEmpty` method it will have inherited. This method must be extended such that the contents of the instance variables is copied. Again, this is only a minor point, but can be extremely annoying when you have spent a great deal of time attempting to track down a *bizarre* bug, only to find this is the root cause of your problem.

24.3.6 Class comments

Every class should have a class comment, no matter whether it is an abstract or concrete class. This comment should act as the basic documentation for the class. It should therefore tell both a developer subclassing from the class, or a user of the class, what they need to know. The comment may also contain information about the author's name, affiliation, history of the class's modifications, as well as its purpose and status. Information which might be placed in the class comment includes the name of the class author, its purpose, who has modified the class, when and why, the type of class, instance and class variables (including the class of object they will hold and their use), collaborations between this class and others, example usage, copyright information and class specific information such as what a subclass of an abstract class is expected to redefine.

24.3.7 A class or an instance

In some situations it may only ever be necessary to create a single instance of a class. This single instance must be created and then referenced where it is required. A point of continued debate is whether it is worth creating such an instance or whether it is better to define the required behaviour in class methods and reference the class (after all a class is an object as well). Invariably the answer to this is no, for the following reasons:

- Such an approach breaks the standards which have been set, not only in the VisualWorks image, but by the majority of Smalltalk developers. You will therefore be reducing the readability and comprehensibility of your system.
- The creation of an instance requires a minimum of overhead. After all this is a key feature in Smalltalk and it has therefore received extensive attention.
- You may require more than one instance sometime in the future. If you have implemented all the code on the class side, it will be necessary to move these methods onto the instance side of the class.
- In doing so, you may be tempted to treat the class as a global reference. This suggests that the implementation has been poorly thought out.

24.4 Methods

24.4.1 Naming methods

Method names should always start with a lower case letter. If the method name is made up of more than one element then each element following the first one, should start with a capital letter. This standard follows that used for variable names. For example:

```
account deposit: 100
account printStatement.
```

If the method is a keyword method containing more than one parameter, then each of the key words should start with a lower case letter, with each subsequent word starting with a capital letter. For example:

```
Dialog request: 'Name' initialAnswer: 'John'
                   onCancel: [Transcript show: 'Error'].
```

The naming of methods is extremely important. An appropriate method name will not only make the code easier to read it will also aid in reuse. Therefore method names should be selected to illustrate the method's purpose. In addition, it is common to try to select a name which makes it possible to read an expression containing the method name in a similar manner to reading a sentence . For example:

```
statement deposit: 100 on: Date today.
```

This is actually helped by the ability to spread the arguments amongst the method name.

Methods which return *true* and *false* as the result of some test follow a common format throughout the Smalltalk system. These methods use a verb such as *is* or *has* concatenated with whatever is being tested, for example :

```
isString
isActive
hasFood
```

Notice that in the first case the method is testing to see if the receiver is an object of class String. It therefore uses the name of the class in the method name. In the next two cases some aspect of the receiver is being tested. For example, the second method may test to see if a process is active or not. In this case, the value being tested for is used as part of the method name.

24.4.2 General comments about methods

In general it is better to percolate a method up as high as possible in the inheritance hierarchy as long as it makes sense. The higher the method is, the more visibility it has to classes in other branches of the hierarchy, and the more method level reuse you can achieve. You should also consider:

The role of a method. Think carefully about the purpose and placement of methods within a class. Just as a class should have a specific purpose, at a lower level a method should also have a single purpose. If a method is used to perform more than one function, then it should be divided into separate methods. In general terms methods should be no longer than one page of A4. Small but beautiful methods are desirable.

Code placement within methods. Deciding how to break up the desired functionality into procedural elements can be difficult in procedural programming languages. In Smalltalk it is made more difficult by considerations of object encapsulation and reuse. However, there are a number of questions which you can bear in mind when determining whether your code is correctly placed within the methods you have defined:

- If a method does not refer to any aspect of the object (e.g. super, self, or instance variables etc.) what is it doing? Should the method be there?
- A method should only send messages to a limited set of objects. This promotes maintainability and comprehensibility and increases the modularity of the method.
- Have you used accessor methods for instance variable access? This is known as *variable-free programming*. This can greatly insulate the method from changes in how the object holds information.
- Is the behaviour encapsulated by the method intended for public or private (to the object) use? If it is a mixture of the two, then the method should be decomposed into two or more methods. The private code should be placed in a method which is defined within a private protocol (see below). This indicates to developers that the method is not intended for external use.
- Does the method rely more on the behaviour of other objects than on its own object (that is, a series of messages is being sent to some object(s) other than "self")? If so, the method may be better placed in another object (or objects).

This last point is worth considering in slightly more detail. The series of messages in such a method may be better placed in a method in the class of the receiver object. This is because it is really describing behaviour associated with that object. By placing it with the receiver object's class, all modifications to the behaviour of the receiver are encapsulated in that object. In addition, this behaviour may be useful to other objects, by encoding it within the receiver's class, they can all gain access to that behaviour (rather than having to duplicate it in a number of places). It is not easy to get good method level code reuse with poorly placed code. To do this most messages should be sent to self. Note: This is probably one of the hardest things to do well in object oriented programming. However, if done correctly it can pay very high dividends.

248

24.4.3 Class methods versus instance methods

It may at first seem unclear what should normally go in a class (side) method as opposed to what should go in an instance (side) method when defining a new class. After all they are both defined in the class! However, it is important to remember that one defines the behaviour of the instance and the other the behaviour of the class (the class side methods). The class side methods should only perform one of the following roles:

Instance creation. This role is very important as it is often used to initialize instance variables of an object to appropriate values. For example, it is quite common to see a class side method called new used to send the message initialize to a new instance.

Class variable access. See below for a discussion of this role.

Inquiries about the class. Such methods answer with generally useful objects, frequently derived from class variables. For example, they may return the number of instances of this object created.

Instance management. To control the number of instances created. For example, some classes only allow one single instance of that class to be created.

A documentation role. Class methods solely for documentation are sometimes used. Generally the class **comment** is a better place for this information unless such a facility is not available e.g. in Smalltalk V.

Examples. Occasionally class methods are used to provide helpful examples which are aimed at explaining the operation of a class. This is good practice.

Testing. Class side methods can be used to support testing of an instance of a class. Such methods can be used to create an instance, perform some operation and then compare the result with a known value. If the values are different an error can be reported. This is a very useful way of providing regression tests.

Support for one of the above.

Anything else should be performed by an instance method.

24.4.4 Class instance creation methods

It is quite common to want to redefine the way in which a new instance is created. This can be because you wish to:

- provide a more meaningful instance creation interface (for example, Line from: (3 @ 3) to: (5 @ 5))
- ensure that certain information is provided which is necessary to instantiate the class (for example Account newBalance: 24.00)
- force an initialization routine to be executed before any user of the object can send it any other messages.

We shall consider the correct way to achieve the last of the above points. That is, we wish to force the execution of an initialization method before returning the newly created instance. To do this we can redefine the message new in the instance creation class side protocol of a class as follows:

new
```
^super new initialize
```

This method says, use the inherited method new to create a new instance of the class and immediately send that new instance the instance message initialize (this is extremely good Smalltalk style). In turn, the initialize method (defined on the class side) should have a format which follows this pattern:

initialize
```
super initialize "to initialize inherited instance variables"
"initialize variables that I define"
```

24.4.5 Programming in terms of objects

It is all too easy when you are first starting with Smalltalk to write procedure oriented code within methods. Indeed, in version 1.0 of VisualWorks there was code which had clearly been written by a C or C++ programmer rather than a Smalltalk developer. In such situations the developer has been thinking in too procedurally a manner. In Smalltalk what the programmer should try to do is to think in terms of objects.

24.4.6 Example methods

Example methods are class side methods which illustrate how the instances of an object should be used. They are particularly useful for complex classes which form part of a framework. In these classes it is often difficult to comprehend how the various classes work together, without seeing them work together. The example methods can then be filed out in a production system as they are not required for the correct functioning of the class.

24.4.7 Test methods

These have already been mentioned above and were discussed at length in the last few chapters. However, they are an extremely useful tool for the developer and should be encouraged at every opportunity.

24.5 Naming message protocols

An important style consideration for any VisualWorks developer is the naming of protocols (or message categories). It is a good idea to follow the conventions laid down in the existing classes for two reasons:

1. your own classes will follow the same pattern as those which have already been encountered and will thus be easier to follow for you and others
2. tools such as the Full Browser will allow you to see methods, defined in other classes higher up the class hierarchy, in a given category. When you want to name a new category you can search for similar methods, when you find them you can merely use the same category name.

Table 24.2: Class message categories

Protocol	Use
instance creation	Used for methods associated with creating instances
class initialization	Methods which initialize class variables
examples	Methods which illustrate some use of the class, e.g. instance creation
private	Methods that provide support for one of the above

Table 24.2 illustrates the common class message protocols and what they are used for. Table 24.3 does the same thing for the instance message protocols. Notice the practice of naming instance message protocols as actions. These actions are intended to indicate the type of activity being performed. An exception to this is the initialize (or its variant initialize-release) protocol. Although this does not conform to the standard it is consistent throughout the VisualWorks image and you are therefore advised to comply with this exception.

Table 24.3: Instance message categories

Category	Use
accessing	Methods used for accessing and updating instance variables.
adding	Used in collection classes for methods which add elements to the collection.
converting	Holds methods which convert one instance into another instance.
comparing	Groups methods used for comparison tests.
displaying	Holds methods which relate to displaying information graphically
initialize	Holds methods which initialize the instance.
printing	Methods associated with printing the instance such as printString
updating	Used to hold methods which cause some change in the instances state.

24.6 Further reading

There are a number of places which can provide very useful further reading, for example [Skublics *et al* 1996] is an excellent little book which really does provide pearls of wisdom on good Smalltalk style. It is a book to be dipped into, rather than read from cover to cover. However, if you do manage to inwardly digest this book, you will be able to write clear, concise, reusable Smalltalk. In addition many of the core system classes also provide excellent examples of the good Smalltalk style.

Graphical interfaces
in Smalltalk

25. The Perform and Dependency Mechanisms

25.1 Introduction

This chapter introduces the use of the perform mechanism which provides an alternative method for sending messages. It then presents a practical discussion of the dependency mechanism. This includes what the dependency mechanism is, why you might want to use it, how to construct a dependency and the effect that it has.

25.2 The Perform mechanism

The perform mechanism is a very important feature of Smalltalk. Some people consider it to be the most powerful feature available to the developer while others consider it essential for the construction of truly reusable classes (it should be noted however than many others consider it a very bad feature!). Those of you who have been exposed to languages such as Common LISP or POP11 will not find this concept too strange, however those of you who have been brought up on languages such as Pascal and ADA may find the perform mechanism horrifying at first glance. As with most language constructs it can be very useful if used judiciously.

Normally, when a message is to be sent to an object, it is specified by the programmer when they write the method. For example:

```
myMethod: anObject
    Transcript show: anObject printString.
```

In this example, I have specified that first the object contained in the temporary variable anObject will be sent the message printString and that the result of this message expression will be used as a parameter with the message show: to the object Transcript. This is all perfectly normal.

However, in some cases the programmer may not know what messages the object passed to them may respond to, or they may not know what type of message should be sent. This may well be the case with a generalist class which is intended to act as some sort of framework which will be reused and customized by the users of the class.

One way around this problem would be to specify that the user of the class should write their own method (e.g. by using a subclass responsibility message) or should modify the current method specifying what the message should actually be. This second approach, (which would be the case, if we know what the method should do, but were lacking the name of one particular message to send to one particular object), is not really desirable.

In some cases, even the person reusing the class may not know what the message to send is; it may only be possible to determine that at *run time*. To get around this, a programmer might have to write a large case-style statement, which tested the object to see what type it was, and then selected the appropriate message to send depending on that type. Again, this is not really desirable as the number of possibilities may be large and each time a new message was used, the programmer would have to update the method accordingly.

Smalltalk provides a way around this which is referred to as the perform mechanism. The `perform:` message (and those associated with it) can be used to request that an object receive a message which is contained within a variable. For example:

```
anObject perform: someMessage.
```

In this example, the object `anObject` is specified to receive a message `perform:` with a single parameter. This parameter will be the contents of the *variable* `someMessage`. Thus at compile time, we cannot tell from this line alone, what action the object will perform. The mechanism essentially allows the method name, as well as the object, to be held in a variable. For example,

```
aVariable := #size.
aCollection perform: aVariable.
```

is equivalent to:

```
aCollection size.
```

The contents of the variable passed with the `perform:` message must be a symbol, otherwise an error will be generated. It must also be a legal message otherwise an error will also be generated. For example, if the variable contained the symbol #abcd, then that would be equivalent to evaluating `aCollection abcd`. Unless this message is defined for this class of object, then the message will generate a "not understood" exception (whether it is sent directly or as part of a perform message).

The perform mechanism can also handle methods which take arguments. The arguments are handled by different versions of the perform: message:

1. for methods with one argument use `perform:with:`
2. for methods with two arguments use `perform:with:with:`
3. for methods with three arguments use `perform:with:with:with:`
4. for methods with more than three arguments use `perform:withArguments:` where the arguments are assumed to be in an array.

For example,

```
anObject perform: aSymbol with: anotherObject.
anObject perform: aSymbol with: object1 with: object2.
anObject perform: aSymbol with: object1 with: object2 with: object3.
anObject perform: aSymbol withArguments: aCollection
```

Note that the symbol held in aSymbol will be the message selector name. That is, if the message to be sent would normally be written as:

```
anObject at: 2 out: 5.
```

then with the perform mechanism this would be written as:

```
aSymbol := #at:put:
object1 := 2.
object2 := 5.
anObject perform: aSymbol with: object1 with: object2.
```

The perform mechanism is very powerful and provides a great deal of flexibility. However, in most normal situations you should not need to use it. Indeed, there are a number of points to remember when thinking about using the perform mechanism. The first is that it is less efficient than directly sending a message to an object. The second is that it can be more difficult to maintain as it is not immediately obvious what message is being sent to the object. Thirdly, it can be an awful lot harder to debug code containing perform: messages. This is because the system back trace displayed in the debugger may not display the same chain of message sends that the user of the class expects.

So where should you use it? The situations where you are likely to encounter it are almost all associated with the user interface. However, you should not try to avoid it just because it may be less efficient at run time and more difficult to debug. There may be situations in which the perform mechanism can allow the construction of very powerful and flexible frameworks. The important point to note is that in this situation there may be a trade off between flexibility and efficiency.

25.3 The Dependency mechanism

There are a number of different relationships between objects in the Smalltalk environment which we have already looked at. In particular we have considered:

- Inheritance (class to class relationships)
- Instantiation (class to instance)
- Part of or contains (instance to instance relationships)

However, there is another important relationship supported by Smalltalk, this is the dependency relationship. This is where the state or behavior of one object is dependent on the state of another object. For example, Figure 25.1 indicates that there are a set of dependency relationships between the objects A to F.

257

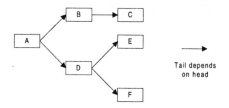

Figure 25.1: Dependency between objects

This figure illustrates that object A is dependent on some aspect of objects B and D. In turn object B is dependent on some aspect of object C and so on.

In Smalltalk dependency is a relationship which can be used to relate two objects such that, as the state of one changes, the state of another automatically changes in an appropriate manner. In such a relationship we say that one object is dependent upon another.

25.3.1 Why do we want it?

The reasons for dependency are all down to *change*. That is, we wish to communicate the fact that one object has changed its value to another object which may be interested in either the fact of the change or the new value effected by the change. The dependency mechanism provides a way of communicating such events in a generic implementation independent manner.

An obvious question is "why not just get an object to send messages to those interested in it?" The answer to this is that if you know what objects you want to send messages to, then do so. However, if all you know is that sometime, at a later date, some object may need to know something about the state of an object (but at present we don't know what that other object might be) then we cannot arrange to send messages to that object - because we don't know what it will be. However, the dependency mechanism allows any object (whose class is a subclass of Object) to be involved in a dependency. A second advantage is that we don't have to know about the objects interested in the object we are working on. All we need to know is that it might be.involved in a dependency relationship and we can let the (hidden) dependency mechanism take care of informing these unknown objects about the updates.

25.3.2 How does it work?

As is hinted at in the above section, the dependency mechanism is implemented in the class Object. This of course means that, as all classes in Smalltalk are subclasses of Object, all objects can be involved in a dependency. You can browse the Object class to explore the dependency mechanism. If you use the implementors option off the message window menu you will find that some of the messages are redefined lower down in the class hierarchy. This is purely for internal efficiency or specific implementation reasons - you will still use the mechanism in the same way.

The basic implementation, inherited from `Object`, associates a collection of other objects with an object. This collection holds the objects which are dependent on the object (collectively these objects are known as the objects dependents). For example, in Figure 25.2 the object `ObjectA` has two dependents `ObjectB` and `ObjectC`. The links to the dependent objects are held separately from `ObjectA` in a dependents list. `ObjectA` can access this list via the message dependents.

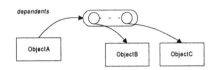

Figure 25.2: An object and its dependents

The message `dependents` can be used to obtain a list of all the dependents of an object (no matter what the class of the object). For example, to obtain a list of the dependents on `ObjectA` we could use:

```
ObjectA dependents.
```

From the point of view of the actual implementation, the dependents are sometimes held in an instance variable inherited from above (so you can see it in an inspector). This is the case for most of the user interface classes. In other cases the dependents list is held as part of an `IdentityDictionary` in a class variable (this is the default mechanism inherited from `Object`).

25.3.3 Constructing dependencies

The `addDependent:` message is used to add an object to another object's dependency list. For example, we can construct the above dependencies using:

```
ObjectA addDependent: ObjectB.
ObjectA addDependent: ObjectC.
```

Note that an object holds (or can access) a list of objects which depend on it. Whereas an object cannot access information about the objects on which it depends. For example, there are no references from `ObjectB` or `ObjectC` back to `ObjectA` in Figure 25.2. Thus an object does not hold a list of objects on which it depends. This may seem a bit strange at first, however, once you gain an understanding of how the dependency mechanism works, hopefully you will see why things are this way round.

It is also possible to remove dependencies once they have been created. This can be done using the `removeDependent:` message. For example:

```
ObjectA removeDependent: ObjectB.
```

This removes `ObjectB` from the dependency list of `ObjectA`. It should be noted that as an `IdentityDictionary` is used (at least in objects which are instances of classes below `Object`), `ObjectB` must be the same object as was used to create the dependency. It cannot be merely equivalent.

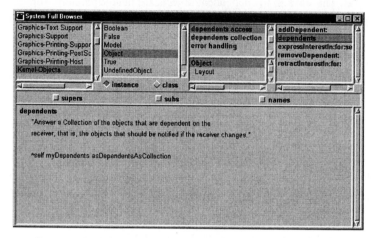

Figure 25.3: The dependents message defined in Object

You can find the methods which implement `dependents`, `addDependent:` and `removeDependent:` all defined in the class `Object` in the *dependents access* protocol (as illustrated in Figure 25.3). Browse these methods yourself, they will help you to understand how the dependency mechanism works.

25.3.4 A simple dependency example

This subsection presents a very simple dependency example, which we will develop further during the chapter. It creates two objects and creates a dependency between them. The objects are instances of a class `DataObject` and `DependentObject`. These classes are direct subclasses of `Object`. Create the classes placing them in an appropriate class category (for example, *dependency demo*). For example:

```
Object subclass: #DataObject
    instanceVariableNames: ''
    classVariableNames: ''
    poolDictionaries: ''
    category: 'dependency demo'
```

Then evaluate the following in a Workspace:

```
| temp1 temp2 |
temp1 := DataObject new.
temp2 := DependentObject new.
temp1 addDependent: temp2.
Transcript show: (temp1 dependents) printString.
temp1 inspect.
```

The result of the show message expression, printed in the Transcript, is:

260

Notice that, although the dependentObject instance was printed in the Transcript, no dependents can be found for the dataObject in the inspector. Indeed no instance variable called dependents can be found at all.

From the point of view of the class DataObject, dependency is an invisible mechanism which works behind the scenes. Of course, this is not really the case. The dependency mechanism has been inherited from Object and is implemented via message sends and method executions just like any behavior provided by an object.

25.3.5 Making dependency work for you

We have now considered how we construct a dependency relationship. However, we want this relationship to be used to inform the dependent object(s) that a change has occurred in the object on which they depend. That is, we want to tell one object that another object, has changed in some way.

To do this we use two sets of methods. One set is used to state that something has changed. These are called "changed" methods. The other set are used to state what type of update is required. These are called "update" methods. They work as illustrated in Figure 25.4.

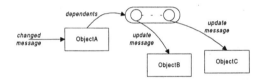

Figure 25.4: The dependency mechanism in action

Figure 25.4 illustrates the sequence of messages which are sent in response to a change message being sent to an object. That is, when ObjectA is sent a changed message (usually by itself) all its dependents are sent an update message. Again from the point of view of ObjectA much of this behavior is hidden. In fact so much so that a point of confusion relates to the sending of one message (i.e. the changed message) and the execution of another method (i.e. the update method). That is, a programmer defining Objects A, B and C will:

1. send a changed message to ObjectA
2. define an update method in ObjectB and ObjectC.

The confusion here stems from the need to send one message but define another. However, if you think about how you are linking into the existing dependency framework, it can make more sense. Essentially the change message is a message to the dependency mechanism asking it to notify the object's dependents about a change. The dependency mechanism is inherited and is generic across applications. However, there is no way that the system developers could know when the change message should be sent. That is application specific. It is therefore the application developer's responsibility to send the changed message. For example, you may only want dependents to get told of certain changes, such as updates to only one field on an input screen etc.

In turn, there is no way that the system developers could have known how you would want the dependents to update themselves. The update message could indicate that the new value produced by the originating object should be displayed, that some calculation should be re-performed, or that a database should be accessed. In fact in the default implementation, inherited from Object, the update methods do nothing. They are only there so that an error is not generated if a message is sent to an object which does not have a new update method defined for it.

In the simple ObjectA, ObjectB and ObjectC example above, we would need to specify what ObjectB and ObjectC should do when ObjectA changed. This would require defining our own update methods.

25.3.6 The "changed" methods

There are three different changed messages which take zero, one or two parameters. They are:

```
anObject changed: anAspect with: aParameter.
anObject changed: anAspect.
anObject changed.
```

The first point to note about the changed messages are that they are sent to the object which has changed in some way. That is, they are used to inform the object that a change has taken place to it and that this change should be passed onto any dependents it may have. That is, the changed message does not effect the change, nor is it sent to the objects which wish to be notified about the change, rather it is telling the changed object that it should notify the dependency mechanism of the change.

Each of the three messages will trigger off the update part of the dependency mechanism. The only difference between the messages relates to the amount of information provided. The first message can be used to not only tell the dependent objects what aspect of the object changed but also what the new value produced by the change was. For example, the aspect that has been modified might be an instance variable and the parameter the new value of the instance variable. In turn the second message only tells the dependents what aspect has changed, while the third only informs the dependents that some change has taken place. Therefore the simplest changed message (and the one with the least information) is the changed message. This can be useful when you want to make sure that the dependents assume nothing about the object to which the change is happening.

A point to note is that the way that these messages are implemented is that the changed method calls the changed: method with nil as a parameter. In turn this method calls the changed:with: method with the parameter passed to it and a nil parameter. Thus if you wish to modify the way that the dependency mechanism works, the changed side is encapsulated within the changed:with: method.

25.3.7 The "update" methods

There are three different versions of the update messages which take one, two or three parameters. They are:

```
update: anAspect with: aParameter from: anObject
update: anAspect with: aParameter
update: anAspect
```

These messages are sent automatically by the dependency mechanism in response to a changed message being sent to the object, on which the object they are sent to depends. That is, if ObjectA is sent a changed message, one of the above will be sent to ObjectB. Which message *appears* to be sent depends on which method has been defined in ObjectB. This is because the method calling process is implemented such that the first message sent to the object will be update:with:from:. Unless this is overwritten, this method calls update:with:. In turn the update:with: method calls the update: method. This method by default does nothing. Therefore, if you define any one of these three methods, that method will be executed.

This means that the developer can decide how much information the dependent object wishes to work with. The parameter values that the developer can work with are:

- *anAspect* the value used for anAspect in the changed message or nil.
- *aParameter* the value used for aParameter in the changed message or nil.
- *anObject* the object which received the changed message.

25.3.8 Extending the dependency example

This section will provide an example of how the dependency mechanism works. We shall use the DataObject and DependentObject classes defined back in section 25.3.4.

The first thing we shall do is to define a couple of instance variables in DataObject. These variables will be age, name and address. For example:

```
Object subclass: #DataObject
    instanceVariableNames: 'age name address '
    classVariableNames: ''
    poolDictionaries: ''
    category: 'dependency demo'
```

Next we shall define an updater method for each of these instance variables. For example, in Figure 25.5, we have defined a new method age: which sets the age instance variable. It then informs the object that we have changed its age and that this fact should be passed onto its dependents (i.e. self changed: #age). This is a typical usage of a changed message. That is, it is sent to self informing self about the change which has taken place. It is very poor style to have one object send an instance of DataObject the message age:, followed by the changed message!

Next we shall define how an instance of DependentObject should respond to the change in a DataObject. That is we will define one of the update methods. The method we will define is the update: method. This method is placed in a protocol called *updating*. The actual method is illustrated in Figure 25.6. As this is just a simple example, all that this does is to print a string in the Transcript which illustrates the change which has occurred to a DataObject instance.

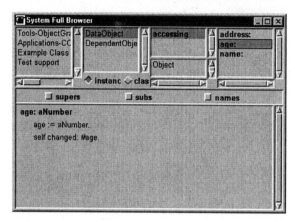

Figure 25.5: Defining an updater for age

We are now ready to try out this simple example. To do this we will use the source code previously typed into the Transcript (minus the last inspect statement). To this we will add three statements which set the dataObject's age, name and address:

```
| temp1 temp2 |
temp1 := DataObject new.
temp2 := DependentObject new.
temp1 addDependent: temp2.
Transcript show: (temp1 dependents) printString.
temp1 age: 32.
temp1 name: 'John'.
temp1 address: 'C47'.
```

The result of evaluating this code, is that the following statements are printed in the Transcript:

```
#(a DependentObject)
The object I am dependent on has changed its #age
The object I am dependent on has changed its #name
The object I am dependent on has changed its #address
```

Notice that the dependentObject has been informed of the changes to the dataObject's age, name and address, even though we have not defined a method which does this directly.

264

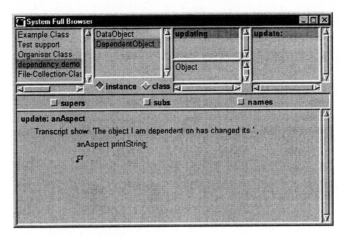

Figure 25.6: Defining the update: method in DependentObject

25.3.9 Discussion

In the simple example presented in section 25.3.8, you should note (and understand) the following points:

1. In DataObject we did not have a reference to, nor did we know anything about, a DependentObject.
2. The DependentObject does not reference a DataObject anywhere internally.
3. The link between temp1 and temp2 was made externally to either object.

It should also be noted that it can be more difficult to debug and maintain relationships which have been implemented using the dependency mechanism (as the message chain is partly hidden from the developer). Therefore care should again be exercised in its use.

25.4 Summary

This chapter has introduced the perform mechanism and the dependency mechanism. The former is relatively straight forward but should be used with care. The latter is more complex, but extensive use is made of it by the user interface classes. You should therefore gain some experience in using it. For example, have a go at modifying the FinancialManager example, add a monitor class which will send the user a message if their bank balance dips below a certain threshold.

26. The Model-View-Controller Architecture

26.1 Introduction

The Model-View-Controller architecture (more commonly known as the MVC) is an oft misunderstood part of Smalltalk. It is the basis upon which the user interface to a system is constructed. Its influence has been so great that numerous other system builders have based their user interface facilities upon it. Indeed so all pervading has the MVC been that at a recent conference an American computer science professor queried whether VisualWorks and Smalltalk was only a user interface development environment!

One of the causes of the confusion surrounding the MVC is that conceptually it is a simple architecture, but in practice it is rather more complicated. Indeed the construction of a good graphic interface, using the MVC, is rather more of an art than a science. There are very many classes involved, which must work together in specific ways. This chapter therefore provides a basic introduction to the MVC. For a detailed understanding of the classes available and how they should be used, the reader is directed to their system manuals and the books listed at the end of this chapter.

The situation is not as bad as it seems however, as many developers will never need to use the MVC. This is because of the user interface building facilities provided by tools such as VisualWorks and Window Builder (for Smalltalk/V). These tools provide interactive drawing tools which allow the user to construct certain types of graphical interface without the need for complex programming. However, these tools build on the basic MVC architecture therefore it is useful to understand at least the basic theory. In addition, in some circumstances, it is necessary to fall back on more basic techniques (especially for highly graphic displays).

26.2 The MVC architecture principles

The Model-View-Controller architecture, often known just by the letters MVC, has been a feature of Smalltalk since Smalltalk-80. It is based on the concept of separating out an application from its user interface. This means that different interfaces can be used with the same application, without the application knowing about it (see Figure 26.1). The intention is that any part of the system can be changed without affecting the operation of the other. For example, in the figure, the way that the graphical interface displays the information could be changed without modifying the actual application or the textual interface. Indeed the application need not know what type of interface is currently connected to it at all.

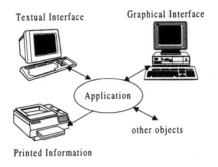

Figure 26.1: Splitting the interface

The intention of the MVC architecture is to separate the user interface from the underlying information model. There are a number of reasons why this is useful:

- reusability of application and / or user interface components,
- ability to develop the application and user interface separately,
- ability to inherit from different parts of the class hierarchy.

In fact, in the MVC, the user interface is further subdivided into the output (to the screen) part and the input (from the user) part. This enables different output elements (look) to be connected with different input elements (feel). Each part of the MVC therefore attempts to provide the functionality required by one of these three areas.

26.2.1 The structure of the MVC

The MVC is actually made up of three cooperating components. These three components are known as the Model, the View and the Controller. These three components are illustrated in Figure 26.2 and are collectively known as the MVC triad.

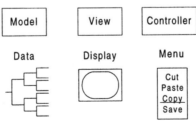

Figure 26.2: The use of the MVC

This division of responsibility in the MVC is broken down in the following way:

- **Model** - The information model which handles data storage and information processing. That is, it manages the behaviour of the data in the application domain.
- **View** - Which handles the visual display (the output part). That is, it handles how the information about the application is displayed on the screen.
- **Controller** - This provides the user interaction to, or control of, the information models processing (the input part). That is, it handles the mouse and keyboard inputs.

The diagram in Figure 26.2 illustrates the idea behind each aspect of the MVC. To use the MVC architecture you must understand the division of labor within the MVC triad. However, you should be aware that in real applications, this division of labor is not always as clean as it should be. For example, controller like behaviour can leak into the view object, while view like behaviour can leak into the controller object!

In addition, you must also understand how the three elements communicate (even if you are using one of the window building tools). Of course in any application there are many objects which aren't models (or which are contained within the *model* but don't realize that they are part of a model or a graphical system). However, they invariably work with the *model* to provide the overall application.

26.2.2 The elements in the MVC triad

26.2.2.1 Models

As has already been stated a model handles data storage and information processing. That is, it handles how the application data is processed (i.e. the functionality of the system). That means that models are responsible for holding data, operating on that data and responding to requests for information. Essentially, they are exactly what you have already been looking at throughout this book: "they are one or more objects which provide some set of operations". For example, the Statement class in the financial manager application, which you have encountered a number of times in this book, could be considered to be a model. It held information on deposits and withdrawals. It responded to new deposits and withdrawals and requests for the current balance. It could therefore be used with a view and a controller as part of a graphic application.

In some versions of Smalltalk (for example VisualWorks) there is an explicit class Model from which models can inherit model like behaviour. Figure 26.3 illustrates part of the Model class hierarchy. It illustrates that classes such as Browser and Inspector are actually models, which hold some data. However, there is no reason why an object which will be used as part of the MVC triad must be a subclass of Model.

The important point to note about an object, which will be used as a model within the MVC, is that it must provide the application functionality independent of the type of user interface being used (ignore the issue of printing the statement in the financial manager example here). In earlier chapters, we explicitly sent messages to the financial manager application via the Workspace. However, these messages could have been sent by another object, such as a banking system object, or by a controller or view object.

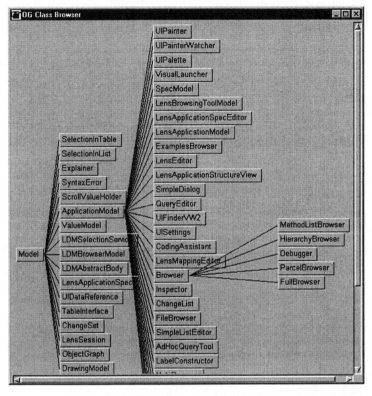

Figure 26.3: Part of the Model class hierarchy

26.2.2.2 Views

The information held by the model is presented to a user via a view. That is, a view obtains information from the model and decides how to present that information to the user. This can be in the form of text, graphics, widgets, or combinations of these etc. However, an important point to note is that the view should not possess any knowledge of what the data means, neither should it change it, initiate some application process because of it, or process it (other than what is necessary for the user interface). Notice that it is the view that decides how the data should be displayed independently of the model.

The result of this is that we could have one view which displays the balance after each transaction as a table, and another as a graph. Depending on which view we connect to the model, we will get a different user interface. However, we will not have had to change the model at all.

Figure 26.4 illustrates part of the View class hierarchy. This hierarchy illustrates how the various elements typically found in a graphical interface are different types of view. For example, a RadioButtonView is a subclass of LabelledButtonView, which in turn is a subclass of BasicButtonView, which is a subclass of SimpleView, which is a direct subclass of View. Similarly ScrollBar, MenuItemView and LauncherView are all direct subclasses of View. This figure also illustrates one of the interesting facilities in VisualWorks. Consider the CheckButtonView class and its subclasses. This class has five subclasses including MacCheckButtonView, Win3CheckButtonView and MotifCheckButtonView. In this case when a user requests that a CheckButtonView is created, one of its subclasses will be used depending on the user interface look requested by the user. For example, either an Apple Macintosh, Windows 3 or X/Motif style button will be displayed. Here different views can be used, without any modification of the model or the associated controller.

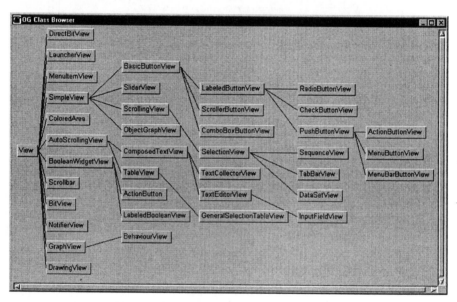

Figure 26.4: Part of the View class hierarchy

26.2.2.3 Controllers

Controllers handle the user interaction with the application. They work in tandem with the view so that when a user clicks on a button (displayed by a view) the controller can decide what to do. For example, the controller can ask the view to confirm that the cursor was within the active area of the button and then call the method associated with that button. That is, when the button is "pressed", the controller will ensure that the appropriate method is evaluated.

As was said earlier, all views have an associated controller (even if it is an instance of the NoController class). Therefore, in many situations there are controller classes available which mirror the view classes. For example, there is a MenuButtonController (to go with the MenuButtonView), there is a ScrollBarController (to go with the ScrollBar view) and there are various ButtonControllers. The StandardSystemController and the ApplicationStandardSystemController are used with the top most application view while many of the other controllers are used to handle input and output for small subviews (such as buttons).

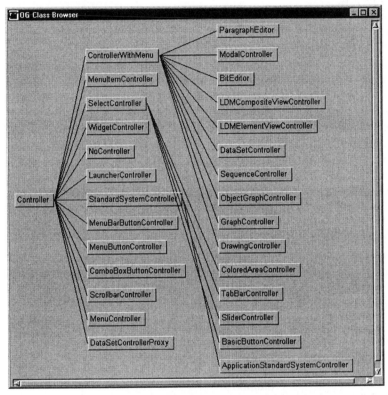

Figure 26.5: Part of the Controller class hierarchy

It might seem understandable that the model should be separated out from the user interface, but why is the input separated from the output? This is for two reasons:

- Firstly, it allows the controllers and the views to inherit from different class hierarchies. This allows the developer to overcome the limitation of single inheritance enforced by Smalltalk (but not all object oriented languages).
- Secondly, it allows different combinations of views and controllers. This may give different looks (views) or feels (controllers).

26.2.3 How the MVC works

You may notice that in Figure 26.6 the arrows only point from the view and controller to the model. There are no arrows from the model back to the view or controller. This is because the model does not directly know anything about its view or controller. This is partly because it does not need to know anything about them and also because it enforces this separation. A common mistake for those new to the MVC is to find that they have created instance variables in their model object which allow them to link the model directly to the view and/or controller. This is *extremely* poor Smalltalk style!

So how do the view and the controller find out about changes in the model. Remember, the view bases what it displays on the data held within the information model. In terms of Smalltalk relationships this means that the view is a *dependent* of the model (see last chapter). The view, must therefore, record itself as a dependent of the model (Figure 26.6 illustrates how interaction occurs between the model, view and controller). This means that it is the responsibility of the model to inform its dependents of any changes to its contents (i.e. its view). This is done by the model sending a message to itself stating that its contents has changed in some way. The changed method is actually defined in class Object and is thus inherited by all classes in the system. This means that any object in the system can act as the model in an MVC triad[1]. This method causes an update: message to be sent to each of the views referenced in the dependents collection.

How the update message is handled is the responsibility of the receiver (in this case the view). For example, in order to find out what change has occurred, the view will need to request some information maintained within the model. Thus the information model only needs to send the change method to itself at the appropriate times, the views must then handle the update: message independent of the model.

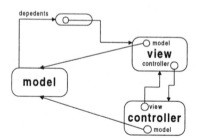

Figure 26.6: The dependency relationship within the MVC

In Figure 26.6 notice that the view and the controller both have direct links to the model and to each other. This means that the controller can send requests for services

---

[1] This actually means that any object, irrespective of whether it is used in the MVC, can have dependents, and that those dependents can be informed of changes to the object is the same way that views are informed of changes in their associated information model.

directly to the model while the view can request state information directly from the model. Also note that the controller and view both possess explicit links to each other which allows them to communicate directly. However, although the model must know that something *may* be interested in it (i.e. it must send itself one of the changed messages), it does not know what that thing is - it could be any type of object including a view. Also remember that it is the view that would have had to make itself a dependent of the model and thus the model developer need *never* know how the model would be used.

This arrangement means that:

- Views and controllers tend to be tightly coupled.
- Views and controllers come in pairs. To support this most views in VisualWorks know what controller they should have and can instantiate it for you.
- More than one view can be associated with a single model.

This last situation is known as having multiple views and is illustrated in Figure 26.7. Thus the same information can be displayed simultaneously by different views. All of which are updated as appropriate, if and when required.

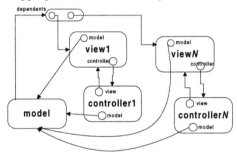

Figure 26.7: Multiple views

26.3 The MVC with the statement model

Using the financial manager application example described earlier in this book, we will look at how the balance might be displayed and updated. The diagram illustrated in Figure 26.8 shows the three elements of the MVC triad, the model (in this case an instance of statement - hence the use of statement in brackets to indicate we mean a statement and not a general type of model object), the view and the controller.

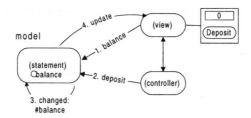

Figure 26.8: Tracing the interactions in the MVC

The view is displaying a very simple window, which can display the current balance and a button labeled deposit. The controller is responsible for responding to the button click.

The sequence of message which would be sent between these objects as the window was created and a user interacted with the window are illustrated in Figure 26.8 and described below:

1. The statement object is instantiated and the view is opened. The view object must first draw the window. To determine the current balance it must send the message balance to its model (the statement). The returned value is then displayed in the output field.

    The user clicks the mouse in the area of the screen used to display the button. The controller sees this click and enters into a dialogue with the view to determine if the click was actually within the button or not[2]. If it was, then the controller must send a message to the model to tell it to deposit ten pounds (we are assuming every deposit equals ten pounds for simplicity). This is done by sending the message:

    ```
    model deposit: 10.
    ```

2. The model (a statement) receives the message deposit and records this. It then updates the current balance and sends itself a changed message, e.g.:

    ```
    balance: newAmount
           balance := newAmount
           self changed: #balance.
    ```

3. Because the model sent itself the changed message, an update message is sent to its dependents, one of which is the view.
4. The view receives the update message. Its implementation of update re-runs the code used to create the balance view in the first place. That is, it sends the message balance to the model as in step 1.

There are a number of points worth noting about this example. Firstly, the view does not record anywhere what the actual balance is. It merely obtains the value from

---

[2] We will come back to this issue of which controller actually catches the input and which view is questioned about the position of the cursor at a later date.

the model and displays it on the screen. From that moment on it forgets it. Secondly, the controller must ask the view to determine if the cursor is within the region of the button. That is, the controller does not know where on the screen the button is displayed, nor does it attempt to obtain that information from the view. Thirdly, even though the controller has direct access to the view, it does not tell the view what it is asking the model to do. The view is unaware of any change in the model until it is sent an update message. At this point it requests the current balance from the model. Note that this means that if the statement was sent a deposit message by some other object (rather than by the controller) it would still result in the view being told to update itself. Finally, the model is unaware that the message:

```
deposit: 10.
```

came from the controller. It could have come from any object and thus the model is completely insulated from the controller and the view.

26.4 Views and subviews

In the example in the previous section, it is unlikely that the button would actually have been handled by the window controller or that the window view would have determined how it was displayed. Rather the button would have had its own ButtonView and associated ButtonController (indeed Figure 26.4 and Figure 26.5 suggest this). The ButtonView would have been a subview of the main window and would have been responsible for displaying the button and checking whether the mouse was over the button.

In fact views are designed to be nested. Most windows actually involve at least two views, one nested inside the other. The outermost view, known as the top component, manages the familiar window features (for example, the window menu bar etc.). It has an associated controller which manages the familiar moving, framing, collapsing and closing operations available from windowing environments.

Inside the top component are one or more subviews, known as components, and their controllers (remember almost all views have an associated controller) which manage specific elements of the view (e.g. buttons, scroll bars, selection boxes etc.). The subview (component) refers to the view it is an element of, as its container. Thus a subview is held within a container and a container possesses components (which are its subviews).

A component may, in turn, have additional components (although this is often not required). The container/component relationships are recorded in instance variables within the views. Each component has a link to its container and a container possesses an ordered collection of components. Thus each window's top component is the top of a hierarchy of components.

Typically, this means that when creating a window you first instantiate the top most view and then create and place subviews within the top level view. Figure 26.9 illustrates exactly this for a very simple window. This is a working example which you can type into a Workspace and evaluate.

The actual source code can be broken down into three sections. The first section creates a new ScheduledWindow. Scheduled windows represent the top connection to the host window system[3]. They are always the top of the view hierarchy (that is they are always the top component). Scheduled windows can have a label, a minimum and maximum size, can possess a single component (which can be made up of multiple views), possess a StandardSystemController (a controller specifically designed to work with scheduled windows) and of course a model. Having created the scheduled window, the code sets its controller, gives the window a label and specifies its minimum size.

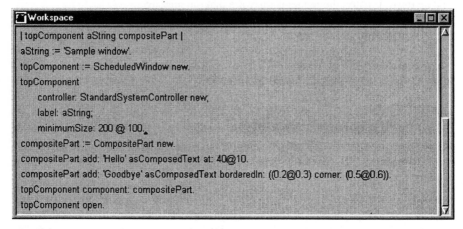

Figure 26.9: Creating a simple window

The second part of the code creates a composite part. A composite part is essentially a view which is made up of one or more subviews. That is, it is a collection of subviews and appropriate behaviour for handling these subviews[4]. In the example in Figure 26.9, two components are added to the compositePart. One is a very simple view which is a composed text. Composed texts allow strings to be displayed as a view. Note that it is the compositePart which determines where the 'Hello' will be displayed. The second component added to the compositePart is another composed text (displaying the string Goodbye). However this time, the string is being bordered. That is, a box is being drawn around that string as a border. This border is actually handled by a Wrapper (Wrappers provide needed bookkeeping information such as translation, clipping, borders, etc.). Note that the border is specified relative to the size of the encapsulating window (this is why the rectangle specifying the border is specified as 0.2 by 0.3 to 0.5 by 0.6. This means that the top right hand corner of the border should start at a position which is 20% of the width of the window by 30% of its depth and should extend to a position which is 50% of its

---

[3] "Scheduled" really relates to the fact that all ScheduledWindows are held by a control manager which determines (schedules) which of them is active at any one moment in time. Note only one window can be active for user input at any particular moment.

[4] There is of course more to it than that, involving Wrappers and VisualComponents, however as these are essentially modifications of the basic MVC we shall leave an investigation of this issue to the reader.

width and 60% of its depth (note windows have their zero, zero position in the top left hand corner of the window).

The third part of the source code in Figure 26.9 adds the compositePart (containing the two strings) to the scheduled window and opens the scheduled window. The result of opening the window is illustrated in Figure 26.10.

Figure 26.10: A simple window

An important point to note is that although a view can contain multiple subviews which it coordinates, only the views are connected; the associated controllers are not. This is illustrated in Figure 26.11. Finally, views can only have one controller and one model. Controllers can also only have one view and one model. However, models may have any number of views associated with them.

26.5 The controller hierarchy

To determine which controller should respond to the user input, there is a controller hierarchy which mirrors the view hierarchy. At the root of this tree is the controller associated with the top component. This controller tries to find a sub controller which will accept control. If none will accept control then it must process the input. Controllers will only accept control if the cursor is within their view. Upon accepting control the first thing a controller will do is see if a subcontroller will accept control. Once a controller has control, it will retain control until the cursor leaves its view. Any input from the user will then be handled by the appropriate controller.

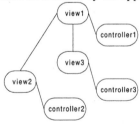

Figure 26.11: The view-subview / controller relationships

The actual mechanism through which this is performed is slightly complicated, however, basically, whenever the cursor enters a window a control manager (see the class `ControlManager` for further details) passes control to that window. This is done by asking each window controller whether it wants to take control or not (via a message `isControlWanted`). The first controller that requests control is given control. This is done via the message `startUp`.

It is then up to the windows controller to decide how it will handle this control. Typically it determines which of its subcomponents wants to gain control via the message `subViewWantingControl`. The window (or top component) then asks its components whether they want control (using the `objectWantingControl` message). The components (or views) then ask their controllers whether they want control. If the controller identifies that it should have control, then it takes over the primary control operation.

26.6 Summary

In this chapter you have encountered the Model-View-Controller (MVC) architecture for the first time. You have seen the basic principles behind the construction of graphical user interfaces to applications and examined the concepts of the View, the Model and the Controller. Remember these are just the basics, not only is the situation much more complicated than indicated here for real world applications, it varies from dialect to dialect (and in some cases from version to version). Windowing systems in general have become very powerful, this means that very large books can be dedicated to explaining the minute of a particular language and its facilities and Smalltalk is no exception. So if you want to get to know more about how Smalltalk handles graphic windows, read the manuals, examine the classes and experiment. Enjoy!

26.7 Further reading

This chapter has only attempted to provide a very basic introduction. However, there are a number of useful places for you to look for further guidance. For example [Lalonde and Pugh 1991b]. This book goes into the user interface side of Smalltalk in great detail. Some parts of it are now out of date, however it is still an excellent reference. As always [Hopkins and Horan 1995] is an excellent reference. In particular see Chapters 29 to 34. You should also have a look at your system's manuals, for example, the following manuals supplied with VisualWorks are also very good references: VisualWorks User's Guide, ParcPlace-Digitalk, Chapters 18 to 20 and the VisualWorks Cookbook, ParcPlace-Digitalk.

27. Graphical User Interface Construction Tools

27.1 Introduction

This chapter provides a brief introduction to the VisualWorks window building facilities. The VisualWorks user interface builder is a tool which allows the developer to interactively construct a window using an object oriented drawing tool (à la MacDraw, xfig or AutoSketch). This drawing tool can then generate the Smalltalk source code required to actually create an instance of the window designed by the user. This Smalltalk window definition can then be easily and simply linked to a user's application. Thus making it particularly easy to construct graphical interfaces to Smalltalk applications.

This chapter is intended to provide a description of some of the features of *the User Interface Painting* tools. It is not intended to be a complete introduction to either the User Interface Builder or to the instance structure of VisualWorks windows.

In the remainder of this chapter we first consider what a window building tool is and then what window construction tools are available in VisualWorks (which are very similar to those tools in other Smalltalk development environments). We then consider the use of associated classes such as `ApplicationModel` and `ValueHolder` as well as how to construct windows using the available tools.

27.2 What is a user interface builder?

A user interface builder is a tool which allows a developer to construct a window by drawing it rather than by defining it programatically. This is a very great advantage as the construction of windows in many windowing systems is unnecessarily complex and difficult to understand. It often takes a great deal of source code just to create a window, give it a label, place an input field, an output field and a button on that window. In many situations the resulting "program" is difficult to maintain and may be error prone. The result is that it is difficult to build and modify windows, whereas windowing systems by their very nature are intended to be easy to use.

One approach to this problem was the construction of window construction toolkit. TCL/TK is an example of such a toolkit [Ousterhout 1994]. It allows the user to specify the structure of a window in a simple scripting language. The resulting window can then be integrated with a program written in another language such as C.

279

The problem with this approach is that firstly the developer must learn the TCL scripting language, secondly they must integrate the windowing system with their C programs (not always a straight forward task) and thirdly when a bug is encountered they must search through two separate systems to identify where the fault occurred. In addition this approach still relies on the developer laying out the window programatically.

Another approach is to use a window drawing tool. The motivation for such tools was to allow users to construct their windows graphically, enabling them to easily and quickly modify the window layout and then to compile the graphic window into source code. The source code could then be compiled to construct the window. In the early days of these systems it was necessary to integrate your application code with the source code generated by the window construction tool. Having done this, if you ever modified the window, you would overwrite any application code. Obviously this was not acceptable, and was caused because the window construction tools were not closely integrated with a development environment.

The age of the visual tool overcame this hurdle. Languages such as VisualBasic, Visual C++, Symantec's Visual Cafe and of course VisualWorks, allow a developer to draw a window on the screen, compile it, add their own application code and modify the window without any loss of information. These tools have greatly simplified the construction of graphical interfaces and enabled a far wider range of applications to benefit from sophisticated windowing environments.

27.3 VisualWorks window painting tools

Figure 27.1: The user interface builder and resource Launcher buttons

The VisualWorks user interface builder is initiated using the canvas tool button on the VisualLauncher. This button has a picture of an easel with an artist's canvas on it (see Figure 27.1). The user interface builder is comprised of three tools. These tools are the *palette*, which contains the elements to be placed on a window, the *canvas*, which is the drawing area for the window and the *canvas tool*, which allows the user to issue specific commands such as the installation of a window.

The user interface builder in VisualWorks allows the user to create the window of an application from a wide range of visual components. These visual components are available from the Palette and include components such as buttons, text, sliders, tables and static visuals like rectangles and lines. Using these components the user can build up a window much in the same way as a diagram might be drawn in an object based drawing tool.

The user interface builder also provides a set of layout options in the canvas tool for relative and absolute positioning and sizing, alignment and grouping of objects. Again this is done in a similar manner to that of an object based drawing tool.

Figure 27.2 illustrates the window painting facilities being used to draw a modified VisualLauncher. On the left of the diagram is the Palette on which iconic versions of graphic objects are made available to the user. On the right of the Palette is the canvas on which the layout of the window is drawn. Additional tools are available which allow the user to specify the properties associated with the graphic objects, for example, it is possible to specify what action should be performed when a button is pressed etc. The Canvas Control is displayed above the canvas window. This window allows the properties of the canvas to be specified.

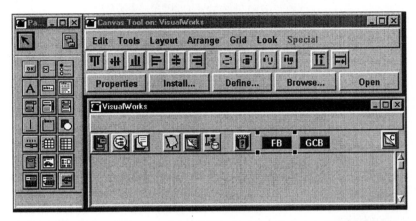

Figure 27.2: Creating a new Launcher using the window painting facilities

It is also possible for the user to generate an actual working version of the window which has just been painted. This can be done by first *installing* the window. This actually generates a class definition for the window. However, this is only the first step towards generating a functioning window. It is then necessary to create the appropriate methods for displaying and updating values displayed in the window and to produce stub methods for any actions which should be associated with the graphic objects in the window. Such information can be entered by the user via the definer option in the canvas tool. This generates accessor methods for the variables referred to or stub methods for the actions entered earlier by the user. These stub methods must then be "filed out" with Smalltalk code using the standard set of browsers.

27.3.1 Palette

The Palette tool provides a set of ready made graphic components (or widgets) which can be placed on the canvas to form part of a window using a simple drag and drop method. This is illustrated in Figure 27.3 where a table component is being placed on a blank canvas.

The top two icons on the palette indicate the single component option (the left hand icon) and the multiple component option (the right hand icon). The multiple component option allows multiple components of the same type to be placed quickly and easily onto the canvas. For example, if you wish to place three buttons on the canvas, then either you have to select the button icon each time you have placed a button on the canvas, or you can select the multiple component icon and then the button icon. This then allows you to place as many buttons on the canvas as you require.

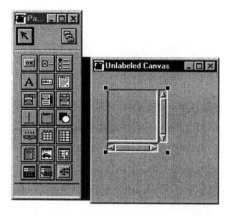

Figure 27.3: The Palette and the Canvas

The remaining icons allow various component parts to be placed on the canvas, these are (from top left to bottom right): button, check box, radio button, textual or graphical label, input and/or output field, text editor field, menu button, list selection box, combo box (a menu and a button combination), horizontal or vertical divider, graphical box (with or without a label), rectangular or circular graphical region, slider, table, data set, notebooks, subcanvas (see later), view holder (see later chapter) and charts icon. The final icon indicates a graph browser (this is an example of a third party widget which is integrated with the palette).

27.3.2 Canvas

The canvas is the drawing area of the user interface builder (see Figure 27.3). In effect it is the window which will be displayed to a user. The developer can place graphic components on the canvas, move them around, give the canvas a label and define its size, background color and foreground color. For further details on how to do these operations see the VisualWorks manuals.

27.3.3 Canvas Tool

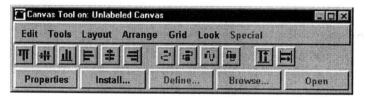

Figure 27.4: The Canvas Tool

The canvas tool (illustrated in Figure 27.4) provides a range of facilities which can be used in conjunction with the current canvas. These facilities can be divided into three: widget layout control, window and widget properties and window specification and construction. Each of these will be considered separately below.

27.3.4 Widget layout control

The widget layout control buttons are presented across the top of the canvas tool window. The first six buttons control widget alignment, the next four control widget distribution and the last two control widget size. Each of the operations is relative to the first widget selected. For example, the first button will align all the currently selected widgets such that their tops are all in line with the very first widget selected.

27.3.5 Properties, aspects and actions

The properties button on the canvas tool brings up the properties tool. This tool displays the information appropriate for the selected widget. If no widget is selected then the window details are selected.

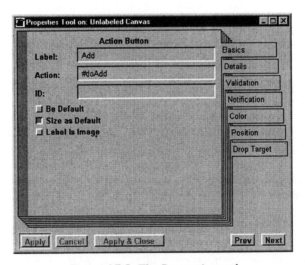

Figure 27.5: The Properties tool

The properties tool allows the user to specify a wide range of details about a widget. For example, it is possible to specify any associated colors, position, etc. The precise details of what can be defined depends on the particular widget.

Figure 27.5 illustrates the properties tool for an action button. In Figure 27.5 the developer has specified that the selected button should have a label '**Add**' (this is a textual label but equally the label could be a graphic image) and the *action* which is the symbol #doAdd. The action is the name of the message which will get sent to the object displaying the window when the button is pressed. The developer therefore defines this method to specify the add buttons' behavior.

283

In a similar manner other widget's details are defined using the properties tools. For example, for an input/output field the tool would request the field's name, and whether it should be output only or input and output (buttons and input/output fields are probably the most common widgets that you will use). The name of the input field is referred to as its *aspect*. Essentially it is the name of an instance variable which will be used to hold the field's data. Other common widgets are the list widget which displays the contents of a list and table widgets which display data held in tabular form. For further details on the properties tool see the VisualWorks manuals.

27.4 Window specification and creation

Once the developer has designed the window to their satisfaction you can install it onto a class (essentially this means that you can compile it into Smalltalk). This is done using the 'Install' button on the canvas tool. This button triggers the installer (illustrated in Figure 27.6). The developer must then specify the name of the class to *install* the window onto. If the class does not already exist it will be created by the system. In such a situation the developer must select what category to place the class into and what the superclass of the class will be.

In almost all circumstances the superclass of the new class will be ApplicationModel, or one of its subclasses. ApplicationModel is an abstract class that provides the functionality required to build a running user interface from the output of the user interface builder. Therefore by inheriting from ApplicationModel, the new class (called ToDoOrganiser in Figure 27.6) is able to create user interfaces.

You may note that in Figure 27.6 I also specified a 'Selector' called windowSpec. This is actually where the window specification will be placed. The selector is actually the name of a class side method defined within a class protocol called interface specs, which returns a windowSpecification. This is actually an array of widget specifications. This approach allows different windows to be defined for the same class and saved under different names. For example, we could construct a welcome window, an input window and an output window for some class and call each of them by different selector names. We could then choose which window we wished to open using the openInterface: message. Note that by default it is the window defined by the specification held in windowSpec which is created in response to an open message. Therefore:

- aToDoInterface open. This opens a window defined by the windowSpec class side method.
- aToDoOrganizer openInterface: #welcome. This opens the window defined by the welcome class side method"

Once the window has been installed onto a class you now have the potential to create a graphical application.

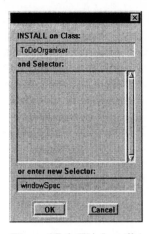

Figure 27.6: The Installer

27.5 Application models versus domain models

In the last chapter we talked about the MVC architecture and that the model was the element of the MVC which held the data. However, in this chapter we have introduced a new class called ApplicationModel (which if you are very observant you will have noticed in the last chapter was a subclass of Model). So where does that leave the good old MVC? Is the ApplicationModel the original model from the MVC or is it something different?

In fact when we talked about the MVC we did actually state that there may be very many objects involved in providing the functionality of the whole system, but that only one of them might act as the model in the MVC. Essentially, the use of an explicit ApplicationModel class is really acknowledgment of this. By creating a class which is intended to provide the behavior necessary to create and manage the graphic user interface the developer can encapsulate all the user interface functionality they need in subclasses of this ApplicationModel.

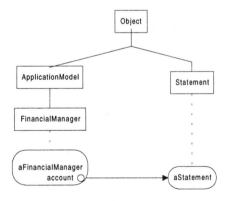

Figure 27.7: Using an ApplicationModel with an domain object

The objects involved in providing the applications functionality (or domain model) no longer need to be involved in the model hierarchy, they can inherit from any class in the system. For example, if we were to link our class Statement into this architecture we would do so as indicated in Figure 27.7. In this figure the classes are indicated by rectangles and instances by round cornered boxes.

The approach of separating out ApplicationModel functionality is extremely powerful as we can now develop the user interface and the system functionality completely separately. The following table summarizes this separation.

application model	Provides user interface processing capabilities
domain model	Provides system functionality

The ApplicationModel class is actually the root of its own application model hierarchy. Figure 27.8 illustrates part of this hierarchy. As can be seen from this diagram many of the graphical tools provided within VisualWorks are subclasses of ApplicationModel. For example, the user interface builder is provided by class such as UIBuilder, UIBuilderWatcher and UIPalette. The browsers are subclass of ApplicationModel as is the inspector, the changes tool and the file browser. The graphical class browser used to display the class hierarchies is also a (user) defined subclass of ApplicationModel.

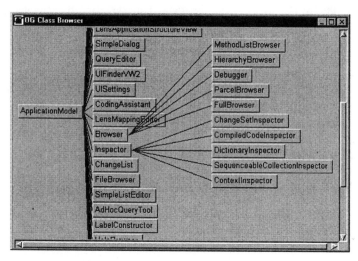

Figure 27.8: Part of the ApplicationModel hierarchy

27.6 Defining a window's functionality

We return now to the process of creating a window. So far we have defined the structure of the window but not yet how information is made available to the window (or obtained form the window), nor what happens when buttons are pressed etc. We have however defined the aspects for input fields (their names) and the actions for

286

buttons (the messages to send if they are selected). We can now get the system to define these for us automatically. This is done using the 'Define' option from the canvas tool. This brings up the definer window as illustrated in Figure 27.9. This allows the user to select which aspects and which actions they wish to define. This can be used to ensure that modifications made to the definitions by the developer do not get over written.

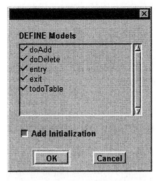

Figure 27.9: The Definer

Different things happen to input fields (and to lists and tables) than to action buttons. In the case of an input field the system defines an instance variable on the class and creates an accessor method as illustrated in Figure 27.10. This accessor method also provides a lazy initialization approach to the instance variable.

For an action the definer merely creates a stub method which returns self. This ensure that when the window is created an exception is not generated when a button is pressed. The user is then able to redefine the action methods to perform the desired operations.

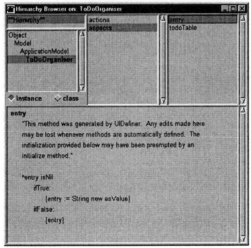

Figure 27.10: The defined entry aspect

287

27.7 Initialization

It is important when using an application model to ensure that any initialization performed does not overwrite that accomplished higher up in the `ApplicationModel` class hierarchy. For example, in Figure 27.11 we define an initialization method for the simple to do list Organizer presented in Figure 27.12. The first thing that this method does is to send a message `initialize` up the class hierarchy using:

`super initialize.`

This ensures that the initialization steps performed by the `ApplicationModel` will be carried out first. This is essential because if `initialize` merely overwrote the inherited method, then the user interface builder would be unable to create the user interface window (this is actually a common mistake even for those used to the VisualWorks system).

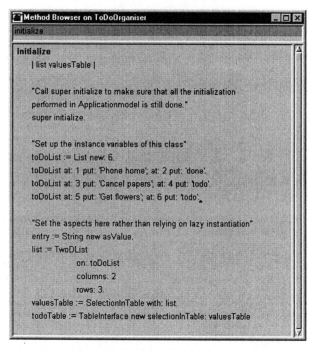

Figure 27.11: Initializing an application model

The remainder of the method in Figure 27.11 can then initialize the application specific aspects of the subclass of `ApplicationModel`. In this case it initializes an instance variable called `toDoList` and a value holder[1] on a string for an instance variable `entry`. Finally it constructs the selection list displayed on the left hand side of Figure 27.12 and stores it in the `todoTable` instance variable.

---

[1] We will come back to value holders later in this chapter.

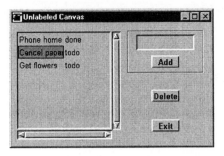

Figure 27.12: The working interface

27.8 Resource Finder

The Resource Finder (also known as the Finder) is a navigation aid for developers. It is intended to help developers to find, edit, delete and execute resources such as windows and menus. Figure 27.13 illustrates the VisualWorks Finder. The left hand selection window presents application classes, while the right hand selection window indicates the resources defined for the selected application class. There are various filter options which can be used to reduce the number of application classes displayed. The filters can be accessed by selecting the classes sub-menu from the view menu.

Figure 27.13 illustrates the resources defined for the `VisualLauncher` class (the class which is used to display the VisualWorks Launcher window). As can be seen from this example, an application can have more than one window specification (in this case it has two: `windowSpec` - the default window specification and `aboutDialogSpec`). If when one of these is selected the user selects the **Edit** button, then the user interface builder is Launcher for the given specification. If the **Start** button is selected then an instance of the application class is created and opened on the specified specification.

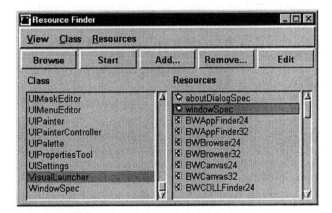

Figure 27.13: The Resource Finder

The Resource Finder is a useful way of finding the specifications provided for various classes, menus, starting applications and editing existing applications.

27.9 ValueHolders

In VisualWorks the biggest departure from the original ParcPlace version of Smalltalk, which was known as Smalltalk-80 and then ObjectWorks, is the use of *ValueHolders*. ValueHolders represent a modification to the way information is exchanged within the MVC architecture. This modification is intended to further buffer the user interface from the application model. The idea is that the model should present only that - a data structure and its associated methods. However in the MVC architecture, information about the interface often crept into the model. For example, the model would have to send the change message to itself at the right times and make the appropriate information available to the view (when the view received the resulting `update:` message). The use of ValueHolders is an attempt to remove this concern from the model.

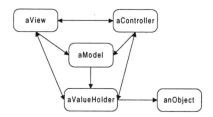

Figure 27.14: The modified MVC architecture in VisualWorks

27.9.1 How they work

The `ValueHolder` acts as an intermediate object which buffers the application model from the actual objects it maintains. The model now refers to ValueHolders, which refer to the actual objects being modeled (this is illustrated in Figure 27.14). Thus the model does not make direct reference to other objects, instead it refers to a ValueHolder. When the model wants to access a value it requests that the ValueHolder provides it. Similarly, if it wants to update a value it sends a message telling the ValueHolder to update its value.

When the object referred to by a ValueHolder changes, it is the responsibility of the ValueHolder to inform the associated view that its value has changed and that the view should display this new value (in the original MVC it was the responsibility of the model). Similarly, if the controller receives input from the user which directly changes the value of the ValueHolder, the controller merely informs the value holder that its value should change.

While this may seem to be a complicated (and rather convoluted) way to change the value of part of the model, it has many advantages in flexibility and modularity. No longer does the model have to inform the interface (view) about any updates; the

ValueHolder does it automatically whenever the value it holds changes. Indeed, it is no longer necessary for the model to concern itself with any aspect of the view (or controller) at all. The model now really is separated from the view and controller. This makes the task of developing highly graphical systems much easier.

27.9.2 Working with value holders

If the user interface builder described above is used to construct a window and the definer has been used to generate the instance variables and accessor methods for the windows aspects, then value holders for these instance variables will automatically be created. However, it is still possible to do this manually (and may be used with non interface instance variables).

A new value holder can be created in two ways:

1. By creating an instance of the class ValueHolder. For example,
```
balance := ValueHolder with: 230.
```
2. By converting an object to a value holder and object. For example,
```
balance := 230 asValue.
```

Whichever approach is used, the contents of the value holder is accessed and updated in the same way. Accessing the valueholder's contents is performed using the `value` message and updating it is performed using the `value:` message. For example:

```
currentBalance := balance value.
balance value: (currentBalance + deposit).
```

If a new value is assigned to a value holder the `value:` message *must* be used, otherwise the value holder will be deleted and the link to a window (if present) and to any dependents will be lost.

27.10 The *onChangeSend:to:* message

In an earlier chapter we discussed the use of the dependency mechanism as a means of informing interested parties about a change in the value of something. Value holders take this concept one step further and makes it more explicit. Whenever the value of a value holder is modified using the `value:` message a check is made to see whether there are any interests recorded on that value holder. If there, then the associated action is performed.

The interest in a value holder is registered using the `onChangeSend: aSymbol to: anObject` message. This message states that when the value holders value changes (via value:) the symbol is sent to the object as a message. A common use of this message is to ensure that some action is performed whenever the user changes a value currently being displayed. For example:

```
balance onChangeSend: #checkInTheRed to: currentAccount
```

states that when the value holder held in `balance` is modified, the message `checkInTheRed` should be sent to the object held in `currentAccount`. Note that unlike the version of the dependency mechanism discussed earlier, this approach explicitly states what action should be performed on what object when a particular value changes.

If at a later date the dependency between the value holder and the message send to the specified object should be retracted, the (less meaningfully named) `retractInterestsFor: anObject` message can be used.

27.11 Visual reuse

The aim of visual reuse is to avoid the necessity to rebuild applications from scratch. There are essentially three types of visual reuse in VisualWorks, these are: *cut and paste* between windows, the use of *subcanvases* and the use of *inheritance*. Each of these will be discussed briefly below.

27.11.1 Cut and paste reuse

It is possible to cut and paste widgets from one window to another using the canvas and the copy edit menu option. Essentially you open the user interface builder on a particular window, select the elements of the window that you wish to copy, use the edit menu to copy them and then go to another canvas and use the edit menu option paste, to place them on the new window. This copy operation also copies all the preference information defined for the first window (although it does not copy any instance variable definitions, initialization or accessor methods). All that is now required for these widgets to be available on the new window is to define them and carry out any initialization operations required.

This approach saves time on building new windows as whole window layouts (such as buttons, input fields, test labels, text boxes etc.) can be copied at once. It is also possible to mix widgets copied from a number of different windows.

However, this approach suffers with problems of maintenance (for both window layout and source code). For example, if the purpose of copying a set of widgets was to ensure that all windows had a similar look (for example, with the same set of buttons across the bottom of the window for operations such as next, last, quit and help). Then whenever a change was made to one window, the same change would have to be performed for every window in the system. Similarly, if the windows were on different classes it would be necessary to ensure that any source code changes were reflected in each class.

Many early graphical user interface building tools provided only this sort of reuse. Indeed there are many systems still in use which provide only this level of support.

27.11.2 Subcanvas reuse

Each window is actually a canvas which has certain properties including the windowSpec. These canvases are by default used to construct the window. However, the layout of part of a window can be defined by a different specification. The top level window handles this by treating the lower specification as a subcanvas. That is a subcanvas takes its layout from a different window specification from that of the result of the window.

There are in fact two ways in which a subcanvas can be used. These are specification based and instance based. We will consider each of these separately.

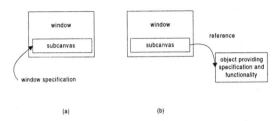

(a)   (b)

Figure 27.15: Subcanvas reuse

Specification based reuse. Specification based reuse uses another window specification (in addition to the current window specification) to define what the area of the window controlled by the subcanvas should look like. This subcanvas can be supplied by another application model (by referencing the other class). This is indicated in Figure 27.15(a). In this situation, the window's application model must provide the necessary functionality required by the widgets in the subcanvas area.

Instance based reuse. Instance based reuse differs from specification based reuse in that in addition to being able to obtain the window specification used to determine the window layout of the subcanvas from another class, the functionality of the widgets is handled by an instance of that class. Thus the subcanvas now relates to a completely separate object from the remainder of the window. This is indicated in Figure 27.15(b).

Instance based reuse is more complicated to achieve but has the advantage that the required functionality is also obtained.

27.11.3 Inheritance of canvases

Subcanvas reuse as described above really relates to *part-of* relationships and must be redefined for each window which wishes to use the same subcanvas even if all the windows relate to subclasses of a common ancestor class.

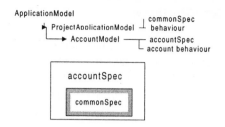

Figure 27.16: Inheritance of subcanvases

One way of alleviating this duplication is to use inheritance with the reuse of parts of a graphical user interface. For example, rather than obtaining the subcanvas specification from another class, the subcanvas specification is inherited from a parent class. This is illustrated in Figure 27.16.

This enables not only part of the window layout to be inherited, but instance variables, accessor methods and value holder relationships etc. This can be done by specifying the inherited window specification containing the required layout, in the canvas property of a subcanvas widget.

27.12 Method of working with the UI builder

At this point it is worth noting the sequence of steps (and their order) which are generally taken when developing a window using the user interface builder. We will assume that we are constructing a new window on a new class. The only differences that you need to bear in mind if this is not the case is to ensure that you don't over write existing window specifications or method definitions (unless that is what you intend to do).

1. Open the user interface builder using the canvas icon on the Visual Launcher and draw the desired window.
2. Once you have drawn the window, select **Install** from the canvas tool. This will bring up the installer window (illustrated in Figure 27.6) with an empty class name. You must enter a class name before you can continue.
3. Having specified a class name the window illustrated in Figure 27.17 will be displayed. As we are defining a new window we select the *Application* option in the *Define As* grouping which results in the ApplicationModel class being selected as the super class of our newly defined class. If we wish the class to be defined in a category other than UIApplications-New, then we also need to specify the category (if this does not already exist it will be created). We can now select *OK*.
4. This returns us to the installer where we have the option of specifying a window specification name other than windowSpec. Remember windowSpec will be used as the default window layout when a window is opened. This is done by typing in a new name into the box below the prompt saying "or enter new Selector".

5. We are now ready to define any action methods, accessor method etc. for the window. This is done using the **Define** button on the canvas tool. This causes the definer window to be displayed (as illustrated in Figure 27.9).

6. You are now ready to define any additional initialization code required. Once this is done you can start the window using the **Open** button on the canvas tool.

7. Any subsequent editing of the window follows a similar pattern. However you will not be prompted for the superclass nor category of the class again.

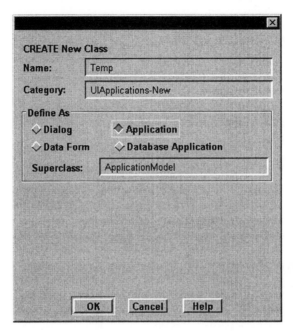

Figure 27.17: Defining the parent class and category

27.13 Summary

In this chapter you have learnt about the VisualWorks window construction tools their use and the concept of value holders. You have also been told about the modifications introduced in VisualWorks to the basic MVC framework and the difference between application models and domain models.

28. A Visual Organizer

28.1 Introduction

This chapter presents a VisualWorks version of the `Organizer` Class described earlier in the book. That is, a graphical front end is constructed that works with the classes previously constructed. The organizer was intended as an electronic personal organizer. It therefore possessed an address book, a diary (or appointments section) and a section for notes. However the version previously described required the user to send the appropriate messages to an instance of `Organizer` using the Workspace. For example, in Figure 28.1 the user has created an instance of `Organizer` and sent it a variety of messages which record addresses, appointments and notes. This certainly works, however, the use of a graphical interface would be preferable. This would allow the user to input the appropriate information via buttons, input fields and text windows.

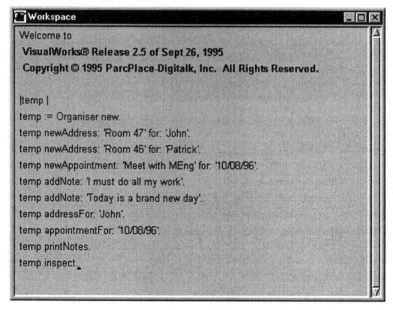

Figure 28.1: Using the (non graphical) Organizer

Figure 28.3 illustrates the type of interface to be constructed for the address input window. As can be seen from this figure, having a graphical user interface (GUI) leads to a far more intuitive interface.

The chapter is structured in the following manner: Section two describes the `VisualOrganizer` class which acts as the class used to define the graphical interface, Section three describes the associated `AddressBook` class and Section four provides a final comment.

28.2 VisualOrganizer class

In the example in this chapter we are going to construct a graphical version of the `Organizer` we constructed earlier in this book. We shall make a number of changes to the architecture of the `Organizer` in order to define the `VisualOrganizer`. The major changes are:

1. The `VisualOrganizer` class will be a subclass of `ApplicationModel` rather than `Object`. This is because we wish to inherit all the facilities used to manage VisualWorks windows. This is important, as these facilities handle everything from creating the window to handling user interaction (e.g. input and output).
2. The other major change is that we have broken the `Organizer` class down into its constituent parts. i.e. we now have separate classes for the address, appointments and notes functionality. the `Organizer` class now acts as a composite class which obtains its functionality from the instances it will possess.

The `VisualOrganizer` now works by displaying a Launcher window when the `VisualOrganizer` is sent the message open. This message is like new except it not only creates a new instance of a class, it also causes that instance to open whatever window is defined in the default window definition method. This method is called windowSpec and is maintained on the class side. The VisualOrganizer Launcher is illustrated in Figure 28.1.

28.2.1 Constructing the Launcher

First of all we need to define the class category we are going to put our classes in. The category will be called 'Visual Organizer Classes'. If you wish to follow the example in this chapter yourself, you should create this category now.

Next we will define the layout of the VisualOrganizer Launcher window. To do this we use the VisualWorks User interface builder. As we are creating a completely new application you should launch the user interface builder from the VisualWorks Launcher using the easel icon (if you are unclear on what the user interface builder does see the last chapter).

Having launched the user interface builder, the first thing to do is to give the window as a whole a label. This can be done using the properties option available from the right mouse button menu (or middle if you have a three button mouse). Note that the properties window will display the properties of the selected widget or the window as a whole if no widget is selected.

I have chosen to use the label "Visual Organizer" for my window, however you can use whatever label you feel is most appropriate as the label is not significant for the operation of the system. Once you have provided a suitable label select accept and close the properties window. Next resize the canvas as appropriate. You are now ready to begin constructing the Visual Organizer Launcher.

The window layout for the Launcher is illustrated in Figure 28.2. It shows that four buttons have been placed on the window. The text boxes with arrows indicate the action properties assigned to each button.

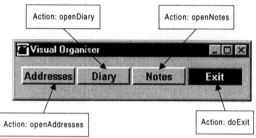

Figure 28.2: Defining the actions for the Launcher's buttons

Each button is a basic action button with a textual label rather than an icon. Place each button on the window using the palette as indicated in Figure 28.2. Remember you can use the button widget with the multiple placement option (the box in the top right hand corner of the Palette) to place more than one button. Then use the properties tool to ensure that the button properties match those in the diagram.

The Exit button also possesses a number of look preferences. These are set using the **Color** option in the properties tool. The actual colors selected are:

- Foreground color: *white* and Background color: *Royal Blue*
- Selection Foreground Color: *Pale Blue* and Selection Background Color: *Red*

The first two colors are used to display the button on the window. The Foreground color relates to the color in which the text on the button is displayed and the background color the is the main color of the button. The selection colors are the colors which the button changes to when a user selects the exit button. The contrast between red and blue helps the user identify that they have selected this button.

You have now defined all that is required to display the window. You are therefore ready to install the window onto a class. To do this you should now select the **Install** button from the Canvas Tool window. You should install the window on a class called `VisualOrganizer` which is a subclass of `ApplicationModel`. The window selector name should be left as `windowSpec`. Don't forget to change the category to *Visual Organizer Classes* otherwise it will be placed in the default category.

Once you have installed the window onto a class you are now ready to define the action methods for the window (a.k.a. the method to run when the button is clicked). You can do this by selecting the **Define** option in the Canvas Tool window. Do this

298

now. The definer should define four methods named after the action properties you defined above.

28.2.2 The VisualOrganizer class

Now go to the System Browser and look at the class definition for VisualOrganizer. You will see that a full class definition has been generated for you by the User interface builder. Your newly created class definition should look like this:

```
ApplicationModel subclass: #VisualOrganizer
        instanceVariableNames: ' '
        classVariableNames: ' '
        poolDictionaries: ' '
        category: 'Visual Organizer Classes'
```

Next add a class comment. This is left as an exercise for the reader.

28.2.3 The "actions" protocol

Methods for each of the buttons in the window are defined by the User interface builder when the Define option is selected (the user can select not to define methods using a scrolling selection window). These methods are placed in the "actions" protocols. By default, these methods are defined to return the value of self. For example, the definitions generated by the User interface builder are:

openAddresses
    ^self
	openDiary
	    ^self

openNotes
    ^self
	doExit
	    ^self

If we wish them to do anything useful, then we need to edit these methods and define what they should do.

We shall first look at the doExit method as this is the simplest method. This method will close the window. To do this we use the closeRequest method defined in the ApplicationModel class. We therefore merely need to send the message closeRequest to self.

```
doExit
        "This method closes the associated window"
        self closeRequest.
```

This method is associated with the "exit" button on the VisualOrganizer Launcher.

The other three actions are associated with the three launch buttons on the VisualOrganizer Launcher. These are used to open the address book, the diary and the notes tool. The openDiary and openNotes methods will remain unchanged. They will return self when called. Extending the application for appointments and notes is left as an exercise for the reader.

The only action method which possesses "content" will be openAddress book. This should send the message open to the AddressBook class. This causes an instance of AddressBook to be created and the default window defined on this class opened:

openAddresses
```
AddressBook open.
```

Define this now and accept it (leave any classes undefined when VisualWorks warns you about them).

28.3 The AddressBook class

28.3.1 The AddressBook window

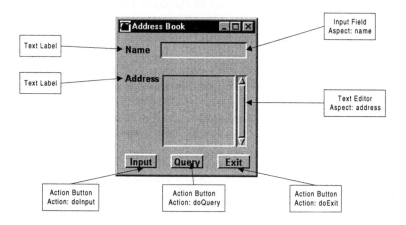

Figure 28.3: The layout and definition of the AddressBook window

Figure 28.3 illustrates the layout of the AddressBook window. As can be seen it has two input fields as well as three buttons and two text labels. The specifications for these different widgets are indicated in the figure. Using the palette and the properties tools define the window following the steps outlined above.

For the window as a whole I have used the label "Address Book" however as before you can use whatever label you feel appropriate. The three buttons along the bottom of the window will be referred to these as input, query and exit (from left to right).

Once you have defined the layout of the window and the various properties you are ready to install the window on a class. To do this select the **Install** button from the Canvas Tool window and install the window on a class called AddressBook which is a subclass of ApplicationModel. Don't forget to change the category to "Visual Organizer Classes" otherwise it will be placed in the default category.

Once you have installed the window onto a class you can select the **Define** option in the Canvas Tool window to define the instance variables and accessor methods for the two aspects (input fields) and the actions for the buttons (a.k.a. the method to run when the button is clicked). You are now ready to define the functionality of the AddressBook class.

28.3.2 The AddressBook class definition

In the System Browser, have a look at the class definition for AddressBook. You will see that a full class definition has been generated for you by the User interface builder. You now need to add the instance variable specific to the functioning of the class (rather than the instance variables specific to the user interface). This variable will be called addressBook. Once you have done that, your newly created class definition should look like:

```
ApplicationModel subclass: #AddressBook
    instanceVariableNames: 'name address addressBook
    classVariableNames: ''
    poolDictionaries: ''
    category: 'Visual Organizer Classes'
```

Don't forget to accept the class definition. The class comment is left as an exercise for the reader (you must get use to defining them). You should also note that when you selected the AddressBook class there were two method protocols defined for you already. These were 'aspects' and 'actions'. The 'aspects' hold the instance variable access methods and the 'actions' hold the methods which will be run when the buttons are clicked.

28.3.3 The "aspects" protocol

The next thing we will do is to look at the methods which have been defined for us by the User interface builder in the "aspects" protocol. If you examine this protocol you should find two methods defined. One called address and one called name. If you examine these methods you should find that their definition matches those presented below:

address
```
"This method was generated by UIDefiner.  Any edits made here may be
lost whenever methods are automatically defined.  The initialization
provided below may have been preempted by an initialize method."
^address isNil
    ifTrue: [address := String new asValue]
    ifFalse: [address]
```

We shall stop for a moment and consider what this method actually says. The method possesses one expression, the result of which will be returned when the method completes. The value will returned is dependent on the result of the isNil test. If the contents of the instance variable address "is nil" then the ifTrue: clause will execute, if not then the ifFalse: clause will execute. We shall take the false case first. If address does not contain nil then the value of address is returned by the ifFalse: clause. However, if the value of address is nil, then the assignment expression in the ifTrue: clause is executed. This assignment expression creates a new instance of the class String. It then sends the message asValue to this new string instance. This creates a value holder around the string. This *value holder with string* construct is then assigned to the instance variable address. The result of this expression is the value of assignment which is returned.

Thus, if the address instance variable has not yet been set (indicated by the value nil) an appropriate value for it is generated, otherwise its value is returned. This form of expression is referred to as *lazy initialization.* That is, address is initialized appropriately when it is required, rather than when the system is initialized. This can be useful sometimes, however it does mean that every time the value of address is obtained an extra expression must be considered (i.e. isNil). This means that is less efficient than initializing the value of address appropriately in an initialize method. The accessor method for the instance variable name is defined in a similar manner.

28.3.4 The "initialize" protocol

Now let us define the "initialize" method protocol. This method protocol will only possess one method, initialize. This method is presented below. It instantiates a Dictionary object to use with the addressBook instance variable. Notice that once again we do not access the instance variable directly. Instead we use an updater method.

```
initialize
    "This method is called whenever an instance of Organizer is created"
    | adBook |
    "ApplicationModel defines its own initialize so send a message to
    super"
    super initialize.
    "Next we set up the address book instance variable"
    adBook := Dictionary new.
    self addressBook: adBook
```

As we are currently using lazy initialization with the 'aspect' methods name and address we have not initialized them here. However, as was indicated above, it would be more efficient to do so. However, it must be remembered that they are "aspect" variables rather than plain instance variables. This means that for the windowing operations to work correctly they must contain a value holder, which acts as a wrapper around the actual value they represent (see the last chapter for more details).

A common mistake (and the cause of much frustration) is to initialize the aspects in an initialize method as a String or a Number (with no value holder). This means that the "aspect" method isNil test fails and the String or Number etc. is returned. The problem is that this is not a value holder and thus cannot respond to input and output properly. Often this manifests itself when values fail to update themselves or updates from the user fail to propagate to the instances etc. Thus appropriate initialization should follow that used in the aspect methods, e.g.

```
address := String new asValue.
name := String new asValue.
```

The aspect methods can then be simplified to just return the contents of the associated instance variable.

28.3.5 The "actions" protocol

Another set of methods defined by the User interface builder are the "actions" methods. These are in the "action" protocol. We have already seen examples of these in the `VisualOrganizer` class. As you saw there, by default, these methods are defined to return the value of self. We therefore need to define them.

We shall first look at the `doExit` method as this is the simplest method. This method will close the window. To do this we again use the inherited `closeRequest` method. We therefore merely need to send the message `closeRequest` to `self`.

```
doExit
        "This method closes the associated window"
        self closeRequest.
```

Next we will look at the `doInput` method. This method takes input from both the name input field and the address input field and stores them using the `newAddress:for:` method which we will define later. Notice that once again we use an intermediate updater method to actually access any instance variables (this is good Smalltalk style). The `doInput` method is presented below.

```
doInput
        "The method is executed when the input button is pressed"
        | aName anAddress |
        aName := name value.
        anAddress := address value.
        self newAddress: anAddress for: aName.
```

Notice that we do not just access the name and address aspects (instance variables) and save them into the temporary variables aName and anAddress. Instead, we send the message value to each of the aspects first. This is because, if we just took the contents of name and address we would obtain a `ValueHolder` object. What we really want is the contents of the value holder. To get this we must send the message `value` to the value holder. Thus `name value`, will return the value held by the value holder in the instance variable name.

Remember when you type this method in and accept it, the system will notify you that the method `newAddress:For:` is undefined. We will define it later!

Next we will examine the `doQuery` action method. This method accesses the name input field and updates the `address` input/output field. Again we must use the message `value` to access the contents of the `name` value holder. We then use the `addressFor:` accessor method (which we will define below) to obtain the address associated with the name. If the address retrieved is not `nil` then we put the address retrieved into the `address` input/output field. If it is nil we display an okay dialog with an appropriate warning message.

doQuery
```
"The method is executed when the input button is pressed"
| aName anAddress |
aName := name value.
anAddress := self addressFor: aName.
anAddress isNil
    ifTrue: [Dialog warn:'There is no address for ' , name value.]
    ifFalse: [address value: anAddress asText.]
```

We will just examine the last statement in the method for a moment. This time we used the message value: rather than the message value with the value holder in address. This is because we were updating the contents of the value holder rather than accessing it. Thus the address value holder is set to the value of the parameter sent with the message value:. This parameter was actually the string returned by the addressFor: method. However, to be displayed it must be converted into a Text object (which understands how to display strings). This is achieved by sending the string in anAddress the message asText. This is necessary because the text editor field assumes that it will display a text (which has special properties such as font and style) rather than just a plain string. When we access the value holder using value, it knows to return the string held by the text object within the value holder. But when we update the value holder we need to wrap the string in a text object.

28.3.6 The "accessing" protocol

Next we shall define the methods in the "accessing" protocol. There are four methods in this protocol. We shall first consider those associated with setting and updating the address book dictionary. The first of these is used to initialize the instance variable addressBook and the second to add new name and address associations to the addressBook. These are addressBook: and newAddress:for: respectively. The addressBook: method is very straight forward and is presented below.

addressBook: aDictionary
```
"This is an update method for the addressBook instance variable. It
is used to accept a new dictionary object to use for the
addressBook. It is intended only for use with the initialization
method of the AddressBook class."
addressBook := aDictionary
```

The newAddress:for: method takes two parameters, the new address and the name. The method uses two different Dictionary methods. The first is used to check to see if there is already an addressBook entry with that name. We could not use the basic at: message as that generates an error if the key provided with the at: message is not present in the dictionary. However, the at:ifAbsent: message allows the code block provided with the ifAbsent: parameter to be run if the key is not present. In our case we do not want it to do anything other than return nil. By default when a block is evaluated it returns nil if nothing else is returned. We therefore only need to provide any empty block which will always return the value nil. We can then test the value of the temporary variable alreadyThere to see if it is nil. If it is nil then we can add the new name and address to the dictionary held in addressBook. If it is not nil we can warn the user that an entry with that key already exists using a dialog window.

```
newAddress: anAddress for: aName
    "This method is used to add a new address to the address book."
    | alreadyThere |
    alreadyThere := addressBook at: aName ifAbsent: [].
    alreadyThere isNil
        ifTrue: [addressBook at: aName put: anAddress]
        ifFalse: [Dialog warn: 'That key is already present']
```

We shall now consider the last two methods in this protocol. These methods are addressBook which returns the contents of the addressBook instance variable and addressFor: which returns the address associated with a particular name (if one is present). The addressBook method is:

```
addressBook
    "This is an access method for the addressBook instance variable"
    ^addressBook
```

The addressFor: method is slightly more complex as it must handle the situation where an address is not available (it uses the at:ifAbsent: message to do this).

```
addressFor: aName
    "This method is used to retrieve an address from the address book."
    | anEntry |
    anEntry := addressBook at: aName ifAbsent: [nil].
    ^anEntry
```

28.3.7 A working application

If you have followed all the steps above correctly you should now have a working application. To start the application, type the following into a Workspace and evaluate it:

```
VisualOrganizer open
```

This will display the window illustrated in Figure 28.2. Now select the Addresses option and you should see a window such as that displayed in Figure 28.3. You can now type in a few names and addresses selecting input between each. Next try out the query option by typing in a name and selecting query. If the name is in the address book, it will be displayed in the address book field. If not a warning message will be displayed.

28.4 Summary

You have now created a VisualWorks GUI application. This application provides you will the basics of an address book. Of course, if you quit from the window you will lose all the names and addresses you have input. We will look later at how you can store the dictionary used for the names and addresses into a file so that you can access it again. The method we will use is called the Binary Object Streaming Service (or BOSS for short). It is better than saving straight ASCII, as it perseveres the objects rather than just plain text (where you would have to reconstruct the dictionary from the text).

An important point to consider is how we have structured this application. We have effectively bound the address book functionality into the user interface. This is not particularly good style, however for such a small application it seemed acceptable. A better structure would have been to construct a graphical interface which used the facilities defined in the original Organizer class.

28.5 The visual Financial Manager application

This is an exercise for you the reader. This application builds on the FinancialManager you have been constructing at various times throughout this book. The aim of this exercise is to provide a graphical interface to this application. The graphic interface should allow the user to:

1. Add deposits to the account for a specified amount.
2. Make payments (withdrawals) from the account for specified accounts.
3. Get the current balance and print a statement of all payments and deposits.

You should define the window independently of the FinancialManager class. This means that you can make the GUIFinancialManager class a subclass of ApplicationModel. You should then provide an instance variable in which the actual FinancialManager object will be held. This could be done in an initialize method. I have assumed that the two input/output aspects are amount and balance. These could also be initialized in this method. For example:

```
initialize
        super initialize.
    . account := FinancialManager new.
        amount := 0.00 asValue.
        balance := 0.00 asValue.
```

In the above example, account is an instance variable used to hold the FinancialManager object. Note that we must first send the message super initialize to ensure that the inherited initialization is performed.

It should now be possible to write methods to handle user inputs in the form of button clicks which pass the appropriate information onto the object held in account. For example (Note this assumes that the amount to be input field is called "amount"):

```
deposit
        account deposit: (amount value).
```

29. Using a View Within a Window

29.1 Introduction

This chapter describes how a custom view can be incorporated into the type of window seen in the last two chapters. This is important because although the user interface builder is extremely good at creating buttons, input/output field style windows, it cannot be used to display graphical information. For example, if you wish to construct a graph of nodes to illustrate a particular route in a path finding application then this must be generated using the basic MVC (Model-View-Control) features.

In this chapter we consider a simple drawing application which we will call SmallDraw. This application is illustrated in Figure 29.1.

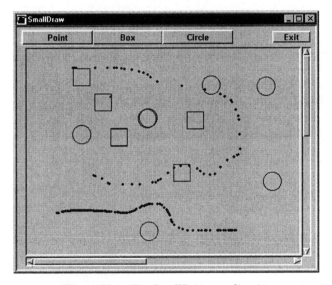

Figure 29.1: The SmallDraw application

SmallDraw allows boxes, circles and points to be placed on a scrollable drawing. The three widget buttons and the exit button have been defined using the user interface builder. The scrollable drawing area is a scrollable view which has be created by the user interface builder but which is controller by a separate model, view and controller.

In the remainder of this chapter we will consider how this application was constructed.

29.2 The custom view widget

29.2.1 What is a custom view widget?

Any widget displayed in a window created using the window building facilities of the canvas, the palette and the canvas tools uses a view to display itself. This view determines what will be displayed, what the associated view does and how it links with your application. However, not everything you will wish to do is covered by the widgets provided by the palette. For example, if you wish to display a network of nodes, then there is no built in widget to do this - you must write the code which will display such a network using a custom view.

Figure 29.2: The View Holder Palette icon

A custom view is held within a view holder which can be placed onto a window using the user interface builder. This is done using the view holder icon which is available on the user interface builder's palette. It allows the user to place a view holder widget onto the canvas being designed. Such a holder can take advantage of some of the widget properties defined by the user interface builder such as sliders etc. However, the developer must supply the majority of the code that connects the graphic contents of the view holder to the application as well as the code which actually generates the graphics.

29.2.2 How do you create a custom view?

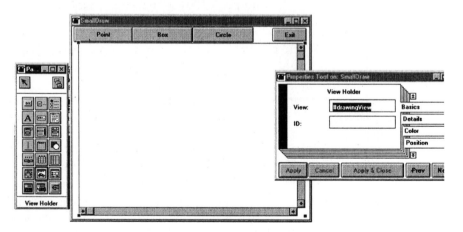

Figure 29.3: Defining a custom view

To create a custom view a user must first place a view holder onto the canvas representing the window being constructed. For example, in Figure 29.3, we have placed a view holder across the majority of the window and added a horizontal and vertical slider. This view is then linked to the window via an instance variable specified in the view's properties window.

The result of this is that when the user interface window building software encounters this window's definition (held in a class side window specification method) it will construct a window with four buttons and a scrollable view. However that is all that it will do. It will not attempt to perform any operations to determine what the interior of the view should look like.

29.2.3 Managing a custom view

Associated with this view holder will be a model, a controller and a view instance. As you will note from these classes custom views are implemented and controlled using the traditional MVC framework described earlier in this part of the book. Remember:

- Views control what is displayed on the screen.
- Controllers handle user interaction.
- Models hold the domain data to be displayed by the view.

Therefore it is in the view class that the developer must define a method which will specify what the custom view widget will display. This method is the `displayOn:` method. It takes one parameter which is a `GraphicsContext`. GraphicsContexts are objects which work with windows to display graphical objects (determining how the graphic object should be rendered).

The `displayOn:` method is sent by the system to the view whenever a change has occurred in one of the objects on which it depends (such as the model) or when the screen needs to be updated (for example, after a window which has been partially covering the view is closed).

For the view to determine what it should display it needs to communicate with the model which holds the data. It must therefore have a link to the model (whether it is a separate object or the instance of application model which holds the parent window).

Finally, the view must also work with a controller. This controller will determine what action the application should take whenever the user interacts with the view widget. Note that this controller does not attempt to control how the user interacts with the whole window, rather it is only concerned with the user's interaction with the view. For example, what happens when the user clicks in the view etc.

We shall now consider how the SmallDraw application is structured.

29.3 The structure of the application

Figure 29.4 illustrates the inheritance structure between the classes used in the SmallDraw application. This class hierarchy is typical of an application which incorporates a custom view. For example, we have an ApplicationModel hierarchy with the main SmallDraw application. We have a `Controller` subclass (`DrawingController`), a `Model` subclass (`DrawingModel`) and a `View` subclass (`DrawingView`). In addition we have three types of object which can be drawn in a `SmallDraw` drawing: `BoxWidget`, `CircleWidget` and `PointWidget`. The only difference between these three classes is what is drawn on to the graphics context representing the view. The `DrawingWidget` class from which they all inherit defines common attributes used by all objects displayed within a `DrawingView` (such as their origin, the extent of their boundary and the size of their border). Each of these classes will be considered in more detail in a later section in this chapter.

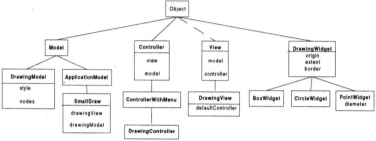

Figure 29.4: Inheritance in SmallDraw

Note that the *dashed* line between the `Object` class and the `View` class indicates that there are a number of classes between these two in the actual class hierarchy. It is useful to examine these classes yourself to see what facilities they add.

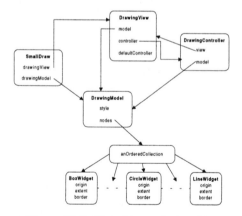

Figure 29.5: The object relationships

However, what inherits from what is only part of the story for any object oriented application. Figure 29.5 illustrates the next part of the story: how the objects relate to one another within a working application (note this diagram only presents the user defined objects within the application. There are other objects such as the `UIBuilder` which are also involved but which are generated by VisualWorks).

As you can see from Figure 29.5 the SmallDraw application model has instance variables which possess links to the drawingModel and the drawingView. The presence of a link to the drawingView object allows the window building facilities associated with the SmallDraw window to inform the view that it needs to redisplay itself. The link to the drawingModel allows the effects of user interaction outside the view to be passed onto it. For example, the user selects which object to add to the drawing by selecting one of three buttons at the top of the SmallDraw window (Figure 29.1). The user's choice must be passed through to the drawingModel so that it can add the appropriate drawing object to its list of displayed objects.

It is also worth noting that if you examine the DrawingModel, DrawingView and DrawingController you will see that these three classes exhibit the classic MVC structure. The View and the Controller have knowledge of each other and the Model, whereas the Model knows nothing about the View or the Controller. This is because VisualWorks records the View as a dependent of the Model when the view records the presence of the model (using the super model: aModel. message expression).

Finally it is worth pointing out that in this case the DrawingModel is a relatively simple model which merely records a set of nodes in an OrderedCollection. These nodes could be anything and could be displayed in any way. It is the nodes themselves which determine what they should look like when drawn.

29.4 The interactions between objects

We have now examined what the physical structure of the application is but not how the objects within that application interact. In many situations this can be extracted from the source code of the application (with varying degree's of difficulty). However, in the case of a custom view within an ApplicationModel, it is useful to explicitly describe the system interaction. There are four different interactions in the system and each will be considered separately.

We shall adopt the following conventions for the diagrams illustrating the interactions between the objects (these diagrams are based on the mechanism diagrams described by [Rumbaugh et al 1991]):

- a solid arrow indicates a message send,
- a dashed arrow indicates instance creation,
- a square box indicates a class,
- a round box indicates an instance,
- a name in brackets indicates the type of instance,
- numbers are used to indicate the sequence of message sends.

29.4.1 Initialization

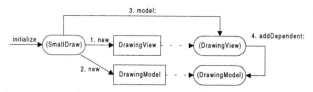

Figure 29.6: Object interaction during initialization

When the SmallDraw application is opened (i.e. when the message open is sent to the SmallDraw class) an instance of SmallDraw is created and sent the message initialize (as illustrated in Figure 29.6). This results in the creation of two further instances one a drawingView and the other a drawingModel. The drawingController is automatically instantiated when the view is displayed (note the type of controller to be used is specified by the drawingView in the instance variable defaultController).

Once the two instances have been created the message model: is sent to the drawingView. This in turn causes the drawingView to become one of the drawing models dependents. Note that this last message send is defined in the DependentPart class, which is one of the superclasses of DrawingView.

At this point the structure required by the custom view is in place. It is now possible for the application model SmallDraw and the user to interact with the drawingView and drawingController.

29.4.2 Changing the type of graphic object to be displayed

Figure 29.7: Changing the graphic object to be added

As we have used the user interface builder to add buttons to the main window which will be used to determine which type of graphic object to add to the drawing, we require some way of passing that information onto the objects involved in managing and maintaining the custom view. That means we must inform the model of the type of object which will be added.

The actual interaction illustrated in Figure 29.7 involves the message setBoxStyle being sent to the SmallDraw application when the **Box** style button is selected in the main window. This message is sent in response to an event being raised (we do not cover how this works in this book: it is left as an exercise for the reader).

When the message setBoxStyle is received by the smallDraw object, a further message is then sent to the drawingModel (which smallDraw has a link to via the instance variable drawingModel) setting the current style to the symbol #box. The style value can currently be one of #box, #circle or #point.

29.4.3 Adding a new graphic object

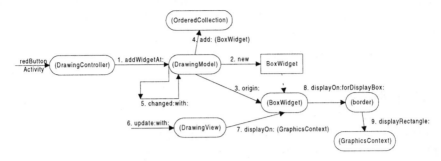

Figure 29.8: Adding a box graphic object

The action of adding a new graphic object to the drawing displayed by the custom view in the SmallDraw application is initiated by the user pressing the left mouse button. Historically the mouse buttons were known as red, yellow and blue for the left, middle and right mouse buttons. This was because the original system on which Smalltalk was developed had multi-color mouse buttons (colored red, yellow and blue). Although Smalltalk is now available on systems with one, two and three mouse buttons (all of which tend to be shades of the same color e.g. white, gray or cream) there are still places in the system where reference is made to the color of the mouse button - this is one of them.

When the left mouse button is pressed a `redButtonActivity` message is sent to the `drawingController` (as illustrated in Figure 29.8). This allows the `drawingController` to decide what action to perform in response to the left mouse button being pressed. For example, an application may specify that a menu should be displayed or that any object under the mouse is selected etc. In the case of the SmallDraw application the action is to place a graphic object (of the appropriate style) at the current cursor location. To do this, the `drawingController` sends an `addWidgetAt:` message to the `drawingModel`.

Next the `drawingModel` creates a new instance of the appropriate type of object. In the diagram illustrated in Figure 29.8 the current style is that of #box. Therefore a new instance of `BoxWidget` is created. This `boxWidget` instance is then sent a message `origin:` which sets its position within the view. The `boxWidget` is then added to the `orderedCollection` used to hold all the graphic objects. Next the `drawingModel` sends itself the `changed:with:` message so that all of its dependents can be informed that a change has taken place.

This results in an `update:with:` message being sent to the `drawingView` via the dependency mechanism. The `drawingView` then sends a `displayOn:` message to the objects to be displayed. The `boxWidget` then uses a border object to display itself on the `graphicsContext`.

This section has outlined the most difficult part of constructing a custom view for the novice - working out what is sent where, by what and when. The thing to remember is that you are slotting your application specific code into a generic framework. However at this stage it is often much easier to look at what someone else has done and to use it as the basis of what you require. While this approach can be extremely useful as a learning exercise it is still important to become familiar with this framework. One way to do this is to place self halt messages into strategic methods (such as update:with: and displayOn: in the drawingView object) and then to use the debugger to explore the objects and messages which have been sent.

29.4.4 Refreshing

The final set of interactions which you should be aware of relate to refreshing the window following some operation which invalidates part or all of the screen display (such as the movement of a partially overlapping window). In such circumstances the message checkForEvents is sent to the applicationWindow, the application controller (which acts as the controller for the overall application). (Note that in Figure 29.9 the large dashed line indicates missing message sends).

The applicationWindow then sends a displayDamageEvent: aRectangle message to itself. This message basically means that an event is raised which indicates that there may be some damage to the displayed area (specified by a rectangle). If the applicationWindow is open, then the message displayOn: will be sent to the drawingView.

The displayOn: method in drawingView (as opposed to that defined in the "widget" classes) obtains a collection of objects to be displayed from the drawingModel using the nodes message and sends each object a displayOn: message as part of a do: message expression. This results in each of the graphic objects being redraw on the screen.

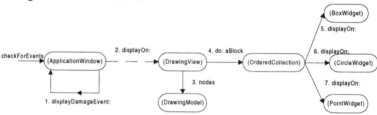

Figure 29.9: Refreshing a custom view

29.5 The classes involved

This section describes how to implement the classes in the SmallDraw application in detail (see Figure 29.4 which illustrates the classes in this application). We will first consider the SmallDraw application itself before considering the three classes involved in the MVC framework (DrawingModel, DrawingView and DrawingController) and will conclude by describing the "widget" classes: DrawingWidget, PointWidget, CircleWidget and PointWidget.

29.5.1 The SmallDraw class

The SmallDraw class is a subclass of ApplicationModel. It possesses two instance variables, drawingView (which is actually an aspect referencing the custom view) and drawingModel. The class definition is presented below and can be typed in using the System Browser. Note that this assumes that the class is being defined in a class category called SmallDraw.

```
ApplicationModel subclass: #SmallDraw
        instanceVariableNames: 'drawingView drawingModel '
        classVariableNames: ''
        poolDictionaries: ''
        category: 'SmallDraw'!
```

The SmallDraw application provides the main window for the application. It possesses four buttons, and a view as illustrated in Figure 29.10. You should use the canvas tool and the palette to create a window which resembles this. Next use the properties tool to define the properties for the four buttons and the view. The figure illustrates the actions defined for each button and the aspect name of the custom view.

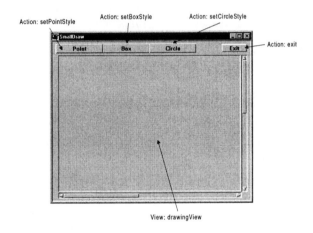

Figure 29.10: Defining the graphic elements of the SmallDraw application

Next use the definer tool from the canvas tools Launcher to create stub methods for the actions illustrated in Figure 29.10.

We shall now define the initialize method in the *initialize* protocol in the SmallDraw class (use a browser to do this). The initialize method creates an instance of the DrawingView class, the DrawingModel class and links them together. The method is presented below:

```
initialize
    drawingView := DrawingView new.
    drawingModel := DrawingModel new.
    drawingView model: drawingModel.
```

You are now ready to define each of the action methods in the *actions* protocol. The first method we shall consider is the exit method which is executed when the exit button is selected. This message uses the closeRequest method we saw in the last chapter to terminate the application:

```
exit
    self closeRequest
```

The next method we shall consider is the setBoxStyle method. This method is executed when the **Box** button is selected. This method sends the style: message to the drawingModel with the parameter #box. That is, it causes the current graphic object style to be set to #box.

```
setBoxStyle
    drawingModel style: #box.
```

In addition there are two other methods which set the style of object to be added. These are setCircleStyle and setPointStyle. They are exactly the same as the setBoxStyle method except that they pass the symbols #circle and #point to the drawingModel via the message style: . The setCircleStyle method is called whenever the **Circle** button is selected and the setPointStyle method whenever the **Point** button is selected:

```
setCircleStyle
    drawingModel style: #circle.

setPointStyle
    drawingModel style: #point.
```

Finally the *aspects* protocol (automatically generated for you if you have used the definer) will contain a single method called drawingView. This is an accessor method for the aspect drawingView:

```
drawingView
    ^drawingView
```

As usual the SmallDraw application is instantiated by sending the message open to the class SmallDraw. For example:

```
SmallDraw open
```

29.5.2 The DrawingModel class

The DrawingModel class is a subclass of Model. It possesses two instance variables nodes and style. The instance variable style indicates the type of object to add to the collection of objects in nodes. The class definition is:

```
Model subclass: #DrawingModel
    instanceVariableNames: 'nodes style
    classVariableNames: ''
    poolDictionaries: ''
    category: 'SmallDraw'
```

The DrawingModel class comment is left as an exercise for the reader.

Having defined the DrawingModel class and class comment we are now ready to define the initialize method. As usual we will place this method in an initialize method protocol. The initialize method initializes the two instance variables nodes and style. A new ordered collection is instantiated for the first and the style: accessor method is used to set the second (with a default style of #box):

```
initialize
    nodes := OrderedCollection new.
    self style: #box.
```

We are now ready to define the *accessing* methods for DrawingModel. These methods (defined within an *accessing* protocol) access the instance variables of the class. For example, nodes and style retrieve the value of their associated instance variables, while style: resets the instance variable style.

```
nodes
    ^nodes.

style
    ^style

style: aSymbol
    style := aSymbol
```

Next we define an *updating* protocol. This protocol will hold a single method addWidgetAt: . This method adds the appropriate type of graphic object to the objects held in nodes. The instance variable style is used to determine the type of object to add. The parameter aPoint indicates the location, within the drawing view, at which the object should be displayed. Finally, the method informs the drawingModel that something has changed and that its dependents may be interested in that change.

```
addWidgetAt: aPoint
    | aNode pos |
    self style = #point ifTrue: [aNode := PointWidget new].
    self style = #box ifTrue: [aNode := BoxWidget new].
    self style = #circle ifTrue: [aNode := CircleWidget new].
    aPoint = nil ifTrue: [pos := 0 @ 0] ifFalse: [pos := aPoint].
    self nodes add: (aNode origin: pos).
    self changed: #object with: aNode.
```

We will also define a single class side method new. This method will extend the functionality of the new method by sending the message initialize to a newly created instance. The method is defined in the class side protocol *instance creation*:

```
new
    ^super new initialize.
```

29.5.3 The DrawingView class

The DrawingView class is a subclass of the View class. It possesses a single instance variable called defaultControllerClass. The contents of this variable will be used to instantiate the correct type of controller (in this case an instance of DrawingController).

```
View subclass: #DrawingView
    instanceVariableNames: 'defaultControllerClass '
    classVariableNames: ''
    poolDictionaries: ''
    category: 'SmallDraw'
```

The class comment for the DrawingView class is left as an exercise for the reader. The initialize method for the DrawingView class is defined as :

```
initialize
    super initialize.
    defaultControllerClass := DrawingController.
```

This method is defined within the *initialize* protocol. To ensure that all initialization done in superclasses is also carried out in this class, the method first sends the message super initialize. It then initializes the defaultControllerClass instance variable.

Following the conventions laid down in the system view class hierarchy we will define a defaultControllerClass accessor method in a protocol referred to as *controller accessing*. This method returns the contents of the defaultControllerClass instance variable:

```
defaultControllerClass
    ^defaultControllerClass
```

In the *model accessing* protocol we will define an updater method for the model associated with the drawingView instance called model:

```
model: aModel
    super model: aModel.
    self invalidate.
```

This method uses an inherited version of the model: method to set the model and then sends the message invalidate to itself. This informs the view that some part of what is currently being displayed may need to be redrawn. This will cause a displayOn: aGraphicsContext message to be sent to self.

In the *updating* protocol we need to define a method which will catch the result of the change message set when a new widget is added to the model. This is the update:with: message. In our case we merely wish to draw the newly added object in the view:

```
update: anAspect with: anObject
anAspect == #object ifTrue: [anObject displayOn: self graphicsContext].
```

We now need to define the `displayOn:` method for the drawing object within a *displaying* protocol. This is sent to the drawing view when what is being displayed needs updating (e.g. when part of the window is uncovered). This method sends the `displayOn:` message to all the elements currently held in the nodes list of the `drawingModel`:

```
displayOn: aGraphicsContext
        self model nodes do: [:node | node displayOn: aGraphicsContext]
```

Finally we need to extend the class side method in the *instance creation* protocol so that it sends the message `initialize` to the newly created instance:

```
new
        ^super new initialize
```

29.5.4 The DrawingController class

The `DrawingController` class is a subclass of the `ControllerWithMenu` class. This is because we wish to catch the left mouse button pressed event. This is simplified for the `ControllerWithMenu` class as a method called `redButtonActivity` is called whenever the left mouse button is pressed.

```
ControllerWithMenu subclass: #DrawingController
    instanceVariableNames: ''
    classVariableNames: ''
    poolDictionaries: ''
    category: 'SmallDraw'
```

The class comment for the `DrawingController` is left as an exercise for the reader. Only two methods are defined for this class: `controlLoop` and `redButtonActivity`. Both methods are defined in the *control defaults* protocol. The `controlLoop` method is called whenever the cursor enters the area of the window displayed by the `DrawingView`. This `controlLoop` method merely changes the type of cursor displayed (to that of a cross) when the user moves the cursor onto the drawing area. It then sends the message `super controlLoop`. This allows the control operations defined higher up the class hierarchy to be invoked:

```
controlLoop
    "Change the cursor to a cross-hair for drawing."
    Cursor crossHair showWhile: [super controlLoop].
```

Finally the `redButtonActivity` method defines what should happen when the left mouse button is pressed. In this case a new graphic object is added to the drawing at the point indicated by the current cursor position:

```
redButtonActivity
"Place widget at the current cursor position when left button pressed"
    self model addWidgetAt: self sensor cursorPoint.
```

29.5.5 The DrawingWidget class

The `DrawingWidget` class is an abstract superclass which captures all the elements which are common to graphic objects which will be displayed within a drawing. The `DrawingWidget` class (a subclass of `Object`) defines three instance variables `origin` (the cursor position when the mouse is clicked), the `extent` (or size of the object) and the `border`:

```
Object subclass: #DrawingWidget
    instanceVariableNames: 'origin extent border '
    classVariableNames: ''
    poolDictionaries: ''
    category: 'SmallDraw'
```

The `initialize` method for this class (defined in the `initialize` protocol) sets the default values for each of the instance variables. For example:

```
initialize
    origin := 0 @ 0.
    extent := 30 @ 30.
    border := Border width: 1.
```

You can experiment with these values by changing the extent or the border (do so and see what the effects are).

Next we will define the methods in the *accessing* protocol. These methods retrieve and set the border, the origin and the extent:

```
border
    ^border

border: aBorder
    border := border.

origin
    ^origin

origin: aPoint
    origin := aPoint.

extent
    ^extent

extent: aPoint
    extent := aPoint
```

The *displaying* protocol has two methods in it: `displayOn:` and `bounds`. The `displayOn:` method is a subclass responsibility. This is because each subclass needs to specify what it should look like independently. This is done in the `displayOn:` method.

```
displayOn: aGraphicsContext
    self subclassResponsibility
```

The `bounds` method calculates the bounds of the object using the `origin` and the `extent`. The return object is an instance of `rectangle`.

bounds
```
^origin extent: extent.
```

Finally, as before we need to extend the basic instance creation method new by sending the message `initialize` to the newly created instance. This is left as an exercise for the reader.

29.5.6 The PointWidget class

The `PointWidget` is a subclass of `DrawingWidget` that specifies how a point should be drawn in a drawing. It defines a single instance variable `diameter`. This indicates the size of the point to draw:

```
DrawingWidget subclass: #PointWidget
    instanceVariableNames: 'diameter '
    classVariableNames: ''
    poolDictionaries: ''
    category: 'SmallDraw'
```

The `initialize` method specifies the default size of the `diameter`. As the `DrawingWidget` defines some initializations as well, we must send the message `super initialize`.

initialize
```
super initialize.
diameter := 4.
```

The *displaying* protocol contains the class specific `displayOn:` method. This method uses the `displayDotOfDiameter:at:` message to draw a point on the graphics context:

displayOn: aGraphicsContext
```
aGraphicsContext displayDotOfDiameter: diameter at: origin
```

29.5.7 The CircleWidget class

The `CircleWidget` is another subclass of `DrawingWidget`, however it only redefines the `displayOn:` method such that it draws a circle within the bounds returned by the `self` bounds message:

displayOn: aGraphicsContext
```
| bnds |
"Get the bnds of the node."
bnds := self bounds.
"Draw the circle representing the object on screen"
aGraphicsContext displayArcBoundedBy: bnds
                        startAngle: 1 sweepAngle: 360.
```

29.5.8 The BoxWidget class

The BoxWidget class is the last subclass of DrawingWidget. Again it only redefines the displayOn: method. This time the border itself is displayed.

```
displayOn: aGraphicsContext
        | bnds rect |
        "Get the bnds of the node."
        bnds := self bounds.
        "Display the nodes border."
        rect := self border insetDisplayBoxFor: bnds.
        self border displayOn: aGraphicsContext forDisplayBox: rect.
```

29.6 Add a *delete widget* option

The exercise associated with this chapter is to extend the SmallDraw application by adding a delete option. This could be done by adding a fifth button to the window labeled delete. This would then set the style to #delete. The redButtonActivity method would then need to be changed to send either an addWidgetAt: message or a deleteWidgetAt: message. It would then be the responsibility of the drawingModel to find and remove the appropriate graphic object, remembering of course to send the changed message to itself.

29.7 Summary

This chapter has introduced the concept of custom views and how they are implemented. The use of custom views provides a great deal of flexibility for developers when constructing graphic user interfaces. In addition the availability of the user interface builder simplifies the task of creating such interfaces and allows the developer to concentrate on the implementation and control of the view rather than issues such as scrolling, or event capture.

29.8 Further reading

One of the best places to look for further guidance on this area is in the VisualWorks Cookbook and Tutorial which accompanies the VisualWorks system. In addition almost any book which discusses the MVC will be a useful reference.

Further Smalltalk

30. Memory Management and Garbage Collection

30.1 Introduction

This chapter describes how Smalltalk manages its memory and how automatic garbage collection is achieved. Automatic garbage collection and memory management are one of the main features lacking from some other object oriented languages (such as C++). We therefore begin the chapter by considering why high level object oriented languages should provide automatic memory management and garbage collection. A discussion is then presented of the way in which VisualWorks manages its memory and identifies those objects whose memory can be collected and reused. The process, by which obejcts can be relocated into permanent memory, is described. This can improve the efficiency of the garbage collector. Following this we consider the exception handling facilities in Smalltalk.

30.2 Why have automatic memory management?

One of the many advantages of Smalltalk over languages such as C++ is that Smalltalk automatically manages memory allocation and reuse. It is not uncommon to hear C++ programmers complaining of the problems they have had spending many hours attempting to track down a particularly awkward bug only to find it was a problem associated with memory allocation or pointer manipulation. Similarly, an often heard problem from C++ developers is that of memory creep - a problem which occurs when memory is allocated at some point but never freed up. The application then either eats up all available memory or runs out of space thus producing a run-time error.

Most of the problems associated with memory allocation in languages such as C++ are because the programmer must not only concentrate on the (often complex) application logic but also on memory management. They must ensure that they allocate only that memory which is required and deallocate it when it is no-longer required. This may sound simple, but it is no mean feat in a large complex application.

An interesting question to ask is "why do programmers have to manage memory allocation?". This is a reasonable question to ask. For example, there are few programmers today who would expect to have to manage the registers being used by their programs, however 20 or 30 years ago the situation was very different. One answer to the memory management question, often cited by those who like to manage their own memory, is that "it is more efficient, you have more control, it is faster and leads to more compact code". Of course, if you wish to take these comments to their extreme, then we should all be programming in assembler. This would enable us all to produce faster, more efficient and more compact code than that produced by Pascal, C++ or Smalltalk.

The point about high level languages, however, is that they are more productive, introduce fewer errors, are more expressive and are efficient enough (given modern computers and compiler technology). The memory management issue is somewhat similar. If the system automatically handles the allocation and deallocation of memory, then the programmer can concentrate on the application logic. This makes them more productive, removes problems due to poor memory management and when implemented efficiently, can still provide acceptable performance.

30.3 VisualWorks memory management

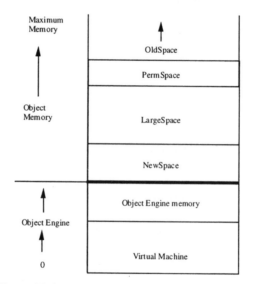

Figure 30.1: Memory organization in VisualWorks

VisualWorks provides automatic memory management. Essentially it does so by allocating a portion of memory as and when required. Then, when memory is short it searches through memory looking for areas which are no longer referenced. These areas of memory are then freed up (deallocated) so that they can be re-allocated. This process is often referred to as "garbage collection". A second process, invoked with garbage collection is memory compaction. This involves moving all the allocated memory blocks together so that free memory is contiguous rather than fragmented. The Smalltalk memory is divided up as shown in Figure 30.1.

As can be seen from this figure there is an area of memory allocated to the Virtual Machine (the object engine). This area, below the black line, holds both the virtual machine and the memory it uses. This area is outside the scope of this book and will therefore not be considered in greater detail.

The regions in the Object Memory are used to hold the objects created by the system and by user programs. It is useful to distinguish between parts of this memory, not least because the VisualLauncher offers the user two different types of garbage collection, one called "Garbage Collection" and one called "Global Garbage Collection". The options relate to which parts of memory are processed.

30.3.1 NewSpace and OldSpace

NewSpace is fixed in size (the default for NewSpace is about 200 K) and is used to hold newly created objects. When the amount of memory used in NewSpace crosses the *scavenge threshold*, the "generation scavenger" is called. This is a program which frees up memory from objects which are no longer referenced. This memory can then be used again. If an object has survived for long enough it may get moved in OldSpace.

References to objects in OldSpace are not quite as fast as those to objects in NewSpace, however, OldSpace is not fixed in size and can grow as long as there is memory available. The scavenger does not operate in OldSpace as it is optimized for NewSpace handling objects which are rapidly created and then de-referenced.

30.3.2 LargeSpace

This is a special area of memory for very large byte objects (typically larger than 1 KB) e.g. bitmaps. This saves the need to move large areas of memory around because of small frequently used areas of memory being repeatedly allocated and deallocated. Objects in LargeSpace are only freed up or moved when LargeSpace is compacted as part of a "compacting garbage collection" or when LargeSpace has filled up.

30.3.3 PermSpace

This is used to house objects which are rarely eligible for garbage collection. Examples of such objects are the system classes, tools and compilers. None of the garbage collections attempt to process this area of memory except the "Global garbage collector". This is initiated by the user from the VisualLauncher. Again this is a performance "tweak" and means that most of the time items such as a class do not have to be checked to see if the memory they occupy should be reclaimed nor must PermSpace be compacted.

30.4 Garbage collection and memory compaction

There are a number of different ways in which garbage collection and memory compaction can occur. The first is the "Generation Scavenger". This is called whenever NewSpace exceeds the *scavenge threshold*. It only processes objects in NewSpace (although it does place objects in OldSpace).

Another garbage collector is the *incremental garbage collector* (or IGC). This is called from Smalltalk code (as opposed to the scavenger which is called automatically by the Virtual Machine). The IGC reclaims objects in OldSpace, NewSpace and LargeSpace. It is called the incremental garbage collector because it works in an incremental manner to avoid disturbing the executing VisualWorks environment.

The two remaining garbage collectors are the "Compacting Garbage Collector" and the "Global Garbage Collector". These two garbage collectors are under user control and are initiated from the VisualLauncher. The compacting garbage collector is run when the user selects the "Garbage Collection" option on the special menu on the Launcher. The global garbage collector is run when the user select the "Global Garbage Collection" option on the same menu (and processes all of the memory available).

Finally, there is a data compactor which runs on the OldSpace which does not do any garbage collection, only memory compaction. This runs considerably faster than the garbage collectors.

30.5 Placing objects in PermSpace

PermSpace is an error of memory which is intended to hold objects which will never die or which will only rarely die. This means that most of the garbage collection methods do not need to worry about what is in PermSpace, thus reducing the amount of memory they must scan. Obviously some of the objects in PermSpace may die off, the global garbage collector therefore scans PermSpace as well.

It is possible to move objects from OldSpace to PermSpace to increase the performance of the garbage collector. This effect is achieved because by moving objects out of OldSpace the number of objects which must be considered is reduced. This can have a major effect on the performance of the garbage collector.

When you start up your "clean" image, most of the objects (including classes) present in the system will be located in PermSpace. When you create new objects these will reside in NewSpace or OldSpace. To relocate them into PermSpace it is necessary to save the current image using the "**Perm Save As ...**" option from the "**File**" menu option in the VisualLauncher. This writes the objects in OldSpace into PermSpace in the saved image. It does not affect where objects are located in the current (executing) image, only in the saved image. It is therefore necessary to exit the image and start up the newly saved image to have an executing image, in which the objects are stored in PermSpace.

There will however be a number of objects in PermSpace which are transient (i.e. likely to die in the short term). These objects will have been placed into PermSpace, because all objects, whether or not you wanted them to, will have been saved into PermSpace. Example of such objects may included windows, objects with which you were working etc. To remove these from the image (thus improving the performance of the garbage collector) perform a global garbage collection. Once you have done this save the image in the normal manner (i.e. "**Save as...**"). Having started up the newly saved image you could increase the time taken to start the image by performing one last save of the image. This is necessary because the global garbage collector compacts the objects in PermSpace. This means that when the image is started up, the system must relocate these objects. If you make one more image, then the objects will already have been relocated and the startup time will be minimized.

It is also possible to move objects from PermSpace into OldSpace. This can be done using the "**Perm Undo As...**" option again from the "**File**" menu option in the VisualLauncher. This will move **all** objects from PermSpace into OldSpace. This will obviously have an impact on the performance of the garbage collector, and is not recommended unless you intend to remove a large number of objects which were previously in PermSpace. You should then save the image again using the "**Perm Save As...**" option.

31. Concurrency in Smalltalk

31.1 Introduction

This chapter presents and explains a short example of how concurrency can be accomplished within Smalltalk. It also considers lazy evaluations (i.e. you only perform the evaluation if you absolutely have to), futures (you start an evaluation now which you will need later) and persistence.

The remainder of the document is structured in the following manner: Section two introduces the concept of concurrency, Section three briefly discusses processes within Smalltalk. Section four introduces the concepts used in the time slicing scheduler and Section five explains how future and lazy evaluators may be implemented in Smalltalk.

31.2 Concurrent processes

The concepts behind object oriented programming lend themselves particularly well to the concepts associated with concurrency. For example, a system can be described as a set of discrete objects communicating with one another when necessary. In most Smalltalk implementations, only one object may be executing at any one moment in time. However, conceptually at least, there is no reason why this restriction should be enforced. For example, the basic concepts behind object orientation still hold, even if each object executes within a separate independent process.

Traditionally, a message send is treated just like a procedural call, in which the calling object's execution is blocked until a response is returned. However, we could extend this model quite simply to view each object as a concurrently executable program module, with activity starting when the object is created and continuing even when a message is sent to another object (unless the response is required for further processing). In this model, there may be very many (concurrent) objects all executing at the same time. Of course this introduces issues associated with resource allocation etc. but no more so than in any concurrent system.

One implication of this concurrent object model is that objects are necessarily larger than in the traditional single execution thread approach. This is because the overhead of having each object as a process. A process scheduler for handling these processes and resource allocation mechanisms mean that it is not feasible to have integers or characters etc. as separate processes. (Note in Smalltalk integers etc. are objects. In such a system there might be a separate type of object which is a concurrent object which is assumed to be a large grained object).

Smalltalk has limited built-in support for concurrency. However, it does support Processes and Semaphores as primitive types. Other conventional inter-process communication and protection mechanisms such as SharedQueues and critical regions, are implemented in terms of these primitives. However, the processor scheduler (part of the virtual machine) implements a naive non-preemptive scheduling policy, with limited support for re-scheduling within a particular priority level. Further, once a high-priority process is running, no lower priority process will run until the high priority process suspends or terminates. For these reasons, the basic Smalltalk system contains only a few processes and typical applications using concurrency do not create more than a few tens of processes.

However, as the source code is available to the developer it is possible to extend the scheduler such that a pre-emptive policy is introduced. This is described in Section 3 following on from a discussion of the facilities provided in Smalltalk which enable the construction of such a scheduler.

31.3 Processes in Smalltalk

For further details on processes in Smalltalk see the appropriate system documentation, for example in VisualWorks see Chapter 8 in the Smalltalk User's Guide, Release 4.1 and pages 25-40 of [Lalonde and Pugh 1991b]. In this section we shall only provide a brief introduction to this subject.

A Smalltalk process is a non-preemptive light-weight process. That is, a Smalltalk process will run to completion unless a higher priority process attempts to gain control Smalltalk does not attempt to share the processor time amongst processes of the same priority. When the highest priority is held by multiple processes, the active process can be bumped to the back of the line with the expression: Processoryield - otherwise it will run until it is suspended or terminated before giving up the processor. A process that has been bumped will regain control before a process of lower priority.

This of course implies that every process has an associated priority. By default a process inherits the same priority as the process which spawned it. The *priority* of a process can be changed using the priority: message.

The process which is currently being executed by the processor is termed the active process. A process can also be waiting to use the processor or stopped, waiting for some resource. There are a number of message related to the state of a process these are:

- aProcess resume. This schedules a process.
- aProcess suspend. This stops the process from executing.
- aProcess terminate. This unschedules the process permanently.

There are a number of messages which are sent directly to the process scheduler which can be useful in working with active processes. These are:

- Processor activeProcess . This returns the process which is currently executing.
- Processor activePriority . This returns the priority of the active process; i.e. the priority of the process which is currently executing.

- Processor terminateActivity . Permanently removes the active process from execution.

Note that the messages are sent to a global variable `Processor`, which holds the instance of `ProcessorScheduler`.

For a process to be spawned from the current process there must be some way of creating a new process. This is done using one of four messages to a block. These messages are:

`aBlock fork`	This creates and schedules a process which will execute the block. The priority of this process is inherited from the parent process.
`aBlock forkAt: aPriority`	This creates and schedules a process executing the block at a specific priority.
`aBlock newProcess`	This creates a new process. It does not schedule the process. The process is created with the same priority as the parent block. It can be scheduled using the **resume** message.
`aBlock newProcessWith: anArrayOfParameters`	This message creates a new process with the same priority as the parent process. An array of parameters is passed to the block.

31.3.1 Semaphores

Semaphores provide a (simple) means of synchronization between multiple processes. For example, if two processes are executing and one must not pass a certain point until the other has completed some operation, then a semaphore between the two processes can be used as a flag to indicate to the first process that the operation has been completed.

The Semaphore class provides facilities for achieving simple synchronization, it is simple because it only allows for two forms of communication `signal` and `wait`. Essentially, a signal puts a 1 in the queue representing the semaphore and wait pops a 1 off the semaphore. The advantage of this approach is simplicity and efficiency. the disadvantage of this approach is that more complex synchronization is not possible. Of course, more complex synchronization can be achieved using semaphores and shared queues, but the key thing is that it is not directly supported.

When a process sends a wait message to a semaphore, that process will only be allowed to proceed if a corresponding signal has been sent to the semaphore. If there is no corresponding signal, then the process will be suspended. It will only be resumed when such a signal is sent.

Semaphores are ordered queues. If five waits have been sent to a semaphore then the fifth wait will only be serviced once five signals have been sent to the same semaphore. This means that they pay no attention to the priority of the process (unlike the scheduler). A high-priority process must wait in line for a signal in just the same way as a low priority process.

There are two instance creation methods for the `Semaphore` class. These are:

`Semaphore new.`	This creates a new empty semaphore.
`Semaphore forMutalExclusion.`	This creates a new semaphore with a single signal in it. This is a special type of semaphore which is used in association with a special message *critical* and provides for mutual exclusion.

As stated above there are two synchronization messages; `signal` and `wait`:

`aSemaphore signal.`	This increments the semaphore *signal* count.
`aSemaphore wait.`	This increments the semaphore *wait* count and causes the sender to suspend if fewer signals were previously sent.

An additional message to a semaphore is `critical:`. This should only be sent to a semaphore which was created using the `forMutalExclusion` instance creation message. The format of this message expression is:

```
aSemaphore critical: aBlock
```

This is useful if the block is accessing shared information. This message only allows the block to execute if no other block controlled by the same semaphore is executing; otherwise, it causes the active process to suspend until the block can be executed. In effect it is performing the following process:

- Send a wait message to the semaphore.
- Executes the block.
- Send a signal message to the semaphore.

31.3.2 Shared queues

When distinct processes access shared objects, then the access to those objects must be carefully controlled. For example, if two objects were to access a common set of data and one was in the process of adding some data, then when another (higher priority) process pre-empts it and attempts to perform a different addition operation, the original changes might well be lost. Since the original addition was not completed the set could be in a partially modified state, this could have extremely unpredictable results.

Smalltalk does not provide protected collection classes (although again these could be implemented using semaphores etc.). Instead, Smalltalk provides a `SharedQueue` class which guarantees that only one process will be able to access it at a time and that the expression being performed will execute to completion without being pre-empted. The design of a shared queue is essentially that presented in the Purple Book [Goldberg and Robson 1989], in Chapter 15 starting on page 258-265.

Elements can be placed in a shared queue using the nextPut: message, while elements can be read from a shared queue using the next message. If no elements are currently in the shared queue when a next message is sent, then the sending process is suspended until a nextPut: message is sent to the queue. If three successive next messages are sent to an empty shared queue by three separate processes, all three processes will be suspended. When a subsequent nextPut: message is sent to the shared queue, the first process to have sent a next message will be resumed. An additional message available is the peek message. This returns the next item in the shared queue, however unlike the next message, it does not remove it from the queue. The instance creation methods for a shared queue are:

```
SharedQueue new.
SharedQueue new: anInitialSize.
```

Both these messages return a shared queue. The three messages used with shared queues are:

```
aSharedQueue next.
aSharedQueue nextPut:
aSharedQueue peek.
```

The following passage is taken from page 36 [Lalonde and Pugh 1991b].

*"In general, creating new shared classes is relatively easy. A specialization of the original class is created with two new instance variables to play the role of the two semaphores (one semaphore for co-ordinating user access and another for mutual exclusion while executing critical code). Then, all operations with side effects are revised using the following template. If a method being revised is called **aMethod**, the critical section code is simply a variant of "super aMethod.".*

For example:

```
aMethod: anObject
        mutualExclusionSemaphore critical: [super aMethod: anObject].
        readingSynchronisationSemaphore signal.
```

or

```
aMethod
        | anElement |
        readingSynchronisationSemaphore wait.
        mutualExclusionSemaphore   critical:   [anElement   :=   super
aMethod].
        ^anElement.
```

31.4 A concurrent Smalltalk example

This section presents an example to show how time slicing could be done within Smalltalk using the current process scheduler (based on an example produced by

Hubert Baumeister - see end of section). The basic idea behind the effective control of multiple processes within Smalltalk is the introduction of a high priority process. This process wakes up every few milliseconds and regroups the processes in the waiting queue of the highest priority that has more than one process. It then goes back to "sleep" for a few milliseconds. It is thus time slicing between the various processes at the lower priority.

The approach taken in this section is that if it is necessary to develop a preemptive scheduler (that is one in which the processor time is shared between a given number of processes, rather than dedicated to a single process), then this can be done by using the facilities provided by the standard scheduler. In effect this results in two schedulers. One, is the system scheduler, the other is a user defined scheduler.

The system scheduler is still used to actually enable a process to execute. For example, it is still this scheduler which can suspend a process when a signal is sent to a semaphore.

The user defined scheduler is used to manage the queues of user processes waiting to be handed to the system scheduler. These queues are controlled by the user scheduler when ever it "wakes up". Of course, in order for it to gain control of the processor it MUST HAVE a HIGHER PRIORITY than all other user processes. It can then interrupt the user processes and select which process to initiate.

The key to the user defined scheduler is that it "wakes up" every few milliseconds. This can be simply and easily achieved using a `Delay`. This will send the process to sleep for the period of the delay. Actually, it will cause the process to suspend until the timer associated with the delay period sends the process a resume. It is this resume which will cause it to take control of the processor again.

Once the process wakes up it can determine which of the processes currently waiting to use the processor should be resumed next. One way in which this can be done is to regroup the processes in the waiting queue of the highest priority queue that has more than one process. Thus ensuring that a different process is at the head of the queue each time the user defined scheduler process "goes back to sleep".

```
Check to see if time slicing is already being used.
If not set up the a new process to sleep for 5 milliseconds
          and then to initiate the time slicing process.
Set the process to have the highest available priority.
Schedule the process for execution.
```

Figure 31.1: The time slicing algorithm

31.4.1 The source code for the example

As explained above the mechanism which allows this time slicing scheduler to work is the user of a `Delay`. This delay forces the user extensions to the scheduler to sleep. When it wakes up it selects a new process for execution using the slice method. It then goes back to sleep.

This continuous sleeping and slicing cycle can be achieved by spawning a new process (with the highest allowable priority). This process continually loops, sleeps and slices. The method which initiates this behaviour is `startTimeSlicing`. This method, defined in *time slice process* protocol, uses the algorithm in Figure 31.1. The actual Smalltalk method is presented below:

```
startTimeSlicing
        "self startTimeSlicing"
        TimeSliceProcess notNil ifTrue: [^self].
        TimeSliceProcess :=
          [[true] whileTrue:[(Delay forMilliseconds: 5) wait.
          Processor slice]] newProcess.
        TimeSliceProcess priority: (Processor highestPriority).
        TimeSliceProcess resume.
```

Of course having set up such a process we must provide some way of killing the process. If this is not done, then this process will always run (until the image is deleted). This is in fact the reason why the new process was stored into a variable named TimeSliceProcess. This is of course a global variable and could easily have been stored as an instance variable of the ProcessorScheduler class. However, for ease of debugging it is often easier to store a process such as this in a global variable. This is because it is at a higher priority level then most user processes. If an unexpected "feature" has been introduced, the process can be killed by sending the message `terminate` to the contents of the `TimeSliceProcess` global variable, either in a normal debugger or an emergency debugger.

The `stopTimeSlicing` method provides a rather more managed way of stopping the time slicing process. This does send the `terminate` message to the time slicing process and then sets the global variable to nil. This method is available in the 'time slice process' method category. The method definition is:

```
stopTimeSlicing
    "self stopTimeSlicing"
    TimeSliceProcess notNil
        ifTrue:[TimeSliceProcess terminate. TimeSliceProcess := nil]
```

So far we have set up the means by which a new, user defined process, can interrupt lower priority processes, and alter the process which will get run next. However, what we have not done is to define how this re-ordering of processes will occur.

The method `slice` in the method protocol *process state change* of the ProcessorScheduler performs this reorder. This is where the real meat of the time slicing operation occurs. The algorithm describing this method's operation is:

1. Find the first process priority queue which contains more than one process.
2. Remove the front process from this list and add it to the end of the list.

This is a very simple algorithm, but it works! The actual implementation of this algorithm is not quite as tidy. It is presented below:

336

```
slice
| aPriority list |
    aPriority := self highestPriority.
    "Find highest priority level with processes in it"
    [aPriority > 0 and:
        [(quiescentProcessLists at: aPriority) size <= 1]]
                    whileTrue: [aPriority := aPriority - 1].
    "Reorder that priority queue"
    aPriority = 0
        ifFalse: [list := (quiescentProcessLists at: aPriority).
                list addLast: (list removeFirst)].
```

To test out the effects of the time slicing try evaluating the following in a Workspace:

```
            ProcessorScheduler stopTimeSlicing.
            ProcessorScheduler example inspect.
            ProcessorScheduler startTimeSlicing.
            ProcessorScheduler example inspect.
```

This executes an example method defined in the *time slice process* method protocol which produces two inspectors. This method forks two processes, each of which puts a number onto a shared queue. The inspectors are opened on the shared queues produced. In the first, all the 1's will come first and all the 2's will follow them. In the second the 1's and 2's will be mixed in together.

```
example
        | queue |
        queue := SharedQueue new.
        [10000 timesRepeat: [queue nextPut: 1]] fork.
        [10000 timesRepeat: [queue nextPut: 2]] fork.
        ^queue
```

This type of example is illustrated in the next section as part of a stand alone application.

31.4.2 Using the example

To see how the time slicing works evaluate the following Smalltalk in a Workspace.

```
        | queue |
        ProcessorScheduler stopTimeSlicing.
        queue := SharedQueue new.
        [10000 timesRepeat: [queue nextPut: 1]] fork.
        [10000 timesRepeat: [queue nextPut: 2]] fork.
        queue inspect
```

In the contents of queue you will find first all the 1's and then all the 2's. If you then evaluate:

```
        | queue |
        ProcessorScheduler startTimeSlicing.
        queue := SharedQueue new.
        [10000 timesRepeat: [queue nextPut: 1]] fork.
        [10000 timesRepeat: [queue nextPut: 2]] fork.
        queue inspect
```

then the 1's and 2's are mixed.

However, you should be aware that time slicing is dangerous in the current implementation of the Smalltalk user interface, as the following example illustrates:

```
ProcessorScheduler startTimeSlicing.
[100 timesRepeat: [Transcript show: 'Process 1'; cr]] fork.
[100 timesRepeat: [Transcript show: 'Process 2'; cr]] fork.
```

This will hang up Smalltalk because some resources are not protected against multiple access. (This is why the example above used `SharedQueue` instead of a `WriteStream`)

31.4.3 Acknowledgments

Acknowledgments are made to Hubert Baumeister, of the University of Dortmund, Germany, who developed the original example. This was from an original idea put forward by Kent Williams of the University of Iowa.

31.5 Further reading

A good article on writing concurrent Smalltalk programs is [Hopkins and Wolczko 1989]. Lazy and future evaluators can also be implemented using these facilities. A good discussion on such evaluators can be found in [LaLonde and Pugh 1993].

32. The Metaclass Framework

32.1 Introduction

The metaclass concept is probably one of the most confusing parts of the whole of Smalltalk. This is partly due to the very confusing names used (for example, `Class class` and `Metaclass class`) but also because almost all of it is hidden from the developer. You are therefore only vaguely aware of it (if you are aware of it at all) during development. This means that developers do not need to understand it in detail and most people avoid trying to understand what appears to be a difficult concept if they don't have to. It also means that developers can only grasp what is happening abstractly, with little chance to see the mechanics of what is going on.

However, contrary to popular myth, the metaclass concept is actually not that difficult (if you can get around the terminology), although it can be confusing especially when its recursive definitions are encountered. We will however leave that aspect of metaclasses until right at the end. This means that you should hopefully gain at least an appreciation of what metaclasses about, even if the fine details of the implementation pass you by. In many ways, it is only an appreciation that you need (if you need it at all) to understand what you observe in the development environment.

As the basic concept being considered in this chapter is the concept of a class, Section 2 provides a review of what is meant by a class etc.

Metaclasses have not always been present in Smalltalk, they were only introduced into Smalltalk with the development of the Smalltalk-80 version of Smalltalk. This is essentially the version of Smalltalk which is used as the basis of commercial versions of the language (such as VisualWorks). Prior to that a number of (simpler) approaches were used. However, each of these provided fundamental problems which were overcome with the introduction of metaclasses.

Section 3 discusses the metaclass mechanism and how it works. As was stated before, it does this without going into the complexities of the implementation of metaclasses. This allows the casual reader to understand where metaclasses fit in and what they do without needing to understand the intricacies of the full metaclass inheritance hierarchy.

The classes `ClassDescription` and `Behavior` are introduced in Section 4. These classes encapsulate what it means to be a class and how classes do what they do. Section 5 considers the relationship between metaclasses, classes and the Metaclass class. This is not actually that complex, but can appear confusing at first sight.

A point to note before reading this chapter are the conventions used for Smalltalk, classes and instances. Remember:

- All Smalltalk code appears in a courier font, e.g. `Collection new`.
- All classes start with a capital letter e.g. `Set`, `Object`, `Array`.
- All instance names start with a lower case letter, e.g. `aSet`, `anObject`, `anEmployee`.

These conventions are adhered to rigidly below.

32.2 What are classes?

All classes are ultimately subclasses of the class `Object` (with the exception of `Object` itself). That is, a class inherits properties form its superclass (which in turn inherits properties form its superclass) up to `Object`. In turn every thing in Smalltalk is an object and every object is an instance of a class. On page 269 of the Purple Book [Goldberg and Robson 1989] the following statement is made:

> "There are two kinds of objects in the system, ones that can create instances of themselves (classes) and ones that can not."

This is a very important point, it highlights the fact that everything in Smalltalk is an object. That is, everything, including classes, are objects and can be sent messages (this of course means that classes are also instances of something, but what this is we will leave until later). However classes are special, they can create new objects called instances. Instances of classes however cannot create other instances (they must ask a class to do it for them).

In fact classes have only a very few roles in the system and these are essentially limited to:

- creating new instances,
- defining what those instances will do,
- holding class information (such as class variables).

Whereas instances hold application data and perform the operations defined by the (instance) methods held by the class. That is, the instance holds the data, but when it is sent a message it looks in the instance methods of its class for a method which implements that message. If no method is found in its class, then its superclass is searched for such a method. This search continues until the class `Object` is reached. If no method is found then the message `doesNotUnderstand:` is sent to the original receiver.

32.3 Classes and metaclasses

32.3.1 Metaclasses

As was indicated in the last section each class is an instance of a class. However we want each class to be able to behave in a different manner to any other class. Therefore each class must be an instance of a different class (as all instances of the same class must behave in the same manner). In Smalltalk-80 the concept of a *metaclass* was introduced. A metaclass is a special class, whose instance is a class. In general a metaclass only possesses a single instance (a class) and a class will be an instance of a single metaclass.

That is, a class is an instance of a metaclass and a metaclass defines how a class behaves. This means that it is actually in the metaclass that the class methods are defined and held. This means that when a class is sent a message, it looks in its metaclass for the method which implements the message. In effect, when you click on the class radio button in one of the various browsers in VisualWorks you are actually examining the classes' metaclass[1].

If you are confused by the terminology try to think of it in this way:

"A metaclass defines information about a class (hence the term meta)".

Metaclasses are not actually named directly, instead their names are a combination of the name of the class they define and " class". Thus the metaclass of `Collection` is `Collection class`, the metaclass of `Object` is `Object class` and the metaclass of a class called `Employee` would be `Employee class`. It is at this point that people begin to be confused by the terminology. We shall therefore attempt to recap.

- A class is an object which can create instances.
- A metaclass is a class which defines a class.
- A metaclass has only one instance (the class it defines).
- A metaclass is named after the class it defines concatenated with the word class.

In addition a metaclass cannot be accessed directly. It can only be access by sending the message `class` to a class. For example:

```
Collection class.
```

If you evaluate this and print the result, you will get the name of the Collection classes' metaclass, which is of course `Collection class` (which confusingly looks exactly like the expression which accessed the metaclass).

---

[1] In fact if you examine the `Browser` class you will find references to `self meta`. This is a reference to whether the user is currently examining the instance side (meta = false) or the class side (meta = true).

32.3.2 The Metaclass hierarchy

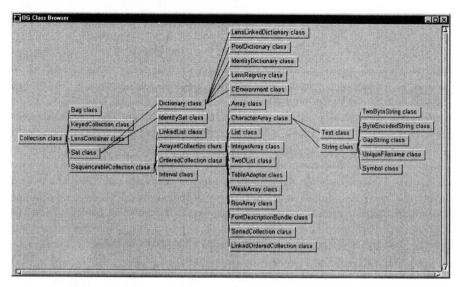

Figure 32.1: The metaclass hierarchy for the Collection classes

As you are aware, the classes in the Smalltalk system form a hierarchy rooted on the class `Object`. Thus the class `Dictionary` inherits from `Set` which in turn inherits from the class `Collection` which ultimately inherits from the class `Object`. This means that when instances of these class are sent messages, the system can search up through the class hierarchy for methods which implement that message.

Metaclasses also possesses a metaclass hierarchy. In this hierarchy one metaclass can inherit from another metaclass. In Smalltalk-80 the metaclass hierarchy was constrained to mirror the class hierarchy. This means that if some class side behavior is defined in `Collection`, then it will be inherited by `Set` and `Dictionary` via their metaclasses. Figure 32.1 presents part of the metaclass hierarchy for the Collection classes. The net result is that if a class is sent a message, the system begins the search for a corresponding method in its metaclass. If it does not find it there, it then looks in the superclass of its metaclass. This process continues until either a suitable method is found or until the `doesNotUnderstand:` message is triggered.

Figure 32.2 illustrates the relationships between the two hierarchies. Note that dashed arrows represent instance relationships, whereas solid arrows represent inheritance. Please note the case used for each label. As can be seen from this figure, this means that each class is an instance of its metaclass and that the metaclass hierarchy exactly mirrors the class hierarchy. In the figure, the instance of the class Dictionary, labeled as aDictionary, is presented in a rounded box, because it is an object which cannot create new instances. Therefore it is a different kind of instance. To make this distinction clear a different box style is used.

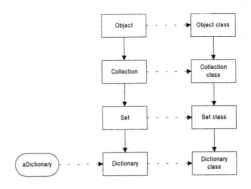

Figure 32.2: Class and instance relationships

32.4 ClassDescription and Behavior

One point we ignored above was "what happens when we get to Object?". That is, Object is the root of the class hierarchy in Smalltalk and therefore Object does not inherit from any superclass. This is not a problem for the class hierarchy as Object encapsulates all the concepts associated with being an object. However, what happens in the metaclass hierarchy? One possibility is that Object's metaclass, Object class, encapsulates all the concepts associated with being a class. However, in Smalltalk-80 a different and more sophisticated approach was adopted. (The reasons for adopting this approach only really become clear later when we discuss the recursive nature of metaclass, for the moment just accept that the following approach was taken).

In Smalltalk-80, Object class, the metaclass of Object inherits from a class called Class (See Figure 32.3). This allows Object class to define how the class Object should behave, while the concepts associated with being a class are encapsulated within Class. In particular, Class defines what instances of a class should look like and how they should behave. It also provides facilities which enable class variable names and pool (shared) variables.

Figure 32.3: The metaclass hierarchy up to Behavior

In turn, Class inherits from ClassDescription. This class provides facilities for naming classes, commenting classes (and this is why we defined commentTemplateString here) and naming instance variables. ClassDescription was provided as a super class of Class so that another class called Metaclass (which we will consider in the next section) could also inherit these facilities.

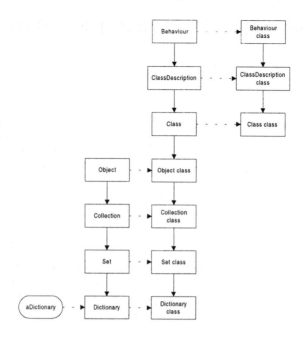

Figure 32.4: The metaclasses for Class, ClassDescription and Behavior

`ClassDescription` then inherits from a class known as `Behavior`. The class `Behavior` defines how classes should behave (for example how to create new instances). In particular it defines the minimum state necessary for objects that have instances.

Together these three classes define what a class is, how it should behave, how new instances should be created and what a class should look like. Figure 32.3 illustrates the metaclass inheritance hierarchy up to the class Behavior.

You may have noticed from the above class names, that `Class`, `ClassDescription` and `Behavior` are not metaclasses (i.e. they do not have class after their names). They are in fact classes, thus at the top of the metaclass hierarchy we find (not surprisingly) that metaclasses are classes after all. This raises two questions, firstly "do Class, ClassDescription and Behavior have metaclasses?" and "If metaclass are really classes, shouldn't they be instances of something?". In this section we will answer the first question, the second question is deferred to the next section.

As `Class`, `ClassDescription` and `Behavior` are classes, they are all instances of their metaclasses. This is illustrated in Figure 32.4. The metaclass of `Class` is of course `Class class` (the terminology can and will get worse!), the metaclass of `ClassDescription` is `ClassDescription class` and the metaclass of `Behavior` is `Behavior class`.

If you are comfortable with the description so far you have learnt most (if not all) of what you need to know to exploit the metaclass structure and the presence of `Class`, `ClassDescription` and `Behavior`. If you find that you become lost in the next section don't worry, much of what is described there is implementation level detail and overly convoluted.

32.5 The metaclass concept goes recursive!

32.5.1 What are metaclasses?

A question which was raised in the previous section (but not answered) was "If metaclass are really classes, shouldn't they be instances of something?". The answer to this question is "yes", just like any class, they are in fact an object and objects are all instances of some class. The next question then is, "of what class is a metaclass an instance?". The answer this time, is the class `Metaclass` (note the capitalization and font).

That is, all metaclasses (such as `Collection class`, `Object class` and `Set class`) are instances of the class `Metaclass`. This is because all metaclasses have the same behavior. They define the structure, definition and behavior of a class. Each subsequent class may have a different behavior, but from the point of view of the metaclass, all classes are constructed in the same way, are structured in the same way (i.e. they have class methods, class instance variables and class variables) and all require the same set of operations (i.e. they must be able to construct instances).

32.5.2 What is metaclass an instance of?

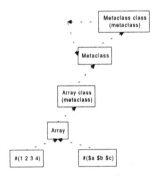

Figure 32.5: Instance relationships between instances, classes and metaclasses for array

`Metaclass`, being a class, must also be an instance of something. Following the standards laid down about it is therefore an instance of its metaclass. This metaclass, like all other metaclasses, has its name derived from the class, it is therefore called `Metaclass class`. However, every metaclass is an instance of `Metaclass`, thus the `Metaclass class` is an instance of `Metaclass`. This is the first point of circularity in Smalltalk and it is worth summarizing:

- All metaclasses are instances of `Metaclass`.
- The metaclass of `Metaclass` is `Metaclass class`.
- `Metaclass class` is a metaclass, it is therefore an instance of `Metaclass`.

- Therefore the metaclass of Metaclass is an instance of Metaclass.

This is illustrated in Figure 32.5. This figure shows that an object such as an array is an instance of the class Array. In turn Array is an instance of its metaclass Array class. This metaclass is an instance of the class Metaclass, which is an instance of its own metaclass Metaclass class. And as has been said, Metaclass class is an instance of Metaclass (see what I mean about the terminology!).

32.5.3 Instance relationships for classes and metaclasses

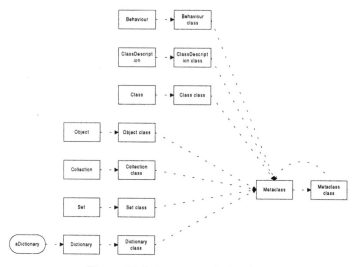

Figure 32.6: Instance relationships

To complete the explanation being given, consider Figure 32.6. This illustrates the *instance* relationships between classes, their metaclasses, the Metaclass and the Metaclass class. Note that no distinction is made between a class being an instance of another class and a user generated instance of the Dictionary class.

32.5.4 Class inheritance

A point we have still not covered is what does the class Metaclass inherit from? Remember all classes (except Object) have a superclass and Metaclass is no exception. Metaclass inherits from ClassDescription, this is because the structure of classes and metaclasses are very similar. For example instances of both Class and Metaclass can have methods. In turn, the metaclass of Metaclass, (i.e. Metaclass class) follows the standard laid down and it inherits from the ClassDescription class. This is illustrated in Figure 32.7.

As ClassDescription is a subclass of Behavior, it also means that both Class and Metaclass inherit from the facilities provided by Behavior. This means that instances of both Metaclass and Class can create new instances etc. (Remember Behavior provides all the protocol for making new instances so this is not surprising).

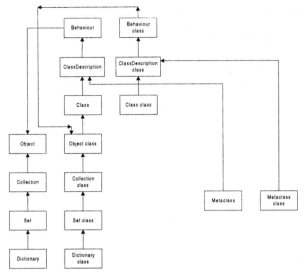

Figure 32.7: Class inheritance

We are now left with the class `Behavior` and what it inherits from. All other classes have been accounted for. What then does `Behavior` inherit from? It inherits from the class `Object`. This closes the loop and ensures that all things in the whole of Smalltalk are objects (i.e. at some point their class inherits from `Object`) whether they are class, metaclasses or ordinary instances.

32.5.5 The whole enchilada

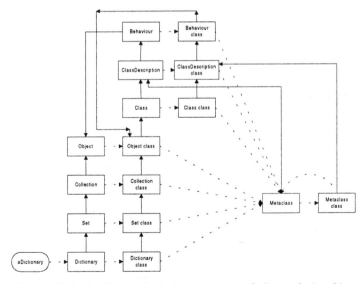

Figure 32.8: Combining both the instance and class relationships

The last two sections have considered the instance relationship and the inheritance relationship between classes in Smalltalk respectively. Each of these in isolation isn't too complicated, however when you put the two together you obtain a diagram such as that illustrated in Figure 32.8.

This figure illustrates the instance and inheritance relationships between classes and metaclasses. As can be seen from this diagram the overall structure is quite complex. However, if you study it closely you should find that it does make sense. Even when there appears to be the potential for excessive circularity it can be seen that this is not the case. There is one point of circularity which should be noted, that is an `Object` is an instance of `Object` class which (eventually) inherits from `Behavior` which inherits from `Object`.

32.6 Further reading

See Chapters 5 and 16 in the Purple Book [Goldberg and Robson 1989] for an introduction to metaclasses and a detailed description of the class `Class`, `Metaclass`, `ClassDescription` and `Behavior`. However, the actual description of the metaclass concept and the diagrams presented with it are a little confusing. Also see Chapter 26 of [Hopkins and Horan 1995] for an excellent introduction to metaclasses.

The Future

33. The Future for Object Technology

33.1 Introduction

This chapter is structured in the following manner: we first consider issues directly relating to the future of the Smalltalk language and then the type of object oriented development toolkits which are, and will be, available. We next consider the impact of the internet on object technology. We then briefly discuss the development of object oriented databases and then address Smalltalk's role as a training environment for object technology before concluding by considering very briefly the future of object technology over the next five years.

33.2 The Smalltalk language

The Smalltalk language is unlikely to change a great deal for the new ANSI standard being produced by the X3J20 standard committee. This committee was formed in late 1993 and draws its members from both the user and vendor communities. This standard is necessary as more and more vendors are producing Smalltalk based development systems which, while similar, all possess (significant but subtle) differences. Although the merger of the two largest Smalltalk vendors ParcPlace and Digitalk in 1996 could be seen as resulting in the creation of an enforced standard, other vendors could still "go their own way".

However there are other aspects of the Smalltalk language which need to be addressed, some of which are fundamental to Smalltalk and others of which are technology oriented. Each of these areas will be considered below.

33.2.1 Smalltalk issues

There are a number of language issues which Smalltalk must address if it is to survive and prosper into the next century. All of these are related to providing better support for large scale, commercially critical systems. Such systems require:

- **Non-interpreted implementations**: All commercial version of Smalltalk rely on the use of a virtual machine which executes byte codes. The byte codes are the "compiled" version of the Smalltalk source code. This means that Smalltalk is compiled into an intermediate language which is then "interpreted" by the virtual machine rather than being compiled into a native code. The result is that Smalltalk does not produce a true executable image which generally results in significant performance and memory overheads.

- **Class-based version control**: Within a software development project, different team members will be developing different parts of the system. In many cases they will maintain their source code using a source code control systems such as SCCS under UNIX. This means that all the source code control operations are outside of the Smalltalk system and require external intervention. For example, if a developer within a project using SCCS, wishes to see how an old version of a class would interact with a set of newly defined classes, they must leave VisualWorks, retrieve the old version of the class from SCCS, file it into VisualWorks, probably having removed the newer version of the class from the image to ensure that no additions remain. When they have finished performing these tests they must then retrieve the new version of the class. Such version control of classes and methods should be inherent to the development environment rather than a third party after sales add-on.

- **Team-based development support**: Smalltalk was originally conceived as a language and development environment for a single user. It therefore has inherent weaknesses when it comes to team development. At present if members of a development team wish to share their work they must file out (all) the relevant classes and methods from their own images and file in those from their fellow workers. This can be problematic as well as cumbersome. This problem stems from the very nature of the image in which all the "source code" is held and within which development takes place. A fundamental change in the way that the image works is required.

- **Typed variables**: Smalltalk is a dynamically typed language. That is, a variable's type is determined by the type of object that it holds. This is all very well for rapid prototyping and for small single user developments, however for large projects which must exist for significant periods of time, this can result in disaster. For example, "type mismatches" cannot be detected at compile time and will only manifest themselves at run time. This places a huge burden on testing which must now catch such mismatches. In addition the performance of a dynamically typed language can be lower than that of a statically typed language as the run time system must now perform various checks which could otherwise be performed at compile time.

- **Improved exception management**: At present Smalltalk possesses only very rudimentary exception handling. If the developer has not defined how the exception should be caught it is merely presented to the user. This is acceptable for a single user/developer system, however for delivered systems this is unacceptable. Even the facilities that are available are extremely limited. For example, class level rather than block or method level support is required, such that if a particular type of exception occurs anywhere within an instance of a class (or one of its subclasses) then that exception is handled cleanly and in an appropriate manner.

- **Private methods**: In Smalltalk all methods are publicly available, that is any object can send a message requesting that the receiving object perform any of the defined methods. In general Smalltalk developers place those methods which are not intended for external use in method protocols such as private (or private-<some-additional-description>). However this is only convention and there is no system support for these "private" methods. Other object oriented languages such as C++ and Java do support the definition of private and public methods. Indeed these languages take the concept of private and public further. For example, in Java [van der Linden 1996] there are a number of classes of access indicated by keywords:

1. public - world access.
2. protected - accessible to any object in the current package or any subclass in any package.
3. default - any class in the package (A Java package is a group of classes which are to be bundled together. They are essentially the same as libraries in C++).
4. private protected - class / subclass access only.
5. private - accessible to the current class only.

Of course some of the above issues are being addressed by current research (for example [Feigenbaum 1995]) however there appears to be little interest in following this lead from the vendor community.

33.2.2 Technology issues

There are a number of technology based issues which will affect Smalltalk's popularity in the coming years. These are less related to Smalltalk itself and more to the way in which software is, and will be, developed.

The majority of software today is developed for use on PCs running either Windows 95, Windows NT or Windows 3.1. Therefore Smalltalk needs to be able to easily and simply interact with these environments. For example, explicit support for OLE and dynamically linked libraries is a must.

In the future it is likely that the influence of the World Wide Web (or Web) and the internet will continue to grow. Smalltalk vendors must provide facilities which will allow Smalltalk to take advantage of this (ParcPlace-Digitalk have already produced a product called VisualWave which is a VisualWorks based Web server).

Object sharing and notification must be made significantly easier. CORBA (see [Ben-Natan 1995] for a summary of the CORBA standard and [Orfali et al 1995] for an excellent compendium of distributed object technology including OLE, OpenDoc as well as CORBA) while providing a possible infrastructure for such object sharing results in large cumbersome ORBs (CORBA stands for the Common Object Request Broker Architecture. It is a specification for an ORB (Object Request Broker) which allows distributed objects within different systems to communicate. Simpler and easier to use solutions are needed which suit the requirements of less technically complex systems, such as a database server which is accessed by a small number of interacting Smalltalk clients.

Improved support for deploying applications is required. The process of removing as many system classes as possible without damaging the application's operation is still largely an art rather than a science. VisualWorks 2.5 does give greater support for this, however it is still severely limited in its operation.

Finally, there needs to be a convergence between the different Smalltalk dialects. This will happen to some extent through the new ANSI standard. However, if this standard does not cover issues such as the user interface, database access, web access, the use of dynamically linked libraries and OLE, then it will have only limited success.

33.3 Object oriented development toolkits

For Smalltalk to maintain its position as a mainstream language it must be supported by appropriate development tools, as well as by a number of language vendors. The merger of Digitalk and Parcplace systems raised the prospect of the emergence of essentially a single language vendor (as ParcPlace and Digitalk between them accounted for the majority of Smalltalk system sales). This has been an impediment to a language's success in the past. For example, developers are unwilling to commit to a language which, on the demise of their system supplier, forces them to re-implement the whole system in a new language. However IBM have entered the market with their range of Smalltalk products thus alleviating the situation to a certain extent.

However we are still left with the issue of the range of development tools and toolkits available. It is possible to classify object oriented development toolkits into a number of categories:

- **Object oriented language compilers and linkers**. These tend to be command line programs which read in a source code file and produce object files which are then combined with other object files to create a stand alone executable. They are typically used in an Edit-Compile-Link-Execute cycle in which the various tools used are poorly integrated (if they are integrated at all).

- **Object oriented application development environments**. Object oriented Application Development Environments (or OOADEs) are comprehensive development environments that not only possess highly integrated development tools but also provide a far greater level of developer support than the basic language compilers. For example, database access, user interface construction, code generation and libraries of reusable components. Typically OOADEs exploit an iterative development cycle in which the developer writes some code, compiles it in-situ and executes it before writing some more code.

- **Object oriented CASE (OOD methodology-based) tools**. OO CASE tools differ from the OO ADEs because they support one or more OOD methodologies. The most common OOD methodologies used with OO CASE tools are OMT and Booch. These two accounted for over 50% of OOD methodologies used world wide in 1995. Given this, it is likely that the Unified Modeling Language (UML) will have a significant impact in the future, as it is the inheritor of both OMT and Booch.

There are in fact two different types of OO CASE tools available: OO analysis and design tools and OO Integrated CASE tools. The former act as diagramming tools while the latter are model-based code generating tools. Most of the code generation tools support C++ although versions for Smalltalk have been appearing since the end of 1995. This is now a significant market which increased in the US by 82% in 1995 to be worth about $138 million.

Smalltalk examples of each of these can be identified. For example gnu-Smalltalk falls into the first category, while VisualWorks itself falls into the second. There are also a growing number of Smalltalk based OO CASE tools. For example, Rational (probably the most influential OO CASE developer having Grady Booch, Jim Rumbaugh and Ivar Jacobson working for them) has a version of its product ROSE for Smalltalk (It also produces versions of Rational ROSE for C++, SQL Windows and Ada).

However it is worth noting that although OO CASE tools are the fastest growing product area, this is an area in which Smalltalk has been a relatively late entrant. OO CASE tools first started appearing commercially , in any number, around 1992. It was three years before many of these tools offered direct Compatibility (or code generation) for Smalltalk. For Smalltalk to continue as a commercial success it is essential that it gains a similar level of support in this area as C++.

33.4 The internet and objects

The world wide web (or just the Web for short) is one of the phenomena of the last few years. It is set to revolutionize the way we think about computers and computing. However, at present most information available on the web is in the form of static web pages. These are useful in providing information but are fairly limited in their ability to do much more. Java has of course allowed Web pages to possess at least some dynamic element, however the majority of Java applets on the Web make little cartoon characters do something. To gain the full benefits of the Web it is necessary to be able to connect applets, downloaded form the Web, into corporate databases or to existing programs. Such an ability will open the Web up to a huge range of applications both within and between corporations.

Java, of course, has already guaranteed that object technology will play an important role in the development of such applications. Java is in many ways just another object oriented language, which like Smalltalk, is not compiled into an executable but into byte codes which are then "executed" by an interpreter (or virtual machine). Thus any Java applet is an object or set of objects which communicate with each other via message passing. Thus these applets should be capable of communicating, relatively easily, with a distributed object system. Indeed developments are already underway to link Java applets to CORBA compliant ORBs, and to OLE/COM.

To simplify this sort of task, special OO WEB site development tools will be (and are being) developed. It is also likely that many of the existing OO CASE tools will provide Web additions so that they too can be used with the Web and for Web development.

However, which language will dominate, and which type of distributed system will be adopted, are two different questions. Java will certainly be the dominant Web language, although there is no great reason why Java should be any better as a Web language than Smalltalk or any other interpreted OO languages such as Objective-C or Eiffel, other than the fact that Java got there first and has the backing of both Netscape and Sun. However, in early 1996, ParcPlace-Digitalk released VisualWave. This is an application development environment (ADE) for building live applications on the Web. VisualWave runs on VisualWorks and hides all the HTML (Hyper Text Markup Language) and CGI (Common Gateway Interface) details from the developer. Instead, the developer can concentrate on creating Web applications in a Smalltalk environment. This allows the user to access multiple databases, use interactive window building tools, Smalltalk classes and the VisualWorks browsers to develop applications. At present VisualWave relies on the use of a CORBA compliant ORB, however it claims that it will be able to access OLE components soon.

It is interesting to compare and contrast Java and Smalltalk. Smalltalk appears to be the better OO language for the internet as it is not a hybrid language and has many features built into it which would work well with the Web. This means that it is likely that companies which already have significant Smalltalk experience will stick with Smalltalk and use VisualWave, although many others will swallow the hype surrounding Java, and go with it.

The question of which distributed object technology will be adopted is more complex. OMG would certainly like CORBA to be adopted as the accepted standard, while Microsoft would prefer their own OLE/COM infrastructure standard. An open question is what will Netscape do? It is probable that Netscape will do both. For example, Sun have already linked Java with CORBA and Sun and Netscape are closely linked, but a great deal of the world uses Microsoft products.

33.5 Object oriented databases

An object oriented database system is one which relies on an object-oriented view of the world, that is, uses classes and objects as the basic storage mechanism rather than forms and tables. In general these databases are also quite flexible about the type of data they hold including text, programs, graphics, video and sound. However OO databases have been fairly thin on the ground until recently. The main players in this field have tended to concentrate on Smalltalk based systems. Either providing Smalltalk binding or in some cases implementing the system in Smalltalk and treating Smalltalk as the database scripting and query language to use. Recently however, a great deal of interest has been shown in using OO databases with the Web.

Web developments are not only based around a variety of different data types, they also require the ability to navigate easily around data in a domain model. Many OODB vendors (as well as many users) are coming to the conclusion that OO databases are ideal for supporting a HTTP server. By storing the Web site within the OO database the process of exchanging data with the database, and modifying the Web pages is simplified.

This trend is likely to increase significantly in the future. It is already the case that other OO database suppliers are adding Java interfaces or making their systems Web compliant. It is also likely that the Web will act as the motivating force which will force many organizations to adopted OO database technology (as opposed to relational database technology).

33.6 Smalltalk as a training environment

It is likely that Smalltalk will reach a point in the commercial sector where its use does not increase. At what level this will occur is still unclear, however I believe that Java is going to have a greater impact on the use of C++ than Smalltalk. If anything, I suspect that Java will help to interest people in OO languages including Smalltalk. At this point I believe that Smalltalk's strengths as an educational language will come to the fore.

Far too many people believe that it is possible to move from a procedural development language, such as C, to an OO language just by reading a book on C++. The result is that they develop C programs but maintain their data within objects. I myself have been involved in discussions with developers who have claimed that object technology is a waste of time because they did not accrue the benefits claimed. When pressed it is almost always that case that they failed to invest in appropriate training for their staff. This was their mistake.

The transition to object technology is not an easy one. Indeed it becomes harder the greater the level of experience of those trying to make the change. This does not necessarily have anything to do with their ability to adapt to new ideas, rather I believe it is to do with the fact that they have a very firm grasp of one paradigm where as less experienced software developers have a poorer grasp of (for example) the procedural paradigm. It is therefore necessary to include in the first object oriented development attempted by an organization, a suitable training budget. This budget needs to be seen as an investment in the future, rather than a cost of the actual project involved. In addition it should not be seen as a language programming exercise. The best approach is to view it as a training in the philosophy and techniques of object technology. The aim of such a training is not necessarily to educate those involved in the use of the tools to be used on the actual project (such as OO CASE tools and the OO language to be used). Such an approach will allow the staff involved to explore the concepts rather than worrying about a particular syntax and how it differs from what they are used to.

Of course educating software developers in abstract concepts is only of limited use, therefore such training courses should re-enforce what is being taught with practical experience of a pure OO language such as Smalltalk. After all it is not possible to write anything in Smalltalk without using objects and message passing. In addition it is easier to spot conceptual problems in Smalltalk (as evidenced by students attempting to write the main program or worrying about procedures rather than objects).

I therefore believe that Smalltalk will have a concrete future as an educator as well as a practical OO development environment. Indeed it may well have a greater influence as an educational language allowing organizations to migrate to object technologies in as painless a manner as possible.

33.7 Object technology: the next five years

What will happen to object technology over the next five years? This is both an interesting and a difficult question. Object technology is certainly gaining an ever increasing share of the market for commercially developed systems, however there is still a great deal of resistance to it in many quarters. This resistance is sometimes due to ignorance and sometimes due to bigotry. In either case it requires someone to champion its cause in the affected organizations. However the Web is here, and despite the hype, is likely to be a major factor during the next ten years.

Thanks mostly to Java, object technology is seen as the developer's Web technology. This therefore means that it is likely that much of the development in object technology will be Web driven (we have already considered some of its effects above). This will probably continue to grow and may have both a positive and detrimental effect. The positive effect will be that many new and existing companies will adopt object technology, many other companies will move to support their requirements and many new start up companies will be created. Over time many of these companies will close down again only to be replaced by other small start up companies. It is within these companies that many of the most innovative ideas will probably be generated (consider Netscape as an example). This will be a very creative and dynamic time.

However there are two possible results of this. One is that object technology becomes so successful that companies such as Microsoft consider it a part of their core business and move into the market with such force that they come to dominate. I have always believed that monopolies (or virtual monopolies) are a bad idea and certainly tend to be bad for any industry. The other concern is that object technology becomes so tightly linked to the Web in people's minds that the technology providers ignore other aspects of the computer world and focus solely on the Web (which I believe would be a mistake). Such a close binding might have a short term benefit, but let us hope that when the Web bubble bursts or when the next great new thing comes along, object technology is not left behind with the Web and ignored.

A.1. Appendix: The Smalltalk Language Syntax

A.1.1 Basic syntax

A.1.1.1 Statement separation

Achieved in Smalltalk by the *period* or *full stop* rather than the semi-colon as in Pascal or C. For example:

```
Transcript show: 'Hello World'.
Transcript show: ' John'.
```

Although it is unnecessary to put a period at the end of the last line of code, as in Pascal it is a good idea.

A.1.1.2 Assignment operator

The assignment operator is the colon equals combination as in other languages such as Pascal. For example:

```
a := 2 + 4.
```

This operator is not a "copy" operator and thus may result in two variables referencing the same object. Not that := is not a message as variables are not objects (whereas + is a message as it relates to two objects even if one is contained within a variable).

Further example are:

```
oldIndex := 1.
newIndex := oldIndex.
myArray := #(1 2 3 4).
myName := 'John Hunt'.
```

Assignments return values (like other expressions), so that several assignments can be made together:

```
nextIndex := newIndex := oldIndex.
```

A.1.1.3 Comments

Comments are defined using " ". Everything between the double quotes is treated as a comment. Note that comments cannot be nested in Smalltalk. This can be awkward if you wish to comment out some code for later.

A.1.1.4 The return operator

This operator is used to return a value from a method. By default a method will return the object that the message which triggers the method was sent to. However, this can be altered using the return operator ^. For example:

```
^24
```

would cause a method to return the value 24. Note that the method will "return" as soon as it encounters a return operator. It is therefore possible, although not necessarily a good idea, to have more than one return operator in a method. Thus allowing a method to return from different points depending on the execution path taken through the method.

A.1.1.5 Cascading

The cascade operator, represented by a comma (,) can be used to send a series of messages to the same object (which is only referenced once). For example:

```
Transcript cr.
Transcript show: 'John Hunt'.
Transcript: tab.
Transcript show: '1995'.
Transcript cr.
```

Can be re-written as:

```
Transcript cr;
        show: 'John Hunt';
        tab;
        show: '1995';
        cr.
```

A.1.2 Literals and variables

A.1.2.1 Literals

Literals are constant objects such as numbers, characters, strings, symbols etc.

Numbers are a sequence of numeric characters with an optional decimal point and an optional minus sing. Example of numbers are:

```
  8       12.7    -44.7    0.0009
```

In Smalltalk a number is positive unless otherwise stated. there is therefore no need for a unary plus sign. Numbers can also be represented in other bases, by preceding them with a radix and the letter "r":

```
  6r145   8r5E
```

Characters are individual letters and are distinctly different to a string containing only a single letter. They are represented by a single character preceded by a "$" symbol. For example:

```
  $a      $d      $'      $+      $4
```

Strings are collections of characters encompassed within single quotes. They can possess spaces, under bars etc. For example:

```
  'Hello World'
```

Symbols are special objects that represent unique entities in the Smalltalk system. These are represented using a leading the hash (#) symbol.

```
  #temp   #john
```

A.1.2.2 Variables

Variable names describe accessible variables. Variable names are identifiers made up of letters and digits with an initial letter:

```
  someObject    MyCar   totalNumber
```

A capitalization convention is used consistently throughout the standard image. Most Smalltalk programmers adhere to this standard which it is therefore advisable to follow:

- *Private* variables (instance variables, temporaries) start with an initial lower-case letter.
- *Shared* variables (class variables, global variables, pool variables) start with an initial upper-case letter.

Message selectors should also start with a lower-case letter. For both variable names and message selectors, if the name is a combination of two or more words, the convention is to capitalize the first letter of the second word onwards. For example:

```
  displayTotalPay      returnStudentName
```

A.1.2.3 Pseudo variable names

A *pseudo variable* name refers to an object which cannot be changed; these include:

- nil. A value used when no other value is appropriate, such as un-initialized variables. nil is the sole instance of class Undefined Object.
- true. Represents truth. The sole instance of class True.
- false. Represents falsehood. The sole instance of the class False.

True and False are subclasses of Boolean which implements Boolean algebra and control structures.

In addition there are two pseudo variables whose value changes depending upon the context. They are therefore not constants, however the programmer has no ability to change their value.

self. This refers to the receiver of a message itself. It literally means "the object within which the method is executing". It is used to send a message to the object requesting the another method defined on the object is executed.

super. Also refers to the message receiver, but the method search starts in the superclass of the class in which super is used. This is often used if the functionality of a method is to be extended rather than overwritten. For example:

```
myMethod: anObject
        new code before super.
        super myMethod.
        new code after super.
```

There is also a pseudo message, which just returns the receiver of the message as the result of evaluating the message. This message is yourself:

yourself. A message which returns the receiver of the message. It can be used in any situation, however its most common use is in a cascade of messages, where it is necessary to return the original receiver of the cascaded messages.

A.1.2.4 Declaring a variable

To declare a *temporary variable*, place the variable to be declared between two bars, e.g. | x y z | indicates that the variables x, y and z are temporary variables.

If you reference an undeclared variable the system will assume you wish to declare a new global variable and do so. Global variables should, by convention, always start with a capital letter. They can be deleted by looking at the Smalltalk system dictionary and deleting the appropriate entry.

A.1.3 Classes and methods

A.1.3.1 Defining a class

The structure of a class definition is:

```
NameOfSuperclass subclass: #NameOfClass
    instanceVariableNames: 'instVarName1 instVarName2'
    classVariableNames: 'ClassVarName1 ClassVarName2'
    poolDictionaries: ''
    category: 'Visual Organiser'
```

Where

NameOfSuperclass is the parent class of the class to be defined.

NameOfClass is the name of the class being defined. (Note that at this stage it does not exist and must therefore be preceded by a #).

instanceVariableNames is used to list the instance variable to be used with this class.

classVariableNames is used to define the class variable to be used with this class.

poolDictionaries defines the pool variables to be used with this class.

category defines the category in which this class will be placed.

Note that this definition may not define all the variables associated with this class, for example, it may have inherited instance variables from its parent.

A.1.3.2 Methods

The structure of a method is:

```
messagePattern: argument1 additionalPattern: argument2 ....
    "comment"
    | temporaries |

    statements
```

Where

messagePattern and additionalPattern: represents the name of the method. Notice that the method name is divided up amongst the arguments and that a part of the message name which precedes an argument has a trailing colon ':'.

arguments the names of arguments in the message pattern are accessible within the method.

"comment" is a comment describing the operation performed by the method and any other useful information.

| temporaries | is used to define variables which are local to the method. They must be declared at the beginning of the method (just after the message pattern) and are initially nil.

statements represents any legal set of Smalltalk statements. These statements are used to implement the behaviour of the method.

A.1.3.3 Message expressions

Message expressions describe messages to receivers. The value of the expression is determined by the method it invokes. For example, the following is a message expression:

```
newStatus := thisPerson marries: thatPerson
```

This expression is made up of an assignment and a message expression. In turn the message expression is made up of a receiver, a message selector and an argument:

- thisPerson is the receiver
- marries: is the message selector
- thatPerson is the argument

As with every message expression it returns a result, which is what is saved into the variable newStatus.

A.1.3.4 Message types

There are a number of different types of message. These are:

- **Unary Message** have no arguments.
  ```
  anArray size.   theta sin.     4 even.
  ```
  the message selector (i.e. size) can be any simple identifier.
- **Keyword Messages** have one (or more) keywords, each with an argument.
  ```
  index max: limit
  anArray at: first put: 'John'
  ```
  In the above examples max: and at:put: are the keywords (termed selectors). This means that the name of a message selector is spread amongst the arguments. These can be any simple identifier with a trailing colon. The argument can be an expression representing any object.
- **Binary Messages** have one argument, and the selector is one or two non-alphabetic symbols. For example:
  ```
  3 > 4.  100 / 17.     oldIndex + 1.
  ```
  The second character in a binary message selector *cannot* be a minus sign.

A.1.3.5 Parsing rules

The parsing rules of Smalltalk can be summarized in the following points:

- Multiple expressions are separated by full stops.
- Unary expressions parse left to right.
- Binary expressions parse left to right.
- Unary expressions take precedence over binary expressions.
- Parenthesized expressions (using round brackets) take precedence over unary expressions.

To summarize then the precedence order is unary - binary -keyword (plus take into account round brackets).

A.1.4 Blocks

A block is a sequence of statements whose execution is deferred. They are evaluated in the context in which they were defined. Each block is an object of class Context. The statements are enclosed in square brackets e.g. []. The block will be executed when it is sent the message "value". The result of the last message sent is returned as the value of the block. For example:

```
| temp |
temp := [Transcript show: 'Hello John'.].
Transcript show: 'Hello World'.
temp value.
```

Blocks are most commonly used with control structures such as:

```
anObject
    ifTrue: [Transcript show: 'Hello Out There'.].
```

They may also be used in iteration statements, for example:

```
[x > 0]
    whileTrue: [.....].
```

This repeatedly evaluates the Smalltalk code in the second block while the result of the first block evaluates to true. Note that **whileTrue:** is a message to the first block, it is therefore a method defined in class Context. Other control structures which use blocks include repetition e.g. **timesRepeat:** and **do:**.

A.1.5 Class Boolean

Class Boolean, although not exactly part of the Smalltalk syntax, is important enough to be considered here. It may at first seem confusing that class Boolean is not part of the language and is in fact a class with methods defined which provide the usual logical operations. However, given Smalltalk's commitment the the philosophy of object orientation, it is perhaps not that surprising that facilities such as Boolean are actually provided by a class definition.

Once you get used to the idea it is not that strange and most of the time you do not need to worry about the fact. Indeed, as long as you learn the "syntax" of boolean operators you need never actually know that they are not part of the basic language.

The class `Boolean` defines the whole protocol for boolean operations. This class has two subclasses `True` and `False` which determine what should happen when different messages are sent to them. Thus the equivalent of C's if statement in Smalltalk is :

```
anObject
        ifTrue: [some code ].
```

There is also the equivalent of the unless statement in some languages:

```
anObject
        ifFalse: [ some code ].
```

These can be combined to form an if-then-else construct.

```
anObject
        ifTrue: [ some code ]
        ifFalse: [some other code].
```

Note the period is only placed after the last line. The message selector used here is actually `ifTrue:ifFalse:`.

The usual range of boolean functions have been defined such as (&) and (|) or as well as specialized versions such as and: and or: which only evaluate the second operator if necessary. For example:

`(a < 2) & (b > 2)`	And
`(a < 2)	(b > 2)`	Or
`(a > 0) and: [b > (6 / a)]`	And where the second expression is only evaluated if the first expression evaluates to true. As here, this construct may be used as a check to ensure that erroneous operations are not performed.
`(a > 0) or: [B > 0]`	Or where the second expression will only be executed if the first evaluates to false.

A.1.6 Collections

As with class `Boolean`, collections are not strictly part of the Smalltalk language, however they are so important that they will be mentioned here.

Collections are the elements used to construct data structures in Smalltalk. They allow any object to be grouped together and manipulated. Complex data structures can be built up by combining collections together. Abstract Data Types (ADT's) can be instantiated by subclasses the default collection classes. They therefore provide a very powerful data construction mechanism.

The most commonly used collection classes are:

Set	A collection of objects in any order. No duplicates are allowed.
Bag	A collection of objects in any order; duplicates are allowed.
Array	Like an array in Pascal, has a fixed size (which can be grown) and accessed by explicit position references.
OrderedCollection	A bit like a linked list in Pascal or C. Elements are added to specific locations specified either as first, last or relative to another object.
SortedCollection	A collection whose order is determined by a sort block. This block is a piece of code which returns true or false depending upon the test performed.
Dictionary	Rather like a hash table. Objects are stored with a key and accessed by a key. Dictionaries are therefore a set of key -> value associations

Elements in collections are in general accessed by the at: and added by the at:put: or add: messages. It is possible to iterate over the elements of a collection using the do: construct.

Bibliography

[Acron and Walden 1992] T. L. Acron and S. H. Walden, SMART: Support Management Automated Reasoning Technology for Compaq Customer Service, pp 3 - 17, *Innovative Applications of Artificial Intelligence 4*, Ed. A. Carlisle Scott and Philip Klahr, (1992).

[Alexander et al 1977] C. Alexander, S. Ishikawa and M. Silverstein with M. Jacobson, I. Fiksdahl-King and S. Angel, *A Pattern Language*, Oxford University Press, 1977.

[Alexander 1979] C. Alexander, *The Timeless Way of Building*, Oxford university Press, 1979.

[Barbey and Strohmeier 1994] Stephane Barbey and Alfred Strohmeier, The Problematics of Testing Object-Oriented Software, in *SQM'94 Second Conference on Software Quality Management*, Vol 2, M. Ross, C. A. Brebbia, G. Staples and J. Stapleton (eds), pages 411-426, July 26-28, 1994.

[Barbey, Amman and Strohmeier 1994] Stephane Barbey, Manuel M. Ammann and Alfred Strohmeier, Open Issues in Testing Object-Oriented Software, in *ECSQ'94, European Conference on Software Quality*, Basil Switzerland, Oct. 17-20, 1994.

[Beck 1994] K. Beck, Simple Smalltalk testing, *The Smalltalk Report*, Vol 4, No. 2, pp 16-18, October 1994.

[Beck and Johnson 1994] K. Beck and R. Johnson, Patterns Generate Architectures, Proc. *Eccop'94*, pp. 139-149, 1994.

[Ben-Natan 1995] R. Ben-Natan, *CORBA: A Guide to Common Object Request Broker Architetcure*, McGraw-Hill, ISBN 0-07-005427, 1995.

[Beizer 1990] B. Beizer, *Software Testing Techniques*, Van Nostrand Reinhold, New York, 1990.

[Binder 1994] Robert V. Binder, Guest Editor, *Special Issue of Communications of the ACM, Object Oriented Software Testing*, Vol. 37, No 9, 1994. ACM Press.

[Binder 1994b] Robert V. Binder, Design for Testability in Object-Oriented Systems, in *Special Issue of Communications of the ACM, Object Oriented Software Testing*, Vol. 37, No 9, pp. 87-101, 1994.

[Birrer and Eggenschmiler 1993] Andreas Birrer and Thomas Eggenschwiler, "Frameworks in the Financial Engineering Domain: An Experience Report:, *ECOOP'93*, pp 21-35.

[Boehm 1988] B. W. Boehm, A spiral model of software development and enhancement, *IEEE Computer*, pp 61-72, May 1988.

[Booch *et al* 1996] G. Booch, I. Jacobson and J. Rumbaugh, *The Unified Modeling Language for Object Oriented Development*, Documentation Set, Version 0.91 Addendum, UML Update, Rational Software Corporation, (available on the web http://www.rational.com/ot/uml.html), 1996.

[Booch 1996] Grady Booch, *Object Solutions: Managing the Object-Oriented Project*, Pub. Addison-Wesley, Menlo Park, ISBN 0-8053-0594-7, (1996).

[Booch and Rumbaugh 1995] Grady Booch and James Rumbaugh, *The Unified Method Documentation Set*, Version 0.8, Rational Software Corporation, (available on the web http://www.rational.com/ot/uml.html), 1995.

[Booch 1994] Grady Booch, *Object-Oriented Analysis and Design with Applications*, 2nd Edition, Benjamin Cummings, Redwood City, California, (1994).

[Booch 1991] Grady Booch, *Object-Oriented Design with Applications*, Benjamin Cummings, (1991).

[Booch 1987] Grady Booch, *Software Components with Ada*, Benjamin Cummings, Menlo Park, California, 1987.

[Booch 1986] Grady Booch, Object Oriented Development, *IEEE Transactions on Software Engineering*, 12 (2), pp 211-221, February 1986.

[Brooks 1987] Fred Brooks, No Silver Bullet: Essence and Accidents of Software Engineering, *IEEE Computer*, April 1987.

[Brown 1989] A. L. Brown, *Persistent Object Stores*, Ph.D. Thesis, University of St. Andrews, 1989.

[Budd 1991] T. Budd, *An Introduction to Object Oriented Programming*, Pub. Addison-Wesley, ISBN 0-201-54709-0, (1991).

[Budinsky *et al* 1996] F. J. Budinsky, M. A. Finnie, J. M. Vlissides and P. S. Yu, Automatic code generation from design patterns, *IBM Systems Journal*, Vol. 35, No. 2, 1996.

[Coad and Yourdon 1991] P. Coad and E. Yourdon, *Object-Oriented Analysis*, Yourdon Press, Englewood Cliffs, NJ, (1991)

[Coleman *et al* 1994] D. Coleman, P. Arnold, S. Bodoff, C. Dollin, H. Gilchrist, F. Hayes and P. Jeremes, *Object Oriented Development: The Fusion Method*, Prentice Hall International, ISBN 0-13-101040-9, 1994.

[Cook and Daniels 1994] S. Cook and J. Daniels, *Designing Object Oriented Systems: Object-oriented modelling with Syntropy*, New York, Prentice Hall, 0-13-203860-9, 1994.

[Cox 1990] Brad J. Cox, There *Is* a Silver Bullet, *BYTE*, October 1990, pp 209-218.

[Cox and Novobilski 1991] Brad J. Cox and Andrew Novobilski, *Object-Oriented Programming: An Evolutionary Approach (2nd dition)*, Pub. Addison Wesley, ISBN 0-201-54834-8.

[Derr 1995] K. W. Derr, *Applying OMT: A Practical step-by-step guide to using the Object Modeling Technique*, Prentice Hall, 0-13-231390-1, 1995.

[Deutsch 1989] L. Peter Deutsch, The Past, Present and Future of Smalltalk, *Proc. ECOOP'89, Third European Conference on Object Oriented Programming*, pp 73-87, (1989).

[Feigenbaum 1995] Barry Alan Feigenbaum, Smalltalk/2: An enhanced Smalltalk, *Journal of Object Oriented Programming*, Vol. 8, No 7, pp. 50-56, 1995.

[Freedman 1991] R. S. Freedman, Testability of software components, *IEEE Trans. Softw. Eng.* 17 (6), pp. 553-564, June 1991.

[Gamma *et al*, 1995] E. Gamma, R. Helm, R. Johnson and J. Vlissades, *Design Patterns: Elements of Reusable Object-Oriented Software*, Addison-Wesley, 1995.

[Gamma *et al* 1993] E. Gamma, R. Helm, R. Johnson and J. Vlissades, Design patterns: Abstraction and reuse of object-oriented design, in *ECOOP'93 (Lecture Notes in Computer Science 707)*, pp. 406-431, Springer-Verlag, 1993.

[Goldberg and Robson 1983] A. Goldberg and D. Robson, *Smalltalk-80: The Language and its Implementation*, Addison-Wesley, 1983.

[Goldberg and Robson 1989] A. Goldberg and D. Robson, *Smalltalk-80: The Language*, Pub. Addison-Wesley, ISBN 0-201-13688-0, (1989).

[Goldberg 1984] A. Goldberg, *Smalltalk-80: The Interactive Programming Environment*, Addison-Wesley, 1984.

[Harel *et al* 1987] D. Harel, A. Pnueli, J. P. Schmidt and R. Sherman, 1987. On the formal semantics of Statecharts, *Proc. 2nd IEEE Sump. on Logic in Computer Science*, pp 54-64.

[Harel 1988] D. Harel, On visual formalisms, 1988. *Communications of the ACM*, Vol 31, No. 5., pp 514-530.

[Harmon and Taylor 1993] P. Harmon and D. Taylor, *Objects in Action: Commercial Applications of Object-Oriented Technologies*, Pub. Addison-Wesley: Massachusetts, (1993).

[Harrold, McGregor and Fitzpatrick 1992] Mary Jean Harrold, John D. McGregor and Kevin J. Fitzpatrick, Incremental testing of object-oriented class structures, in Proc. of the 14th *International Conference on Software Engineering*, pages 68-79, May 11-15, 1992. ACM Press.

[Hoffman and Strooper 1995] Daniel Hoffman and Paul Strooper, The testgraph methodology: Automated testing of collection classes, *Journal of Object Oriented Programming*, Vol. 8, No 7, pp. 35-41, 1995.

[Hopkins and Horan 1995] Trevor Hopkins and Bernard Horan, *Smalltalk: An Introduction to Application Development Using VisualWorks*, Pub. Prentice Hall, ISBN 0-13-318387-4, 1995.

[Hopkins and Wolczko 1989] T. P. Hopkins and M. I. Wolczko, Writing Concurrent Object-Oriented Programs using Smalltalk-80, in *The Computer Journal*, 32 (4), Oct. 1989, pp 341-350.

[Hunt 1995] Neil Hunt, Automatically tracking test case execution, *Journal of Object Oriented Programming*, Vol. 8, No 7, pp. 22-27, 1995.

[Jacobson 1992] I. Jacobson, M. Christerson, P. Jonsson and G. Overgaard, *Object-Oriented Software Engineering: A Use Case Driven Approach*, Addison-Wesley, Reading, MA, ISBN 0-201-54435-0, 1992.

[Johnson 1992] Ralph. E. Johnson, Documenting Frameworks with Patterns, *Proc. OOPSLA'92, SIGPLAN Notices* 27(10), pp. 63-76, 1992.

[Jorgensen and Erickson 1994] P. C. Jorgensen and C. Erickson, Object-Oriented Integration Testing, in *Special Issue of Communications of the ACM, Object Oriented Software Testing*, Vol. 37, No 9, pp. 30-38, 1994.

[Kemerer 1987] Chris F. Kemerer, An Empirical Validation of Software Cost Estimation Models, *Communications of the ACM*, Vol. 30, No. 5, May 1987, pp 416-429.

[Krasner 1983] G. Krasner (ed.), *Smalltalk-80: Bits of History, Words of Advice*, Addison-Wesley, 1983.

[Krasner and Pope 1988] G. E. Krasner and S. T. Pope, A Cookbook for Using the Model-View Controller User Interface Paradigm in Smalltalk-80, JOOP 1(3), pp. 26-49, 1988.

[Kuhn 1962] Thomas Kuhn, *The Structure of Scientific Revolutions*, The University of Chicago Press, 1962.

[Lalonde 1994] W. Lalonde, *Discovering Smalltalk*, Benjamin/Cummings Pub. Co. Inc. ISBN 0-8053-27207, 1994.

[LaLonde and Pugh 1993] W. LaLonde and J. Pugh, Idle time computing with futures, *Journal of Object Oriented Programming*, Vol 6 (6), pp 69-76, 1993.

[Lalonde and Pugh 1991] W. Lalonde and J. Pugh, *Inside Smalltalk Volume I*, Pub. Prentice Hall, ISBN 0-13-468414-1, (1991).

[Lalonde and Pugh 1991b] W. Lalonde and J. Pugh, *Inside Smalltalk Volume II*, Pub. Prentice Hall, ISBN 0-13-465964-3, (1991).

[Lalonde and Pugh 1991] Wilf Lalonde and John Pugh, Subclassing /= subtyping /= Is-a, *Journal of Object Oriented Programming*, Janurary 1991, pp 57-62.

[Lewis 1995] Simon Lewis, *The Art and Science of Smalltalk: An Introduction to Object Oriented Programming* Using VisualWorks, Hewlett-Packard Professional Books: Prentice Hall, Pub 1995. ISBN 0-13-371345-8.

[Love 1993] T. Love, *Object Lessons: Lessons Learned in Object-Oriented Development Projects*, SIGSBooks: New York, (1993).

[Meyer and Nerson 1993] B. Meyer and J. Nerson, *Object-Oriented Applications*, Prentice-Hall: New Jersey, (1993).

[Meyer 1988] B. Meyer, *Object-Oriented Software Construction*, Prentice Hall International, Englewood Cliffs, NJ, (1988).

[Moser and Nierstrasz 1996] S. Moser and O. Nierstrasz, The Effect of Object-Oriented Frameworks on Developer Productivity, pp 45-51, *IEEE Computer*, Sept. 1996.

[Myers 1979] G. J. Myers, *The Art of Software Testing*, Business Data Processing: a Wiley Series, John Wiley and Sons, 1979.

[Orfali *et al* 1995] R. Orfali, D. Harkey and J. Edwards, *The Essential Distributed Objects Survival Guide*, John Wiley & Sons, ISBN 0-471-12993-3, 1995.

[Ousterhout 1994] John K. Ousterhout, *TCL and the TK Toolkit*, Pub. Addison-Wesley Professional Computing Series, ISBN 0-201-63337-X, 1994.

[Perry and Kaiser 1990] D. E. Perry and G. E. Kaiser, Adequate testing and object oriented programming, *Journal of Object Oriented Programming*, 2 (5), pages 13-19, January 1990.

[Pyle 1991] I. C. Pyle, *Developing Safety Systems: A Guide Using Ada*, pp. 177-195, Pub. Prentice Hall, 1991.

[Rational 1996] *Unified Modeling Language for Real-Time Systems Design*, Rational Software Corporation, (available at http://www.rational.com/ot/uml.html), 1996.

[Rumbaugh *et al* 1991] J. Rumbaugh, M. Blaha, W. Permerlani, F. Eddi and W. Lorensen, *Object-oriented modeling and design*, Prentice Hall, 1991.

[Shan 1995] Y-P Shan, Smalltalk on the Rise, *Communications of the ACM*, Vol. 38, No. 10, pp 103-104, October 1995.

[Siepman and Newton 1994] E. Siepmann and A. R. Newton, TOBAC: A Test Case Browser for Testing of Object-Oriented Software, *Proc. of the International Symposium on Software Testing and Analysis (ISSTA)*, ACM 1994.

[Skublics *et al* 1996] Suzanne Skublics, Edward J. Klimas and David A. Thomas, *Smalltalk with Style*, Prentice Hall, ISBN 0-13-165549-3, 1996.

[Smith 1994] David N. Smith, *IBM Smalltalk: The Language*. Benjamin/Cummings Pub. Co. Inc. ISBN 0-8053-0908-X, 1994.

[Sparks, Benner and Faris, 1996] S. Sparks, K. Benner and C. Faris, Managing Object-Oriented Framework Reuse, pp 52-61, *IEEE Computer*, Sept. 1996.

[Taylor 1992] D. A. Taylor, *Object-Oriented Information Systems: Planning and Implementation*. John Wiley, N.Y. 1992.

[van der Linden 1996] P. van der Linden, *Just JAVA*, SunSoft Press, A Prentice Hall Title, ISBN 0-13-565839-X, 1996.

[Wirfs-Brock *et al* 1990] R. Wirfs-Brock, B. Wilkerson, L. Wiener, *Designing Object Oriented Software*, Pub. Prentice Hall, ISBN 0-13-629825-7, (1990).

[Yourdon 1994] E. Yourdon, *Object-Oriented Systems Design*, Prentice Hall: New Jersey, (1994).

OOPSLA/ECOOP'90, Joint Conference, on Object-Oriented Programming: Systems, Languages and Applications, Ed. Norman Meyrowitz, Pub Addison Wesley, ISBN 0-0201-52430-X, (1990).

OOPSLA '91, Conference on Object-Oriented Programming Systems, Langauges and Applications, Ed. Andreas Paepcke, Pub Addison Wesley, ISBN 0-0201-55417-8, (also as ACM SIGPLAN Notices Vol 26, No. 11), (1991).

OOPSLA '92, Seventh Annual Conference on Object-Oriented Programming Systems, Languages and Applications, Ed. Andreas Paepcke, Pub Addison Wesley, ISBN 0-201-53372-3, (also as ACM SIG PLAN NOTICES Vol 27, No. 10, (1992).

OOPSLA '93. OOPSLA'93 Conference Proceedings. ACM/SIGLAN, Pub. Addison Wesley, ISBN 0-201-58895-1, 1993.

ECOOP '89, Third European Cnnference on Object-Oriented Programming, Ed. Stephen Cook, Pub. Cambridge University Press, (in the British Computer Society Workshop Series), ISBN 0-521-38232-7, (1989)

ECOOP '92, European Conference on Object Oriented Programming, Ed. O. Lehrmann Madsen, Pub. Springer-Verlag, ISBN 0-387-55668-0, (Published in the Lecture Notes in Computer Science series), (1992).

ECOOP '93. European Conference on Object Oriented Programming, Pub. Springer-Verlag, Lecture Notes in Computer Science Vol 707, 1993.

ECOOP '94, European Conference on Object Oriented Programming, Pub. Springer-Verlag, Lecture Notes in Computer Science Vol 821, 1994.

ECOOP '95, Ninth European Conference on Object-Oriented Programming, Lecture Notes in Computer Science, Vol. 952, Springer Verlag, 1995.

[ISO 1993]. *Information technology, software packages, quality requirements and testing,* ISO Draft International Standard, ISO/IEC DIS 12119. 1993.

Workshop on Testing Smalltalk Applications, held at the OOPSLA '95 Conference, Monday October 16, 1995. For more information contact Barbara Yates, OOPSLA Workshop, 2002 Parkside Court, West Linn, Oregon, 97068-2767, USA (Email: barbara.bytesmiths@acm.org).

Index